The Art Museums of New England

The Art Museums of New England

S. Lane Faison, Jr.

David R. Godine · Publisher · Boston

Gratefully dedicated to the directors and staff members of the institutions here surveyed, and to hospitable friends along the road

This edition first published in 1982 by
David R. Godine, Publisher, Inc.
306 Dartmouth Street
Boston, Massachusetts 02116

Library of Congress Cataloging in Publication Data
Faison, Samson Lane, 1907-
    The art museums of New England.

    (Godine guides ; 3)
    First ed. (1958) published under title: A guide to the art museums of New England.
    Includes index.
    1. Art museums—New England—Guide-books.
    2. Art—New England—Guide-books.   I. Title.
    N510.5.N4F2 1982   708.14   80-83952
    ISBN 0-87923-372-9
    ISBN 0-87923-373-7 (pbk.)

This is a revised and expanded version of Mr. Faison's *Guide to the Art Museums of New England*, published in 1958 by Harcourt, Brace & Co.

Manufactured in the United States of America

Contents

Rhode Island

Massachusetts

How to Use This Book

The survey of museum collections is arranged south to north by states, Connecticut to Maine, and alphabetically by towns within each state. It comes in two forms: a complete hardcover volume that covers all six states and three individual softcover volumes, one for Connecticut and Rhode Island, the second for Massachusetts, and the third for New Hampshire, Vermont, and Maine. Each of the four volumes has an index. The complete hardcover volume is paged consecutively; the separate paperback volumes are paged consecutively as the complete volume is paged: Connecticut and Rhode Island from page 1 to page 111, Massachusetts from page 113 to page 358, and the northern three states from page 359 to page 463.

The map that introduces each state is dotted to indicate proper locations. Each location refers to an adjacent identification list in alphabetical order, which will allow you to turn to the appropriate entry in the main text. In planning a tour these maps should be helpful.

A major feature of the book is a network of cross references to examples in other museums related to the work under discussion. Each reference is therefore followed by a number in parentheses, indicating first the state where the item appears, then the item number. For example, the Degas pastel at the Hill-Stead Museum in Farmington, Conn. (CT 3) is placed in a larger critical and historical context by reference to other works of Degas in the museums of Boston (MA 81), Northampton (MA 179), and Providence (RI 18).

Rather than appending a bibliography, which in a book of this kind would be either too long or much too short to be useful, I have included occasional references to books and articles in the text itself. These are for the general, but curious, reader. The scholar will understand their introductory purpose, and pass on.

Preface

This work surveys, critically and historically, some 550 works of art selected from the *permanent* collections of over one hundred art museums, historical societies, and libraries open to the public in the six New England states.

·While the text is directed to the general reader, I have reason to believe that the scholar, too, will be surprised to learn what artistic riches exist in out-of-the-way places. Over twenty years ago, when I first undertook such a survey, I had little idea that sixty institutions would fall within its scope. Since then, many of those originally covered have doubled in size, twenty-four new ones have been established, and eighteen others have subsequently developed collections worthy of inclusion or were originally omitted through oversight.

My earlier book, published in 1958 by Harcourt, Brace and Company under the title *A Guide to the Art Museums of New England*, went out of print within six years. So it has remained, but in the meantime I have filed away corrections and additions in the hope that an updated version would someday be forthcoming. This happy event took place when David Godine, in search of an author for such a book, discovered mine in limbo. He had recently published *New England Gardens Open to the Public*, by Rolce Redard Payne, as the second in a projected series of all–New England handbooks (the first, *The Boston Basin Bicycle Book*, was published in 1975). The present book now becomes the third; it is to be followed by a comparable volume, *A Guide to Historic Houses of New England Open to the Public*, by Margaret Supplee Smith and R. Jackson Smith.

The word "guide" has been eliminated in the new title because it suggests a purely descriptive compilation à la Baedeker, whereas I propose an excursion into art criticism and art history based on the vast treasure available to the public in New England. Some of the present text repeats selections and comments in the older one. While masterpieces of art are not quite so dependable as the heavenly bodies, and in the interim connoisseurship has reduced the magnitude of a few of them, for the most part the original text has been greatly expanded rather than cut. Everywhere it has been corrected, refined, or reoriented as the case seemed to demand.

Twenty-odd years ago I did not suspect that even if the Boston Museum of Fine Arts were eliminated, the whole range of world art—from antiquity to the present, and from Western art to Far Eastern, Pre-Columbian, and so-called primitive art—would still be abundantly represented in fine original examples in New England's museums. Today, if we leave out of account the world's great metropolitan centers, it is fair to say that no region of comparable size anywhere can boast such a concentration of art museums as New England. Yet the area of the six New England states is about the size of Oklahoma and less than a third of that of France, and under one-sixth of France's size if we subtract the museumless expanses of hinterland Maine. Even more extraordinary is the concentration in Massachusetts alone—an area just half the size of Denmark. Almost half the museums and nearly three-fifths of the works of art surveyed here are in the Bay State.

Arranged south to north state by state, this is not a book to be read in the usual sequence. The informed student of art will find what is wanted by consulting the table of contents or the index; these will lead to quick answers as to what is to be seen in any given institution, or which of them have significant examples (cited in these pages) of the work of a given artist or of types of art, such as African, Chinese, or Pre-Columbian. The general reader who wishes to get an overview of the development of art history might well start with the section on the Boston Museum of Fine Arts. This provides a kind of miniature survey of Western art, and it contains the book's most significant coverage of Far Eastern art. Less comprehensive surveys will be found in the sections on other leading museums. The fullest discussion of primitive art is contained in the entry on the Peabody Museum at Harvard University.

In a selective project of this sort, injustices inevitably occur. For omissions and misplaced emphases I can only ask the reader's indulgence. Some explanation, however, is necessary for the treatment of historical societies and libraries. As the number of these in New England is very large, it was possible to include only those that own works of art of consequence, or more modest ones that interestingly supplement the discussion of works commented on elsewhere. The exclusion of such an institution is in no way to be taken as a judgment of its intrinsic eminence.

The total of some 550 works illustrated and discussed is a compromise between the claims of broad coverage and portable size. *Portable*: a book to be carried with you into the museum and, it is hoped, read in the presence of the original works of art. *Coverage*: this or any other total could easily have been devoted to the Boston Museum of Fine Arts alone. While it was obvious from the start that B M F A should receive more emphasis than any other, it became equally obvious that to allow the total for all the museums of Boston and Cambridge to exceed a quarter of the selections for the whole book would mean eliminating many small museums elsewhere. (As it has worked out, Boston and Cambridge are represented by 128 works, or about 23 percent of the whole.) Smaller places contain works that are worth a pilgrimage; and the experience of traveling to see a fine object becomes part of the experience the object itself can provide. I do not mean that you will come upon a Chartres Cathedral or an Arena Chapel in rural New England, but who could wish that these shrines were in Paris or Florence? In somewhat the same way a watercolor, a precious ivory, or a superb impression of a Rembrandt etching, suddenly come upon in a small museum, or a modest painting by a hitherto unfamiliar artist, can have a greater effect than if the same work were seen—or very possibly missed —in a major institution.

The reader will discover, with a few exceptions in the case of prints, that furniture, photographs, and prints are not discussed in these pages.

The same holds true, again with a few exceptions, for the decorative arts in general. This policy was dictated by limitations of space and by the theory that all these arts are "multiples," in the broad sense that identical or nearly identical examples are usually to be found in several institutions. Where it is appropriate, however, reference is made to important collections of decorative arts, furniture, photographs, and prints.

Visitors are warned not to expect that my selections (often made from works in storage) will always be on display, museum by museum, to welcome them. Shortage of exhibition space often dictates a policy of rotation, and temporary shows can mean that whole galleries have to be cleared and their contents stored. Loans to other museums can account for other absentees, yet there is an extra dividend of pleasure in finding a work in unexpected surroundings and new contexts.

Within the limits defined above, each entry attempts a selection of what is outstanding in the museum under discussion. On many occasions you will naturally question why certain works were not included. There are many answers, and I will leave to your judgment which of the following are appropriate: (1) limitations of space in the book; (2) discussion of a generally similar work in some other museum; (3) too many works by the same artist to warrant inclusion of yet another one; (4) poor condition of the work in question; (5) attribution of the work to the given artist doubtful; or, finally, (6) my opinion of it less enthusiastic than yours.

Two pairs of terms frequently appearing in these pages seem to require explanation. By *classical*, I mean pertaining to the art of Greece and Rome. By *classic*, I mean characterized by such restraint, high idealism, and formal discipline as is found in Greek art of the fifth century B.C., in Chinese art of the T'ang dynasty, in Gothic sculpture of the thirteenth century, in the painting of Raphael and Titian and Poussin, and in the nineteenth-century painting of Corot, Cézanne (especially in the 1880s), and Seurat. I hope I have used these terms consistently.

The second pair of terms is *size* and *scale*. By *size*, I mean physical dimensions. By *scale*, I mean the size that the work *seems to suggest*, irrespective of its actual measurements. In this connection, Viollet-le-Duc pointed out in his *Dictionnaire Raisonné de l'Architecture* that although Notre Dame in Paris is approximately the same height as the Arc de Triomphe, the former is scaled to human beings and does not dwarf the neighboring houses; whereas the latter—scaled, we might say, to Napoleon's ambition—is restrained by no such modesty. Contrariwise, a self-portrait in the Louvre by the fifteenth-century French painter Jean Fouquet, painted in gold enamel on a black ground, seems to expand to life size even though this little roundel measures only 3 inches in diameter. It was once attached to the frame of a small two-paneled altarpiece.

Before acknowledging my indebtedness to many kindly persons, I am happy to add a concluding word about the present state of admission fees to art museums in New England and elsewhere in the United States. Many make no charge whatever. When fees are imposed they are modest indeed as compared with the cost of concert or theater tickets, or with golf or ski-tow charges. Free or not, museums often provide a prominently displayed opportunity for the visitor to make a contribution. The need for such support is both real and pressing.

In each of the institutions discussed in these pages, staff members have been generous in providing information, advising me in my choice of works, and in supplying photographs. Many friends along the road have housed and entertained my wife and me, and made our more than four thousand miles of New England travel the more enjoyable. A list of all these benevolent people would inevitably be so long as to defeat its purpose. The book itself is therefore dedicated to them *en masse*. In so doing we hope they will understand that no such screen of collective anonymity clouds our grateful memories of kindnesses received.

Vivian Patterson, a graduate student in the Williams College / Clark Art Institute Master of Arts Program in the History of Art, has been enormously helpful as my research assistant and amanuensis-without-portfolio. The sections on the two museums in Williamstown are in large part her work.

It has been a continuing delight to work with David Godine, my publisher, and William B. Goodman, his editorial director. Their enthusiastic collaboration in my task is warmly appreciated.

The original text and thereby the present one owe much to the cultivated mind and eye of my friend, the late Professor John McAndrew, a former director of the Wellesley College Museum. For scholarly assistance in Rhode Island, I am indebted to my friend Winslow Ames, a distinguished collector and art historian. I must especially thank Cornelius Vermeule, Curator of Classical Art at the Boston Museum of Fine Arts, for extensive and sustained support, not only within and beyond the confines of the museum itself, but also beyond his professional field.

Colleagues in the Williams College Department of Art have given generously of their time and expert knowledge and have saved me many a slip. If flaws remain despite all the assistance outlined above, or if my critical estimates sometimes seem eccentric, the *culpa* is *mea*.

Finally, there is the problem of thanking my wife adequately for her participation in this venture. In truth she is all but the joint author of this book. It is *not* true that without her it would have been written sooner—as occasional dedications have slyly suggested.

> S. Lane Faison, Jr.
> *Director Emeritus*
> *Williams College Museum of Art*

Williamstown, Mass.
October 15, 1981

Connecticut

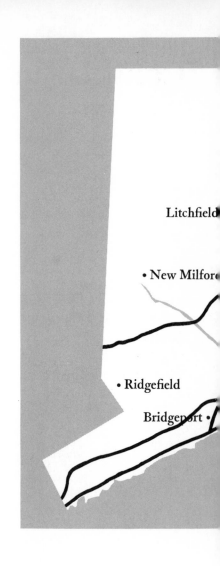

Litchfield

• New Milford

• Ridgefield

Bridgeport •

Connecticut

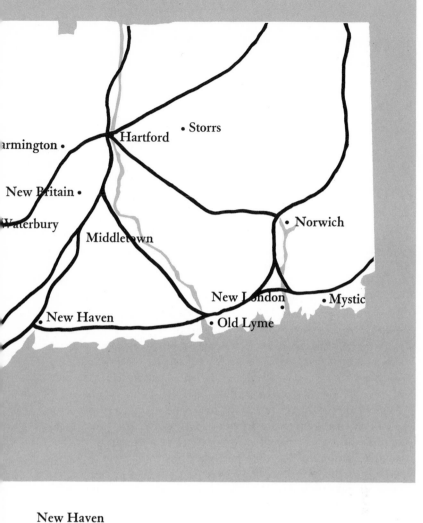

Housatonic Museum of Art

Location: 510 Barnum Ave. From exit 28 on I-95 take East Main St. north to Barnum Ave. Parking across the street
Telephone: (203) 579-6400
Hours: Mon.-Thurs. 8-9, Fri. 8-4
Admission: Free. Ⓗ partially (advise phoning)

Our first museum offers one of the largest and finest public collections of contemporary and ethnographic art in Connecticut. Begun in 1967, shortly after the founding of Housatonic Community College, it was conceived as a facility as essential to visual education as the library is to learning through verbal media. This important idea has been realized through the efforts of Burt Chernow, Chairman of the Art Department and Director of the Museum. It has been accomplished at minimal expense: most of the works of art have come to the college through gifts from artists and collectors, sometimes even from the student body. Collecting began long before the college moved to its present quarters, at a time when it was leasing space in churches, schools, and other buildings in nearby Stratford.

Rather than developing a separate museum building, a decision was made to provide a gallery for temporary loan exhibitions (often supplemented by works from the permanent collection), and to display changing selections of the permanent collection throughout the college buildings. In this way, it was felt, works of art would make the greatest impact on students and at the same time be more than customarily available to the community and the general public. Tours of the collection can be arranged on request.

The growth of the collection has been phenomenal. Within the first year it already numbered several hundred works, and today there are well over a thousand paintings, sculptures, drawings, prints, and photographs. An illustrated catalogue, published in 1980, lists over four hundred artists who are represented by one or more unique works, that is, other than prints or photographs. Among them are oils by Giorgio de Chirico and Milton Avery; a tempera, *Chorus Line*,[1] by Reginald

I

Marsh, one of five works by this artist (see VT 8); *Alphii*, a marble sculpture by Isamu Noguchi (ME 45); bronzes by Charles Despiau (two unique portraits), Auguste Rodin, and Alexander Archipenko (*Egyptian Motif*, 1917); and a welded metal sculpture by Richard Stankiewicz.

The focus of the collection is on contemporary American and European art and on ethnographic art, which is also represented in quantity and quality. Outstanding among African works are a terra-cotta Ashanti head 17 inches high and a Zaire mask.

The collection as a whole is fast becoming a major resource in New England for the study of contemporary art, supported by a considerable coverage of its historical origins, especially under the inspiration of what is too blithely called primitive art. Plans are under consideration to provide more gallery space, but not to the extent of concentrating the permanent collection in a museum building. The original idea of making it easily available throughout the college will continue to be respected.

Museum of Science, Art & Industry

Location: 4450 Park Ave., 1 mile south of Merritt Pkwy., exit 47; 4 miles
north of Conn. Tpke., exit 27 (via South Ave. to Park Ave.)
Hours: Tues., Wed., Thurs., Sat., Sun. 2-5; Fri. 10-5
Admission: Charged, except on Fridays. Ⓗ

An interesting place for all tastes and ages, intelligently managed.
While Science and Industry are primary here, Art is decidedly worth
a visit. A special Tactile Gallery for the blind will also fascinate those
not so deprived. The museum is active in temporary exhibitions, including work of local artists, and in discussions on historic art. There
are many programs for schools and groups. The permanent collections
have a wide range, including American folk art and Colonial art,
Indian artifacts, European and American paintings, and an enthralling
array of objects associated with P. T. Barnum (1810–91), Bridgeport's
most spectacular citizen and for one stormy year its mayor.

While the downtown Circus Museum is a Barnum heaven (the part-
nership with Bailey did not occur until 1880), a group of models built
for the great showman is a major attraction in this uptown one, and
Barnum's own "scolding chair"—a Baroque extravaganza of 1860 in
Louis XIV style—outdazzles the Sun King himself.

The Captain John Brooks Collection forms the core of the museum's
Colonial and Early American exhibits. A prosperous merchant and ship-
owner, he built a house in 1787 on the Old Boston Post Road. Now
in the process of reconstruction on museum grounds, the house will be
an important reminder of Bridgeport's long-forgotten past. The furniture is impressive and there are several good portraits, including one
of Captain Sir William Wallace, of New Haven, attributed to Reuben
Moulthrop.

The painting collection is dominated by a very large portrait of Jenny
Lind, a souvenir of Barnum's triumphal tour of "the Swedish nightin-
gale" through American cities and Havana in 1850/51. The work of
F. X. Winterhalter, it can stand comparison with the master's images
of Queen Victoria. Jenny Lind's American debut at Castle Garden, in
New York City's Battery Park, sold 5,000 tickets at auction at prices
up to $225. She gave 93 concerts under Barnum's flamboyant manage-
ment at $1,000 per concert plus a share in the profits and salaries and
expenses for a retinue of accompanists and servants. Barnum's daring
venture brought him not only riches but greatly desired prestige as an
impresario rather than merely the showman of Tom Thumb (the five-
year-old midget discovered in Bridgeport), the dead mermaid, and
other such oddities.

From the Samuel H. Kress Foundation come twelve Italian pictures,
fourteenth to eighteenth centuries. Other paintings include a fine Dutch

still life by Willem Heda, Barbizon oils by Diaz, Daubigny, and Millet (a late portrait); four large sea pieces by Edward Moran (1829–1901); and small works by Maurice Prendergast and Arthur Dove. Modern American sculptures include a saucy terra-cotta plaque by Reuben Nakian and an extensive group of bronzes by Mahonri Young.

Hill-Stead Museum

Location: Enter from either Mountain Rd. or Farmington Ave., about ½ mile east of the village center
Hours: Wed., Thurs., Sat., Sun. 2-5, and at other times by appointment
Admission: Charged. Ⓗ projected

Commanding a fine view of the Farmington Valley, Hill-Stead was built in 1901 by Mr. and Mrs. Alfred A. Pope from Stanford White designs altered by their daughter, Theodate, who later married John W. Riddle, U.S. ambassador to Russia and the Argentine. Upon Mrs. Riddle's death, five years after that of her husband, the house, left exactly as it had been lived in, was opened as a museum.

I maintain a discreet silence on this aspect of Hill-Stead (and of similar perpetuations) in order to discuss its works of art, for which I have unbounded enthusiasm. Outstanding among them are paintings by the French Impressionists, which Mr. Pope collected in the early 1890s, when these artists were little known in America. There are four Claude Monets, two Edouard Manet oils and a sepia wash drawing for his first important work, *The Absinthe Drinker*, an oil and two pastels by Degas, several Whistlers, and a Mary Cassatt. Related to these is a large collection of Japanese woodblock prints, much favored by the Impressionists for their flat patterns and unexpected angles. In addition, there are oils by Puvis de Chavannes and Eugène Carrière, and, on the staircase, etchings by Whistler, Millet, and Charles Meryon, whose romantic *Towers of Notre Dame from the Seine* is especially moving.

Woman with Guitar[2] by Edouard Manet (1832–83) is among his finest early works in America. The model was Victorine Meurend, who posed for the *Olympia* and the *Déjeuner sur l'herbe* (both in the Louvre) in 1863, and for the *Street Singer* (Boston). Seldom was Manet's touch more masterly in laying on flat tones of subtly related hues. This brought upon him the scorn of the critics of the day, understandably so if we recall the meticulous modeling of forms demanded

2

by such leading academic painters as Gérôme (several in the Clark Art Institute, Williamstown, Mass.). Note here the indescribable "white" of the dress, the brilliant play of oranges on the guitar, the green of the parrot, and the red-violet cord hanging from the guitar in a shape that echoes the line of the full sleeve. Such purity of color was revolutionary in the 1860s. We should realize this when we read the critics' invective, especially when the subject is at once tasteful and traditional, as it is here. Critics today date the modern movement in art from such works as these of Manet. The flat planes of Cubism and collage (the pasting of flat strips of textured material) function in much the same way as Manet's areas of clear tone. To achieve his effect, he used a kind of spotlight illumination. The sculptural modeling exists, nevertheless, but it is achieved mainly by the three-dimensional quality of Manet's outlines.

There can be little doubt that Degas's large square pastel, in the drawing room, is among his consummate masterpieces in this medium. Even the Louvre can provide no more spectacular example. The composition of *The Tub*[3] is a wonderful interlacement of circular and angular forms, both brought to climax in the shapes of the bending nude figure. But the most memorable achievement here is the shimmer of gray-blue light, starting at the distant window and brought to its culmination in the modeling of the figure. The date of this work, c. 1885, marks the middle of the career of Edgar Degas (1834–1917). His interest in the pastel medium, increasing steadily from this period onward, seems to have responded to a desire for greater fluidity and surface movement. In his early work (MA 179), under the influence of fifteenth-century Italian masters and Ingres (MA 126), Degas depended on strong outline to define form. Another fine pastel is discussed at Providence (RI 18).

The Blue Wave[4] by James A. McNeill Whistler (1834–1903) is hardly less astonishing, especially since we tend to think of Whistler as a somewhat anemic variant on Degas, who deeply influenced him. It hangs over the mantelpiece in the library, above two fine bronze groups by A. L. Barye, Delacroix's alter ego in sculpture (VT 1). The date is 1862, when Whistler was closely associated with the group later known as Impressionists and with Courbet, whose marines this

3

4

composition superficially resembles. I have selected it, despite its close proximity to another fine Whistler of the same period in the Wadsworth Atheneum at Hartford (CT 27), because it is doubtful that he ever painted a greater picture. It has much, if not all, of Courbet's power, but the drama of the sea is suggested by indirection, not by Courbet's sledgehammer blows. There is no "story" whatever: only the play of dark blue against brown, and the framing of the concave wall of water by the rocks, with the foam fanning outward into the corners. It has been said that only the great master knows when to stop.

Three of the Claude Monets, including two of the celebrated *Haystack* series, date from 1889/90, when he was fifty, in the full bloom of his fragmentation of form through light. Increasingly thereafter, the subject of the picture yielded to symphonic color effects and complex surfaces with a life of their own. But *Boats Leaving the Harbor,*[5] c. 1865, shows that the hard-won achievement of Monet's maturity came only after mastery of sharp line, strong contrasts of dark and light, and careful placement of echoing flat shapes. Nevertheless, the bright pink streak across the horizon and the fugitive lavenders in the sea tones are omens of the Impressionist palette to come. Comparison with Edouard Manet's *Beach at Berck* (CT 23) will illustrate the great divergence, even within the same subject, between these closely related leaders of the new movement. Manet is all sensibility and deftness; Monet seems driven by a somber power.

A brochure on these and other major pictures at Farmington, by Jean Harris, is warmly recommended.

5

The Connecticut Historical Society

Location: 1 Elizabeth Street at Asylum Avenue. Parking free
Hours: 9-5 except Sun. and holidays; in summer closed on Sat.
Admission: Free. ⓗ

The society was founded in 1825 as a research library and record museum on Connecticut history. In its spacious contemporary quarters, it serves both functions actively.

The art collections are important and extensive. Some 10 percent of the holdings are on view at a time in the upstairs galleries in frequently changing exhibits. Storage, however, is "live," that is, available to interested persons by appointment. Connecticut furniture of the seventeenth and eighteenth centuries, the most celebrated of the society's varied treasures, compares in quality with the collection in the Wadsworth Atheneum. In the large auditorium the walls are covered with some sixty tavern and hotel signs, many of them proclaiming a policy of Temperance.

The visitor would do well not to miss, among the many superb quilts, *The Star*—red and blue on white, mid-nineteenth century. This example was lent to the U.S. pavilion at the Osaka World's Fair. The same recommendation applies to a truly unique, 6-foot-long silhouette, the work of one William Henry Brown and given to the society as early as 1851. It memorializes the De Witt Clinton locomotive and includes profiles of the inventor and his wife. Silver, pewter, glass, pottery, stoneware, and prints of documentary interest are here in great abundance. The number of clocks suggests that at one time Connecticut was the American Switzerland.

Among the six hundred portraits, dating from the seventeenth century to the present, I have space only to mention an early John Trumbull (1756–1843), stiff but strong, of his parents. The *Portrait of Stephen Mix Mitchell*,[6] painted in New York c. 1825–27 by Samuel F. B. Morse (1791–1872), is perhaps the finest of them all on a basis of competence

6

and quality. Chief justice of the state and a U.S. senator, Mitchell appears at about the age of eighty-three, alert and determined, his ruddy face echoed in the rich red background and dominating the stark black and white of his costume and wig. This picture and the companion image of Mrs. Mitchell are of what was called "cabinet size," 30 by 24 inches.

The full-length seated *Portrait of James Eldredge*,[7] over 4 feet high, carries the date July 5, 1795, but no signature. The subject, a merchant of Brooklyn, Conn., was then aged fifty. The artist was almost certainly John Brewster, Jr., of whom more is said in the section on Saco, Maine, where there is a large group of his pictures (ME 34). Clearly this artist was more concerned with shapes and patterns, and much less with characterization, than Samuel F. B. Morse. We learn a great deal about Eldredge's mode of life, but as a person he remains strangely frozen and aloof. The basic source for study of Brewster's career is an article by Nina Fletcher Little in the Connecticut Historical Society's *Bulletin* for October 1960.

I conclude this too brief survey with the powerful if impassive image of *Mrs. Isaac Hawley, Jr.*, dated 1798 and signed "R. J. pinx[t]."[8] As with the Morse portrait, it is one of a pair and of "cabinet" size. For the identification of the monogram with Richard Jennys and an unraveling of his complicated relationship with William Jennys, another Connecticut portraitist whose work sometimes closely resembles his, the reader is referred to two long articles, in the society's *Bulletin* for October 1955 and April 1956, by William Lamson Warren. Richard Jennys, active from 1776 to 1799, appears to have originated in Boston; by 1783 he was advertising his wares in Charleston and from 1785 to 1791 busily at work in Savannah. In 1792 he painted in New Haven, and thereafter in the New Milford area. There are but three signed portraits known, and the existing attributed ones are all from the Connecticut period. William Jennys, active from the 1790s to 1807, painted first in central and western Connecticut, and then journeyed north to western Massachusetts, Vermont, and finally New Hampshire. A putative third Jennys, J. William, has been shown to be the same

7

8

William, the *J* being merely a flourish on the *W* of his signature. As the society owns no certain work by William Jennys, he is discussed in the sections on New London, Manchester (N.H.), and the Williams College Museum of Art, Williamstown (Mass.). Suffice it to mention here that there is no definite proof that he was related to Richard Jennys, but the evidence is strong that he may have been a younger brother or even a son. The early Connecticut portraits by William closely resemble Richard's, and it is not surprising that attributions have moved back and forth between them; but as William traveled northward his style changed markedly toward that harsh, almost Expressionist realism fortified by the astringent color for which he is best known. Curiously, we know very little about William's early life even though he was much more prolific than Richard, whom we know as an artist only from his work of the final few years.

Mrs. Hawley, who was born and died in Brookfield, appears here at age thirty-one, capable and unruffled. The faintly marked oval inner frame adds additional emphasis to her unsmiling presence. A knowing compositional twist, often seen in Richard's portraits, extends up the scarf, to be completed by the strongly projecting cap. It also serves to keep our eyes from wandering off into the corners of the picture. (William Jennys seldom bothered with such subtleties.) Color is somber and modeling, which is pronounced and convincing, depends less on contour lines than on light and shade.

Wadsworth Atheneum

Location: 600 Main Street
Hours: Tues., Wed., Fri. 11-3; Thurs. 11-8; Sat., Sun. 11-5
Admission: Free (contribution suggested). Ⓗ

The Wadsworth Atheneum, together with the museums of Worcester, Providence, and New Haven, ranks among the leading art museums of New England outside the Boston-Cambridge area. Its complicated history began in 1842 with the construction of the Gothic Revival building that still stands on the Main Street side of Atheneum Square. The gift of Daniel Wadsworth, it contained not only a library but also a gallery of fine arts.

The construction of the Colt Wing and the Morgan Memorial, in the years 1907 to 1910, greatly expanded the museum functions of the Atheneum. The memorial was the gift of J. Pierpont Morgan. His son donated collections of porcelain and decorative arts that are among the most important in America today. They rival the painting collection for first rank in the Atheneum's holdings. A subsequent donation by Mr. J. P. Morgan, Jr., added the famous Wallace Nutting Collection of Early American furniture.

The painting collection has grown rapidly since 1927, when the Sumner bequest was received. It is best known for its seventeenth- and eighteenth-century examples. In the field of Baroque painting the Atheneum acquired important works before other museums, and its influence on American collecting has been considerable. In more recent years it has also assembled an important collection of modern art.

The Avery Memorial, completed in 1934, provided a much-needed series of modern galleries around a central court, as well as generous studio facilities and a finely equipped theater. The theater opened in February 1934 with the world premiere of Gertrude Stein's *Four Saints in Three Acts*. The Atheneum thus became the first museum in the United States, and perhaps in the world, to include theater and ballet in its regular program.

Much of the extraordinary development of the Atheneum was due to the energy, inventiveness, and taste of the late A. E. Austin, its director from 1927 to 1944, who made it one of the most dynamic art museums in the United States.

Renovation of the original building in the late 1960s and construction of the Goodwin Wing connecting it with the Avery Memorial have now provided a total of thirty-six galleries for display of a collection totaling over thirty thousand objects.

Considering the importance of the collections of furniture and decorative arts (areas in which many good museums are poor), we shall begin our survey with two examples. They make an extraordinary contrast. The ebony and silver *Cabinet*,⁹ 2 feet high and one of the most magnificent items in the Morgan Memorial, is attributed to Christopher

Jamnitzer of Nuremberg (1563–1618). The silver reliefs, almost aggressive in their display of knowledge of Italian perspective and classical forms, incorporate a German love of small detail and heavy ornament. The workmanship is so exquisite, however, and the material so pure against its polished black foil that we can only confess our utter admiration at the way in which all this conspicuous waste was sublimated into a work of art.

The silver-gilt *Centerpiece*[10] was made at Augsburg by Bernhard Heinrich Weye, about 1757–59. Also 2 feet high, it represents a concert in a "Chinese" pagoda. The musicians' offerings are supplemented by *putti* blowing vigorously on their instruments. One near the summit beats out a spirited rhythm on two kettledrums. The fronds above him suggest antlers, such as are found in the corridors and banqueting halls of all self-respecting German castles. This is a special German note, for hunting flourished there as perhaps nowhere else, and antlers gave rise to many kinds of ornamental variations, including candelabra and chandeliers; even Dürer drew such metamorphoses. The centerpiece itself might be compared to the shrine in the nave of Vierzehnheiligen, the most famous of the eighteenth-century German churches. Both are everywhere animated by irregular C-shaped curves—a hallmark of the prevailing Rococo ornamental style.

My reference to Albrecht Dürer leads us to his most famous German contemporary, Lucas Cranach the Elder (1472–1553). The *Feast of Herod*,[11] a signed oil on wood panel, dated 1531 and 4 feet in length, is the earliest and finest of several known versions of the subject by Cranach or his workshop. German precision, notable in the cabinet and the centerpiece already discussed, here produces a tour de force, especially in the figure of Salome, richly caparisoned and starkly

9

10

11

silhouetted against the nearly bare white tablecloth. Salome arrives, presenting the Baptist's head on a salver to a troubled Herod, just as fruit is about to be served at the end of the repast. As a symbol of woman's power over man, Salome joins the biblical Eves, Delilahs, and Judiths as well as the Omphales of classical mythology. Since Herod clearly resembles Cranach's chief patron, Frederick the Wise, Duke of Saxony, a contemporary warning may be implied. A second Cranach painting, *Diana and Her Nymphs Surprised by Actaeon*, of weaker execution, may be the work of Lucas's son of the same name. Here the antlers of the stag (into which the offending huntsman was transformed and thereupon attacked by his hounds) bring to mind the crowning element of Weye's silver-gilt centerpiece.

Among the Atheneum's Italian Early Renaissance paintings, *The Finding of Vulcan*, c. 1490, by the quixotic Piero di Cosimo is outstanding. It is closely related to the Worcester Museum's *Discovery of Honey* (MA 298). A superb fifteenth-century *Portrait of a Member of the Van Busleyden Family*, on the traditional medieval gold ground, indicates how little the Franco-Flemish master (name unknown) was concerned with contemporary Renaissance mastery of anatomy and spatial illusion. *Hercules and Antaeus*, a large oil by the great Venetian Tintoretto or his school, demonstrates how far such mastery had progressed by the end of the sixteenth century.

The Ecstasy of St. Francis[12] is one of the very few works by Caravaggio (1573–1610) in America. Of the great climactic painters, Caravaggio is, with Giotto, Masaccio, and Leonardo da Vinci, least well represented in this country. Like them, Caravaggio initiated a revolution in the whole conception of painting. This example shows his dramatic darks and lights to good advantage, and his journalistic actuality. He shocks us into believing that the scene is taking place before our eyes. What a transformation of the Giotto-inspired version of the theme at the Fogg Art Museum (MA 114), nearly three centuries earlier! There is a sudden crash of diagonals in the foreground, while the distance shows one of the first moonlight landscapes in postmedieval art. This is a youthful work (c. 1593–95) by one of painting's great prodigies. The contours are still sharp, as in the marble sculptures of Michelangelo and the nude athletes on the Sistine Ceiling, which Caravaggio eagerly

12

studied. By coincidence Caravaggio's first name was also Michelangelo. He came from northern Italy, where painters took much interest in the night pieces of Gothic art, but he worked in Rome, until a street murder forced him to flee to Naples.

The immediate impact of Caravaggio's style may be seen in the *St. Serapion*[13] by the Spanish master Francisco Zurbarán (1598–1664), surely one of the outstanding works of art in New England. This early example (1628) is closely related to the first phase of Zurbarán's great contemporary Velázquez (see the *Portrait of Luis de Góngora* in Boston, MA 72). The figure of the dead saint hanging from ropes tied to his wrists may have been cut from a full-length picture. The wonderful cream whites are Zurbarán's specialty, but the whole effect curiously presages Goya's *Disasters of War*.

If the relatively stable forms and hard edges of Caravaggio and Zurbarán continue the classicism of the Italian High Renaissance, the art of Bernardo Strozzi (1581–1644) is much more characteristic of the Baroque. Born in Genoa, Strozzi worked in Venice from 1631 to the end of his life. The Atheneum's *St. Catherine of Alexandria*[14] dates from this period. In this ravishing image, all is in movement, twisted on diagonal axes, and theatrically spotlighted as in the sculpture of Bernini (for example, the celebrated *St. Teresa* altarpiece in Rome). The saint reaches out with mobile fingers for her wheel of martyrdom and clasps a scimitar-bladed palm frond (a more general symbol of martyrdom). A restless contortion begins abruptly at the base (binding-strings of the book), to end finally at the very top with Catherine's spiked crown on her tilted head. All this is enhanced by flickering strokes of subtle color, in which lavenders and pale blues play a major role among the creamy whites. Such painting comes only from an artist hopelessly in love with the *act* of painting. By contrast, Caravaggio and Zurbarán seem to have given us illusions of painted sculpture. But remember: Strozzi was a longtime resident of Venice.

14

13

The inspiration for such "painterly" painting—from Rubens to Fragonard to Delacroix and on to the Impressionists—came from such great Venetian masters as Titian and Veronese. During his early sojourn in Italy, Peter Paul Rubens (1577–1640) drew heavily and enthusiastically from this source. *The Return from the Flight to Egypt*,[15] nearly 8 feet high, dates from about 1613, when the artist, firmly established at Antwerp, was at work on his great triptych for the cathedral, the *Descent from the Cross*. Indeed, the Virgin takes a pose, in reverse, similar to that in the Visitation in the left wing of that altarpiece. The *Return* has a distinguished pedigree, having hung for nearly two hundred years in Blenheim, the palace of the Duke of Marlborough. There are other versions and many later copies of this celebrated work. In his later career, Rubens broke up the surfaces more freely than here and softened the edges, in closer accord with his small oil sketches, of which we discuss examples at Amherst, Harvard, and Yale.

In the Baroque seventeenth century there was a powerful counterforce of quiescence. In Paris, champions of this persistent classicism hailed the work of Nicolas Poussin (1594–1665), and the battle between the Rubénistes and the Poussinistes waged long and clamorously. *The Crucifixion*,[16] set in a thrall of darkness but shot with electric reds, is one of Poussin's most remarkable pictures. He painted it in Rome in 1645. While its personae are engaged in an ancient Roman tableau (and Poussin's career evolved almost entirely in Rome, despite his French origin), Baroque drama nevertheless asserts itself. Yet even in such a context, Poussin controls the dramatic tensions by static balance and symmetry. Note how the diagonals cancel each other, and how the extremities of the composition turn inward, as in any well-behaved Greek or Roman relief. This work, as Dr. Walter Friedlaender has suggested, was perhaps inspired by Andrea Mantegna's *Crucifixion*, now in the Louvre. For a more typical, classicizing Poussin, the reader is referred to the Fogg Art Museum's *Holy Family* (MA 123).

The extravagances of Baroque art seldom found much welcome in the staid Dutch north. Among the Atheneum's many fine pictures from

16

15

this area, *A Moor Presenting a Parrot to a Lady*,[17] by Nicolaes Berchem (1620–83), is a brilliant exception. Three feet high, signed and dated in the artist's final year, this showpiece presumably represents no incident of Dutch life but a dream world of Mediterranean luxury. Standing against the heavily clouded sky and balanced against the warm grays of the nude statue, the lady wears a bodice of electric blue and a white satin skirt worthy of a Ter Borch. At her bosom are some gems rendered with such precision as to remind one of Jan van Eyck. The glistening black Moor is sheathed in a torrent of oranges and vermilions. Note how the parrot connects the two figures—in color.

The intensely preoccupied types in *Gossiping Women*[18] by Francisco Goya (1746–1828) strike a psychological note completely absent from the Berchem picture. Nearly 5 feet long, it was painted about 1790 as a cartoon for an overdoor tapestry. The composition is directly borrowed from Giovanni Battista Tiepolo, the great Venetian decorator who ended his career as court painter in Madrid and died there in 1770. But Goya shifted from Tiepolo's high allegory to everyday genre, and from Tiepolo's gamut of sky blues, pinks, and ivory tones to a more lowering one of olives, russets, and fugitive greens. Already Goya announces himself as a man of the modern world. It should be added that the picture has darkened with time, for the underpainting has eaten through the surface pigments. The Atheneum also owns a work by Goya's brother-in-law, Francisco Bayeu—whose work is rarely seen in American museums—the fine *Portrait of Don Pedro Arascot*. Painted in 1786, it seems tight and stiff by Goya's standards, and distantly touched by the emerging Neoclassicism of Jacques Louis David.

David's art, crisp and taut, is superbly represented in the Altheneum by *The Lictors Bringing Back to Brutus the Bodies of His Sons*, signed and dated 1789—the oil sketch for his large composition in the Louvre. How the new generation of the Romantics, led by Théodore Géricault (1791–1824), reacted against David's domination of the arts during the Revolutionary and Napoleonic periods is seen in *The Coal Wagon*,[19] a

18

17

19

watercolor of exceptional power, probably painted in England about 1820. Here Géricault follows Goya's turn to everyday scenes without a hero. An English connection appears in the low horizon and sweeping distances of Constable and Bonington (examples at Yale's Center for British Art). The massive strength felt in these beasts of burden— Géricault preferred percherons, whereas his follower Delacroix, the chief Romantic of them all, chose elegant Arab chargers—is Géricault's own.

Concern for the common man also marks the art of Honoré Daumier (1808–79). Too often and too glibly he is called a "realist." Realist he certainly was, but his vision was filled with fantasy. Thus, in his *Mountebanks Changing Place*,[20] a pen, chalk, and wash drawing of about 1860, persons on the fringe of society wander as in a nocturnal dream. Daumier's world has so much in common with that of Charles Dickens—including humor not seen here—that it is surprising they neither met nor influenced one another. There is hardly anything finer than the *Mountebanks*, no matter at what size or in what medium, by this giant of nineteenth-century painting. Balzac, Daumier's alter ego in French literature, indeed knew him, and once said of him, "there is something of Michelangelo in that fellow"—the Sistine Ceiling, as it were, brought down to the back streets of Paris. In the presence of such work we can understand Balzac's admiration, and as well Daumier's for Cervantes and Molière. All four dealt with the Human Comedy, that is, with the great passions.

We turn to three beach scenes by French Impressionists in holiday spirit. Eugène Boudin (1824–98), a sailor's son from Honfleur, at the mouth of the Seine, worked there while running a stationery and picture-framing shop at nearby Le Havre. It was only a short trip up the Norman coast to the fashionable watering place of Deauville, where he painted this beach scene[21] in 1863 (signed and dated). Boudin's range was limited, but he had a sharp eye, a deft hand, and a poetic soul. A critic once wrote that "his art had only one window, but it looked out on infinity." Infinity, beneath a slightly domed sky, is in-

20

21

deed what lies beyond this charming cluster of well-heeled urbanites on vacation. Not much larger than the top of a cigar box (on which Boudin often worked *en plein air*), this little canvas seems all the more magical in its spatial extension, and magical also *as painting*, as we have observed in Strozzi's *St. Catherine of Alexandria*. Proof that Boudin's appeal is not limited to the charm of his subject matter can be found in a rare still life in the Atheneum's collection, dating from about 1860.

It was Boudin, apart from academic training in Paris studios, who was the most important formative influence on Claude Monet (1840–1926). Monet spent his childhood in Le Havre and worked with Boudin from about 1856. He too visited the fashionable Norman resorts. *Beach at Trouville*,[22] painted about 1870, is one of the finest of many such compositions. The figures strolling by the Hotel des Roches Noires recall Boudin's, but in their isolation they are more aggressive as they establish positions in the abruptly receding distance. The horizon is dimmed because the emphasis here is on a sequence of flat planes: green staircases up to the terrace, pink building facades, and dark shadows drawn or spotted with a relatively wide brush. The squarish format (21 by 23 inches) plus the many vertical accents, including a steeple that reaches the top edge of the picture, all tend to keep the eye forward despite the pull of the perspectives; as a result, Boudin's serenity gives way to jolts of visual activity. Other Trouville scenes by Monet have large-scale close-ups of figures in the front plane.

In the summer of 1873, Edouard Manet (1832–83) painted the *Beach at Berck*,[23] a resort not far from Calais. In this virtuoso per-

22

23

formance, Manet—the supreme "painter's painter"—implies rather than directly states the holiday animation: it is the *paint* more than the boats that activates the scene. In these black shapes—the glistening blacks of Velázquez—laid so confidently against the blue-green plane of the sea, we find that revolutionary shorthand by which Manet was to inspire much of the painting of our century. It is not surprising to learn that he had been in Holland during the previous summer and that his old enthusiasm for the art of Frans Hals was there renewed. A look at the gloved hand of the Atheneum's *Portrait of Coymans* (or CT 73 at Yale) will clarify the connection.

Only the competing claims of other museums force me to pass over Degas's remarkable late pastel, *Before the Curtain Call* (1892), a symphony of yellow greens and oranges in a collapsed space much more "modern" than that of the Farmington example (CT 3). Such art, properly called Post-Impressionist, is nearly as advanced as *Nirvana: Portrait of Meyer de Hahn*[24] by the younger and more revolutionary Paul Gauguin (1848–1903). It was executed about 1890, shortly before the artist left for Tahiti. In the dwarflike figure of his friend, a Dutch painter, Gauguin found a striking affirmation of his own emerging concept of the primitive human figure. This concept had been nourished by constant visits to the ethnological museums of Paris. In such flat-plane execution the art of Matisse is here directly foreshadowed; yet the oils (and turpentine) betray the broken brush strokes of Impressionism, to which Gauguin had earlier been trained. The image looms like a great icon—so much so that I regret to destroy the visitor's surprise by revealing that it is only 8 inches high.

Before venturing further into modernity, let us backtrack to survey some of the Atheneum's masterworks by American painters. It was not often that the Colonial painters attempted large canvases, their passion for intense detail being more suited to the modest scale—and their houses seldom running to palatial size. Chief Justice and Mrs. Oliver Ellsworth, however, ordered a 6-by-7-foot double portrait from Ralph Earl (1751–1801) in 1792, showing them fiercely at ease in their Windsor residence and, curiously, showing *it* in the distance out the window. While this is Earl's most ambitious work, his "bite" is perhaps better seen in the portraits at Litchfield (CT 36) and in the *Roger Sherman* at Yale (CT 75). The same can be said for Copley's full-length pair of the Jeremiah Lees of Marblehead, Mass., which have neither

24

the flair nor the penetration of his seated *Mrs. Seymour Fort.*[25] John Singleton Copley (1738–1815) painted her in England about 1780, several years after his arrival from Boston. While the rich coloring and showy brushwork betray the influence of prevailing British style, the face, hands, and gesture continue Copley's direct and honest approach. We discuss his superlative Boston work in examples at three colleges: Bowdoin, Dartmouth, and Smith.

By the mid-nineteenth century, the nation had expanded, houses grew larger with the fortunes to support them, and mural-size painting accommodated current excitement over the natural wonders of Hudson River scenery, Niagara Falls, the Rockies, and the Big Sky country. Painters like Thomas Cole (1801–48) traveled afar in search of awe-inspiring sights, especially those affording an opportunity to meditate on the glories of the past; thus we have the Atheneum's 6½-by-11-foot panorama of *Mt. Etna from the Ruins of Taormina*[26] (signed and dated 1843—there is a modest 3-by-4-foot version of it a year later in the Lyman Allyn Museum, New London). Purchased directly from the artist in 1844, *Mt. Etna* is the largest of eleven works by this master in the Atheneum. Note here the plunging perspective through a dark arch down to the greenish sea, and the pale, Fujiyama-like ghost of the snowcapped volcano towering in the distance. Note, too, that the premise of such art was to find an astonishing subject.

James A. McNeill Whistler did not share this attitude, perhaps because he had the advantage of study and contacts abroad. Born in 1834, in the same year as Degas, he went to Paris in 1855 in search of a

25

26

career in art. He quickly made his way into the circle of young painters later called the Impressionists, and exhibited with them in the Salon des Refusés of 1863. At this promising moment he went off to England, where his famous verbal battles in the name of "art for art's sake" perhaps brought about too much affectation in his creative work. But *Coast of Brittany*,[27] signed and dated 1861, preceded all these public manifestations. It is strictly painting and very beautiful painting. The subject is adequate to attract our interest, but what sustains it is the color, the design, the rhythmic sequences across the rocks, the clarity of the air, the clean sweep into distances beyond the sleeping figure. A year later, Whistler painted *The Blue Wave*, now at Farmington (CT 4). If either or both of these pictures remind us of the early Winslow Homer, the suggestion is illusory, for Homer's very first oils date from around 1860.

The mid-nineteenth century in England saw the rise of the Pre-Raphaelite Brotherhood, of whom one of the leading figures was William Holman Hunt (1827–1910). The Atheneum enjoys possession of one of his finest works, *The Lady of Shalott*, begun about 1886 and not completed until some twenty years later.[28] Hunt had been attracted to Tennyson's narrative ballad as early as 1857 and at that time made preliminary drawings. He settled on the single episode of Sir Lancelot riding by and the Lady tearing herself away from her mirror to behold the real image. In the painter's visual equivalent of the poet's neo-medieval magic, there is a wonderful contrast between the dark plush and mauve foreground and the brilliant yellow and green landscape reflected in the cracked round mirror—thus separating the world of reality from the world of dreams. All of this, including an amusing account of a squabble between Hunt and Tennyson over this picture, is detailed in an article by Samuel J. Wagstaff, Jr., in the Atheneum's *Bulletin* for summer 1962.

Although Paris was the art capital of the world from 1900 to the Second World War, when New York supplanted it, the whole twentieth-century scene grew increasingly international. The Norwegian painter Edvard Munch (1863–1944) leads off our survey of the Atheneum's

27

28

important holdings in modern art. *Aasgaardstrand*,[29] an oil of c. 1904, is a beach scene, but what a contrast it makes with the three nineteenth-century examples previously discussed! Figureless, drenched with the color of blood, it whirls us back into nothingness. It is an Expressionist's wild nightmare. As in a dream, there is no physical substance, not even in the rocks or the houses. Smeared surfaces and ribbons of liquid paint limn a psychological state somewhat akin to that of the last works of Vincent van Gogh. Born ten years after him, Munch lived a long and troubled life to the age of eighty-one, whereas Vincent's career was cut short by suicide at thirty-seven. To a considerable degree Munch took up where Vincent left off, and through periods of residence in Berlin helped turn modern German art in the direction of Expressionism —once well described as the sense of the person in a psychological predicament.

Strident color and signs of violence appear in the tilted and saw-toothed elements of the design mark *Military: 1913*,[30] by the American painter Marsden Hartley (1877–1943). One of our pioneers of modern abstract art, he followed a strange pattern in the development of his art. His work of about 1913–15 is perhaps his best; at any rate, he seldom matched its quality until the end of his life, as in the example at Andover (MA 21), when he settled down in his native Maine and softened the abruptness of his abstractions by a loving observation of nature. He spent much of the year 1912 in Paris, where he was attracted to the art of Kandinsky, and lived in Berlin most of the following three years. *Military: 1913* reflects the prewar mood of Germany and its celebrations of the anniversary of a major defeat of Napoleon's

29

30

armies. Among several modern German artists whose influence is visible in this painting, that of Franz Marc is especially strong.

The Atheneum's *Bather*,[31] by Pablo Picasso (1881–1973), dates from 1922, in a period of strenuous variations on classical themes—soon to be softened and sweetened in a reprise of Picasso's early sequence from the "Blue Period" pictures of c. 1901–03 to the "Circus-Rose" ones of 1905 (as in the celebrated *Family of Saltimbanques* at the National Gallery, Washington). From the illustration one might suppose that the *Bather* is a very large canvas. The owner of a *Nude* similar to it in appearance and size enjoyed telling about lending his picture to an exhibition. The borrower agreed to have it called for at the owner's home. To the latter's astonishment, a huge trailer truck drew up. The driver announced he had come for a big picture. The owner, James Thrall Soby, had it in his hand.

Picasso, the master of Cubist interpenetrating planes and the obliterator of sculptural mass and spatial illusion, could also vie with the ancient Greeks and Romans when it came to massiveness. Yet some of his finest Cubist pictures date from the same period as the Hartford *Bather*, for example, Smith College's *La Table* of 1919/20 (MA 185). How could two such opposed styles coexist in the same artist? I think the anecdote suggests an answer. Appearances aside, this is no classical nude, and its 7-inch height has nothing to do with its scale or proportion. The Atheneum owns a fine bronze statuette of a draped warrior, late archaic from south Italy, of about the same height: it makes an interesting comparison in monumentality. Picasso's figure seems overlarge, overripe, seized with a kind of megalomania. Its classical loveliness is deceptive. The "other" Picasso is here.

Joan Miró (born 1898), a fellow Spaniard and younger friend of Picasso, is superbly represented at the Atheneum by *Composition*, painted in the vintage year of 1933.[32] In the dreamlike vein of Surrealism, of which he was one of the leading figures, he combines his gay Catalan fantasy—redolent of Barcelona street fairs—with ominous dark colors. His forms, aptly called biomorphic, have had an enormous influence, on the mobiles of Alexander Calder (NH 2) and all the way to the now forgotten fad of the "shmoo."

32

31

Among black artists in the United States, Romare Bearden (born 1914) is perhaps the most widely respected. The Atheneum's *She-Ba* (1970),[33] 4 feet high, combines collage with other media to produce an impressive evocation of Bearden's cultural heritage. In the catalogue of an exhibition of his work, organized by the Museum of Modern Art in 1971 and circulated nationally, the following statement by the artist is placed beside a reproduction of *She-Ba:* ". . . You have to have some object to harness your affections to; I mean, if you're in love, you're not just in love with life, you're in love with a particular woman."

The art of Jackson Pollock (1912–56), who came into prominence at the end of the Second World War, depends on no such object to harness the attention. The Atheneum's *Painting Number 8, 1952*[34] departs from Pollock's famous "drip" paintings of only two or three years before (MA 22) : very black on white, it is brushed with furious strokes in a frenzy surpassing even that of Edvard Munch. Having no "subject," the work is simply numbered and dated—a practice begun early in the century by Kandinsky on the model of composers of music. (What is the subject of Mozart's Piano Concerto no. 23?) Pollock's signature indicates the "bottom" of the composition, yet upside down the picture would have an equal effect. It was not painted on an easel, but on the floor, with the artist constantly moving around its edges to "wollop" it—Winston Churchill's expressive word for attacking a bare canvas. In an age of space travel, Pollock achieved an art of gravity-defying weightlessness. His "music" is, as you may wish, the clamor of city life or an extension of Vincent van Gogh's excitement over the rush of the stars across a night sky. For such concepts only a very large canvas would suffice.

The visitor will hardly have missed Alexander Calder's enormous red *Stegosaurus*[35] in Burr Mall, off the Main Street side of the Atheneum.

33

35

34

It has an extraordinary history. In her will, made out in 1906, Ella Burr McManus bequeathed fifty thousand dollars for a drinking fountain with sculpture as a memorial to her father. The Connecticut State Capitol Commission was to be in charge of the project, which must be "artistic in design and humane in purpose." She did not insist on a drinking fountain should another form of memorial be considered more appropriate; but she *did* insist that the commission employ "the most competent and gifted sculptor" known to them. For half a century the project ricocheted between commissions and the courts, with more than thirty locations being considered—and the fund inexorably growing. By the 1960s it had reached 1.2 million dollars and the location was finally settled: between the Atheneum and the Municipal Building, happily across from the *Hartford Times*, which Mr. Burr had founded and where he served as editor and publisher for some sixty years. Eventually Alexander Calder was chosen: there was no contemporary American sculptor more eminent than he, and, moreover, he maintained a studio at Roxbury, Connecticut. Mrs. McManus's original idea presumably called for a drinking fountain for *horses*, so Calder created a prehistoric variant, a stegosaurus—the fifth leg a tail?—set before a fountain that no horse is likely to imbibe from. Its double wings suggest a kind of super-Pegasus. Beneath it, people enjoy a relaxed stroll or, in summertime, a peaceful picnic lunch. Calder's moving sculptures ("mobiles"), when not suspended, required a base on which to revolve (see NH 2); and such bases gradually became elaborated into sculptures themselves ("stabiles"), and finally into stabiles without mobiles. *Stegosaurus* is one of the most impressive of them. Calder's 18-inch maquette is exhibited in the Atheneum itself.

In conclusion, attention is directed to the extensive collections of this museum in classical and medieval art and the decorative arts, especially furniture, porcelain, and glass. In conjunction with the local interest in ballet, it is most appropriate that the Serge Lifar collection of ballet set and costume designs is now an added, and great, attraction among the Atheneum's holdings. Lifar was a leading member of the celebrated Diaghilev Ballet. Among many renowned—but then little-known—artists represented are Matisse, Picasso, Juan Gris, Derain, de Chirico, Rouault, and the sculptor Gabo. Specialists in such design include the Russians Leon Bakst and Alexandre Benois.

An ongoing series of catalogues of the various collections is a model of scholarship (and typography). A well-illustrated account of the museum as a whole will be found in the special December 1968 issue of the British magazine *Apollo*.

Litchfield Historical Society

Location: Museum in the Noyes Memorial Building, corner of South and East Sts.; on Routes 202, 118, 63

Hours: Open mid-April to mid-November, Tues.-Sat. 11-5; closed holidays and Tues. following Mon. holidays

Admission: Free. Ⓗ projected

While historical societies are, generally speaking, beyond the scope of this book, the concentration of portraits by Ralph Earl (1751–1801) at Litchfield provides a most welcome reason for an exception to the rule. We refer the reader to the discussion of Earl's *Roger Sherman* at Yale University (CT 75) and of Earl's subsequent career. After his return from England in 1785, he worked in Providence, New York, Stamford, and Greenwich before he began to paint in New Milford and Litchfield around 1789/90. These towns seem to have provided a great many commissions in the final decade of his life, though he also painted in Hartford, Windsor, Middletown, New London, Sharon, and Fairfield; in New York City and Long Island; in Bennington, Vt.; and in Northampton and Worcester, Mass. The Wadsworth Atheneum at Hartford owns the most ambitious work of this period, the *Portrait of Justice Oliver Ellsworth and His Wife,* but some of the Litchfield examples equal it in quality.

The finest of these are two life-size portraits with landscape prospect: *Benjamin Tallmadge and His Son William,* and *Mrs. Tallmadge with Her Son Henry and Her Daughter Maria,*[36] both signed and dated 1790. They give a wonderful impression of Earl's power as an artist. Compared to the *Roger Sherman* of some fifteen years before, they are more sumptuous in dress (for a more bizarre headgear of 1791, see MA 283 and text) and surroundings, and more complex in silhouette and surface. These changes no doubt reflect an English influence on Earl's style as well as the improved economic conditions of the time.

36

The landscape views are a further English touch. Nevertheless, the most superficial comparison with Gainsborough's portrait of his daughters at the Worcester Museum (MA 306) shows how strongly Earl felt the pull of native tradition, and how sparingly he employed the virtuoso Rococo refinements of fashionable English painters. Benjamin Tallmadge had settled in Litchfield in 1784 after a brilliant career in the Revolution. He became a wealthy merchant, a member of Congress (1801–17), and president of the Connecticut Society of the Cincinnati, the insigne of which he wears in Earl's picture of him. In portraiture of this time it is often hard to tell the sex of small children. In the portrait with his mother, Henry is identified, in part, by the little coach, clearly a boy's plaything. The landscape prospects should be compared to the large horizontal *View near Sharon*, also at Litchfield, with the *View from Denny Hill* at the Worcester Museum, and with the view of Hartford behind *Mrs. Moseley and Her Son Charles* (1791) at Yale. One gathers that Earl, like Gainsborough, nursed a secret desire to be a landscapist, but that prevailing fashion made this financially impossible. One could hardly mistake his work, however, for English landscape art.

The Historical Society also owns a pair of portraits securely attributed to Richard Jennys (CT 8), three by Ammi Phillips, and a number of miniatures by Anson Dickinson (1805–51), who flourished in the Litchfield area. The collections include prints and paintings by George Catlin, First World War posters, and many examples of nineteenth-century mourning-pictures. Costumes, Connecticut pewter, and local clocks are also well represented.

Davison Art Center, Wesleyan University

Hours: Tues.-Fri. 12-4; Sat., Sun. 2-5; during summer, appointment suggested
Admission: Free

Through the generosity of Mr. and Mrs. George W. Davison, Wesleyan University acquired one of the finest print collections outside the nation's largest museums; for that reason we make an exception to the decision not to include prints in our survey. The collection may be seen in Alsop House (1838–40), one of the most distinguished Classical Revival mansions in America, renovated in 1952 as an art center. During the 1970s on adjacent property a cluster of eleven buildings was constructed to house the departments of art, music, and theater. One of these includes a spacious gallery for temporary exhibitions.

The print collection, numbering several thousand items, covers the entire field of printmaking since its beginnings in the fifteenth century. All the major masters are represented in impressions of superb quality. There is also an important collection of photographs.

Much of the history of printmaking, and of its expressive potential, is embraced by this striking contrast between two interpretations of the Crucifixion. The first,[37] a German engraving by the so-called Master E.S. (active 1440–67), lies near the invention of making prints on paper from a copper plate. The second, Rembrandt's famous etching *The Three Crosses*[38] (1653), is perhaps the culmination of its development before the invention of lithography.

A word of technical description may be helpful here. Engraving is known to have originated in goldsmiths' shops not long before 1450. Incising a soft metal plate with a burin had been standard procedure with these artisans for centuries. All that was lacking for engraving to be born was paper and the idea of transferring to it an impression from the incised copper surface. Paper became sufficiently available by the mid-fifteenth century to make possible the realization of the idea. After

37

38

the copper plate was incised and the curls of metal cleaned away, the plate was inked. The surface was then wiped clean (a difficult and laborious maneuver), leaving the ink only in the incised troughs. The plate was then put under considerable pressure against a sheet of damp paper, so that the ink was pulled out from the troughs and deposited on the paper. This constituted a single "impression," and the process had to be repeated each time. At a certain point the copper showed signs of wear and the incised lines lost their precision. The conscientious craftsman then destroyed his plate. Sometimes, when he failed to do this, the plate, no longer able to hold the desired amount of ink in its little trenches, went through posthumous editions, the resulting impressions being mere ghosts of what the artist intended.

Etching originated primarily in the workshops of armorers and gunsmiths about the same time as engraving. Again, the unavailability of paper was the only thing that delayed its arrival. Armorers and gun-smiths worked in steel and iron, and because the burin was soon blunted by such hard metals, they used acid to cut their lines. An acid-resisting varnish was first placed over the entire surface, then incised with a stylus down to the surface of the metal; thereupon, the plate was laid in a bath of acid, which ate into the exposed line surfaces. At first all lines were "bitten" to the same depth, and the first etchings were made from iron plates. (Dürer made several of these, one of them, interest-ingly enough, featuring a cannon.) The real "invention" of the process came early in the sixteenth century, when some craftsman had the bright idea of using the softer and more manageable copper plate, and of exposing it to repeated baths by stopping out some of the lines with more acid-resisting varnish, so that any quality of line, from the faintest suggestion to the darkest blur, could be obtained. Etching had reached this technical stage well before the birth of Rembrandt in 1606. A further refinement had also been worked out: the plate could be worked directly with a needle, "dry point," with and without the use of acid. (Dürer made three drypoints.) The resultant "burr" held the ink in such manner that a soft, velvetlike line was deposited on the paper. The effect of drypoint was entirely different from either engraving or etching; its sole technical disadvantage was that the plate quickly dis-integrated under repeated pressure.

The Master E.S. is known by his monogram, but he has not been further identified. Scholars have assigned over three hundred different prints to him on the basis of stylistic analysis from the few examples on which his monogram appears. Many of these are ornamental designs similar to those in vogue among the goldsmiths of the time; and it is possible that his monogram originated as a kind of goldsmith's hallmark. "E.S." was the first engraver who signed his name in any manner what-ever. *The Crucifixion* in the Davison collection is one of only four impressions known to exist today, and it is in mint condition. Its clarity of edge is related, of course, to late Gothic painting in northern Europe; indeed, painting was increasingly influenced by engraving. Some of the chief painters, like Martin Schongauer and Albrecht Dürer (1471–1528)—seen here in a magnificent impression of the *St. Jerome in*

Penitence,[39] c. 1497—were primarily printmakers. "E.S." may have been a painter as well.

In the case of Rembrandt, the relation between painting and printmaking was reversed. Rembrandt was primarily a painter, and his etchings should be thought of as concentrates of a painter's vision. Authorities accept about three hundred of them as authentic. *The Three Crosses,* one of the finest of all, seems to run the whole gamut of natural color, even though it is nothing but ink on paper. That is its miracle, and we may be grateful that such a magnificent impression is still preserved to communicate all that Rembrandt wanted to express. For him line was almost never outline; it was movement, shadow, light, atmosphere, and psychological emotion. *The Three Crosses* is one of Rembrandt's few large plates. It had an astonishing life history. Normally a printmaker perfects his plate, takes his impressions from it, and destroys it. Many of Rembrandt's plates went through different "states"; that is, he made alterations in the plate itself at various stages, and took impressions of all of them. Instead of destroying the plate, he reworked it, in this case with an unheard-of use of drypoint on top of the etched work. He even left the ink on the surface of the plate, to increase the tonal range. The example illustrated is an impression of State IV, the most celebrated of the "states" of this plate. Among the novelties is the horseman below the cross at the left: Rembrandt took it bodily from a bronze medal of Giovanni Francesco Gonzaga by Pisanello, a north Italian sculptor of the fifteenth century. He had a miscellaneous collection of art objects in his studio and occasionally borrowed details from them. In the seventeenth century nobody cared about Pisanello as such; for Rembrandt, the horseman served the same purpose that pseudo-Romanesque architecture had for Jan van Eyck: to provide a wondrous setting for a miraculous event.

It is hard to believe that a virtually unknown print by a great master can still turn up in the attic of a university library, but that is what happened at Wesleyan. In January 1957, Dr. Heinrich Schwarz, the then curator of the Davison collection, found the *Portrait of Gaulon*[40] by

39

40

Francisco Goya (1746–1828) in a scrapbook. It is the first state of the lithographed portrait of the man who printed Goya's wonderful *Bullfight* series at Bordeaux. The only other impression known of this state came to the Bibliothèque Nationale in Paris from the collection of Eugène Delacroix. There is a second state, with a slight alteration, of which only a single impression is known. Goya's stormy career ended in exile at Bordeaux, and in those final few years he divided his time between oil painting and the virtually new technique of lithography. Only the *Bullfight* lithographs were printed in any quantity (one hundred impressions). The Gaulon portrait was done about 1825, when Goya was eighty. Observe the delicacy of touch, and how Goya utilized the grain of the stone and the rich luster of the ink to achieve a soft, atmospheric effect.

Lithography was invented (literally "come upon") by Aloys Senefelder, working in Bavaria just before 1800. As the late William Ivins pointed out in *Prints and Visual Communication* (Harvard University Press, 1953), "it is the only great historic graphic process of which we know the name of the inventor. What is even more remarkable is that he worked out most of the technical capabilities of the medium even as we have it today. Here at last was a graphic process in which the only person who had to have a technical training in process was the printer—for literally anyone who could make marks with either a pen or a pencil [or a crayon or a brush] could, with the services of the printer, make a lithograph . . . . I have myself, in a demonstration, made a print from a drawing that I made on a stone with a lipstick borrowed from a lady in the audience." As in woodcuts (also superbly represented in the Wesleyan collection), impressions are made from the *surface* of the material used—originally a highly porous stone that absorbs the grease of the medium applied to it. The process of transferring the drawing onto a page of paper is based on the incompatibility of oil and water. The number of impressions that can be taken is virtually unlimited.

We have already sensed the graphic power of Honoré Daumier (1808–79) in a wash drawing at Hartford (CT 20). A lithograph, *Rue Transnonain, le 13 avril, 1834*,[41] is universally acknowledged as one of his most magisterial in that medium. It depicts the results of a savage police murder that became a scandal of the day. The three innocent victims are strewn about in colliding diagonals in a Rembrandtesque dusk shot with the whites of tumbling bedsheets and the father's rumpled nightgown and his bare limbs. Daumier often had impressions

41

taken on fine paper (as in the Wesleyan example), but such work was normally destined for popular newsprint brochures, and in mass production on inferior paper much of the subtlety of the inner tones was lost. In the special case of the *Rue Transnonain*, however, the sheets were sold at one franc apiece to defray the fine imposed on the journal *Caricature* for printing it. Appearing two or three times a week in the popular press, Daumier's four thousand different lithographs must have reached a total number of impressions rising into the millions. The production was cut short only by blindness in Daumier's old age. It ranged from bitter political satire to good-natured comment on human foibles.

Mystic Seaport Museum

Location: On Route 27, one mile south of I-95 at exit 90
Hours: Daily 9-5; Memorial Day through mid-September grounds are open until 8; closed Christmas and New Year's Day
Admission: Charged. Ⓗ

Mystic Seaport was the scene of shipbuilding activity even before 1700, but its great days as a whaling center came in the first half of the nineteenth century. With the object of rescuing Mystic's traditions from oblivion, and in the belief that Mystic's pioneering spirit, its craftsmanship, and its inventiveness could be an inspiration even today, the Marine Historical Association was founded in 1929.

The remarkable assemblage of buildings, ships, and exhibits that the association has brought together is primarily of historical and technical interest. Nevertheless, the visitor who is more interested in the visual arts will be well rewarded. The fine proportions of the several houses, stores, taverns, and places of worship, some of them originally built here, most of them moved from neighboring villages and towns, and their interesting furnishings, often of excellent design, lie beyond the scope of this book. The same must be said for the group of sailing ships that has found a permanent home in the quiet harbor. All these exhibits are well described and illustrated in the indispensable *Mystic Seaport Guide*, on sale in the Seaport Stores.

Ships' figureheads offered the artisan carver a wide range of possibilities and a free use of his imagination. The specimens, British as well as American, housed mainly in the Aloha Meeting House and the Wendell Building, comprise a collection of unique interest and importance. Other pieces may be seen in changing exhibits in other buildings, including the ship-carver's shop. Native oak or pine served as the basic material, and color was liberally applied for emphasis and decorative appeal. These figureheads were so highly prized that the shipmasters often had them removed during a voyage and mounted again when the ship entered port.

The collection offers a great variety, both in size, which, of course, depended on the ship's dimensions, and in theme. The carver's problem was to personify the ship's name. The most obvious solution, and perhaps the least interesting, was the stock allegorical female gesticulating with right hand over the heart like some figure from a German Baroque church. We may assume that at the lowest level the artisan copied a well-established model according to his ability. Other examples are more memorable: *Columbia* in liberty cap, *Orlando* in armor (British, 1811), a disdainful *Alexander Hamilton*, a sartorial *Sir Francis Drake* from an eighteenth-century British man-of-war, a horrendous sea serpent from the schooner *Phantom*, a Turkish merchant from the British ship *Aleppo* (1810), a Knight of Malta, and a blackamoor from the *Asia* (Bath, Maine, 1855). Outstanding for size and sculptural power is the 8-foot *Donald McKay*[42] (1855), the latter from a ship of 2,595 tons, the second largest clipper built in America, which was wrecked in the Cape Verde Islands. The vigor of the carving of this clansman seems surprisingly modern; in our century, the Swedish artist Carl Milles has struck a similar note in his wood sculpture. But the *Admiral Farragut* (on indefinite loan), however impressive, would look strange indeed atop Saint-Gaudens's stone base for his Farragut monument in New York City (NH 4).

Also displayed here are several important collections of scrimshaw, ivory, or bone carvings made by sailors during long voyages. As one might expect, the quality varies considerably, in both the carved examples and those in which the surface of whalebone or walrus ivory is engraved or drawn upon with India ink. Many pieces show technical skill in the service of a playful imagination. Others might be described as pinups in Victorian dress.

One returns again and again to the wood-carvers. Figureheads gave them their main opportunity, but stern boards, skylights, and gangway boards presented other occasions for elaborate carving. A fine example, *in situ*, appears on the stern of the *Charles W. Morgan* (1841), the last of the wooden whaleships, one of the main attractions of Mystic Seaport.

The making of scale models of ships is, of course, a related art. The collection of these models is a notable one and it has been brought up to date by including models of twentieth-century ships. If we think back to the great ninth-century Viking ship housed at Oslo, Norway, and to the vessels of classical antiquity, a whole sweep of maritime history can be surveyed.

42

The New Britain Museum of American Art

Location: 56 Lexington St. *From I-84*, take exit 35, follow signs to downtown, take Columbus Blvd. exit, turn left at light onto Lake St., at stop sign turn right onto West Main St. and then immediate left onto Lexington St. *From I-91*, take exit 21, follow Route 72 West through downtown, take Corbin Ave. exit, and at light turn right onto Corbin Ave.; at next light turn right onto West Main St. and follow it .8 mile, turn right onto Lexington Ave. You will appreciate these directions!

Hours: 1-5 daily except Mon.

Admission: Free. ⓗ, also special tour for the deaf and the visually impaired (by appointment)

Outside a few major city museums of the United States, the New Britain Museum of American Art has one of the largest, finest, and most representational collections of American paintings, sculpture, and graphics in the country, numbering some thirty-five hundred works. It is closely followed by that of the Addison Gallery at Andover, Mass. The historical range runs from the eighteenth century to the present. While most leading figures of the nineteenth century are represented at New Britain, the bulk of the collection is devoted to American painting since 1900, with a strong showing of members of the so-called Ashcan School and of more recent work of a relatively conservative character. The collection is being rapidly expanded through purchases, but it is possible to study here the main outlines of American art, except for recent avant-garde developments. The quality is often of a high order, and the pictures are displayed in well-lighted galleries.

A branch of the New Britain Institute, the museum moved in 1937 from the library to its present quarters. At that time the collection numbered only twenty-four paintings. Additions to the well-appointed house bequeathed by Mrs. Grace Judd Landers include three galleries opened in 1964 and an East Wing opened in 1977. It has an active program of temporary exhibitions, especially of living artists. Because these are normally suspended during the summer, these months are the best time to see the permanent collection as a whole.

Eighteenth-century American paintings being no rarity in New England museums, I regret only to mention the excellent examples of such major figures as Smibert, Charles Willson Peale, Badger, Copley, Earl, Trumbull, and Stuart.

Among characteristic early works of the Hudson River School, *Haying near New Haven*,[43] by Frederic E. Church (1826–1900), is of outstanding quality. Painted in 1849, it has none of the exotic wonder of the master's *Icebergs*, painted twelve years later, and now in the Mattatuck Museum at Waterbury (CT 102)—nor of the large version of the same theme that brought a record price for an American painting at a recent London auction. The haying scene exudes a sense of gentle peace, while the intense detail indicates the love that the painter devoted to it.

Albert Bierstadt (1830–1910) may be described as the most Wagnerian of the Hudson River masters. After peaceable but poetic beginnings (as in my selections at Framingham and Harvard, Massachusetts), he explored the Great West, capturing on vast canvases the grandeur of the Rockies and Yosemite (MA 154). In 1872 he painted *Seal Rock*,[44] near San Francisco. That he was born in Germany seems no coincidence when, in the presence of this thundering drama, we think of Wagner's wave-tossed Rhine Maidens in *Das Rheingold*. Indeed, Bierstadt's almost exact contemporary, Arnold Böcklin, Swiss born but active in Germany, in a preposterous picture at Munich called *The Play of the Waves* limned these very Maidens, as fat and complacent as Bierstadt's seals. The violence of Bierstadt's Romanticism comes close to matching the stormiest late works of Turner—but with an extra dose of melodrama. I suspect the visitor will long remember the ominous power of the great green wave, towering and translucent.

With the charming *Portrait of Miss Cara Burch*,[45] painted in 1888 by John Singer Sargent (1856–1925), we are suddenly transported to an elegant normality. It is like a close-up of Sargent's unforgettable Boit girls at Boston (MA 84). Miss Cara is neatly framed in the curvature of the chair: a wistful evocation of the Age of Innocence. Her white dress glistens against the chair's lush red foil. It was against such comfortably restricted social attitudes that the so-called Ashcan School (soon to be discussed) reacted.

In the same year, Childe Hassam (1859–1935)—like Sargent, deeply indebted to training in Paris—painted *Le Jour du Grand Prix*,[46] with its file of elegant folk driving past the Arc de Triomphe. (Note that in those gentle days there was two-way traffic on the Place de l'Etoile.)

43

44

45

46

The title indicates that this is the day of the great races, but it was Degas who painted the races themselves. In this picture we are in the world of the French Impressionists, but Hassam, twenty years younger than Monet and Renoir, is more hesitant about adopting their prismatic color and dappled brush strokes. Also, as a good American, he insisted upon a detailed description of the scene. Hassam's delight in spotting his composition with gaily colored parasols foretells their appearance in the early watercolors and oils of Maurice Prendergast (MA 19 and CT 99). Later and more thoroughly Impressionist pictures by Hassam are discussed in the sections on the museums of Colby and Smith colleges.

Innocent of the pleasures and temptations of Paris was John Haberle (1856–1933) of New Haven, a contemporary nonetheless of Sargent and Hassam. A longtime American tradition of "fool-the-eye" painting came to a climax at the end of the nineteenth century in such artists as Harnett (MA 220) and Peto (MA 187), but none was more resourceful than Haberle. *Time and Eternity*,[47] dating from about 1890, takes its title from the news clipping, which, believe it or not, is painted. So is everything else in this assemblage of mementos, including the cracked watch crystal. Do not miss the nails with their shadows cast on the "board"—as if this were the back of the painting itself. The museum owns a second oil and several pencil sketches by the artist.

Everett Shinn (1876–1953), who painted *French Vaudeville*[48] in 1937, was the youngest member of a group variously known as The Eight and the Ashcan School. The leaders of this group, Robert Henri and John Sloan, are discussed in the sections on the museums of Mount Holyoke and Bowdoin colleges. Shinn preferred the more oblique reality of the theater to Sloan's teeming New York streets and parks or Henri's brusque middle-class portraits. He also adored Paris, which the others, in their excitement about American city life, refused to visit. Thus his art absorbed much of the Impressionists' feeling for light and atmosphere. Characteristically, he preferred popular vaudeville to ballet at the Opéra—Degas's particular obsession (RI 18). But his intention was more purely illustrative than Degas's; we look in vain here for the latter's intricately interwoven design. In the foreground portraits we catch overtones of George Bellows and Guy Pène Du Bois.

47

48

A strain of nostalgia marks the realism of Charles Burchfield (1893–1967), who lived and worked in the Buffalo area. *Lavender and Old Lace*,[49] on which Burchfield labored from 1939 to 1947, is a giant-sized watercolor measuring over 3 by 4 feet. It is one of his masterpieces. "Now at last," he later wrote, "it seemed to embody all that I felt about the old abandoned house, the tragedy of the decay of a beautiful place contrasted with the ravishing beauty of the lilacs in bloom." He might have added a note about the contrast between the harsh spikes atop the Gothic structure and the luminous curvilinear explosion of the branches of the great trees. To achieve his effect, Burchfield pasted together several wide strips of paper, and thickened the watercolor with opaque material.

A very different picture of America appears in *Arts of the West*,[50] painted in 1932 in tempera with oil glaze by Thomas Hart Benton (1889–1975). This is one of a series of five murals executed for the library of the Whitney Museum of American Art in its old quarters in downtown New York. When the Whitney moved to West Fifty-fourth Street (prior to moving again to its present location), the murals stayed behind. The New Britain Museum acquired them in 1953 and installed them in a special new gallery eleven years later. Known as *The Arts of Life in America*, they are among the most ambitious examples of the movement called Regionalism—fashionable in the Depression years and currently returning to favor with the rise of the new Photo-Realism. Both movements marked a swing of the pendulum away from European-inspired abstract art. If the exaggerated contortions of the figures seem gratuitously borrowed from El Greco, nonetheless a keen observation and a lively sense of rhythmic design are at work here. Color, however, is perhaps more blatant than expressive. The museum's

49

50

excellent 1975 catalogue lists, in addition to Benton's murals, five oil studies for them, six other paintings and drawings, and no fewer than eighty-five lithographs. There is no museum outside Missouri in which Benton's work can be better studied.

Sanford Low, the first director of the New Britain Museum, founded the now extensive collection of original works by magazine illustrators in 1965. Prominent among them is Norman Rockwell, whose oil (33 by 31 inches), *Weighing In*[51] (1958), for a *Saturday Evening Post* cover, is surely among his most spectacularly convincing. What an eye, and what a steady hand! It is worth recording that Rockwell, the friendliest of men, was also a modest one. He insisted that he was not an artist, but an illustrator. I know from conversations with him that he admired modern art and wished he could "do" it. There was neither animus nor surprise when I rejected, as juror, one of his modernistic attempts from an exhibition in Pittsfield. For further discussion of this much-loved master, see the entry on The Old Corner House, Stockbridge, Mass.

I regret that restrictions of space preclude my discussion of fine oils by Winslow Homer, Thomas Eakins, Asher Durand, Fitz Hugh Lane, John Twachtman, George Inness, and George Bellows; and watercolors by Maurice Prendergast, John Marin, and Charles Demuth.

51

New Haven Colony Historical Society

Location: 114 Whitney Avenue
Hours: Tuès.-Fri. 10-5; Sat., Sun. 2-5
Admission: Free, except for a charge to use the library

A visit to this beautifully appointed institution, with its artistically mounted exhibits, is sure to be rewarding. The history of New Haven begins with the first English Puritan settlers in 1638, and until 1873 Hartford and New Haven alternated as the state capital.

Among the painters represented here are Reuben Moulthrop (1763–1814), a local artist whose style reverted to the flattened images of Elizabethan or of Dutch provincial art of the sixteenth century; and Joseph Blackburn, George Henry Durrie, John W. Jarvis, Eastman Johnson, and John Ferguson Weir. A fascinating picture of the *Monitor* and the *Merrimac*, signed and dated in 1883 by Warren Sheppard, was lent in 1939 to "Life in America," an important exhibition staged by the Metropolitan Museum of Art.

The furniture is of superb quality, and it is complemented by exhibits of silver, pewter, ceramics, and glass.

Peabody Museum of Natural History, Yale University

Location: 170 Whitney Avenue
Hours: Mon.-Sat. 9-5; Sun. 1-5; closed major holidays
Admission: Free. Ⓗ

Evidence of skilled arrangers of exhibits abounds here, as in the neighboring New Haven Colony Historical Society. Natural history takes precedence in this museum, from giant dinosaur skeletons on the ground floor to ravishing vitrines of stuffed birds upstairs. But archaeology and ethnology are also in the museum's purview, and that means the presence of art. If we mention the contents briefly, it is only to concentrate on the so-called primitive cultures at Harvard's vaster Peabody Museum—the gift of the same George Peabody (1795-1869) who founded the Peabody Museum at Salem, Mass. Yet the range and the quality of Central and South American and of Oceanian arts are considerable. For African art, however, one fares better in a special large gallery in the university's major art museum.

Not to be missed are two enormous murals by Rudolph Zallinger (born 1919) representing *The Age of Reptiles* (completed 1947) and *The Age of Mammals* (completed 1967). Executed in the Italian fresco medium, each mural took several years to complete. *The Age of Reptiles* measures 110 by 16 feet, and it was awarded a Pulitzer Prize.

Yale Center for British Art

Location: Chapel St. between York and High Sts. (opposite the Yale University Art Gallery); parking at rear
Hours: Tues.-Sat. 10-5; Sun. 2-5; closed major holidays
Admission: Free. Ⓗ

The gift of Paul Mellon, who attended Clare College, Cambridge, after his graduation from Yale, the Center is housed in a much-praised building designed by Louis I. Kahn. It opened in 1977. For many years Mr. Mellon had been collecting British art: his gift includes over twelve hundred paintings, ten thousand drawings, twenty thousand prints and an equal number of rare books, and a small but representative group of sculptures. The historical range runs from Elizabethan times to the mid-nineteenth century. Storage is completely "live"; that is, the public may inspect these picture-lined galleries without prior appointment.

From this vast assemblage we have selected ten paintings to give an overall introduction. Well-designed scholarly catalogues are available at the entrance desk for those who wish to explore in greater depth. Our selections are normally on view in the subtly lighted galleries on the fourth floor, but the largest pictures are hung in one of two sky-lit, oak-paneled courts, onto which these galleries open.

We begin with two of England's most distinguished visitors. In June 1629, Peter Paul Rubens (1577–1640) arrived in London as the diplomatic envoy of the King of Spain, charged with negotiating a treaty with England. King Charles I was reported as well satisfied with the mission and as wishing to know "a person of such merit." An excellent account of Rubens's enthusiastic reception (including an honorary degree at Cambridge) and of the success of his visit, which was extended to March 1630, is given in Ruth S. Magurn's edition of his letters (Harvard University Press, 1955). It was during this time that he painted the ceiling of the great Banqueting Hall of Whitehall Palace, as well as the *Portrait of the Earl of Arundel* in the Gardner Museum, Boston (MA 47) for which the Clark Institute has the preliminary drawing (MA 264). A major attraction at the British Center is *Peace Embracing Plenty*,[52] Rubens's oil sketch (on a panel 2 feet

52

high) for one of the compartments of the Whitehall ceiling. Such
sketches as this and Harvard's *Neptune Commanding the Waters*
(MA 119) all but allow us to look over the master's shoulder as he
swirls his brush in bold serpentine strokes, and shapes his massive
Baroque forms. The color is deliciously fresh, the embrace as joyously
ardent. The great Solomonic columns, which echo it rhythmically, are
taken from Bernini's colossal baldacchino at St. Peter's, admired by
Rubens on earlier visits to Rome.

As it turned out, Rubens's favorite pupil, Anthony Van Dyck (1599–
1641), was not only a visitor to England, but from 1632 until his
death a resident. It has been said of this Fleming that he created the
English gentleman. Indeed, his images of aristocracy have shaped official
British portraiture down to our own time. The full-length *Mountjoy
Blount, Earl of Newport*,[53] painted c. 1637/8 and 8 feet tall, ranks
high among Van Dyck's works of this kind. Compared with Rubens's,
the color glows with a more subdued flame—much closer to Titian's—
the pose is more refined and even languid (gentlemen don't have to *do*
anything), and the finery is carried to an unheard-of virtuoso sheen. If
there were a dog here, it would have to be a greyhound. Earlier paintings
of Van Dyck have much more of Rubens's heft and fleshiness; and
echoes of his master's power persist until the final decade, for Van Dyck
did his best to keep in touch with an Antwerp dominated by its native
colossus. But the Mountjoy portrait belongs securely to Van Dyck's
"English period"; and it is fair to suggest that this arbiter of English
taste was in turn deeply affected by English culture. The same can be
said for two other famous immigrants: Hans Holbein and George
Frederick Handel.

With Thomas Gainsborough (1727–88), we come to a later English
disciple of Van Dyck, that is, in the fashionable portraiture of the latter
half of Gainsborough's career. *Girl Seated in a Park*,[54] however, dates
from the early 1750s, and here the connection is closer to the Rococo
art of Paris. Yet this is no Boucher soubrette. A degree of stiffness—as

53

54

it were a faint echo of Elizabethan images—and a certain naive self-consciousness give the work a rural and provincial air. Ellis Waterhouse, the leading authority on Gainsborough, has pointed out a Dutch influence, conflicting with the French one, that brought him back to nature. *Girl Seated in a Park* was painted only a little later than the most celebrated of the master's early works, the *Portrait of Mr. and Mrs. Joseph Andrews*, in the London National Gallery; in that masterwork, Waterhouse notes, "for the first time, the old tradition of the 'conversation piece' becomes transmuted in the hands of an artist for whom the portrait and the landscape are both of equal concern." The same can be said for our lady and the park in which she sits so demurely. For Gainsborough's more confident and more psychologically penetrating later work, see our selection from the Worcester Art Museum (MA 306). For examples of the "conversation piece," in which landscape is clearly secondary to the figures, see the Center's *Drummond Family*, by John Zoffany (1734/5–1810) and the same master's *Judge Suetonius Grant Heatly with His Sister, Temperance*, c. 1783–89, at Springfield (MA 217).

Gainsborough's contemporary George Stubbs (1724–1806), generously represented at the British Center, seems to prefigure Géricault and other painters of the Romantic nineteenth century in his passion for animals. He obviously preferred them to humans as subjects for his art. The very large *Lion Attacking a Horse* announces a theme later exploited by Delacroix and, in bronze sculpture, by Antoine Louis Barye (1796–1875). But *Turf, with Jockey Up*,[55] painted c. 1765 in the relatively modest dimensions of about 3 by 4 feet, is far subtler. The meticulously delineated silhouette of *Turf*, magically expressive of the racer's potential speed, makes the whole range of British sporting prints seem animated by mere types. Here indeed is a horse portrait, and that of the jockey is hardly less telling. The adjacent rubbing-down house, properly subdued, and the pale fringe of distant trees combine to project the main element of concern, and to give it an impressive scale.

Among the many masterly human portraits from the end of the eighteenth century, we have chosen the half-length *Admiral Sir John Markham*,[56] painted c. 1793 by Sir Thomas Lawrence (1769–1830),

56

55

third president of the Royal Academy and the most fashionable artist of his generation. As invariably in his work, the textures sparkle as they catch the light, while the rapidly brushed passages, comparable to Van Dyck's, imply the sort of bravura of which there is little evidence in American painting before John Singer Sargent. (Gilbert Stuart developed his virtuosity in London—and for that matter Sargent developed *his* in Paris.) Psychologically, the admiral's portrait probes more deeply than many of Lawrence's ceremonial images of royalty and other Very Important Persons.

British landscape painting of the first half of the nineteenth century was dominated by J. M. W. Turner (1775–1851) and John Constable (1776–1837). We discuss the former in works at other museums (MA 165 and MA 253), but the Yale Constables are so numerous—thirty-five oils in one gallery—and of such superb quality that examples elsewhere in New England must yield to them. *Dedham Vale with Ploughman*,[57] only 16¾ inches high, is a masterpiece of the "early" Constable—he was already some forty years old, but, unlike the prodigious and immediately successful Turner, he developed very gradually against a tide of public discouragement that today seems inexplicable. *Hadleigh Castle, the Mouth of the Thames—Morning, after a Stormy Night*[58] (note the very explicit title) dates from 1829. Four feet high, it represents Constable's later and more ambitious phase, marked by churned-up surfaces and flecks of high-intensity color that were to have a revolutionary effect on landscape painting on the Continent. Yet the two pictures have this in common: they depict a specific place at a specific time of day under specific atmospheric conditions. This sounds like the art of the French Impressionists; and indeed Constable was one of their chief precursors. His small oil sketches and

57

58

watercolors, *painted out of doors* with incredible spontaneity and freedom, were especially admired by them. Furthermore, Constable virtually rescued the color green from the "Old Master" brown sauces of traditional landscape painting.

Constable seldom traveled beyond his native Suffolk and its southern neighbor Essex. He was born at East Bergholt, near Dedham; and Hadleigh is on the Essex side of the Thames as it meets the sea. There were trips as far afield as Salisbury, but Constable never left England. Turner, on the contrary, crisscrossed western Europe in search of scenic wonders. If Constable, moved by the serenity of his own homeland, is England's closest parallel to Wordsworth in painting, Turner comes nearest to Byron's majestic apostrophes to the sea.

Richard Parkes Bonington, born in 1801 and dead only twenty-seven years later, could hardly rival the careers of these two giants, but he was an outstanding example of what Erwin Panofsky has called a "major-minor artist." The range was small, though he produced history pictures as well as landscapes, and he traveled extensively in France, where he was admired even more than in England. *River Landscape*,[59] painted about 1825–27 in characteristically small format (9⅝ by 13¾ inches), shows him at his best. The very low horizon has Dutch precedent, and the scene as a whole echoes that tradition, but the drenched atmosphere is his own, as are the rich colors that plunge into dark intensities. Bonington's skies are very special: not the densely massed clouds of Constable, nor yet the swirling effects of Turner, but long horizontal fingers of cloud-film against the sky's fresh blue, often tapering toward yellow at the horizon. Perhaps it is irrelevant to mention Masaccio, the great Florentine, whose dates are 1401–28, for he was truly a major-major master, but like him Bonington charted new paths of human vision.

The case of John Martin (1789–1854), whose *Deluge*,[60] nearly 6 feet

59

60

high, was painted in 1834, is highly exceptional in British art. Even Turner at his stormiest did not plunge so deeply into the prevailing Romanticism. *Deluge* brought Martin a gold medal at the 1835 Paris Salon. Moons, suns, and lightning assist here at a cosmic catastrophe in which Byron and the Bible seem conjoined. The color, violent but perhaps more literary-associative than directly expressive, owes much to the later work of William Blake. Modern enthusiasm for Martin can probably be attributed to a spin-off of Surrealism's wilder fantasies.

The phenomenal revival, currently, of nineteenth-century Academic art has included that of Frederick Leighton (1830–96), who may be thought of as the English equivalent of William Bouguereau (see MA 257). President of the British Royal Academy and member of all the prestigious academies of Europe, created a baronet in the year of his death, Leighton turned out a vast number of pleasing historical pictures and pretty nude confections based on classical mythology. He had all the skills, but his imagination was at best defective. What a stunning surprise, therefore, to come upon his full-length *Portrait of Mrs. James Guthrie*!61 Painted about 1861, she stands statuesquely in an interior beside two vases of flowers. Like Van Dyck's ladies and gentlemen, she is not very busily occupied, nor is her face marked by much character. But like Herrick's Julia, how sweetly flows the liquefaction of her clothes! What a rustle of black taffeta! What a happy placement of the figure between the elegant flowers and the elegantly inlaid chair! But why the current excitement, notably among the middle-to-lesser aged, about Academic art, apart from its documentation of the taste of a certain period? Could it be because the supply of more profound art of the time has dwindled, or because in today's paucity of messages of complexity and depth, technique and exploration of novel media have captured the market?

61

Yale University Art Gallery

Location: 1111 Chapel Street (opposite the Center for British Art)
Hours: Tues.-Sat. 10-5; Sun. 2-5; and during the academic year Thurs. 6-9
P.M.; closed Mon. and major holidays
Admission: Free. Ⓗ

Among the art museums of Connecticut, the Yale University Art
Gallery—even without the Center for British Art—ranks at the top with
the Wadsworth Atheneum at Hartford. Outstanding bequests have
come to it, notably the Jarves and Griggs collections of Italian painting;
the Garvan collection of early American silver, painting, and furniture;
the Moore collections of textiles and of Near and Far Eastern art; the
Société Anonyme collection of modern art; the Linton collection of
African sculpture; the Stoddard collection of Greek and Roman vases;
the Rabinovitz collection of paintings; and the Stephen C. Clark collection of paintings, sculpture, and drawings. In addition, the gallery
displays antiquities from the Yale excavations at Dura-Europos, a Roman
outpost in the Syrian desert. Medieval sculpture is well represented, and
the collections of drawings and prints are among the finest in New
England.

Yale's was the first art gallery opened to the public in the United
States. Its history began in 1832 with the Trumbull Gallery, housing
the work of Colonel John Trumbull (1756–1843), "patriot artist" of
the Revolution and aide-de-camp to General Washington. The building,
torn down in 1901, was designed by Trumbull himself.

Street Hall (1864), across High Street from the present complex
and connected to it by a bridge, originally contained the James Jackson
Jarves collection of Italian paintings, the first assemblage of original
works of art made by an American collector. Jarves, a portraitist of
repute, was a pioneer in public education through the study of art, and
it is fitting that his pictures have found a university home. That they
did is the result of an elaborate piece of irony. Jarves offered his
collection of 119 paintings, virtually at cost, to the Museum of Fine
Arts in Boston and to the Metropolitan in New York; both institutions
allowed the opportunity to slip through their fingers, and in 1871 Yale
got the collection because it was on deposit with the university as security
against a twenty-thousand-dollar loan.

The present complex is composed of two connecting units. The first,
with a bridge to Street Hall, was constructed in 1928; its design was
based on a Gothic palace at Viterbo, Italy. The second, extending along
Chapel to York Street, was opened in 1953; it was designed in starkly
functional style by Louis I. Kahn and Douglas Orr, Associated Architects. The visitor will note the advantages of the latter approach to
planning a museum, as against the older method of adapting a modern
building to a gem culled from the past.

Art-historical studies at Yale cover the whole range of world art;

it is not surprising, therefore, that its gallery is more encyclopedic than even the Wadsworth Atheneum. An overview of the contents thus presents difficulties as to procedure. For the sake of clarity, we shall discuss sculpture first, and then turn to paintings—the only two arts for which we have space in this section. The sequence will be roughly chronological, but the reader will note as we go along that, as the great French art historian Henri Focillon often pointed out in his classes at Yale, art has not always evolved in chronological order.

The large glazed-tile *Lion*[62] is Babylonian work of about 600 B.C. It once decorated the processional street leading to the Ishtar Gate in the time of King Nebuchadnezzar. The fierce animal strides alertly along the brightly colored wall, of which it is an integral part. Consider the artistic loss if the lion had been, instead, merely applied as a relief. As the Romanesque sculptors well understood, one way to achieve monumentality is to make the sculpture literally a part of the monument.

The marble relief of *Five Divinities in Procession*,[63] 4 feet long, is from no earlier than 50 B.C. and possibly as late as the second century A.D. Its style is Archaistic, in the revival of Greek art of the sixth century that became fashionable in Rome's Augustan Age. The work has such refinement, however, that a Greek artist is certainly its author. Represented from right to left—in processional order—are Zeus, Hera, Athena, Aphrodite, and the lyre-carrying Apollo. Revivals, like forgeries, always manage to betray their own era—though, as everyone knows, not always immediately. Here the sophisticated knowledge of anatomy indicates the later Hellenistic phase of Greek art, as do the freely flowing rhythms so smoothly linking one figure to the next. The marble itself is Greek, its crystals sparkling in the light. Comparison with the sixth-century amphora at Worcester (MA 288) will quickly show the source

62

63   64

of this figure style, as well as the differences resulting from the passage of half a millennium.

Our next selection demonstrates what happened to the tradition of high Greek sculpture after it moved with Alexander's conquests into a foreign land. The *Seated Buddha*,[64] in black schist, first to third centuries A.D., comes from the region of Gandhara, in Afghanistan. Its cultural orientation is ancient Indian, but the crisp cutting, the powerful modeling, and the very character of the head all betray a Greek spirit. Beneath this network of abstract lines is a human body understood, as the Greeks understood it, as an organism.

The 1970 catalogue of Yale's Far Eastern art, by George J. Lee, contains nearly five hundred entries, but this is only a selection. We have chosen a single towering masterpiece—towering in quality but not in actual size, for it is only 3½ feet high. Carved from a single piece of wood, with traces of the original polychrome on a gesso base, the Buddhist deity *Bon-ten*[65] is Japanese work of the tenth century (Fujiwara period). There is a faint residue of Hellenistic sculpture here, via Indian and then T'ang dynasty Chinese sources, but the stiff, bow-legged stance retains little of Greek resilience, while the drapery folds have become also purely decorative. But the figure has a commanding presence, partly through the aggressive lift of the arms and especially through the proud attitude of the head (with its impassive face), tightly framed between the strong vertical accents of the elongated ears and the clumpish force of the flat cylindrical headdress.

Equally prized among the Yale Far Eastern sculptures is a Chinese seated *Kuan-yin*, a Bodhisattva, of the twelfth century, somewhat stiffer and less elegant than the comparable figure in Boston (MA 93).

The *Bon-ten* makes a fascinating comparison with our next selection, a twelfth-century French Romanesque figure of a *Standing Saint*.[66] This life-size image is an architectural element transposed with great restraint into the human form. It is one of a series that ornamented the church of St. Martin at Angers; they were placed either on the facade or at

65

66

the base of the ribs of the choir vault at the point where the ribs joined
the side walls. They were carved from the same limestone used for the
building itself; and the carvers differed from ordinary stonemasons
only in the sense of their superior skill. Sculpture in Romanesque Europe
was inspired by a revived interest in the molded forms of ancient Roman
art—at a distance of nearly a millennium—but the presence of actual
Roman remains in Europe helps account for the much closer relationship to that source than the distant echo we have observed in the
Japanese *Bon-ten*. In the Angers *Saint* we seem to watch the coming into
life of the human figure, just prior to the Gothic era, after its long
hibernation through the Dark Ages.

As for Gothic sculpture at Yale, a small ivory *Madonna and Child*,
French fourteenth century, of the greatest elegance and sweetness, is
comparable to the wonderful ivory relief of the same theme in Worcester
(MA 294).

We skip now to the French eighteenth century, superbly represented
by the plaster *Bust of Denis Diderot*,[67] painted to resemble terra-cotta, by
Jean Antoine Houdon (1741–1828). Modeled about 1771, it tempers the
prevailing Rococo liveliness with a taste of the fast-developing solemnity
of Neoclassicism. Houdon was an almost exact contemporary of Jacques
Louis David, whose *Oath of the Horatii* (Louvre), painted in Rome
in 1784, marked the arrival, full force, of the new movement that swept
all before it through the Revolution and the Napoleonic era. For a
comparison with the portraiture of David, consider his *Emmanuel Sièyes*
at Harvard (MA 125), a work of 1817. In Sièyes's severe company,
Diderot, the great critic and encyclopedist, exhibits qualities of informality, high wit, and a Voltairean intelligence.

We skip again, this time to our own century, with sculptures by
Constantin Brancusi (1876–1957) and Henry Moore (born 1898).
Thanks to the bequest of the Société Anonyme collection and the ac-
quisitions of the former director of the gallery, Andrew C. Ritchie,
Yale is rich indeed in modern sculpture. Brancusi's *Yellow Bird*,[68]

68

67

painstakingly carved and smoothed in tawny marble and set on a lime-stone base, dates from about 1912. It precedes by a few years his celebrated and still more elegant *Bird in Space*, of which a version in polished brass may be seen at New York's Museum of Modern Art. For thirty years Brancusi made variations on the bird theme, those in stone coming before the brass ones in each step of the sequence (he was first and foremost. a carver). The well-known dictum of the architect Mies van der Rohe, "less is more," surely applies to the work of Brancusi, but the latter put it differently: "Simplicity is not an end in art, but one reaches simplicity in spite of one's self by approaching the real meaning of things." Brancusi approached the very essence of sculpture: the *expressive* arrangement of solid masses in space. Surely his evocations should not be classed as "abstract" without further qualification, be-cause they start and end with a deep study of nature. Born in Rumania, Brancusi settled in Paris in 1904. Brief training in the Ecole des Beaux-Arts was followed by a period of work under the powerful in-fluence of Rodin, but soon the growing interest in the art of primitive cultures (initiated essentially by Gauguin) turned him in the new direction—one absolutely revolutionary for the whole range of twentieth-century sculpture. In this connection it is worth recalling that the art of Picasso underwent similar metamorphosis a few years earlier, specifically in 1906/7, as a result of his exposure, first to the ancient "Iberian" art of his homeland, and then to African sculpture. Thus the seminal phenomenon of *Les Demoiselles d'Avignon* (Museum of Modern Art, New York), which had an equally potent effect on modern painting.

Among several major sculptures in the peaceable outdoor area at the rear of the gallery, the bronze *Draped Seated Woman*,[69] 1957/8 and purchased from the artist in 1959, proclaims the powerful presence of Henry Moore. The effect is so majestic that it is a surprise to learn that the piece is only 6 feet high. At the time of its purchase the artist wrote Mr. Ritchie a most revealing statement of what sculpture—and his own work—is all about. "Beneath surface interest there must be a satisfactory arrangement of forms—an alert alive pose, for power in sculpture is given by a strong tense spring in the relationship of the large masses to each other." And concerning the drapery: "Besides revealing the form it covers, drapery can have infinitely varied surfaces and rhythms, larger or smaller folds going round the form showing

69

its section—or along it emphasizing its direction, lying slackly between points or stretching taut from one point to another, showing thrusts from within."

One of the oddities of cultural history is the dearth of fine sculpture in England up to the last half century. As compared with what was achieved on the Continent, English medieval sculpture was decorative rather than figurative; and from Elizabethan times onward much of the work was done by foreigners—as visitors to the Yale Center for British Art will have noticed. So why the extraordinary emergence in our own day of sculpture by English artists? Outstanding among them is Henry Moore, a Yorkshireman. It should be pointed out that Moore traveled widely, that he is thoroughly at home with all manifestations of modern art, especially in its concern for primitive arts—including, in his case, Pre-Columbian sculpture. But Moore also reveres the great sculpture of ancient Greece, as may be divined from his *Draped Seated Woman.* It would appear that the opening up of Britain, like so much of the modern world, through technological advances in transportation and communications, provides the answer to our query. I leave to others an explanation of why the literary genius of Albion had no counterpart in its feeling for plastic form.

Those interested in tracing the emergence of Italian painting from its Byzantine origins into the Gothic age will find in the great Jarves collection a better opportunity than is provided anywhere else in New England. Such thirteenth-century artists as Guido da Siena and the anonymous Magdalen Master lead on to major figures of the next century in Florence and Siena.

We pass on to the continuation of Gothic attitudes in Italy and the Flemish North during the Renaissance era. Two superb paintings, totally disconnected, will illustrate the point. *Allegory of Intemperance*[70] was painted by Hieronymus Bosch (c. 1450–1516) in the region between present-day Belgium and Holland, while *The Temptation of St. Anthony*[71] is the work of the Sienese artist Stefano di Giovanni, called

71

70

Sassetta (1392–1450), or of a close associate. The Bosch is related to a painting in the Louvre, *The Ship of Fools*, and may even have been cut from it. The Sassetta is one of a series of little episodes from the life of St. Anthony Abbot. Among others of this series, *The Torment* is also at Yale, while *The Meeting with St. Paul Hermit* is in the National Gallery, Washington.

Though Bosch painted long after Sassetta, he rejected all outward interest in Renaissance forms of expression. Instead, he couched his spiritual messages in the manuscriptlike space of Flemish art, and in those spidery marionettes that seem so suggestive of the art of Paul Klee. Like Klee, too, his art is freighted with symbolism and shrouded in magic. Bosch's theme was not man's nobility but his waywardness in the sight of God. Nevertheless, Bosch could scarcely disguise his delight in sin, and so he reminds us of those carvers of hell scenes in the Last Judgments of the great cathedrals, who clearly found Damnation more interesting than Paradise. Gluttony is the main theme here: the figure striding a barrel suggests a devotee of Bacchus and one of the men shoving him along wears a monk's black hood; the tavern sign stuck in the tent where an amorous couple imbibe has an unmistakably symbolic pig's foot; and the adjacent coat of arms is that of a family from Hertogenbosch, the painter's own birthplace. Satire bites hardest when it is most specific.

Being Sienese, Sassetta (or his associate) did not stray far from the forms of Duccio and Simone Martini. (For the latter, see MA 34 and MA 115.) The discoveries of Renaissance Florence held little interest for him, or for his fellow townsman Giovanni di Paolo, several of whose works Yale owns (but see MA 35). A medieval air wafts gently across this solemn but enchanting *Temptation*. The slit in the skirt of the devil-woman was not put there to reveal a knowledge of Renaissance anatomy. Approximately 15 inches square, this tempera panel was painted c. 1430.

Even as late as about 1470, Sienese art reverently perpetuated its Gothic origins. The lovely lunette *Annunciation*,[72] over 4 feet long, once crowning an altarpiece, was formerly attributed to Neroccio di Bartolommeo Landi (1447–1500), but today it is given a double authorship to include Francesco di Giorgio (1439–1502), with whom Neroccio was closely associated from about 1469 to 1475. Francesco di Giorgio was a leading Renaissance architect and as a painter very knowledgeable in the ways of perspective. Thus the advanced Renaissance setting, including its wall reliefs animated by anatomically

72

liberated figures, is assigned to him, while the Virgin—strikingly reminiscent of the comparable figure in Simone Martini's great *Annunciation* in the Uffizi at Florence—is the work of the stay-at-home Neroccio. The Angel, however, more sprightly and Botticellian, may well be Francesco's work. An exquisite silvery tone, common to the art of both masters, pervades this lovely dream world. We should add that Simone's *Annunciation*, though now in Florence, was in Neroccio's time on an altar in Siena's cathedral, whence it held most Sienese painting in thrall for a century and a half. Look again at the colors of Neroccio's and Francesco's lunette: the lavender pinks, cool grays, and orange-rust tones as subtle and oblique as those of Antoine Watteau.

Among seventeenth-century paintings at Yale, the *Portrait of Mevrouw Bodolphe*,[73] signed and dated 1643 by Frans Hals (c. 1581–1666), is perhaps the outstanding masterpiece. AETAT SUAE 72, as the inscription reads, this elderly woman embodies all the qualities that produced Dutch prosperity in its Golden Age. Here in mid-career Hals has tempered the exuberance of his early shooting-company pictures, not to mention their brilliant array of oranges, sky blues, and blacks, with a sober palette of blacks, browns, and whites befitting the occasion. The English critic Roger Fry once wrote that "some of the greatest works of art in the world are portraits, but they are very rarely the work of portrait painters." We think of Rubens, Rembrandt, Velázquez, Degas, and Cézanne and agree, but Hals, the supreme portrait specialist, is one of the very rare exceptions.

From the superb collection of American portraits at Yale, I have chosen three examples to illustrate a certain continuity in the American view of life. The first is a large group portrait of *Bishop George Berkeley and His Entourage*[74] by John Smibert (1688–1751). The second is the stark image of *Roger Sherman*[75] by Ralph Earl (1751–

73

74

75

1801). The third is *John Biglen in a Single Scull*[76] by Thomas Eakins (1844–1916). One can scarcely argue that this trio is unrepresentative, since it spans a century and a half, and juxtaposes artists born in Edinburgh and trained in London (Smibert), born in the interior of Connecticut and of unknown training (Earl), and born in Philadelphia and trained there and in Paris (Eakins).

Smibert painted the Berkeley entourage in 1729 at Newport, while the bishop was awaiting a parliamentary grant for his projected university in Bermuda. They had met in Italy, and in 1728 Berkeley invited him to join the faculty as an instructor of painting and perspective. Had the plan materialized he would have become the first member of an academic art department in the Western world. Since it did not, Smibert moved on to Boston, where he became the leading portrait painter. His style was based on that of Godfrey Kneller in England, but his first American work already shows a marked simplification of silhouette and surface over the imported Baroque style. That Smibert became "Americanized" and eventually embraced the blunt realism of Colonial portraiture with its forbidding, archaic stiffness may be seen in a work after 1745, the standing *Sir William Pepperrell*, at Salem (MA 196). In the Berkeley group the bishop's wife, holding their child, sits next him. The seated man is probably the bishop's secretary. Smibert's signature and the date, 1729, will be found on the edge of the small volume at the very center of the composition.

With Earl's *Roger Sherman* we reach a very high, if taut, moment in American culture. Earl painted this picture about 1776/77, just before he went to London to study with Benjamin West. As E. P. Richardson points out in *Painting in America*, John Adams had occasion to observe Roger Sherman in the Continental Congress, and noted in his diary that Sherman's movements were "stiffness and awkwardness itself." It often happens, however, that a really memorable portrait, such as this one, is as much a self-confession by the artist as it is a record of the sitter's character and appearance. In this instance we can be sure that the "stiffness and awkwardness" were Earl's own way of expressing his attitude toward life. The *Portrait of William Carpenter* in the

76

Worcester Museum, signed and dated 1779, is very similar to the *Roger Sherman*, even though the sitter was only twelve years old, and—still more remarkable—the picture was not painted in America but in England. Ralph Earl went there in 1778 and stayed until 1785. It is clear that he took his American outlook with him. How much of the English accent he contracted as a result of his seven-year sojourn may be discovered in his late portraits, such as the *Mrs. Moseley and Her Son Charles* (1791) at Yale, or the Tallmadge portraits at Litchfield (CT 36).

Thomas Eakins's *John Biglen*, painted in 1874, seems to me to speak the same visual language as Earl's *Roger Sherman*, despite the passage of time and the change in social scenery. There is the same intense silence, the same uncompromising honesty and precision, the same psychological tension. Hard line and sharp angle are of the essence of this art, no matter what else the painter may call upon to produce his effect. Both works are masterpieces, American to the core. Yet there are important differences. In Eakins a special mood prevails, almost as if his subject were under the spell of unheard music. Musicians, in fact, were a major theme in his work, and we discuss two of them in other museums (MA 17 and MA 176). Eakins's many rowing pictures—on the Schuylkill River in his native Philadelphia—and boxing pictures are invariably *inactive*, or caught at a moment between actions, as in the *John Biglen.* It is the same with the celebrated medical groups of Dr. Gross and Dr. Agnew, both in Philadelphia. Yale is rich in works by this perhaps greatest of American painters, and most of the examples come from what seem to me to be his vintage years, the 1870s.

A survey of the Yale collections can hardly fail to include a work, among many here, by the founder, John Trumbull (1756–1843). As a patriotic gesture I have selected his spirited oil sketch for *The Death of General Warren at the Battle of Bunker's Hill*.[77] Painted in London in 1786, eleven years after the battle, this brilliant little sketch (25 by 34 inches) was a study for the large canvas, more sedately executed, in the Rotunda of the U.S. Capitol. Trumbull studied with Benjamin West in London, where he absorbed the fluency of European methods of painting. It is certainly unfair to criticize him because he was so obviously different from Copley and Earl, and one must admit that for American art to progress in Trumbull's time it had to cast off its provincialism. I still believe, however, that Trumbull's gift was more the virtuoso's than that of the profound interpreter of life.

77

In the preface to his first volume on *Modern Painters* (Goya to Courbet), Lionello Venturi recalls being asked why, in considering nineteenth-century art, "one confines oneself exclusively to the French." Venturi's reply: "That you must ask of God." The book was written over thirty years ago, and in the interim much more attention has been paid to other European painting and to work across the Atlantic. Still, expatriates aside, it is hardly an exaggeration to say that American art can offer only Eakins and Homer—and such exquisite minor masters as Fitz Hugh Lane and Martin Heade—as against the roster of French giants from David to Cézanne.

Our next four selections, by Corot, Manet, Homer, and van Gogh, all came to Yale in the great bequest of Stephen C. Clark, which also included the *Portrait of Mevrouw Bodolphe* by Frans Hals.

The Harbor of La Rochelle,[78] painted in 1851, is widely regarded as one of the mid-career masterpieces of Jean-Baptiste Camille Corot (1796–1875). It is an early example of the so-called feathery type of painting, influenced by the growing popularity of photography in blurred focus for "poetic" effect, that brought Corot a great, and much delayed, success. His starker, more geometric early work, rediscovered by the Cubists, had attracted no purchasers whatever until the 1840s. As we look through the lovely diaphanous film of atmosphere that pervades *The Harbor of La Rochelle*, we find a classic order and calm produced by a lucid sequence of planes parallel to the picture's surface (in the foreground group and the row of cast shadows, for instance), and by the severe Cézanne-like cylinders and cubes of the fortifications and the houses. An untroubled sky of gentle grays and pale blue completes the peaceful scene. All too often Corot's "feathery" paintings fail to have such solid form; it was the prolific supply of these fragile evocations that brought Corot fame and fortune—and also the unwelcome activity of clever forgers. A new-rich American clientele (as well as a French one) was unmercifully duped by these impostors. It used to be said that of two thousand works by Corot, three thousand were in America.

Although Edouard Manet (1832–83) dedicated his *Young Woman Reclining in Spanish Costume*[79] to his friend Nadar, above his signature at the lower right, we should be cautious about assuming any strong influence of photography here from one of the nineteenth-century greats in that medium. This is first of all a symphony in reddish purple,

78

79

pale pinks, oranges, off-whites, and black. Secondarily it is a Romantic evocation of Spain, in response to a wave of fashion introduced in literary circles by such works as Victor Hugo's *Ernani* (1830)—by 1844 already an opera by Verdi—and continuing in the 1870s with Bizet's *Carmen*. Manet's picture dates from 1862/3, at a time when he did a whole series of Spanish pictures inspired by the visit of a dancing troupe to Paris. It apparently just preceded his famous *Olympia* of 1863. Whereas that masterpiece brought a modern-day Titian courtesan into the demimonde of Paris, here Manet transported Goya's *Maja Vestida* into his own studio. Spanish art was known to him through engravings and an important collection of original works then on view in Paris. He did not visit Spain until 1865—and thereupon virtually stopped painting Spanish pictures. The figure was posed by Victorine Meurend, Manet's favorite model. The strongly silhouetted figure, spotlighted directly from the front, is molded by a line of amazing plasticity and by subtly differing inner tones within a very close value range. The paint is laid in very flatly. Such a technique, radically different from accepted Academic procedures, stimulated some of the most vicious critical attacks ever endured by an artist. Manet's later development toward Impressionism may be easily seen in a comparison with *Le Repos*, a magical work of 1870 at Providence (RI 15).

Winslow Homer (1836–1910), born in Boston of a middle-class family whose English forebears were among the early settlers of Massachusetts, is with little doubt New England's most distinguished nineteenth-century artist. (In making such a statement we exclude expatriates like Whistler.) Locally trained as an illustrative lithographer, soon after his move to New York in 1859 he became one of the most popular illustrators for *Harper's Weekly*, supplying drawings that were coarsely reproduced by the wood-engraving process. During the Civil War he regularly sent in his visual reports to that magazine, and from about 1863 to 1865 developed a few oil compositions from them. It was not until the fall of 1866, when he was thirty, that he went to Paris, to spend ten months of study, during which he presumably visited the great World's Fair of 1867. Here, or in the studios and art galleries, he must have been exposed to the work of young artists who were later to form the Impressionist circle, and of their predecessors in nascent Impressionism, like Eugène Boudin (see CT 21).

Morning Bell,[80] an oil 24 by 38 inches, generally dated 1866, would seem to have been painted by Homer just prior to this trip. If so, it is

80

even more of a miracle than its intrinsic magic proclaims it to be. Homer apparently trained himself in oil painting, yet his mastery of outdoor light stands up well in comparison with that of most European masters with the exception of Claude Monet (as in the example at Farmington, c. 1865; see CT 5). We observe the beginning of a day at a small New England factory as the young girls—in straw hats and the calico bonnets so abhorred in the columns of a Boston critic named Henry James— arrive to work. No hint of Dickensian social sermonizing can be found here, only the haunting beauty of the moment. What a marvelous passage is the long inclined plane leading up to the work space— presumably above the stream and waterwheel that powered this modest plant. To give Henry James his due, he managed to praise Homer for seeing "everything at one with its envelope of light and air." But then he ruined it all by adding, "It is damnably ugly!"

Imagine what Henry James would have said of *The Night Café*[81] by Vincent van Gogh (1853–90)! Fortunately, he seems never to have heard of the tragic Dutchman, although he continued to write art reviews as late as 1897. But we do know what Vincent himself thought of it. Writing to his brother Theo from Arles in September 1888, he poured out his emotions: "I have tried to express the idea that the café is a place where one can ruin oneself, run mad, or commit a crime, so I have tried to express as it were the powers of darkness in a low drink shop, by soft Louis XV green and malachite, contrasting with yellow green and hard blue greens, and all this in an atmosphere like a devil's furnace, of pale sulphur." And in another letter: "I have tried to express the terrible passions of humanity by means of red and green."

Here speaks the modern Expressionist. Stirred with the fervor of an evangelist, van Gogh dared to set down these passions of humanity (including love) from his early work in Holland (MA 85) until his death by suicide at thirty-seven. A relatively serene interlude occurred in Paris from 1886 to the spring of 1888, when he worked with the Impressionists, introducing their "rainbow colors" into his previously sunless palette; but all this was transformed during his year at Arles. Even greater violence was yet to come.

Our next four selections, which take us far into the avant-garde of twentieth-century art, came to Yale in 1941 with the massive donation of the Société Anonyme collection of Katherine S. Dreier, or, in the

81

case of Marcel Duchamp's *Tu M'*, by a later bequest of the same donor.

Marcel Duchamp (1887–1968) was the intellectual *enfant terrible* of modernism, challenging many of art's basic assumptions and, though the soul of modesty himself, exerting an enormous influence on movements as varied as Surrealism and the recent explosion of Conceptual art. *Tu M'*,[82] a work of 1918, consists of an oil mural 10 feet long with a painted rent fastened by real safety pins, a sequence of painted color samples "attached" to the canvas by a real bolt, an illusionistic pointing hand painted by a commercial artisan hired for the task (and signed A. Klang by him), and other oddities. Over this strange assemblage three of the artist's already notorious "ready-mades" (a bicycle wheel, a corkscrew, a hat rack—all proclaimed by him to be works of art because chosen by an artist) cast mysterious and ominously warped shadows. In the lower left corner is a painted image of Duchamp's "three standard stoppages," his personal units of measurement arrived at by dropping three meter-long strings to the floor. *Tu M'*—which may signify *tu m'emmerdes*, "you bore me"—was Duchamp's last oil painting, but by no means the end of his puzzling career. What have we here? Painting of great beauty (the color samples); witty shifts between reality and illusion, between shadow and substance; a proclamation that non-art is art because the artist says so; and an apotheosis of chance as a major element in the creation of art—all this and, perhaps the visitor will agree, a work of both power and beauty, its complex messages and allusions relieved by flashes of Voltairean humor.

Composition Number 238: Bright Circle,[83] by the Russian artist Wassily Kandinsky, was painted in 1921, three years later than *Tu M'*, but its author belonged to an earlier generation than Duchamp's. It is not surprising, therefore, that he ignored Duchamp's revolutionary challenges. Kandinsky (1866–1944) had recently joined the faculty of the Bauhaus at Weimar, where his "painterly" exuberance underwent a rapid change under the influence of the discipline promulgated by Walter Gropius, the architect-founder of that celebrated School. Kandinsky's brilliant Slavic color, however, still dominates the canvas. If the main

83

82

forms seem to have been laid out with a compass and T square, and the edges ruled with an architect's sharp pencil, the rhythms of the design weave in gay abandon, fully supporting this coloristic orgy.

Architectural discipline is much more marked in the work of Fernand Léger (1881–1955). A somewhat hesitant Cubist in the company of Picasso and Braque, his exact contemporaries, Léger subsequently adapted Cubist principles to incorporate machine forms and urban imagery in boldly scaled abstract designs. During the 1920s these took on a classical look with their severe vertical and horizontal armature and their compact forms—sometimes strongly modeled to resemble sculpture, at other times completely flat. This stage of Léger's career is superbly represented by *Composition Number 7*,[84] an oil of 1925. (Note the appropriateness of numerical titles, a practice initiated several years earlier by Kandinsky, for subjectless pictures.) During the 1920s Léger was a member of the movement known as Purism, in association with Amédée Ozenfant and Charles-Edouard Jeanneret—the latter a major architect under the pseudonym of Le Corbusier. As George Heard Hamilton has expressed it so succinctly, "the very purity of Purism was its undoing." After Léger's break with it he sought and found the humanity he had temporarily lost. Nonetheless, *Composition Number 7*, with its squat Italianate baluster, its industrial lettering (of the sort used on freight shipments), and its complex of rectangular frames within frames, has an undeniably powerful impact.

Modern abstraction reached a point of *ne plus ultra* in the 1920s in the mature work of the Dutch artist Piet Mondrian (1872–1944). Although such works normally have abstract titles, our selection, signed and dated 1929, is called *Fox Trot B*.[85] While it does not differ significantly from works without such a reference, we know that this Calvinist of modern art was an enthusiastic fan of American jazz; and fifteen years later, in residence in New York City during the war years, he was to produce such multicheckered variations on this theme as *Broadway Boogie-Woogie*, now in the Museum of Modern Art. People familiar with Mondrian's development are aware that in the very early 1900s he was painting landscapes and portraits in a darkened version of the manner of Vincent van Gogh. They observe with fascination a process of ever greater simplification through the years in Paris under the

84

85

spell of Cubism and, toward the end of the First World War in 1917, in his activity as co-founder of the Dutch movement known as De Stijl. "The Style" was strongly oriented toward architecture and city planning, with a Platonic ideal of providing an environment for a better, cleaner life. Although the architectural side of the movement was deeply affected by the art and theories of Mondrian, it has been suggested that he in turn responded in his paintings to right-angled street intersections of a gridiron city plan, and to the clean, planar surfaces of modern architecture. The range of his variations within the improbable limits of the rectangle and a palette of black, white, yellow, red, and blue is phenomenal. His off-center balances are extremely exact, and they respond at once to the force of gravity and to Western habits of reading from left to right. Try *Fox Trot B* (our illustration of it, that is!) in all four possible positions and you will discover that he knew what he was about. The monogrammed signature and date (lower right) is your security as to how Mondrian intended the picture to be hung. Every street-corner telephone booth in America is witness to his influence.

We conclude this survey with *First Steps*,[86] painted by Pablo Picasso (1881–1973) in 1943. Scaled for giants despite its moderate size of 51 by 38 inches, it has much in common with the great mural *Guernica*, painted six years earlier. At first look the violent distortions of the figures seem perverse in such an innocuous, sentimental theme. But those who have satisfied themselves that *Guernica* is a major masterpiece of our time will have little trouble in accepting these very distortions as artistic means toward a deeply emotional expression. How moving the sheltering curve of the mother, how convincing the startled insecurity of the child! But the gigantism (already noted in the little "classical" *Bather* at Hartford, CT 31) and the harshness convey an altogether different message. A cold color scheme of slate blues, dull greens, ashen grays, and blacks—contrasting with the sour pinks of the flesh tones—additionally removes Picasso's image from expected clichés about tender loving motherhood. Indeed, we can *forget* the subject matter and discover here a masterfully organized design expressive of a dislocated world.

86

We shall meet Picasso again in other museums, in works from 1901 to 1941, but this is the latest one we shall discuss. His paintings of the 1950s begin to show a falling off of creative power, and those of the 1960s are decidedly slapdash and repetitive—unlike the work of other octogenarians like Michelangelo, Titian, Hals, Claude Monet, and Matisse. Still, we are hardly in a position to complain when we remember that Picasso began to paint *mature* pictures by the age of fourteen.

The Yale Gallery has a good collection of Pre-Columbian art and a very fine one of African sculpture. For discussion of these cultures see the entry on the Peabody Museum of Harvard University. As we go to press, announcement is made of the Ordway bequest of modern art, especially rich in the work of the New York group of Abstract Expressionists.

In addition to scholarly catalogues on the various divisions of Yale's holdings, there is an admirable general one on the paintings and sculpture, by Andrew C. Ritchie and Katherine Neilson. The sharp-eyed reader will discover my debt to it.

Lyman Allyn Museum

Location: 625 Williams St. From I-95 take the Briggs St. exit and follow signs to museum entrance. Free parking
Hours: Tues.-Sat. 1-5, Sun. 2-5; closed major holidays
Admission: Free. Ⓗ

The museum opened in 1932 in a building designed by Charles A. Platt. Three additions have provided a total of nine galleries for the permanent collection and four for changing exhibitions. The permanent exhibits, which have a broad range through world art, are especially fine in the decorative arts. Furniture, silver, glass, and porcelain are of sumptuous quality, and the taste with which they are displayed is exemplary. The collections of drawings and prints are large and important. The Museum Shop, unlike the miscellaneous bazaars that disfigure too many institutions, sells original works of quality—due care having been taken vis-à-vis their donors. Storage, cleverly contrived in an added top floor, is immense, but there are limits to piling duplication upon duplication.

(A word here about storage: at the Lyman Allyn Museum it is admirably organized, but in too many museums we have visited, storage seems to begin at the front door.)

Administration of this institution is under the trustees of the neighboring Connecticut College, although the two are legally separate entities; but their connection is a very close one because many of the college's art courses meet here.

As may be expected, the museum's greatest strength is in Connecticut painting and decorative arts of the eighteenth and early nineteenth centuries. The more important Connecticut painters seen here are Ralph Earl, William Jennys, John Frederick Kensett, and Frederic E. Church. Other members of the Hudson River School on view include Thomas Cole (a small version of the *Mt. Etna* at Hartford (CT 26), Jasper Cropsey, and Thomas Doughty.

The *Portrait of Major Reuben Hatch*[87] and its companion canvas of his wife, signed and dated (on the back) April 20, 1802, are among the

87

finest surviving examples of the art of William Jennys, whom we have discussed in some detail at the Connecticut Historical Society, Hartford. In every way they are comparable to the superb pair in the Currier Gallery of Art at Manchester, N.H. (NH 17). Much more than Richard Jennys (see CT 8), William continued the hard precision and the uncompromising realism of Ralph Earl's *Roger Sherman* (CT 75). The contour lines on Hatch's face are sharp to the point of cruelty, and his intense gaze manages to compete with his incredibly emphatic hairdo. The origins of William Jennys are obscure, including the date of his birth. He may have been a near contemporary of Ralph Earl (1751–1801), but he seems never to have traveled abroad as did Earl. Thus Jennys's surviving work, all of it from the 1790s and early 1800s, shows no trace of what happened to Earl's later style (see CT 36).

The life-size *Standing Portrait of James Francis Smith*,[88] aged six, is by a New London painter, Isaac Sheffield (1798–1845). It is included to show how a local craftsman could meet the challenge of an interesting occasion. The boy's father ran a whaling ship, the *Chelsea*, shown in the background, and the family had just returned in 1837 from a voyage to the Desolation Islands. James proudly displays his coat of penguin skins. It is pleasant to learn that young James became a sea captain himself.

Our first selection from the many fine examples of European art is the terra-cotta bust of *Dr. Apollonio Massa*,[89] by the Venetian sculptor Alessandro Vittoria (1525–1608), dating from about 1587. Massa was a highly respected doctor of anatomy at the medical school in Padua. The fact that four other identical busts are known (one of them on his tomb) attests to his fame. Stylistically the work is pure Mannerist —a flattened and elongated version of High Renaissance sculpture showing no sign of the Baroque twists and turns already visible in the work of Giovanni Bologna. Certain oil portraits by Vittoria's great contemporary, Tintoretto, are roughly similar.

The collection of drawings, which includes fine examples by Tintoretto, the two Tiepolos, Boucher, Rowlandson, and John Singleton Copley, boasts a remarkable black and white chalk *Portrait of Philip V*

88

89

of Spain,[90] 2 feet high, by the French court painter Hyacinthe Rigaud (1658–1743). Born at Versailles in 1683, Philip was a grandson of the reigning Louis XIV. He appears here dressed for his coronation in 1700. The large oil developed from this drawing is in the Louvre.

Another important preparatory drawing is the pencil study for the *Portrait of Madame Moitessier,*[91] in the National Gallery, Washington, by Jean Auguste Dominique Ingres (1780–1867). Squared to facilitate transfer to the large canvas—artists today prefer slide projectors for this purpose—it was used in the production of the Washington picture. The date is 1851, in the fashionable period of the Second Empire. Tastes change: the visitor may be surprised to know that Madame Moitessier was regarded as one of the great Parisian beauties of her day. But there remains the question of how much Ingres's own style intervened in the representation. A look at his *Odalisque with Slave*, in the Fogg Art Museum at Harvard (MA 126), will be helpful in a decision.

An *English Overmantel Mirror*[92] in the Chinese Chippendale style, c. 1750, is so outstanding as to warrant an exception to our exclusion of "multiples" (explained in the Preface to this book). It deserves comparison with the silver-gilt *Centerpiece* at Hartford (CT 10) as a somewhat soberer response to the Rococo indulgence in *chinoiserie*.

90

91

92

The three paintings, charming but of no special distinction, were executed on the back of glass panels. Pagodas sprout from the frame, and everywhere the typical Rococo C-shape appears in the curvatures. Expectedly, there are stands for two Chinese vases.

The mirror may serve as a reminder that the museum's collection of Far Eastern art is extensive, particularly in the decorative arts.

Modern sculpture includes works by Wilhelm Lehmbruck, a cast stone replica of the bust of his famous *Kneeling Woman* at the Museum of Modern Art; Pierre Auguste Renoir's *Maternity*, a late bronze of 1916; and *Singing Boy*,[93] a bronze of 1928 by Ernst Barlach (1870–1938). The Barlach is intensely Northern, with its roots deep in German Gothic art (compare the *Crippled Beggar* at Harvard University, MA 110). The figure is shaped like an anchor, but it is vitalized by the stretch of the arms clasped about the knees, and by the facial expression. The main theme of this visual sonata is harshly angular; its secondary theme is globular (knees, shoulders, head); and Barlach interweaves them in a complex development. One should not fail to observe *Singing Boy* from all angles. Surprisingly, it is only 20 inches high.

93

New Milford Historical Society

Location: 6 Aspetuck Avenue
Hours: Thurs.-Sat. 1-4
Admission: Free

The society's collection of portraits includes the *General John Logan* by Eastman Johnson (1824–1906), James Stuart's replica of Gilbert Stuart's *George Washington*, four by Ralph Earl (1751–1801), and four by Richard Jennys (active 1776–99).

The Earls, of *Mr. and Mrs. Sherman Boardman* and *Colonel and Mrs. Nathaniel Taylor*, signed and dated 1796, are late works in the vein of the Tallmadge portraits at nearby Litchfield (CT 36).

The attribution of the unsigned portraits of *Colonel and Mrs. Elisha Bostwick* to Richard Jennys is convincing when they are compared with the Hawley pair discussed at The Connecticut Historical Society (CT 8). That they are not by William Jennys becomes immediately clear on comparison with his portraits at New London (CT 87) and Manchester, N.H. (NH 17). In addition to the oil portraits of the Bostwick parents, the Historical Society owns two miniatures of their children, Jared and Betsy Ann.

The Slater Memorial Museum

Location: The Norwich Free Academy, Boswell Ave., in the uptown (northeastern) part of the city; approach from Route 12
Hours: Mon.-Fri. 9-4; Sat., Sun. 1-4 during the school year; in summer open Tues.-Sun. 1-4; closed holidays
Admission: Free

The museum opened in 1886 in a brick Romanesque building of imposing size, embellished with a German round tower, a projecting semicircular bay, porches, corner entrance portico, and vast roof. That in itself is worth the trip to Norwich. A plaster, painted black, of an ancient Egyptian statue, which greets you in the entrance hall, may give rise to doubts about the contents; but upstairs there are wonders to behold. Suddenly you enter an enormous three-storied Hall of Casts.[94] The plaster cast is not dead! The best view is from one of the galleries above. Here are pediments from Olympia and the Parthenon (the latter looking exactly as the *original* once did in the British Museum!); here is the major part of the great Hellenistic altar from Pergamon; here are Greek friezes, the *Winged Victory, Harmodius and Aristogiton,* the *Victory* by Paeonius (at Olympia). Higher up are masterpieces of the Italian Renaissance, including works of Donatello and Luca della Robbia, and—crowning the end wall—Michelangelo's *Moses*. But nothing from the Middle Ages: in the age of the Chicago World's Fair of 1893 and the gleaming classical revival of McKim, Mead, and White, only the art of ancient Greece and Rome, and of the Florence and Rome of the Italian Renaissance, would do—the Romanesque building notwithstanding.

In the United States today, I believe only the great collection of casts at the Carnegie Institute in Pittsburgh is more inclusive; but the assemblage at the George Walter Vincent Smith Museum in Springfield, Mass. (page 285), ranks high in the competition.

Interestingly enough, the Norwich collection was an early venture of its kind. In 1894, when a new wing of the Metropolitan Museum of

94

Art opened in New York, the entire ground floor was planned to contain a huge collection of casts of sculpture and architectural models. By 1908 it had reached a total of 2,607 items. Among the experts enlisted to advise in assembling this accretion were Edward Robinson, of the Boston Museum, and Henry Watson Kent (later to join the Metropolitan and become its longtime and influential secretary), then the director of the Slater Museum at Norwich. It was felt at the time that "such collections must undoubtedly in the future be the main dependence of our American fine-arts institutions." Later, of course, all that changed, and casts disappeared into storage, or were sold, or even broken up. During that period of disgrace for casts, Norwich quietly enriched its own collection, which had always been found indispensable to its teaching program.

Today the cast is in favor again—if grudgingly—and many museums regret their precipitous action.

The Slater Museum, as a part of Norwich Free Academy, has an extensive collection of world art, displayed in galleries around and overlooking the Hall of Casts. Far Eastern, Oceanian, African, American Indian, Pre-Columbian, and Egyptian objects and textiles, and American furniture from the seventeenth century to the present are all well represented. The painting collection has good examples of the Hudson River School and of local painters, notably John Denison Crocker (1822–1907); and among twentieth-century artists examples by George Luks, Karl Knaths, and William Thomson (born 1931 and working in Bristol) are noteworthy. There is also a print collection, including rare examples by Amos Doolittle and a large assortment of Japanese woodblock impressions.

Lyme Historical Society:
Florence Griswold House

Location: From I-95 take exit 70; second house on the left on the *north* side of the overpass. (Old Lyme Church is at the far end of the street, *south* of the overpass)
Hours: Tues.-Sat. 10-5, Sun. 1-5 except in winter; in winter open Wed.-Fri. and Sun. afternoon
Admission: Charged

The house, a fine mansion of 1817, became a finishing school in 1884 and, at the end of the century, an artists' summer home under Miss Florence Griswold's benign guidance. A portrait of her in white lace, playing a golden harp, by Alphonse Jongers, tells much; but there are pleasant surprises. These are delightfully recounted by Arthur Heming, one of the boarders, in his reminiscences written shortly after her death in 1937. *Miss Florence and the Artists of Old Lyme* was published, for the first time, by the Historical Society in 1971. The colony itself was founded by Henry Ranger (1839–1916), a loyal follower of the Barbizon painters, with whom he had studied in the forest of Fontainebleau.

In 1966, the Museum Seminar of Connecticut College, in cooperation with the Lyman Allyn Museum of New London, organized an exhibition entitled "The Art Colony at Old Lyme, 1900–1935." Works by sixty-nine artists were included. The list encompasses most of the leading figures in American Impressionism, notably Gifford Beal, Frank DuMond, Will Howe Foote, Childe Hassam, Eugene Higgins, Willard Metcalf, and Edward F. Rook. (Virtually the entire colony is represented by examples in the collection of the Florence Griswold House.)

We quote from the foreword of the exhibition, by Jane Hayward. "The role played by the art colony at Old Lyme in the artistic development of the United States has been largely overlooked by the art historian. We have tended to ignore that it was the first and largest art colony of its kind and that many of the more forward spirits in the art world during the first decades of this century either worked at Old Lyme or were closely associated with the group. At one period in its history, the colony was also a summer school for the Art Students League of New York and as such had an even wider influence upon artistic thought. Its annual summer exhibitions drew an audience from all parts of the country and included critics, collectors and dealers. But most important, the art colony at Old Lyme developed a style—a way of looking at nature that was uniquely its own."

In appreciation for Miss Florence's support and hospitality, the boarders turned to and repaired the dilapidated house—something her meager income had not allowed her to do. They also adopted the agreeable habit of leaving mementos of their own work, singly and in unison. Thus the door panels sported little oil paintings, and over the big dining-room fireplace they jointly created—twenty-four of them—

a narrow overmantel, full of jolly quips animated by their caricatured portraits. The adjoining walls of the paneled *Dining Room*[95] became a veritable museum of the Old Lyme School. The narrow door panels at the center of our illustration are the work of Childe Hassam (1859–1935), best known for his pictures of Old Lyme Church at the other end of the village, but discussed in examples at Colby and Smith colleges.

95

The Aldrich Museum of Contemporary Art

Location: 258 Main Street
Hours: Wed., Sat., Sun. 1-5; Sculpture Garden open daily
Admission: Charged (Sculpture Garden free)

Since New England museums are not in the vanguard of support for contemporary art, the exception here (along with academic institutions) is particularly welcome. But there is a difficulty from the viewpoint of this book, which is limited to permanent collections. For the Aldrich Museum, "contemporary" means within the last fifteen years; therefore its policy is to dispose of most works as they reach that time limit. Sculpture, especially of monumental size, is, however, likely to remain undisturbed.

Accordingly, I must merely mention works of the late 1950s and the 1960s—all worthy of discussion and illustration—by Grace Hartigan, Jean Dubuffet, Charles Hinman, Roy Lichtenstein, and Robert Indiana, and prepare the visitor to find that they may have been replaced by more recent work by other artists.

A probably permanent fixture in the Sculpture Garden is *La Ruota* (The Wheel),[96] by Arnaldo Pomodoro, a leading figure in modern Italian sculpture. The hefty bronze cylinder, nearly 4 feet in diameter, dates from 1961. Within the pure geometry of the circular band all is scarified and in disrepair: a dislocated modern world hungering for order and security. Another characteristic Pomodoro can be seen in the contemporary wing of the Worcester Art Museum (not illustrated)— a gilt bronze sphere, similarly attacked and robbed of its purity.

Study of Falling Man: 3-Box Landscape,[97] by the American sculptor

96

97

Ernesto Trova and executed in 1966, is only 9 inches high, but extends to a length of 41 inches and to 28 inches in depth. It is made of Plexiglas, plastic, and enameled bronze. What a chilly world is this, and how devious and difficult our passage through life! In a long series devoted to this theme (also in painting and graphic media), Trova's simplified Everyman often falls or is actually recumbent. This piece is so highly prized by the museum that you are likely to see it—unless it is temporarily in storage. I would recommend tracking it down.

The Aldrich Museum opened in 1964 in the historically distinguished quarters of a frame house dating back to 1783. It performs a notable service in acquainting the public with developments in the most advanced art. Exhibitions change frequently, and if you are adventurous in the spirit of the museum itself, you can acquire a work at a modest price—before the artist's reputation has had a chance to expand the charges.

The William Benton Museum of Art, University of Connecticut

Location: The university grounds are so extensive that the visitor is strongly advised to arrive by Route 195 at the university information booth, located a brief distance south of the intersection of Routes 195 and 44A. Ask for a map and for permission to park. The museum, marked number 39 on the map, is near the university library. On Saturdays and Sundays, proceed to the center of the campus and park on Fairfield Rd. in the library area

Telephone: (203) 486-4520

Hours: *During exhibitions,* Mon.-Sat. 10-4:30, Sun. 1-5; since the museum closes for several days between exhibitions, it is advisable to telephone ahead

Admission: Free. Ⓗ projected

As our directions may have indicated, changing exhibitions form a major part of the museum's activities, and they are frequently of high distinction, accompanied by excellent catalogues. Space being limited by rapid growth since the 1966 opening, there may be difficulty in seeing the permanent collection; hence telephoning ahead is again advised.

The museum is in the process of obtaining such a large selection of the work of Reginald Marsh (1898–1954) that—assuming a happy outcome to this venture—it will become the leading center for study of this important American artist (see VT 8). It owns the inclusive Walter Landauer collection of 103 prints in superb impressions and 6 drawings by the great German Expressionist Käethe Kollwitz (1867–1945). The donor was a member of the university faculty for forty years, in the Department of Animal Genetics. Onward and upward with hobbies like this!

If three of our four selections are by American artists, that is roughly proportional to the range of the museum's impressive holdings; but, as we shall indicate, European art is well represented. Scholarly studies of works in the museum appear regularly in the museum's annual *Bulletin.*

The theme of the *Mother and Child,*[98] by Mary Cassatt (1845–

98

1926), was a favorite of hers, as was the pastel medium in which this image is so tenderly chalked. Her oils and her prints, however, are regarded equally highly. Often her appeal is frankly sentimental and the color brightly charming; but here in the blacks and dark olive tones of this portrait of Madame de Septeuil and her son, and in their averted gazes, a more detached statement emerges. The date is about 1890, long after Miss Cassatt's early years in Paris working with the Impressionists (especially Degas), and now at the height of her career. Nevertheless, some echo of Degas's astringency is felt here, and of his tightly compacted compositions. A return to Paris in 1890, when an important exhibition of Japanese prints attracted great interest, increased Cassatt's emphasis on flat design, so striking in this memorable pastel.

Born in St. Johns, Newfoundland, but reared in Boston, Maurice Prendergast (1859–1924) worked mostly in New England. But he made several trips to Europe, some of long duration. During a three-year stay centered in Paris, 1892–95, and in return trips in 1907 and 1909, he frequented the bathing resort of St. Malo, near the border between Normandy and Brittany. His 1907 and 1909 St. Malo watercolors differ markedly from such early New England ones of c. 1896 as the *Revere Beach* in Andover (MA 19). The color is more intense, especially the rich blues; and the surface patterning by jagged strokes is much more pronounced. *Lighthouse at St. Malo*,[99] in the Benton Museum's collection, an oil of 1909 about 20 inches high, demonstrates that in the oil medium Prendergast made similar departures from his earlier style. We know from his letters that he was excited in Paris by the new works of the Fauve painters, especially Derain and Vlaminck, and by the mottled flat designs of Édouard Vuillard (see MA 183). For further study of his development I recommend *Watercolors by Maurice Prendergast from New England Collections*, the catalogue for an exhibition prepared by Gwendolyn Owens and shown in 1978 at the Clark Art Institute, Williamstown, Mass.—particularly in view of the New England source of the exhibits.

While late nineteenth- and twentieth-century art is primarily in evidence at the Benton Museum, there are many fine earlier works. *Rye Beach, New Hampshire*,[100] an oil only 8½ inches high by Martin J. Heade (1819–1904), is signed and dated 1863. We discuss two more oils by this subtle master in other museums (ME 30 and ME 14), for

99

one of the joys of an art tour through New England is the repeated discovery of his luminous, but vaguely ominous, nature poems. Heade, the subject of a penetrating chapter in Barbara Novak's *American Painting of the Nineteenth Century* (New York: Harper & Row, paperback edition, 1979), shares with Fitz Hugh Lane (see MA 156) a leading position in what is now called American Luminism. *Rye Beach* has his characteristic deep distance, led into by the swirling curve of the shore, his leaden sky suddenly bright at the horizon, his low-keyed color. A lonely receding cart, trailed by a diminutive dog, adds scale to this vastness. A fringe of trees at the horizon echoes the ridge of the wave breaking at the end of its journey. Heade worked mostly in the Newburyport and Narragansett areas and also at Lake George, but he traveled as far afield as Jamaica and Brazil.

Moving back to the seventeenth century, we illustrate the *Seated Portrait of the Poet Jan Vos*,[101] painted in 1679 by the Haarlem artist Jan de Bray (1627–97). While this refined image lacks the penetration (and the expressive brushwork) of de Bray's fellow townsman Frans Hals (see CT 73), it has an elegant, if sober, sheen, and the poet's right hand is sensitively observed.

Other Old Master paintings not to be missed are the life-size, full-length *Noblewoman and Child*, attributed to the Spanish court painter Sanchez Coello (1515–90); two classical pictures by Angelika Kauffmann, the eighteenth-century Swiss painter who became celebrated in London; a big allegorical piece by the American Benjamin West, successor to Sir Joshua Reynolds as president of the Royal Academy; the Rembrandt Peale *Portrait of Captain Paul Ambrose Oliver and His Daughter Mary* (1825); the very dark and Spanish-looking *Portrait*

100

101

of the Artist's Mother, by the nineteenth-century French painter Théodule Augustin Ribot; and a 1908 landscape by Gabriele Münter, the protégée and inamorata of Wassily Kandinsky—her work a tame version of the latter's "painterly" exuberance in those years. An interesting contrast can be made between paintings by two American painters born in 1882: Edward Hopper and George Bellows. The Hopper is a self-portrait, the artist seated at the easel, of 1903—very dark and most unlike his later work (see MA 278), but resembling, at least in value tones, his etchings of the early 1900s. The Bellows, *Criehaven*, an oil of the Maine coast painted in 1916, is a fully characteristic work of the same year as the *Farm of John Tom*, at Duxbury (MA 150).

Mattatuck Museum

Location: 119 West Main St.; exit 21 from I-84 to West Main St.; the museum is on the near right side of the Green
Hours: Tues.-Sat. 12-5, Sun. 2-5 (except July and August)
Admission: Free

The Mattatuck Museum offers an active program of adult and children's programs, including art classes and workshops. There are elaborate displays of local life in period rooms in an addition at the rear of the main building, an Italianate Revival brick and sandstone mansion. Upstairs, the permanent collection emphasizes paintings, drawings, and prints by Connecticut artists from the late eighteenth century to the present. An illustrated checklist is available.

Icebergs,[102] by Frederic E. Church, is perhaps the most arresting among the many works by older masters. Signed and dated 1863 at the lower right, it is a moderately early example of the art of one of the most extraordinary members of the Hudson River School. Though Church was born in New Haven in 1826, he settled, as is well known, on the banks of the Hudson itself, where he built "Olana," a Moorish-style residence that has to be seen to be believed. We have discussed Church's very early work in the example at New Britain (CT 43), *Haying near New Haven,* 1849. Inspired by the writings of the great German naturalist Alexander von Humboldt, he visited Ecuador in 1853 and again in 1857, and in the 1860s Jamaica, Europe, and the Near East, ever in search of awesome natural spectacles. But our chief interest here is in his 1859 trip to Labrador—to study icebergs. From the studies he brought back (several are in the Cooper-Hewitt Museum of Design, New York City), he developed the large oil that recently made history at a London auction. The Waterbury oil, only 8½ by 11½ inches, is a variant of that composition. Touched by strong green and orange lights, the gigantic white pile is truly a Gothic nightmare.

Among other earlier painters with Connecticut associations, good examples are seen here of the work of John Trumbull, Ammi Phillips, George Loring Brown, and John Twachtman; and there are numerous plaster groups of pre–Norman Rockwell flavor by John Rogers. Securely

102

attributed to William Jennys (see CT 87) is the superb *Portrait of Jonah Bronson, Aged Eighty-three*, painted in 1795; but the smaller image of *Miss Martha Pike as a Young Girl* lacks his precision and "bite."

A figure composition in watercolor, 1914, by Maurice Prendergast (see CT 99), takes us into the twentieth century. In 1964/5 the museum received an extensive bequest of modern art from Kay Sage (1898–1963), a distinguished American Surrealist painter. This included sixteen of her oils and many in watercolor, charcoal, and mixed media; and over a dozen works by her husband, a leading French Surrealist who came to America in 1939. Among Kay Sage's oil paintings, *The Instant*[103] (1949, 3 feet high) is the most memorable—partly for its unexpected affinity with Church's *Icebergs*. Sage's "mountain," however, is a dream construction veering off into limitless space; its cold grays and harsh reds add to its sense of inhumanity. An earlier work, *Egg on Sill*, shows the strong influence of the Italian Giorgio de Chirico on her art, as on that of many other Surrealists.

Kay Sage and Yves Tanguy lived in Roxbury, not far to the west of Waterbury; here too their friend Alexander Calder maintained a studio. Leading avant-garde artists frequently visited them, and exchanged works with them. From these contacts the Mattatuck Museum later benefited, again through the bequest of Kay Sage, or by earlier gifts from her. Thus we have the opportunity here to enjoy a mobile, a watercolor, and a color lithograph by Alexander Calder; a crayon drawing by Arshile Gorky—who in his short career became the commanding figure in American Surrealism; and a small Plexiglas construction by the Russian-born Naum Gabo.

Painters of more limited reputation are of course here in great number. Among them, I especially admired the work of the Bristol painter William Thomson (born 1931) and of Robert Vickrey (born 1926), whose *Flower Wall*, in egg tempera on Masonite panel, casts the startling white and blue silhouette of a nun against a pockmarked floral and foliated gray background.

In closing, I would like to add a word of praise for the intelligently written and instructive labels that accompany the exhibits in the Mattatuck Museum. Would that more than a few other museums did likewise!

103

Rhode Island

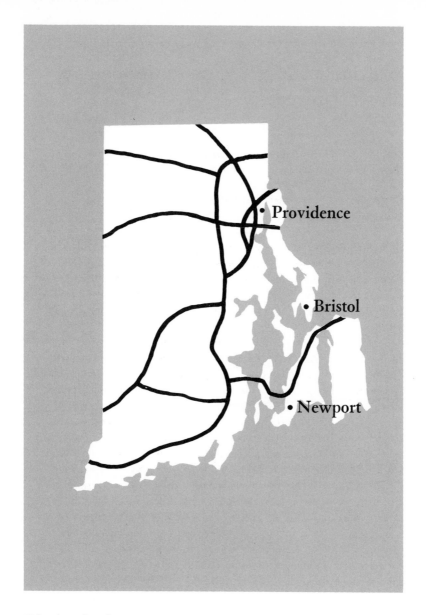

Rhode Island

Haffenreffer Museum of Anthropology, Brown University

Location: Mt. Hope Grant, Bristol, east of the town and overlooking Mt. Hope Bay. From Metacom Ave. (Route 136) turn east on Tower St. and follow the signs for 1¼ miles
Hours: Sat.-Sun. 1-5; weekdays during special exhibitions
Admission: Charged

Unlike the Peabody museums of Harvard and Yale, Brown University's anthropological museum is not on the Providence campus, but about twenty miles to the southeast on a point of land of great beauty. The museum is an active scientific and research institution, and its exhibitions, both temporary and of the permanent collection, are displayed with taste and care.

Because we concentrate the coverage of so-called primitive art in this book on the rich collections of the Peabody Museum at Harvard, only a brief survey is attempted here. American Indian cultures (from Alaska to South America) form the main focus of interest at the Haffenreffer Museum, but Southeast Asia is also a sphere of interest.

In 1956 the R. F. Haffenreffer Foundation, from which the museum derives its major support, gave a magnificent 12-foot *Totem Pole*, from the Pacific Northwest coast, to the Museum of Art of the Rhode Island School of Design. We discuss this work on page 109.

The visitor will find the photographic exhibits of excavations conducted by the museum most informative. Artifacts, often of great beauty, have a wide range: baskets, pottery, blankets and other textiles, wooden bowls, feather collars, and feather headdresses of the type discussed at Harvard's Peabody Museum (MA 141). Among recent expeditions conducted by the museum, in conjunction with Brown University, is one of 1975 to the Arhinahua of eastern Peru.

A Newport Miscellany

Apart from the Redwood Library, separately considered, and apart from its many celebrated examples of historic American architecture, Newport offers an interesting selection of works of art in institutions open to the public.

Old Colony House, completed by Richard Munday in 1742 and crowning the Mall on Washington Square, contains one of two identical full-length portraits of George Washington ordered by the state legislature from Gilbert Stuart in 1800, one for each of Rhode Island's capitals at the time. The other is in the executive chamber of the state capitol in Providence.

The Newport Historical Society, nearby at 82 Touro Street, has four portraits of the Ellery family, painted before 1721 by an unknown artist and mysteriously close to a large group of portraits of Dutch patroon families in the Albany area. Most of these are in the Albany Institute of History and Art and in the New-York Historical Society, Central Park West, New York City. Generally called the work of "the Schuyler Master," from the full-length *Peter Schuyler* in the mayor's office in City Hall, Albany, they appear to be by more than one master. Appearing some twenty years before the emergence of Robert Feke (see ME 10), and adapted as to poses and composition from British mezzotint reproductions of oil originals, they are marked by great native vigor and the sharp grasp of character that is so striking in American portraiture from Feke and Copley to Eakins and Bellows. Another related group is in the Virginia Museum at Richmond, painted in that area. It seems doubtful, but not impossible, that an itinerant painter traveled so far beyond the upper Hudson limits to which he was more likely confined.

In the autumn 1980 issue of the *American Art Journal*, however, Mary Black attributed the Ellery portraits to Nehemiah Partridge, a previously unknown artist, whom she identified on the basis of documentary evidence as the author of certain Wendell family portraits in the Albany Institute (among the "Schuyler Master" portraits referred to above). Since many of these portraits are inscribed "Aetatis Suae," with the age of the sitter and the date of execution, the master is also known as the "Aetatis Suae Painter." Mrs. Black's article, "Identification of the Aetatis Suae and Wendell Limners" (pp. 5–31), attributes the whole corpus, including the Virginia portraits, to Nehemiah Partridge. Despite her exciting discovery concerning the Wendell portraits, I still believe several masters were involved in the production of these many portraits during a brief decade beginning about 1717.

In addition to the Ellery portraits, the Newport Historical Society owns examples by Feke and by Joseph Blackburn (see ME 11), and important drawings by Michele F. Corné (see page 93) and Charles du Saint-Mémin, both from abroad, and by the Philadelphia engraver Francis Kearny. The *Portrait of an American Indian* by Charles Bird

King (1785–1862), active for forty years in Washington and in summers at his home in Newport, relates to a commission from the superintendent of the Indian trade for the War Department, who conceived the idea of a portrait gallery of Indians who visited Washington. Most of these portraits, by King and others, were destroyed in a fire at the Smithsonian Institution in 1865, but the Peabody Museum at Harvard owns a set of copies by Henry Inman. (Further discussion will be found in E. P. Richardson, *Painting in America*; New York: Crowell, 1956.) An interesting Marine Museum occupies the basement level of the society's building.

The Preservation Society of Newport County, with offices at 118 Mill Street, administers a large group of historic buildings (admission charged, map and strip ticket available, open daily from 10 to 5 at varying periods of the year). Apart from their architectural significance and their furnishings of high quality, some of them contain works of art that fall within the limited scope of this book. The Nichols-Wanton-Hunter House (1748), on Washington Street, has been restored to its former beauty by the society; in addition to examples of the work of Newport's finest furniture makers, it has a rare overmantel painting. Vernon House (1758) has a unique series of Chinese murals painted on plaster, in the front north room on the ground floor. Trinity Church (1726) owns important examples of eighteenth-century silver. The Breakers, completed in 1895 for Cornelius Vanderbilt, contains a beautiful fountain under the grand staircase by Karl Bitter, sculptor of the Pulitzer Fountain in New York City, Fifth Avenue at Fifty-ninth Street. The great stables of The Breakers has a magnificent array of carriages and other vehicles.

Redwood Library and Athenaeum

Location: 50 Bellevue Ave., corner of Old Beach Rd. Follow Touro St. north from Newport Historical Society, turn right on Bellevue Ave. for two blocks
Hours: Mon.-Sat. 10-6 (10-5 in August); closed holidays
Admission: Free

Founded by Abraham Redwood in 1747, this is one of the oldest libraries in America. The building itself, a masterpiece of the architect Peter Harrison, was completed in 1750. It contains an important collection of American portraits by such masters as John Smibert, Robert Feke, Gilbert Stuart (whose career began in Newport), and Chester Harding.

Among the most interesting is Stuart's very early portrait of his life-long friend *Benjamin Waterhouse*,[1] painted in 1776, when Stuart was twenty-one and Waterhouse was a year older. After pursuing medical studies in England, where Stuart also knew him, Waterhouse became famous for introducing Jenner's vaccination against smallpox into America. Stuart's reputation has suffered from too many portraits of George Washington, not all of them by Stuart himself, and it must be confessed that in his later work the face of the first President managed to insinuate itself onto many of Stuart's other portraits. Here we see him under the strong influence of Copley (see ME 12), insisting on small detail, and conferring upon the sitter the same sharp eyes with which he must have looked at him. The Redwood Library also owns a self-portrait at the age of twenty-four, painted in London; already Stuart was absorbing the style of Sir Joshua Reynolds, a style that profoundly influenced his later work (see ME 13).

1

The *Portrait of President John Quincy Adams*[2] is by Chester Harding (1792–1866), an itinerant master of many crafts who finally settled down to portrait painting in Washington, Boston, and Northampton. The red ground makes the black coat stand out well and helps provide a foil for the bald head and the gimlet eyes. For further discussion of Chester Harding see MA 25.

The many portraits by Charles Bird King, mentioned in our account of the Newport Historical Society, were bequeathed by the artist himself.

2

A Providence Miscellany

For the architectural splendor of this old city, the reader is referred to the companion volume in this series, *A Guide to Historic Houses of New England Open to the Public,* by Margaret Supplee Smith. For information, brochures, and (if desired) guided tours, the Providence Preservation Society, with headquarters at 21 Meeting Street, is recommended.

The gilt-domed State Capitol, on a hill overlooking downtown Providence, has the full-length *Portrait of George Washington,* by Gilbert Stuart, mentioned in connection with its twin at the Old Colony House in Newport.

Benefit Street, two blocks uphill from the east bank of the Providence River, is the site of the majority of the fine houses and churches, the Providence Athenaeum, and the Museum of the Rhode Island School of Design. Streets leading farther uphill from it take you to the campus of Brown University and other great houses, including that of John Brown (1786), now the elegant home of the Rhode Island Historical Society, at 52 Power Street. Apart from its magnificent furnishings and chinoiserie (brought back by the ships of China trader John Brown), it offers portraits by Robert Feke and John Greenwood, and *The Bombardment of Tripoli,* painted by Michele Felice Corné (1752–1832), an artist from Naples who claimed the distinction of having introduced the tomato to the United States. (Long before the Spanish Conquest, it was in fact cultivated in Central and South America, and its very name comes from the Aztec *jitomate.*)

The Providence Athenaeum, at 251 Benefit Street in a Greek Revival building of 1836 by William Strickland, is a famous old library whose history goes back to the Providence Library Company of 1753. It contains a full-length *George Washington* of the so-called Lansdowne type by Gilbert Stuart, presented in 1838. A miniature on ivory by Edward Malbone (1777–1807), representing *The Hours,* is remarkable for its large size, but its quality is below the usual standard of this leading American figure in miniature portrait painting.

Brown University

Close association with the Museum of the Rhode Island School of Design makes it unnecessary for the university to develop an ambitious collecting program to serve its art department. Nevertheless, three buildings on the campus should be visited: the John Carter Brown Library, the Annmary Brown Memorial, and the Bell Gallery. In addition, Sayles Hall contains a large full-length *Portrait of Nicholas Brown* (1836), one of Chester Harding's major works.

While the John Carter Brown Library is chiefly famous for Americana, including Latin American manuscripts illustrated by Indians still working in preconquest traditions, it contains a precious Romanesque manuscript, an antiphonary illuminated at the Bavarian monastery of Ottobeuren in the late twelfth century. There are also important Books of Hours of the Gothic period.

The Annmary Brown Memorial contains the collection of paintings, manuscripts, and incunabula assembled by General and Mrs. Rush C. Hawkins. After Mrs. Hawkins died in 1903, General Hawkins erected the building in her memory, giving it her maiden name. It has been open to the public since 1907, and was transferred to Brown University in 1948 by its board of trustees. A printed catalogue of 1913 describes the 116 paintings in the original collection, which has gradually been supplemented by later acquisitions. Attributions in the old catalogue have frequently fallen victim to the cross fire of modern connoisseurship. Thus an impressive *Holy Family* is no longer given to Andrea del Sarto (1486–1531) but to a follower; and the same has happened to the panoramic *Grand Canal, Venice*, formerly ascribed to Canaletto (1697–1768)—for reasons that will become clear in a close study of Boston's *Bacino di San Marco* (MA 76). In general, but with exceptions of note, the collection may be described as problem pictures from the fifteenth to the early twentieth century; and the display has been so treated, with admirable forthrightness, by the curatorial staff. Informative labels discuss each attribution intelligently, and the visitor soon feels invited to participate in a game of sharp looking. Among unquestioned works of quality here, I was especially impressed by a work (acquired by gift in 1978) of Pompeo Batoni, a polished Romanist of the eighteenth century, and by *Girl in a Blue Dress*, painted by Pieter Nason, Dutch seventeenth century.

Museum of Art of the Rhode Island School of Design

Location: 224 Benefit St. From I-95 take I-195 exit onto Wickendon St.; traveling west on I-195, exit onto South Main St.

Hours: Tues., Wed., Fri., Sat. 11-5; Thurs. 1-7; Sun., holidays 2-5. June and July: Tues.-Sat. 11-4:30, Sun., holidays 2-4:30. Closed in August and major national holidays

Admission: Charged

Established in 1877 as part of the Rhode Island School of Design, the museum occupied its present building in 1926. Since then the collections have grown so rapidly that they now represent most of the world's art in characteristic, often outstanding, examples. As a result, they not only serve the school but the city of Providence as its museum. They also provide an important complement to the liberal-arts program of Brown University, nearby. The museum ranks easily among the six or seven best in New England. It publishes a bulletin and picture books of the collection.

The sequence of galleries is roughly chronological, with Western art on the ground floor, while the upper floor displays Far, Middle, and Near Eastern art and the more primitive and exotic cultures. The visitor will gain much from observing what is exhibited next to what. Painting, sculpture, graphic art, furniture, and decorative arts are freely inter-mingled, and national boundaries freely traversed to establish contemporaneous connections. Yet the individual object is left unencumbered, as it should be, to make its unique aesthetic effect. It is not submerged in a "period room." Period rooms can be beautiful as wholes and yet fatal to the masterpiece (as distinguished from the period piece), for the special quality of the masterpiece is often its power to rise above its period.

The collections of Classical art, nineteenth-century French painting, and Far Eastern art are outstanding. The important Pendleton collection of eighteenth-century English and American furniture is shown in the former Pendleton residence adjacent to and incorporated with the museum.

Like Yale University (see CT 62), RISD—as we shall call the Providence museum for the sake of brevity—has a glazed brick *Lion Relief* from the Ishtar Gate at Babylon, c. 600 B.C. In the field of ancient art, however, its great glory is the collection of Greek and Roman art, in which it probably ranks second only to the Boston Museum of Fine Arts among New England museums.

Our earliest selection is from its excellent assemblage of the art of the Etruscans—those warlike people who are generally supposed to have invaded Tuscany about 850 B.C. and to have come from Asia Minor. Much more imposing than its 9½-inch height would suggest, the *Standing Bronze Warrior*,[3] dating from c. 500 B.C., once held a spear in his right hand and a shield in his left. Such a work was probably offered to Mars, the god of war. Its sharp-edged, attenuated forms give it a kind of wiry vitality markedly different from the more anatomically concerned Archaic Greek art of the same period; and in our own time such figures have inspired the ghostly proportions of the later bronze figures of Alberto Giacometti. Subsequent Etruscan art shows the harmonious influence of mainland Greek art, but the insistent realism, seen in the *Warrior*, persisted to form the main basis of Roman Republican sculpture (see RI 6).

The marble *Polykleitan Torso*,[4] 45 inches high, is a superb Roman copy, perhaps of the first century A.D., of the celebrated *Athlete Tying a Fillet around His Head* (Diadoumenos) of c. 430 B.C. It would be hard to choose between this magnificent reflection of Greek sculpture of the Parthenonic era and the *Torso* at Wellesley (MA 232), also a Roman copy of a work by the great Polykleitos. Strictly speaking, the RISD *Torso* is an adaptation rather than a copy; the contour of the figure's right side is straighter—and somehow more heroic—than the S-curve swing in known copies of Polykleitos's lost masterwork. Arms and head were attached separately by iron dowels. A large cavity received the neck and head; but the ugly square hole in the center of the back was almost certainly gouged in for a modern fastening. How Greek art developed in the fourth century in the direction of greater elegance may be seen in a marble *Torso of Hermes* (?) at RISD, a Greek copy of c. A.D. 130 after an original of c. 340 B.C. This is number 16 in the fine catalogue of Classical sculpture at RISD by Brunilde S. Ridgway (1972); the example we have discussed is number 13. The Baroque direction taken by Hellenistic sculpture (see MA 111) is superbly exemplified by a *Torso of a Fighting Giant* (Hadrianic, after an original of the second century B.C., and number 25 in the catalogue).

Among a fine collection of Greek bronzes, a *Standing Aphrodite*,[5] 18½ inches high, exudes a Praxitelean beauty. Compared with the Polykleitan torso just discussed, it demonstrates the complete liberation

3

4

5

of the figure as a self-supporting organism. So conceived, the freestanding nude female seldom appears as a theme in Greek sculpture much before c. 400 B.C.; but within the next few decades Praxiteles had made Aphrodite undraped one of its most popular subjects. The studied grace of this little bronze, its flowing lines, its intricate tilts and balances, its invitation to the eye to follow around behind the frontal plane, and its position in a gently curving S shape all suggest the world of Praxiteles. Although it is now considered to be a Roman copy, it is an exceptionally fine one.

The *Portrait Head of a Man*,[6] from the Roman Republican era of c. 60 B.C., has the grim look of death that Imperial Roman portraiture, oriented more strongly toward Greek idealization, generally avoided. The skin is stretched tightly over the cranium, but toward the lower half of the head it sags with expressive folds. The deep-set eyes, marked by no pupils, stare out blankly—into eternity? Such heads were normally carried separately from the toga-draped body, and usually by a different sculptor. For a contrasting intention in ancient portrait sculpture, see MA 60.

The gallery of Classical art features a large marble sarcophagus, Graeco-Roman of the late second century A.D., of Asia Minor type. On one face it shows *amorini* fighting lions; on the other, Achilles dragging Hector around the walls of Troy. The lid gives us some idea of how the roof of a late Greek or Roman temple was constructed. There are fine Roman wall paintings here as well, and a superb mosaic, also second century A.D., representing Apollo. Acquired by exchange from the Worcester Museum in 1940, it came from that museum's excavations at Antioch. In style it is much closer to the mosaic head at Williams College (MA 269) than to Worcester's great floor mosaic (MA 291), which dates from about A.D. 500.

Of approximately the same date, but from a very different part of the world, is a magnificent *Peruvian Mantle*,[7] of wool fabric some 40 inches

6

7

long. From Paracas, on Peru's southern coast, it belongs to the early Nazca culture. Its preservation is as spectacular as its beauty. To call it a triumph of decorative art is not enough, for it is filled with symbolic meanings, and with those special deviations from an abstract norm that mark the creative imagination. Its skin can be imitated, but not its substance.

Gothic sculpture, to which we now turn, was dominated by the masters of the great French cathedrals. In a larger view, however, it embraced such wide variations as RISD's harsh 7-foot-high Spanish wooden *Crucifix*, a belated Romanesque work of the early thirteenth century, and a gracious little *Ivory Diptych*[8] under 10 inches high, thoroughly Parisian in style but possibly made elsewhere. This small private altar dates from the years just before or just after 1300. The left wing represents the Annunciation and the Nativity (combined) below the Crucifixion and the Coronation of the Virgin (also combined); on the right, we see the Adoration of the Magi beneath the Last Judgment. Such elegant portable art as this—or illuminated manuscripts—may have provided the impetus for the liberation of Sienese painting from its Byzantine heritage, as seen in the *Crucifixion* by Simone Martini at the Fogg Art Museum (MA 115). To a lesser extent, RISD's large tempera panel on gold ground by Spinello Aretino expresses a similar fourteenth-century turn toward elegance in Florentine art as painters reacted against the blunt strength of the art of Giotto (reflected in MA 114).

Late Gothic art was seldom more flamboyant than in the superb *Verdure Tapestry*[9] of Tournai workmanship c. 1520. Such tapestries reflected Indian fashion stimulated by Vasco da Gama's voyages of discovery around Africa in 1497–99 and 1502. In an elaborate article for the museum published in 1947, Phyllis Ackerman, the well-known

8

9

tapestry expert, discussed this example with several other related ones. Almost certainly the models for the designs were Indian, but the motifs originated long before in Syria. She pointed out that the wildly floral plant that springs from the center of the RISD example is purely imaginary, exhibiting as she said "a gorgeous irrationality." Spotted around, but in a more organized way than in the normal *millefleurs* designs of about the same period, are a griffin, a strangely bearded lion, a wildcat (above the lion), a monkey, a crane, a peacock in full splendor, deer, and an array of lesser birds. The tree trunk, resembling drapery, derived —deviously and over a long period of time—from the Serpent in representations of the Fall of Adam.

That theme, with the Serpent approaching from above, is the subject of an unusually large pen-and-ink drawing[10] by the Antwerp Master, Jan Gossaert, called Mabuse (c. 1478–1532)—one of the "Antwerp Mannerists," so called because they attempted to graft the forms of Italian Mannerism (see MA 70) onto the intense realism of their own native tradition. At 31 by 22 inches it is the largest known drawing by the master; this fact and the unfinished condition of the tree can be explained if we assume that the drawing was made to preserve for Gossaert's studio the arrangement of Adam and Eve in a picture he had just sold. The theme itself absorbed Gossaert for many years. It is a late example, from about 1525, with the figures twisted in a relatively Baroque manner. In an article in the *Gazette des Beaux Arts* (November 1953), Dr. Heinrich Schwarz demonstrated Gossaert's sources for his drawing: Michelangelo's reclining *Adam* from the Sistine Ceiling, various classical motifs, and some of Dürer's engravings. He argued convincingly that the Adam is a self-portrait. The connection of this drawing with a picture (NH 20) at Manchester, N.H., which he also identified as a self-portrait, is therefore all the more interesting.

Jacopo Robusti, called Tintoretto (1518–94), was the greatest Venetian after Titian. Indeed, he was easily the greatest Italian painter of the later sixteenth century. (El Greco, who was strongly influenced by him, lived into the next century.) This 28-inch high oil sketch of *The Combat between Tancred and Clorinda*,[11] from Tasso's *Jerusalem Delivered*,

10

11

allows us to watch him in the very act of creation. The canvas has been sized a deep brown, and upon it Tintoretto is drawing (one cannot avoid the present tense) in livid-tinted lines of opaque oil paint. The effect is nocturnal and phosphorescent, almost like El Greco. Tintoretto was deeply affected by Michelangelo's later paintings and sculptures in Florence and Rome, but his light was all his own. His biographers tell us that he hung up small figures in his studio and observed them by candlelight to achieve his remarkable effects. It is no great step from such work to fully Baroque art. This brilliant sketch dates from late in Tinoretto's career, c. 1584–88.

Sebastien Bourdon (1616–71), like his older contemporary and chief inspirer, Nicolas Poussin (see MA 123), accepted much of the Baroque art prevalent in the seventeenth century, but muted it with a strong feeling for classical restraint. His *Landscape with a Mill*[12] is one of his masterpieces, marvelously fluid, lyrical as a Giorgione, and yet cool as Cartesian logic. Harmonious greens and browns are accented by small touches of white and yellow and brightened by the lovely blue of a Mediterranean sky. Arranged in planes parallel to the picture surface and receding in almost military precision, the forms have the sort of geometric purity that we associate with Poussin, and later with Corot, Cézanne, and Seurat. Bourdon was born at Montpellier—on the Mediterranean—and studied in Italy from 1634 to 1637. It is thought that RISD's picture, so Italian in aspect, may be a much later reminiscence, as in Corot's *Souvenirs d'Italie.* In his next to last *Discourse* (December 1788), Sir Joshua Reynolds praised Bourdon for his ability to inspire "sentiments of grandeur and sublimity." "By continual contemplation of such works," he urged on the students of the Royal Academy, "a sense of the higher excellences of art will by degrees dawn on the imagination."

By contrast, Baroque drama projects from a large (40 by 50 inches) Dutch canvas representing *St. Peter in Prison Summoned by the Angel.* Close to Rembrandt in feeling and in subtlety—no angel appears here except through the startled recognition of St. Peter, and the helmeted guards are totally unaware of what is happening—it is too soft, too silvery, and too closely packed into the front plane to be Rembrandt's own work. An attribution to his most original pupil, Carel Fabritius (c. 1622–54), seems a likely solution to the authorship of this fine paint-

12

ing, but not all authorities agree. If Fabritius painted it, the date must be in the late 1650s when his connection with Rembrandt was still strong.

Rococo art of the eighteenth century is splendidly represented here by a Louis XV console table of carved and gilded oak with a green marble top, and by the magnificent porcelain collection of Lucy T. Aldrich. Outstanding among the exhibits are figurines by Franz Anton Bustelli, who led the Nymphenburg Palace manufactory outside Munich from 1754 to 1763. If Antoine Watteau (see MA 265) set the tone, early in the century, for the style that was to prevail until the French Revolution, Bustelli was his closest parallel in three-dimensional art.

The Spartan crispness and purity of Neo-Classicism appears in a little watercolor drawing, *Man on Horseback*, by Wilhelm Kobell (1766–1853), a Biedermeier-Bavarian variant of Jacques Louis David's Napoleonic style. Close to David himself, however, is the *Portrait Bust of Madame Récamier*[13] by Joseph Chinard de Lyon (1756–1813). In dazzling white Carrara marble, it appears to have been cut down from a half-length figure holding a shawl around one shoulder, the left breast bared. A not quite identical version, in this more complete state, is in the Museum of Lyon, where the sculptor worked and Madame Récamier was born. An article in RISD's *Bulletin* for December 1938 convincingly argues that an old tale of the reduction of the portrait to a state of Victorian decorum was in fact true, and that Chinard's signature is a crude copy of the one originally on the base. Madame Récamier, who died in 1849 at the age of seventy-one, is best known for her portrait by Jacques Louis David (Louvre) of c. 1800, when she was twenty. Chinard's marble portraits would have been carved not long afterward.

Thomas Couture (1815–79) is not among the great pathfinders of nineteenth-century French painting, but he was the master of one of them, Edouard Manet, who learned much from him. *Little Gilles*,[14] an oil study for Couture's painting in the Philadelphia Museum of Art, dates from c. 1878, and was possibly influenced by his more gifted pupil. However that may be, the flat brush strokes and the concern for

13

14

"painterly" surfaces were constants in Couture's art, though his reputation was launched by such Salon successes as the huge *Romans of the Decadence* (Louvre, small version also at RISD). In his Providence study of a small confectioner, he appears to have thought of his subject not as a manifesto of prevailing fashion, but as an occasion for fine painting. The same is true of Manet, whom we now consider.

The beneficent effect of six years' study with Couture on the art of Edouard Manet (1832–83) has been indicated above. Curiously, it happened despite a strong antipathy between master and pupil, but that was caused by widely diverging temperaments and by Couture's dedication to history painting. Manet, who soon found a supporter in Emile Zola, turned to contemporary life and thereby earned Couture's scathing comment that he would never be more than the Daumier of his day. That turned out to be true, as we know, only in the sense of the choice of subject matter. RISD owns one of Manet's finest oils from mid-career, *Le Repos*,[15] painted in 1870, bought by the dealer Durand-Ruel in 1872, and lent by him to the Salon of 1873. It represents Manet's favorite pupil and protégé, Berthe Morisot (1841–95), who was soon to marry his brother Eugène. She first appeared as the most prominent figure in Manet's *Balcon* (Louvre, 1869). In *Le Repos*, which is nearly 6 feet high, the ease of the pose—accented by the remarkably fluid Gardner wrists—rivals Van Dyck's most gracious images (see MA 46), but in no way interferes with the expression of forceful character. Since the time of the somewhat comparable *Young Woman Reclining in Spanish Costume* (1862, Yale University, CT 79), Manet's painting had become more fluid, and the Spanish overtures had been succeeded by an interest in Japanese art. On the rear wall is what appears to be a screen by Kuniyoshi, but Manet brushed it so freely that it could be taken for an oil sketch by Delacroix (see MA 120). A mauve sofa sets off the foamy white of Berthe Morisot's dress, with its subtly played-down polka dots. Manet's full adoption of the prismatic color of Impressionism was delayed until 1874, as seen in the masterly *Blue Venice* at Shelburne (VT 22). As nearly always in Manet's appearances at the Salon, *Le Repos* was savagely—and to us incomprehensibly—attacked.

15

Among the critical epithets: "the goddess of slovenliness," and "a lady resting after having swept the chimney herself."

Manet declined to exhibit with the Impressionists because he persisted in his hopes to win recognition at the official Salon, but he remained in close touch with them. Following their first group exhibition, mid-April and May 1874, in quarters provided by the photographer Nadar, he joined Monet and Renoir at Argenteuil-sur-Seine, some fifteen miles north of Paris. In that summer, or the next, Claude Monet (1840–1926) painted *Le Bassin d'Argenteuil*,[16] a picture that can be considered the very model of the Impressionist point of view. Color sparkles, textures dance, sailboats bob peacefully on the bright blue water. A specialty for Monet is the screen of intense green foliage that closes off this happy scene. How different it is from the boating picture of ten years earlier at Farmington (CT 5) or again from the Rouen Cathedral series of twenty years later (see MA 254)! In RISD's painting do not miss the splash of brilliant orange below the white hull of the nearest sailboat, or the absence of grays and blacks in all these rainbow hues.

A Boating Party, expertly brushed by John Singer Sargent, who was sixteen years Monet's junior, makes an interesting comparison with the picture just discussed. Painted about 1889, its concern is more with the indolent gentry depicted than with the luminous spatial environment. Indeed, the landscape serves merely as a backdrop.

We turn now to the American Thomas Eakins (1844–1916), in a fascinating watercolor, *Baseball Players*,[17] of 1875—the same year as two of his major oils already discussed (MA 17 and CT 76), and within a year of Claude Monet's *Bassin d'Argenteuil*. No need to emphasize here Eakins's concern with the American scene! By Impressionist standards his color is muted, with only the green of the playing field and the grayed blue stockings of the alert players to enliven the dull whites, ashen grays, and Rembrandtesque browns that dominate this intense little vignette. With the spectators only dimly suggested, as in Eakins's boxing and medical compositions, the focus is held on batter and catcher—poised, as always in Eakins, in a moment before action. The very small and precise signature and date appear on the wall near the batter's hands. The hush of this picture, its action frozen in suspense, is entirely foreign to Impressionist *joie de vivre* and excitement

16

17

in the passing moment. For American interest in that point of view we must await painters of a younger generation, like Childe Hassam (see MA 182).

Although Edgar Degas (1834–1917) was a leading organizer of the Impressionists' exhibitions, his work stands apart. Painting outdoors, essential to the effects of a Monet or a Renoir, seldom interested him. While he enjoyed the races, he painted them in his studio; but indoor scenes were his true métier. RISD's pastel *Danseuse au Bouquet*[18] ranks as high among his ballet pictures as Farmington's *Tub* (CT 3) among those devoted to women bathing. Unlike Monet, Degas cared greatly about composition. This pastel provides a wonderful example of his expressive utilization of abstract design. Turn it upside down and observe the reverse-Z arrangement, the sequences of semicircles and half ovals, the rhythmic flutter of feet, and the final frieze of dancers (now at the base) that diagonally echoes the dark horizontal formed by the top of the loge in which the foreground lady sits (that is, when the picture is right side up). In its proper position you quickly notice how important that lady is, even though you see only half of her head. Her great size and that of her fan establish the foreground. The fan introduces the sequence of semicircles—continued in reverse by the dancer's skirt and bust, by the group at upper left, and most subtly by the chalked lines on the stage floor. Her jeweled earring provides the motif for the half ovals seen in the dancer's bouquet and elsewhere. Color indeed sparkles, but it avoids Claude Monet's honest primaries and Renoir's lush tones to favor more oblique hues: russets, apricots, watered blue-greens, smudged grays, and the startling black of the spectator's fan. At the date of 1878, it exemplifies the degree to which Degas accepted, and altered, Impressionist color. Always the draftsman, he found the pastel medium more sympathetic to his aims than did others in his circle. I hope that in the foregoing I have not made the tricks and turns of Degas's abstract design seem like passionless mechanics. On the contrary, it was through them that he transformed what might have been just a pretty picture into something formidable, surprisingly astringent, and even vaguely sinister. RISD's enchanting oil portrait *La Savoisienne*, from c. 1873, is much more conservative, in the tradition of Ingres; but another major pastel, *Six Friends of the Artist*, dating from 1884, offers a remarkable grouping in two vertical panels with each figure totally

18

self-absorbed: a group created by composition, but psychologically a non-group.

Ces Dames des Chars,[19] a circus scene in the Hippodrome de l'Alma, was painted 1883–85 by James Tissot (1836–1902). Five feet high, it shows three sequin-sheathed young women driving Roman chariots around the ring. A tonal symphony of reds and pinks, it is marked by sharp outlines, crisp detail, and smooth surfaces—all approved by the Academy. But the subject is drawn from contemporary life, and this subject in particular had already attracted Degas, as in his *Miss Lala at the Cirque Fernando* (1879, Tate Gallery, London). Degas was a close friend from the early years and did a fine portrait of Tissot in 1868 (Metropolitan Museum of Art, New York). Painted in Tissot's studio, it includes a Japanese picture high on the rear wall. While this was one of Tissot's enthusiasms, it did not lead him, as it did Degas, to absorb Japanese methods of flat composition. Yet the chopped-off figures of these circus girls reflect that source—supported, as again in Degas, by the influence of candid-camera photography. Degas tried hard to persuade Tissot to exhibit in the first Impressionist show of 1874, but Tissot, now well established in London, declined. It is worth noting that Degas's appeal was based on the necessity of founding a school of Realism. *Ces Dames des Chars* formed a pair with *The Amateur Circus*, now owned by the Boston Museum of Fine Arts; and Tissot produced a fine etching of RISD's picture.

The superb collection of drawings at Providence offers an opportunity to study at their finest two of the greatest masters of the later nineteenth century: Vincent van Gogh (1839–90) and Paul Cézanne (1839–1906). Both artists were schooled in Impressionist technique—primarily by Camille Pissarro (see MA 255)—but soon rejected its easy acceptance of nature's beauties. Neither of them had any interest in Renoir's delight in a summer holiday (MA 83). Although van Gogh was much younger than Cézanne, we consider him first because he developed more rapidly and because his reed-pen *View of Arles*[20] slightly predates Cézanne's watercolor study of a *Card Player*.[21] The dates are 1888 as against c. 1890–92.

20

19

As we observe van Gogh's drawing, its arrangement by diagonal planes diverging from the picture surface will gradually become clear. This is the pictorial reason for the large dark accents in the foreground, and it should be noted that they begin well off center to our left. In the distance, the small buildings are likewise placed on the bias. Everywhere the shapes are interrupted by overlapping ones, and the whole surface is broken up by staccato strokes of the reed pen. This is an art of nerves, not of dense masses, an art of deep space, not of sculptural modeling. If the illustrations are turned upside down, van Gogh's image recedes as before, but Cézanne's still exists in one major plane running from top to bottom.

Cézanne's *Card Player* is a preparatory drawing for the main figure at the right of the great composition at the Barnes Foundation, near Philadelphia (a smaller variant is in the Metropolitan Museum of Art). The Worcester Art Museum owns an oil study for the central figure of the Barnes example. Note how Cézanne juxtaposes the curving masses of the figure to the rectilinear masses of the table and how a single wash defines the cheekbone and sets the position of the eye socket. It is hard to believe that pencil and watercolor can approach the carving of a limestone block, but here it has been done. In the whole range of art there is no more extraordinary example of the economy of means.

Like Edgar Degas, Henri de Toulouse-Lautrec (1864–1901) belongs to a phase of French art that has little to do with the world of Cézanne. The difference between these two worlds may be stated, perhaps too simply, as the difference between Paris and France. By France is meant the provincial towns, villages, and farms that make it possible for Paris to exist. By Paris is not meant the city of Daumier, which is really any great city, but the Paris that is fashionable and sophisticated and yet often tawdry and cynical behind its elegant mask. Essentially, this is an aristocratic Paris, or at least a Paris stamped with aristocracy, no matter what its mode of life may be. It is assumed that Paris, and only Paris, has defined the pattern of French aristocracy, and that aristocratic French art, no matter where it may emerge, is inevitably Parisian. If Degas and Toulouse-Lautrec are the archetypical Parisian painters of their century, it seems relevant to point out that Lautrec was born an aristocrat, and

21

Degas's family once called itself De Gas (with the *s* pronounced). Though they lived in a bourgeois world, they viewed it with an aristocrat's detachment and refinement. So did Edouard Manet, though he was no aristocrat by birth.

It would be easy to point up the salient fact that Toulouse-Lautrec was a devoted disciple of Degas, for his direct borrowings are numerous, yet in each case he effected a complete transformation. The watercolor and chalk drawing of *Yvette Guilbert*,[22] for example, descends from a long line of Degas's cabaret pictures, notably a magnificent pastel of a singer—also featuring a black glove—at the Fogg Art Museum. But unmistakably Lautrec's own are the attenuation, the spidery lines, and in the face a simplification that approaches caricature. Of his many representations of the celebrated entertainer, none is so mordant as this one. The date is 1894.

With the purchase in 1966 of a bronze cast of *The Naked Balzac*,[23] the RISD museum acquired one of its finest works of sculpture. A study by Auguste Rodin (1840–1917) that led to the much larger robed version of 1897 (a cast is in the garden of the Museum of Modern Art), it measures 50 inches in height, and it has a dark gold patina. The original plaster is in the Rodin Museum at Meudon, outside Paris, where the sculptor maintained a large studio for the completion of works of a size too great to be accommodated in his Paris residence and smaller studio. The long and frustrating story of Rodin's *Monument to Balzac*, from the original commission of 1891 to its sad denouement, is recounted in several studies by Albert Elsen (especially in *Rodin*, Museum of Modern Art, 1963) and in a special article by Jacques de Caso in the RISD *Bulletin* for May 1966. The *Naked Balzac* is the most definitive of many attempted versions prior to arrival at the final clothed form. Probably conceived as early as 1892, it appears to have been completed by 1895. Its vigor has to be seen to be believed; yet the final version surpasses it in grandeur and majesty. No bronze was cast of *The Naked Balzac* before 1898, but the RISD example is one of the earliest known. As for the great monument, vituperatively rejected, it was never cast in Rodin's lifetime; and not until 1939 was a bronze erected, at the junc-

22

23

tion of the Boulevard Montparnasse and the Boulevard Raspail. The cast in the Museum of Modern Art was especially made for a presentation to that museum in 1955. Rodin took the great plaster to Meudon, to contemplate it, love it, and sometimes even to doubt it. Here the American photographer Edward Steichen made his famous moonlight studies of it in 1908.

In 1914, three years after his *Bust of Baudelaire*, discussed at Wellesley College (MA 241), Raymond-Duchamp-Villon (1876–1918) created the *Seated Woman*,[24] of which RISD owns a bronze cast of 1915 and also the preparatory drawing for the completed design. This gold-washed bronze, 28 inches high, once belonged to the American collector John Quinn, an enthusiastic supporter of modernism at the New York Armory Show of 1913, at which the artist was represented by five sculptures. At Quinn's request, the original plaster was shipped to him in New York, cast there, and then returned to the sculptor. Other casts were made after the Second World War, with a dark patination. A cast of the same earlier date as the RISD example is owned by Yale University. Duchamp-Villon's considerable development toward Cubism since the 1911 *Head of Baudelaire* is partially obscured by the traditional modeling transitions from plane to plane. Later in 1914 he was to take the full step, already achieved in painting by his brothers Marcel Duchamp and Jacques Villon, with *Head of a Horse* (Hirshhorn Museum, Washington) and *Horse* (Museum of Modern Art). The tenuously balanced pose of the *Seated Woman* has been compared with that of Michelangelo's *Madonna and Child* in the Medici Chapel of San Lorenzo, Florence. The evidence of a manikin, rather than a human form, as the model is strong here; and it appears about the same time in the painting of Giorgio de Chirico, then working in Paris. Such depersonalization likewise suggests the anonymity of the machine, with which the painter Fernand Léger (see MA 245) was already deeply concerned. Not for this true sculptor was the network of flat planes in kinetic sequence of Marcel Duchamp's *Nude Descending the Staircase*, of 1911 and 1912 (Philadelphia Museum of Art).

24

In the field of twentieth-century painting RISD is not rich, but the collection is growing. Picasso is represented in small oils of 1901 and 1911/12 and a pencil drawing of c. 1906 (shortly before the *Demoiselles d'Avignon*). Post–gray-and-tan Cubism examples are by the lesser masters Jean Metzinger and Albert Gleizes, and by the very major Georges Braque (1882–1963)—a *Still Life* of 1918 in characteristic horizontal format and rich in deep browns and greens. Its clean geometry, relating Braque to such French forebears as Chardin and Cézanne, is in direct contrast with Picasso's precarious house-of-cards constructions (see MA 185). The Austro-German Expressionist Oskar Kokoschka is seen in the superb pre–First World War *Portrait of Franz Hauser*—sold by the Nazis from a German state collection. An admirable watercolor, *The Antelope*, c. 1913, shows the German Franz Marc at his best.

From our brief survey of modern art at RISD we turn now to cultures outside the mainstream of Western art. A *Haida Totem Pole*[25] over 12 feet high came as a gift in 1956 from the R. F. Haffenreffer Family Foundation; and it is exhibited with other native American objects owned by RISD or lent from the Haffenreffer Museum's collection (see RI 25). Haida culture centered in the Queen Charlotte archipelago off the coast of British Columbia. The pole was carved from a single trunk of red cedar with representations (top to bottom) of a thunderbird, a killer whale, a beaver, a bear, and a frog, and was painted. These are clan "crest" figures, equivalent to the heraldic devices of European nobility. While such poles are for the most part of relatively recent origin, some examples still standing, weathered silvery gray and marked by moss growing in the cracks, attest to a tradition of considerable duration. For a general introduction to this subject, Philip Drucker, *Indians of the Northwest Coast*, published for the American Museum of Natural History (paperback edition 1963), is recommended. A special account of a Haida village containing a small forest of totem poles *in situ* will be found in John and Carolyn Smyly, *The Totem Poles of Skedans* (Seattle: University of Washington Press, 1973).

While totem-pole imagery is subordinated to the shape of an architectural element, Chinese dragons are beings of such importance that no such limitation prevails. A *Clay Figurine of a Seated Dragon*,[26] 12½

25

26

inches high and dating from the Wei Kingdom (A.D. 220–265), owes its remarkably fine preservation to the fact that it was buried in a tomb with other figurines of humans and animals. In the words of an article in the *Bulletin of the RISD* for October 1930, such figurines "projected into the expansive future of the human race a vivid record of contemporary life; they staged a puppet show for remote generations of men." However horrific a dragon may be, for the Chinese it was a beneficent creature. This one can be described as eager. Here the unnamed artist has combined great energy (especially in the head and horns) with great repose (in the hooped body and neck and the recumbent limbs). For some much wilder dragons, see MA 94.

Preeminent among Indian sculptures at the museum is the *Dancing Siva*,[27] a south Indian bronze of the twelfth century about 4 feet high. Appearing as Natajara, Lord of the Dancers, Siva is one of the great Hindu Trinity, with Brahma and Vishnu. While he is primarily the Lord of Death, as such he is also the Lord of Life (through rebirth from death); here he performs a mystic dance in his joy of creation. Such art as this flourished in the time of the Chola Kings in the Madras region, from the ninth to the thirteenth century. It was cast by the lost-wax process and four metals were used in addition to the basic copper. Siva's supernatural power appears in his four arms and three eyes. A moon is set on his head, and the outer hands hold a drum and a sacred flame. Underfoot is the dwarf Muyalaka, the spirit of evil, with a cobra. The ensemble is encircled by a mandala with a double fringe of flames. Siva's dance, performed as the cosmos is destroyed, expresses his joy in its recreation through Brahma. It symbolizes the eternal flux of energy in all matter, the sequence from disintegration to renewal. While Indian plastic forms owed much in their early history to the spread of Hellenism through Alexander's conquests, they were profoundly modified in the intervening centuries. The sinuous grace, of unbelievable elegance, somehow masks those awkward junctures of the "extra" arms, in themselves an indication of how far Indian thought had moved from the Greek glorification of the organic human body.

27

28

It is unfortunate that considerations of preservation and security require that the colossal *Japanese Sun Buddha*[28] be displayed indoors. This magnificent wood figure of the tenth century (Fujiwara period) was once the chief image of a subtemple across the Inland Sea from the holy mountain of Koya, southeast of Osaka. Carved from many blocks of cryptomeria wood, it is nearly 10 feet high and hollow within. While its size is no match for that of the Great Buddha at Nara, fashioned in bronze and 53 feet high (completed in 752), the latter has suffered much damage and repair. The Providence statue is seated in the pose of Buddha Vairocana—the central point of the universe. Clothed in monastic garment, the utterly serene figure is topped by a high pointed hairdo symbolic of Vairocana's ineffable wisdom. The mountain sanctuaries of Koya were created by the Shingon sect of Buddhism, which was imported from China at the end of the eighth century. Imported with it was Chinese sculptural style of the T'ang era, as may be seen in a comparison with Buddha figures like the stone image in the Fogg Art Museum (MA 137) and the head at Worcester (MA 311). In Japanese, Vairocana becomes Dainichi-nyorai: Buddha in relation to the material world. From this central image four other manifestations of Buddha are conceived as emanating. If the Japanese interpretation lacks some of the energy of T'ang Chinese ones, as a physical presence it is unsurpassed. Yale University's wood figure of a Buddhist *Bon-ten* (CT 65) is of the same period as RISD's Buddha, and it conveys a similar impassiveness.

Further discovery of high aesthetic achievement in Oriental art will be afforded by careful examination of the many costumes in the Lucy T. Aldrich collection, and as well by the Japanese prints Miss Aldrich also gave the museum.

A superb bronze *Head of a Prince* from the Benin region of western Africa rivals one in the Peabody Museum at Cambridge and the *Head of a Princess* discussed at the University of Vermont (VT 2).

Massachusetts

Massachusetts

Mead Art Building, Amherst College

Location: Routes 9 and 116
Hours: Mon.-Sat. 9-5, Sun. 11:30-5; closed August and summer weekends
Admission: Free. Ⓗ

The building was erected in 1949 from funds bequeathed by William R. Mead, an alumnus and member of the firm of McKim, Mead & White. Its symmetrical plan is in the tradition of that great Beaux-Arts triumvirate. Interior rearrangements have increased the exhibition space, which was originally concentrated in the main entrance gallery so that students on their way to art courses would pass through it. This plan was linked to a policy of frequent rotation of the exhibits, and since the collection has grown rapidly through the years a great proportion of it is stored in well-appointed areas on two lower floors. For works not on view, apply to members of the staff.

A special gallery contains Assyrian reliefs from the palace of Ashurnazirpal at Nineveh (ninth century B.C.). Approximately the size and shape of one of the smaller rooms of the palace, it has been decorated to suggest the opulence of that ancient court. These reliefs and the similar ones at Bowdoin, Dartmouth, Middlebury, and Williams colleges, at the University of Vermont, and at Yale were presented in the 1850s by alumni of the respective institutions who were missionaries in the Middle East. The stones were cut for shipment across the desert by camelback, and across the seas by sailing vessel. Amherst owns six of these reliefs. One of the largest, nearly 8 feet high, represents King Ashurnazirpal himself. A smaller one depicts a *Winged Bird-Headed Deity*[1] who fertilizes the sacred date palm (highly stylized) with a pinecone dipped in pollen from a square pail. The cuneiform inscriptions cut across the surface of the larger reliefs are repetitious in their celebration of the king's exploits. Close study of the reliefs themselves will reveal differences of workmanship—not surprising in view of the immense number of such slabs that once decorated the palace. The British Museum has the greatest number of them, but no less than seventy-three are in the United States. For further information, see the excellent brochure published by Dartmouth College, which, like Amherst, owns six examples (J. B. Stearns and D. P. Hansen, *The Assyrian Reliefs at Dartmouth*; Hanover: Dartmouth, 1953).

A second permanent installation in the Mead Art Building is the banqueting hall from Rotherwas House (1611), an outstanding example of Elizabethan decoration. It is fully paneled in walnut, and its richly polychromed oak mantelpiece shows Virtues supporting the crest of the original owner, Roger Bodenham of Herefordshire. This Baroque accent gives the hall a Jacobean flavor, but Elizabethan and Jacobean styles merged so thoroughly that a composite term, "Jacobethan," is gaining acceptance. Normally used as a student reading room, on special occasions this hall is furnished with pieces from the college's collection, supplementing the wall cupboards and chests that are permanent fixtures of the room. The molded plaster ceiling is, of course, a modern reproduction, but the chandelier is a fine example from the period.

European and American furniture at Amherst, especially of the eighteenth century, can be termed, without exaggeration, magnificent. The collection is also rich in porcelains, silver, and textiles, and in small bronzes. An array of miniatures features work by Edward G. Malbone (1777–1807), the leading American practitioner in this field. It also includes the only known portrait of Patrick Henry. In the Far Eastern section, Chinese art and Moghul painting are strongly represented, as are drawings and prints, including Japanese color woodblock impressions. The example of Rembrandt's smaller etching of *Christ Preaching* is rightly prized.

Early on, Amherst received many gifts of ancient classical art, and later acquisitions have developed the collection into one of considerable importance. In the fall of 1979 a catalogue was published, including special essays on the three objects we are about to discuss. A marble *Cycladic Figure* from Neolithic times yields to the larger one at Boston (MA 56) in size, but at a height of nearly 2 feet it nevertheless ranks as the largest known example of its particular kind. Even in this distant era the individuality of the artist asserted itself. The Boston example, by comparison, is sveltely elongated with the arms tightly crossed against the lower thorax; the Amherst one is squatter in proportion, its stubby arms barely meeting at the front, the hips much more swollen. A date of c. 2700 B.C. is suggested.

A small bronze handle from an *oenochoe* (wine pitcher) ornamented with a fierce Gorgon's head is a great rarity in Archaic Greek art, especially because this monster sprouts horns. It comes from Magna Graecia, the Greek colony in south Italy. Its beautiful green patina is, of course, the work of ages in an underground deposit.

Most impressive of all is an *Attic Grave Stele*[2] in Pentelic marble 4 feet high, dating from about 340 B.C. In his article on this fine piece,

Cornelius Vermeule hails it as a precious relic from Athens "in the twilight years of the city's glory." The invasions of Philip of Macedon were soon to come. The relief represents a large amphora (for the shape compare MA 288), but with greatly elongated neck and handles of the type known as *loutrophoros-amphora*, used on ceremonial occasions to memorialize young men in their prime. (A differently shaped vessel was used for young women.) Above this vase is a floral offering flanked by two "tear bottles." Expertly carved in very low relief on the body of the amphora are four mourning figures. The stele presumably stood in the family "plot" of a cemetery.

The Amherst collection of Greek ceramic vases is noteworthy for its range and its quality.

Medieval art includes a sixth-century pavement mosaic from Syria, depicting animals and birds; Coptic textile fragments; and a fragment of a sixth-century sarcophagus. A crude but strong echo of a Roman Corinthian capital, from the ninth-century Rhineland, foreshadowing the achievement of the great twelfth-century Romanesque sculptors, is seen here in an example hardly surpassed by any in the United States today. This limestone *Double Capital*,[3] 15 inches high, comes from the Toulouse area in southwestern France. Comparable ones are in the Toulouse Museum. Note the refinement of the carving of the winged birds, joined at the head (replacing, as it were, the Corinthian rosette in this position). The abacus has a decorative meander of acanthus leaves (flattened reminders, only, of their once luxuriant growth on Roman examples). Monastic cloister arcades supported on paired columns, of which there are many examples, required such capitals as this. The theme of interlaced birds and animals derives from the arts of the barbarian invaders (echoed in the Merovingian buckle at Worcester, MA 292), and ultimately from the ancient art of China.

Purchase in 1941, at the important Brummer sale, of a life-size Catalonian fresco of *St. Sylvester*,[4] from the Cathedral of La Seo de Virge, was a major addition in the Gothic field. Its thirteenth-century date is indeed Gothic, but conservative Spain continued to maintain its Byzantine and Romanesque traditions, as may be seen in the rigid

3

4

frontality, the flattened and angular hand, and the staring eyes. Comparison with Boston's great twelfth-century apse (MA 61), also from Catalonia, will show how little of the style of the thirteenth-century French Gothic cathedrals penetrated south of the Pyrenees. This remarkable fresco is yet another illustration of the statement of Henri Focillon that the development of art is not always in chronological order.

The gift in 1961 of twelve Italian Renaissance paintings filled an important gap in the museum's coverage of Western art. Of these *The Madonna and Child with St. Ambrose*, by the Bergamask-Venetian Girolamo da Santa Croce, is perhaps the finest. An earlier gift from Professor Charles H. Morgan, former director of the museum, a *Holy Family* by the early sixteenth-century Florentine Domenico Puligo, is a good example of Raphaelesque art just beginning to turn toward Mannerism. Puligo was a close follower of Andrea del Sarto.

Baroque painting is superlatively represented by *Charity*,[5] an oil sketch by Peter Paul Rubens (1577–1640). Freely brushed on a wood panel 14 inches high, it is in the master's developed late style, about a year or two after his design for the Whitehall ceiling in London (CT 52). The astonishing degree of Rubens's transformation of High Renaissance symmetry, pyramidal composition, and linear clarity can be quickly measured by comparison with the Puligo *Holy Family* just mentioned. The sketch was made for an additional tapestry in a celebrated series he had designed for the royal court at Madrid in 1625–28. The series represented the Triumph of the Church and the Eucharist.

Indications of the impact of Rubens and of Bernini, his counterpart in seventeenth-century sculpture, can be seen in a marvelous little gilt-bronze *Seated Hercules*, 6 inches high and probably by a French artist. As in the contrast between Rubens and Domenico Puligo, its Baroque fluidity can be set against the elegant frontality and grace of a small gilt-bronze *Crucifix*, from the atelier of France's major sixteenth-century sculptor, Jean Goujon.

To facilitate his enormous output, Rubens employed a small army of students and assistants, some of whom, like Anthony Van Dyck, went on to major careers of their own. He also employed collaborators of established reputation to whom he could entrust the execution of landscape backgrounds, floral elements, still lifes, and the like. One of these

5

was his contemporary Frans Snyders (1579–1657), the showiest exponent of still life and animal painting of the whole Baroque era. Amherst's acquisition of a *Still Life*,[6] oil on panel measuring 55½ by 78½ inches, brought to America an outstanding example of Snyders's specialty. Glowing in vibrant color, its forms crisscrossed in serpentine profusion and energized by the figure at the right and by the hounds at the base, it affords a release of tensions by a view of the sky through a not quite absolutely geometric window grille. Observe this window carefully. An extra small diagonal is surely there to complete the all-important thrust of the dead peacock. Long before current inflation, the flaming red crustacean at the right was already known as "the fifty-dollar lobster." Of special local appeal is the fact that the picture came from the collection of the first Earl Amherst.

In his book *The Art Collection of Amherst College*, published in 1972 on the occasion of the college's sesquicentennial anniversary, Charles H. Morgan lists the extraordinary heirlooms of the Amherst family that the college has acquired: letters, documents, and maps relating to the French and Indian Wars, a Worcester dessert service of 123 pieces (early nineteenth century, belonging to the first earl, who also owned the great Snyders *Still Life*), a handsome tureen, and no fewer than twelve family portraits, including those of Sir Jeffery himself by Reynolds and Gainsborough. Subsequently a third, by Blackburn (see ME 11), was added by gift. Morgan's statement that "there is no comparable collection of English family treasures in the United States" appears to be no exaggeration.

Although the metric rhythm of "Jeffery, Lord Amherst" would be ruinous if applied to the first line of the college's great song, that in fact was his correct title—as were Jeffery, Baron Amherst, and Sir Jeffery Amherst, and General Jeffery Amherst. He lived from 1717 to 1797, and not the least of his achievements was to become the eponym of a Massachusetts town and a Massachusetts college. The first earl was his nephew; *our* Jeffery had refused that title.

The fine Blackburn and Gainsborough portraits, painted in 1760 and c. 1785 respectively, are not housed in the museum (and it will probably be difficult to see them), but the version painted in 1765 by Sir Joshua Reynolds (1723–92)[7] not only is one of the museum's

6

7

major treasures, but must rank as one of Reynolds's masterpieces. No other example in New England, at least, comes close to it in subtlety of color and expressive content. At the generous size of 49 by 24 inches, it shows the brilliant general in full armor at the age of forty-eight after his many victories over the French in North America (Louisburg, 1758; Ticonderoga, 1759; Montreal, 1760). He was governor of Virginia from 1759 to 1768. The portrait itself became famous through engravings, but these give no idea of the beauty and ease of the brushwork, nor of the glinting silver-grays of the armor, the strange pallor of the face, and, most memorable of all, the lavenderish pink of the wide sash. The insigne of the Knight of Bath gave Reynolds another opportunity to indulge his love of painting for painting's sake—something that is less apparent when he browned up his palette in emulation of Old Master works darkened by time.

Amherst has other important British portraits, including one of *Vice Admiral John Amherst,* a rare early work by the landscapist Richard Wilson, painted in 1749; but we pass on to a dashing oil sketch of *Charles Baring Wall*[8] by Sir Thomas Lawrence (1769–1830), third president of the Royal Academy and the most fashionable European artist of the early nineteenth century. This is a study for a family portrait in one of the great English residences. As in Yale's portrait of *Admiral Sir John Markham* (CT 56), Lawrence dazzles us with textures sparkling as they catch the light. The rapidly brushed passages in black and white beneath the youth's chin imply an Old World confidence and ease altogether foreign to the plain and hard-won competence of American Colonial painting.

Most of Amherst's important collection of American portraits came as the gift of Herbert L. Pratt, donor of the Rotherwas banqueting hall. While those of George Washington by Charles Willson Peale and his son Rembrandt, and the Blackstone pair by Copley, are standard fare, the *Portrait of James Peale*[9] painted in 1789 by his brother Charles Willson Peale (1741–1827) has the unfussy observant look of Copley at his best, as in Bowdoin's *Thomas Flucker* (ME 12). In the presence of qualities like these one can hardly complain at the lack of Gilbert Stuart's brilliant, but acquired, European stylishness, or of Sir Thomas Lawrence's indigenous flair.

8

9

An excellent coverage of nineteenth-century American landscape painting begins with a splendid example by Asher Durand (1796–1886), *In the Woods*. Durand was a pioneer in what came to be known as the Hudson River School. Its landscapes were approved by William Cullen Bryant and even apostrophized in his poetry. But the great prize here is a pair—we might almost say a diptych—by Thomas Cole (1801–48), English-born but entirely American as to career. *Past*[10] and *Present*[11] were painted in 1838. We have discussed an Italian extravaganza of Cole's at Hartford (CT 26), but in *Past* and *Present* he introduces the idea of a time sequence already initiated in a more ambitious series, *The Course of Empire*, a quartet now in the New York Historical Society. Cole, Bryant, and Durand maintained a close friendship. At Cole's death, Bryant read a long eulogy and Durand painted his most famous picture, *Kindred Spirits* (New York Public Library), showing Cole and Bryant on Table Rock, overhanging a gorge in the Catskills.

In his writings about American scenery, Cole expressed the feeling that it lacked "historical and legendary associations," and that it was "not so much of the past as of the present and future." Thus, in the Amherst pictures, he turned to the Romantic appeal of the Middle Ages. *Past* evokes the pageantry of a medieval tournament before the walls of a great castle; but *Present* shows the same castle as a glamorous ruin in the poetry of a fading light. Amherst also owns oil sketches for both pictures.

For study of the work of George Bellows (1882–1925) Amherst can offer his papers (in the college library), a large selection of his drawings and prints, and a bewitching portrait of his daughter, *Anne in Black Velvet*,[12] painted in 1917. The subject was a favorite one for him; a portrait of her four years later, in a purple wrap, is at Andover.

10

11

Bellows waxed melodramatic in prizefights and street scenes, but in the portraits of his family he eschewed all such protestations. If his observation is less searching than that of a Copley or an Eakins, it is in the same honest vein. The color is wonderfully fresh, especially here in its contrast with a black that glistens like Velázquez's. Further discussion of Bellows is included in the sections on Rockland (ME 32), Duxbury (MA 150), and Springfield (MA 221).

Nineteenth-century sculpture at Amherst includes bronzes by Barye (a fine *Jaguar*), Saint-Gaudens (small replica of the Springfield *Puritan* and the tondo *Portrait of R. L. Stevenson*); genre plaster groups by John Rogers; and Rodin's early bronze head, *Man with a Broken Nose*. Post-1900 sculpture is on the conservative side, with bronzes by Kolbe and Despiau lingering in the memory. But a truly modern note is struck by *Stringed Figure*,[13] in gold-patinated bronze by Henry Moore (born 1898). It is in his most abstract period, restricted to the years 1937–39. Reminiscing a quarter-century later about his "string sculptures," Moore recalled a visit to the Science Museum in London's South Kensington, where he was enthralled by mathematical models with strings attached "to show what the form between would be." So he decided to make some—as it turned out, many. "They were fun," he discovered, "but too much in the nature of experiments to be really satisfactory. That's a different thing from expressing some deep human experience one might have had. When the war came I gave up this type of thing. Others, like Gabo and Barbara Hepworth, have gone on doing it. It becomes a matter of ingenuity rather than a fundamental human experience" (Philip James, editor, *Henry Moore on Sculpture*; London: Macdonald, 1966).

Among Moore's works of this kind, the Amherst piece is exceptional in retaining much of the master's profundity. Reclining in its boat-shaped container, the "figure" is partially defined by the tautly stretched strings, which indeed help to show "what the form between would be." But the main purpose of their startling introduction into sculpture is to create tension and energize the heavily static forms beneath. Roughened surfaces suggest weathering, as if this object had descended from a timeless past. While it lacks the grand conception of Yale's *Draped Seated*

13

12

Woman of 1959 (CT 69), even at its modest size it obliquely suggests that conception.

Not everyone will agree with Moore that Gabo and Barbara Hepworth (born 1903) were merely ingenious in their string sculptures. One of Hepworth's studies for such a piece, executed in oil and pencil on a gesso board, can be seen at Amherst. Cleanly designed and light as air, it has a poetry of its own.

University Gallery,
University of Massachusetts

Location: Route 116, north of the town
Hours: Tues.-Fri. 11-4:30, Sat.-Sun. 1:30-4:30; closed Mon., holidays, and during academic recesses
Admission: Free. Ⓗ

The gallery forms part of the impressive Fine Arts Center of the performing arts. Active in temporary exhibitions of very recent American arts, the gallery has developed an extensive permanent collection in this field of works of art on paper: drawings, prints, and photographs. It also owns one of Joseph Cornell's magical boxes.

Addison Gallery of American Art, Phillips Academy

Location: On Route 28
Hours: Tues.-Sat. 10-5, Sun. 2:30-5; closed Mon. and holidays
Admission: Free. Ⓗ by arrangement

Housed in a dignified building of 1931 with a highly imaginative new wing by Benjamin Thompson, a collection that includes the very finest paintings of Homer, Eakins, Inness, and Hopper makes the Addison Gallery one of the leading museums of American art in New England. The whole development of American painting from the eighteenth century to the present, and to a lesser degree that of sculpture and the decorative arts, can be studied here in superb examples. The collections of drawings (including many cartoons), prints, and photographs are extensive, as are those of silver, pewter, glass, and furniture. A series of ship models illustrates American maritime history in the era of sail.

Andover maintains an active program of temporary exhibitions, including student work, and it has an enviable reputation for developing shows of an educational nature. During the 1970s the gallery was the center of a foundation-supported program of studies in art as therapy.

Because of our extensive coverage of Colonial and Early Republican art in other museums, selections here are limited to the nineteenth and twentieth centuries; but the visitor will not be disappointed in the representation of the distinguished tradition that gave later American art its momentum and confidence.

I am happy to seize the advantage whenever it presents itself to bring home the point that art is not restricted to painting, nor to what is glibly called fine arts. Some "fine" art is very bad indeed; and humble items often surpass it in quality. Avoiding invidious comparisons, I invite the visitor to inspect a large *Firehouse Sign* from Portsmouth, N.H.[14] The designer is unknown, as is the carver, who may have been the same person. I present this object as good sculpture, in somewhat the same spirit as one might call a Greek vase sculpture on the basis of its shape. This is not to imply that the Kearsarge sign is on the same artistic level, but only that its maker was highly skilled. We are told that 1870, when General Grant was President (and when "3 Kearsarge 3" was organized), was a bad time for the arts in America. How much later than 1870 this sign was made is not known, but it was certainly well before 1900.

Figured sculpture at Andover includes one of the best-known works of Elie Nadelman (1882–1946), *Seated Woman*,[15] in cherry wood (the

14

chair made of iron) about 3 feet high, dating from 1917. It provided the cover illustration of the catalogue for a memorial retrospective offered in 1948 by the Museum of Modern Art, and also shown in Boston and Baltimore. (If a pair of *Circus Women* is still better known today, that is for extracurricular reasons: the architect Philip Johnson had the original group, of papier-mâché 5 feet high, greatly enlarged to form presences in the foyer of his New York State Theater, Lincoln Center.)

Born in Warsaw, Nadelman made his reputation in Paris, and after his triumphant debut in 1917 at a New York gallery became a leading figure in the New York art world. Lincoln Kirstein, in his essay for the Museum of Modern Art's catalogue, points out that while Nadelman absorbed much of European modernism, from the art of Seurat onward, in America "he provided precedents" for George Bellows, Guy Pène du Bois, Gaston Lachaise, and the caricaturist John Held, Jr., of *Vanity Fair*.

We turn now to the gallery's superb array of nineteenth-century American painting. A fair proportion of the leading figures can be studied to advantage here, and I regret to pass over fine examples of the work of such artists as Thomas Doughty, Fitz Hugh Lane, John Quidor —whose eccentric creations make the pages of Washington Irving come visually alive—Eastman Johnson, Whistler, and William Harnett (see MA 220). Masterpieces by George Inness, Thomas Eakins, and Winslow Homer must now claim our attention.

The White Monk[16] (also called *The Pines and the Olives*), an oil over 3 by 5 feet, is signed and dated 1873 by George Inness (1825–94). Comparison with *The Elm* (ME 23) of a decade earlier will quickly show his rapid advance from Hudson River School derivatives to something with great originality. Youthful trips to Europe before and after 1850 had laid the foundations for what was to happen, but it was an extended stay in Italy from 1871 to 1875, particularly in the environs of Rome, that profoundly altered his vision. The scene of *The White Monk* was inspired by the view from the Villa Barberini at Albano. Beyond the umbrella-frieze of the pines, a brilliant red orange streaks the horizon against turquoise greens higher up. Feathery olive trees

15

16

cluster mysteriously in the foreground—and then we notice the brooding figure of the white-robed monk, expressively off center and facing the edge of the composition. We have the feeling, as nearly a century later in the horizontal canvases of Jackson Pollock, that the picture extends indefinitely past the frame, both at left and at right. It is this sideways expansion (not to mention the color) that makes Inness's effect so different from the "classical" landscapes of Claude Lorrain, by which he was clearly affected.

Outside Philadelphia, where he lived and worked, and—secondarily —New York, the places to visit for the best view of the art of Thomas Eakins (1844–1916) are Andover and the Yale University Art Gallery. It is difficult to choose, at Andover, among three masterpieces: *Elizabeth at the Piano*[17] (1875), the *Portrait of Professor Henry A. Rowland* (1891), and *Salutat* (1898). In my earlier version of this book I opted for the great portrait, with its elaborate scientific notations ornamenting the frame. In the intervening years my enthusiasm for Eakins's work of the 1870s has continually risen (but not at the expense of the later works), so this time I have selected *Elizabeth*, seated in black Spanish gloom relieved by touches of red, with shafts of light accenting her face, her right hand, and the sheet of music on the piano.

Eakins's all-important four-year exposure to European art and study in Paris under Gérôme (examples of whose work are in the Clark Art Institute, Williamstown, Mass.) ended in the winter of 1869/70 in Spain. In the Prado at Madrid, Velázquez and Ribera were the masters he most loved—not the great Venetians and emphatically not Rubens. Seville, where Eakins decided to stay, was the home of Ribera until that seventeenth-century painter of shadowy mysteries moved on to Spanish-dominated Naples. The impact of the art of Velázquez and Ribera is particularly strong in *Elizabeth at the Piano*. Whether Eakins's near obsession with musical subjects was stimulated by the musical interests of Degas and other Impressionists (he was their slightly younger contemporary) is unclear, and at any rate unlikely. The fact remains that throughout his career Eakins painted pianists (see MA 176), violinists, cellists, guitarists, singers, and at least one music critic (*John Neil Fort*, a portrait in the Williams College Museum of Art). As we have

17

suggested in an example at Yale (CT 76), even his scullers seem to pause between strokes as if enthralled by distant musical strains.

Among Andover's works by Winslow Homer (1836–1910), a difficult choice is made easy because *West Wind*,[18] an oil 30 by 44 inches signed and dated 1891, stands near the top of any list of his later masterpieces. In a major Homer retrospective of 1973 at the Whitney Museum of American Art (also shown at Los Angeles and Chicago), it was accompanied by two other oils from Andover, *Eight Bells* (1886) and *Kissing the Moon* (1904). Sometimes Homer's lonely women against a storm-tossed sea prey too much on our sympathy (will her man come back safely?); but not in *West Wind*. Here the woman's shape, like a Whistler butterfly monogram, is intrinsically expressive. She leans hard against a gale that blows everything along an upward left diagonal. In *Winslow Homer at Prout's Neck* (Boston: Little, Brown, 1966), Philip C. Beam points out that the cliffs are actually sixty feet high and that the near waves can be seen only in a great storm. He also recounts an exchange between Homer and his good friend John La Farge (whose Venetian-oriented art we have discussed at Bowdoin College, ME 16). La Farge criticized Homer for using too much brown, whereupon Homer bet him a hundred dollars that he could paint a picture in browns only and that it would be accepted and admired. Homer won the bet. This marvelous composition seems to have inspired the Clark Institute's *Sleigh Ride* (MA 259), painted about two years later—but in blues that must have pleased his friend.

Near the turn of the century, Maurice Prendergast (1859–1924) painted a magical little watercolor, *Float at Low Tide—Revere Beach*[19] (c. 1896). It sparkled brightly at an exhibition of the artist's water-colors in New England collections (see CT 99). This early work came soon after Prendergast's return to Boston from two years of study in France. The theme, introduced by Boudin (see CT 21), and the design, which echoes the flat patterns of Japanese prints, are reminders of that experience; but the magic is Prendergast's own.

George Bellows and Edward Hopper, both of them born in 1882 and trained by Robert Henri, took their start in the urban world of the so-called Ashcan School—well represented here by John Sloan's

19

18

Sunday Morning—Women Washing Their Hair (painted in 1912 and included in the Armory Show of 1913). Bellows's career was cut short by his death in 1925. The excitement of city life remained with him to the end, but he also found an escape from it in his Maine landscapes and marines (see MA 150) and in his serene family portraits. Andover has a very fine one of his daughter, *Anne in a Purple Wrap*, where she appears growing up, four years later than the example we have discussed at Amherst (MA 12).

Hopper lived—and worked unremittingly—until 1967. His early painting, much of it bequeathed by his widow to the Whitney Museum of American Art, has Henri's *brio*, but gradually a pervasive calm, strongly tinged with loneliness, settled on his spirit. It is often pointed out that as modern "isms" came and went, Hopper plodded his own solitary path. Nevertheless, we see some similarity with the vacant streets and squares of Giorgio di Chirico, painted around 1915, which had their spell on him. By 1928, when he executed *Manhattan Bridge Loop*,[20] Hopper was in full stride. At the impressive size of 3 by 5 feet, it remains one of his finest works, even in the competition of such later ones as *Morning in a City* (MA 278). The emptiness of an early Sunday forenoon is accentuated by the single figure at the far left—a device we have just seen in Inness's *White Monk*. As in that picture, too, the scene appears to stretch beyond its frame at the two sides—in Hopper's composition aided by a wide belt of deep shadow across the whole front, tilted enough to the left to lead us to that little Everyman. The skyline, with its harsh metallic rhythms, is a concentrate of the American metropolis. Note Hopper's discoveries in shape repetition: the iron structures of different sizes and their relationship to the corniced buildings. The more we study this picture the more its selectiveness and design emerge. Its realism is only its skin.

In collecting contemporary American art Andover has been imaginative and daring. Visitors interested in this field should observe the dates of acquisition of many works by artists now on the verge of becoming Old Masters. One of these, Jackson Pollock's *Phosphorescence*, signed and dated 1947, came three years later by gift from the pioneering Mrs. Peggy Guggenheim. Purchases of other artists, in a list too long to detail, include Alexander Calder, Hans Hofmann, Franz Kline, Loren MacIver, George Rickey, Ben Shahn, Bradley Walker Tomlin, and Andrew Wyeth. A museum that can show the early stage of careers like these is automatically important.

20

A superb example of the work of Marsden Hartley (1877–1943) is in a different category. *Summer, Sea, Window, Red Curtain*[21] was painted in the year before he died (but purchased in 1944). We have seen Hartley's extraordinary change from a small 1909 oil at Bates College (ME 18) to the Berlin-inspired *Military* of 1913 at Hartford (CT 30); but without some study of the steps leading to his final transformation we should be totally unprepared for Andover's rich, deep-toned poem about a Maine summer. The composition echoes that of Matisse's window views, but not the scumbled surfaces, the dark reds of the foreground, or the high-keyed blues in the distance. If Matisse sacrificed everything else for a final triumphant statement in pure color and silhouetted shape, Hartley fell in love with the action of stroking oil paint on canvas.

Phosphorescence,[22] by Jackson Pollock (1912–56), signed and dated 1947 at the lower left center, is only five years earlier than the frenetic example we have discussed at Hartford (CT 34). In a career, however, that developed so rapidly, and one cut short in the artist's mid-forties (like George Bellows's), five years can make a great difference. While it is easy to make such a statement from hindsight, in the meteoric rush of some brief lives of genius (shall we adduce those of Watteau and of Mozart?) we sense a race against time. However that may be, *Phosphorescence* appeared when Pollock was just beginning to gain recognition beyond a small fringe of avant-garde, but astute, critics— and of a group of like-minded artists, all of whom were surprised to learn later that they were classed as Action Painters, Abstract Expressionists, or even New York School. Pollock's full-blown statement —in his painting, that is, for he never went in for verbal explanations— came around 1950, in such immense canvases as *Autumn Rhythm* (Metropolitan Museum of Art). The Andover example has a relatively modest size of 44 by 28 inches, it is executed in oil and aluminum paint (the silvery parts), and it is vertically conceived. While the long silvery lines were drawn with a stick or the wrong end of a paintbrush, this is not yet one of Pollock's "drip" paintings. James Thrall Soby, one

21

22

of the too few critics of modern art who was both sensitive and verbally articulate, liked to recall that Pollock, who enjoyed escaping the New York scene in solitude at the farthest end of Long Island, used to lie in tall grasses to watch the migration patterns of birds. That is surely not the subject of *Phosphorescence*, but it may help to demonstrate that Pollock's abstraction is not without reference to the phenomena of nature.

In a selection of works ranging from prehistory to the present, we must use caution in including artists whose reputation is not already established. The penalty of not doing so is, unfortunately, the omission of some major figure. Nevertheless, in view of the success of the Addison Gallery in guessing "right" about new artists, I reproduce a big oil,[23] 95 inches square, by Deborah Remington (born 1930), whose work is otherwise unknown to me. It was purchased in the year of its execution, 1971. Its title, *Axios*, is not particularly helpful beyond suggesting the symmetry of ancient Greek art. (Quartet opus 59 no. 3, by Beethoven, is not very helpful either.) Titles are necessary for reference, but one of the phenomena of modern art is their appearance after, or during, the completion of a work, not beforehand.

We should not ask, therefore, what *Axios* represents, but what it *is*. It is at least a very handsome ornament, but unfortunately praise on that score is too often regarded as a kiss of death. So what *else* is it? An echo of Euclidean perfection in the timeless beauty of an equilateral triangle? A search for order in a disjointed world? As always, time will tell—I hope, with some confidence—that Andover chose well.

23

A Boston Miscellany

New England's greatest city has two museums of great art and two libraries where art can be found. Accordingly, we devote special sections to the Boston Athenaeum and the Boston Public Library, as well as to the Isabella Stewart Gardner Museum and to that Grand Central Station of art in New England, the Museum of Fine Arts.

Art of quality in the home of the Red Sox is of course not limited to these four institutions. In the following brief account we survey others, open to the public, which the reader should not miss. We are not concerned here with architectural history, that being the province of another volume in the Godine series of New England handbooks. But the contents, or adornment, of such buildings should not be neglected because they fall, as it were, in a no-man's-land between jurisdictions. We cannot include them all, but the reader would be well advised to start at the Boston Park Visitor Center, 15 State Street, opposite the Old State House. It provides information, brochures, and data on tours of the city. Another helpful center is the Society for the Preservation of New England Antiquities, with headquarters in Bulfinch's celebrated First Harrison Gray Otis House at 141 Cambridge Street. The society publishes an illustrated listing of the many historic houses it owns and operates in New England, the great majority of them being in the Boston area.

The Old State House (1712), a gem of Colonial Georgian architecture, now contains the Museum of Boston History, maintained by the Bostonian Society (admission charged). Many of the portraits are of more than historical interest, and the harbor views include notable examples by Fitz Hugh Lane (MA 155) and John White Allen Scott (1815–1907). The commercial signs often display typographical talent, and the maritime exhibits (including scrimshaw) make a small complement to major collections discussed elsewhere in this book. Scrimshaw, by the way, seems to have derived from the French word, *s'escrimer*, to work hard for small results.

Faneuil Hall, close by, has atop its cupola a gilt weather vane in the form of a grasshopper. Such weather vanes (see NH 16) are usually a nineteenth-century phenomenon in America, but this one dates from 1742, when the original building (before its 1806 enlargement by Bulfinch) was completed. The Colonial builders dedicated Faneuil Hall to Liberty and Loyalty—the latter meaning to the British king. In that spirit the weather vane had symbolic ties with the Old Country: "Deacon" Shem Browne copied it from one atop London's Royal Exchange, which in turn reproduced the crest of Sir Thomas Gresham, founder of the Exchange in 1558. The Grasshopper survived Faneuil Hall's tumultuous history—until 1974, when it was stolen, but soon recovered and reinstalled, freshly gilt. If you want to see its considerable beauty, a visit to the Heritage Plantation at Sandwich is suggested: here is displayed, at eye level, a small variant of about 1882, with a lovely green patina, but no golden skin.

The reopening of Quincy Market, beyond Faneuil Hall, as a combined commercial and cultural center has been hailed as one of the great innovations of urban renewal. The joys of this place will become immediately apparent, but it would be easy to overlook the fact that on the fifth floor of the South Market Building the Museum of Fine Arts has opened a downtown extension (open free, Tues.-Sun. 11-6). This venture has met an extraordinarily enthusiastic response; as a result, you might find here, in the changing exhibitions from the museum's permanent collections, something you missed at Huntington Avenue.

At the New State House (new in the sense that Bulfinch's masterpiece of 1789 plan and 1795–98 execution retired the old Georgian one for such use), there are portraits and sculptural memorials in abundance, not infrequently of artistic interest. More certain in that respect, however, is Saint-Gaudens's Shaw Memorial, at the foot of the entrance stairs, across Beacon Street. We discuss the work of this great sculptor in the section on Cornish, New Hampshire.

Across Copley Square from the Boston Public Library is H. H. Richardson's Trinity Church, with more sculpture by Saint-Gaudens, and painting by John La Farge. Farther out Boylston Street is the Institute of Contemporary Art, with its active program of changing exhibitions.

For adults, preferably accompanied by one child or more, there is joy to behold at the old Congress Street Wharf, superbly reconditioned to house the Children's Museum and the Museum of Transportation (admission charged). Who is to say that art is not present in the Elegant Car Gallery, or in the actual performance of children, their imaginations so skillfully enlisted? On the Congress Street bridge, a few yards away, is the Boston Tea Party Ship and Museum, accurately billed as An Adventure in History. That might persuade you to trek northerly to Charlestown to visit the U.S. Frigate *Constitution*, "Old Ironsides" herself.

The Boston Athenaeum

Location: 10½ Beacon Street
Hours: October through May, Mon.-Fri. 9-5:30, Sat. 9-4; closed holidays
Admission: Free

Although this august institution, incorporated in 1807, is owned and maintained by some 1,050 shareholders, visitors in small numbers are welcome to the limit of the available guide service. The address suggests compactness and great antiquity, but the building, designed by Edward C. Cabot in 1846 in Palladian style, is large. Two floors were added in 1913. Cabot was the grandson of Thomas Handasyd Perkins, whom we shall meet shortly, a major donor with his brother James in the era before the Athenaeum moved to its present quarters.

As everyone knows, the Museum of Fine Arts had its origin in the art collections of the Athenaeum, and certain paintings, including Stuart's original oil sketches of George and Martha Washington, passed to the museum on an indefinite loan basis. Protracted discussion of the "gentleman's agreement" by which this was accomplished was resolved in 1980. At three-year intervals these patriotic icons will move between the Museum of Fine Arts and the National Portrait Gallery in Washington.

Much of the art collection, however, remains; and to see it, a tour of these lovely surroundings is, happily, necessary. A beautifully designed illustrated booklet, *Change and Continuity*, published by the Athenaeum in 1976, is warmly recommended. A recent innovation is a series of changing exhibitions of contemporary Boston-area artists in the second-floor gallery.

The very large collection of prints emphasizes eighteenth- and nineteenth-century examples depicting Boston and New England scenes and daily life. These, together with daguerreotypes and photographs, run into the thousands.

I regret to pass over a multitude of white busts of important personages that pop up in alcoves, hover on balustrades, rest on tables, or glower from pedestals. They are somewhat relieved by a squadron of equally spotless Venuses, Medicean and otherwise. Truth to say, the paintings are more distinguished.

Nevertheless, among the busts is a Houdon plaster of George Washington, which came from Monticello. There are other plasters and many versions in marble, but this one is thought to be the "original." It may well be, but that brings up a problem too complicated to go into here. A plaster model of Thomas Ball's equestrian *George Washington* (1858–64) in the Boston Public Gardens presents no such difficulty.

I do not mean to ignore the historical interest of all those busts. An authoritative article on them, by the late director of the Athenaeum, Walter Muir Whitehill, appeared in the June 1973 issue of *Antiques* magazine.

Thomas Sully (1783–1872) suffers from a plethora of canvases of soulful ladies in white playing the harp. That he was a portraitist of great distinction may be seen in a series painted between 1815 and 1830 for, and preserved at, the U.S. Military Academy, West Point. The Athenaeum's *Portrait of Colonel Thomas Handasyd Perkins*,[24] 44 by 58 inches, full-length, and painted 1831/2, is their equal. With his brother James, Thomas established trade centers linking Boston and London with Canton—hence the Oriental ewer in the lower right corner. This portrait made a powerful impression at a major exhibition of the China Trade, held in 1979 at the De Cordova Museum in Lincoln. The colonel was an important patron of many fine artists, including not only Sully but also Washington Allston and Fitz Hugh Lane. Above his long brown coat and gleaming white collar, his commanding face is convincing testimony of his abilities. The pose is comfortably relaxed, and allows full play of a long curve—suggesting Hogarth's "line of beauty"—that extends from his left foot to the extended left arm. A top hat completes the colonel's elegant attire. The Athenaeum's commission for this portrait was to have gone to Gilbert Stuart, but his death in 1828 gave Sully the opportunity to create what many consider his masterpiece. Like Stuart, Sully studied in London, and his art has a European flair often compared with the stylishness of Sir Thomas Lawrence (see CT 56). He was, in fact, English-born, but brought up in the United States.

Chester Harding (1792–1866), whose memorable portrait of Amos Lawrence can be seen at the National Gallery, Washington, and also at the Williams College Museum of Art, is again in top form in the Athenaeum's *Portrait of Hannah Adams*,[25] painted about 1827 in her early seventies. Miss Adams had many distinctions. She was the first American professional woman writer, the first woman to use the Athenaeum, the first person to be buried in Mt. Auburn Cemetery, and the author of *Alphabetical Compendium of the Various Sects* (1784) and of *A Summary History of New England* (1799). A much less spontaneous portrait by Harding, a full-length of Daniel Webster, hangs in the

24

Athenaeum's entrance vestibule near his comparable image of John Marshall.

Among four Gilbert Stuart portraits in the collection, that of William Smith Shaw is perhaps the most accomplished.

European painting is represented, and certainly dominated, by an *Interior of St. Peter's*,[26] over 5 by 7 feet, painted in 1756/7 by Giovanni Paolo Panini (1691–1764). A companion piece, representing a *Roman Picture Gallery*, was sold in 1975 to the Museum of Fine Arts, where there is room for it. It is safe to say that no photograph can catch the spaciousness and at the same time the multifarious details of the vast interior of St. Peter's; and Panini has fortunately peopled it to give what is so easily missed in the actual building: its scale. If the occasion seems more festive than religious, that is altogether in the spirit of the eighteenth century. A less strenuous Panini is discussed in the section on Springfield (MA 214).

25

26

Boston Public Library

Location: Copley Square at Dartmouth Street

Hours: Mon. 1-9, Tues.-Thurs. 9-9, Fri. 9-5; closed holidays (the Print Dept. and the Rare Books and Mss. Dept. close at 5 P.M. Mon-Fri. and are also closed on Sat. and Sun.)

Admission: Free

If this were a book on architecture, I should launch into superlatives over the magnificent design of the original building by Charles Follen McKim (of McKim, Mead & White), erected 1888-92, and over the large addition at the rear, completed in 1972 from designs by Philip Johnson. The latter has become the functioning Public Library, allowing the McKim building to serve as a research library—and, to no inconsiderable degree, a public art museum.

The great facade on Copley Square opposite Trinity Church once had as a near neighbor the Victorian Gothic Museum of Fine Arts (1870), replaced by the Copley-Plaza Hotel after the museum moved in 1909 to its present building on Huntington Avenue. The entrance is embellished by the work of three sculptors of reputation: the three heraldic seals above are by Augustus Saint-Gaudens, the bronze doors by Daniel Chester French, and the large seated bronze figures of Art and Science by Bela L. Pratt. The commission for the figures was originally assigned to Saint-Gaudens, but at his death in 1907 the work had not progressed beyond preliminary models. He did, however, complete one of the four bronze memorials (a medallion portrait of benefactor Robert C. Billings) in the spacious, Renaissance-inspired Court.

As for the Main Staircase, I shall not compete with Henry James's paean: "its amplitude of wing and its splendour of tawny marble, a high and luxurious beauty." Here, framed in yellow Siena marble, specially quarried for the purpose, are murals by the celebrated Pierre Puvis de Chavannes (1824-98). These peaceful, reticent canvases, painted in film of dirt. One must look carefully, and lean on one's knowledge of the setting or its lighting, are thoroughly appropriate but they do not make the impact that is their due. Also they have acquired with time a film of dirt. One must look carefully, and lean on one's knowledge of the master's great murals in Paris, Lyons, or Amiens, to find in them what the French art historian and critic Henri Focillon rightly saw: "le bleu de la mer, l'azur du ciel—le ciel et la mer des dieux." We have chosen one of the smaller panels, *Physics*,[27] for its greater visibility. Here, as in the others, a lovely play of white drapery about these reborn divinities heightens the purity and serenity of the blues of sky and sea. While the elaborate allegories may be hard for the tough modern mind to digest, the beauty and sureness of the composition carries them. A description of the whole project, by the artist himself, is available at the library (as also for the Abbey and Sargent murals we are soon to discuss). "I have sought," he wrote, "to represent under a symbolic form and in a single view the intellectual treasures collected in this beautiful building." Of *Physics* he wrote, "By the wondrous agency of Electricity, Speech flashes through Space and swift as lightning bears tidings of good and evil."

A very different series of murals, by Edwin Austin Abbey (1852–1911), adorns the Delivery Room (serving the Main Reading Room), to the right of the top of the Main Staircase. An 8-foot frieze representing the *Quest of the Holy Grail* tops a Venetian-style *salone* 64 feet long, wainscoted and timber-ceilinged, where all is deep brown, dark red, and gold. Unlike Puvis de Chavannes, Abbey had control of the décor of the whole room; and his late Victorian version of the Arthurian cycle suits to perfection its equally Victorian mixture of the Middle Ages and the Venetian High Renaissance. Abbey was one of the outstanding illustrators of his day, and from his earliest beginnings in Philadelphia he became obsessed with the romance of English medieval legends. The murals were installed in 1895, and Henry James wrote a fine account of them (available on request). We start with the child Galahad, descended by his mother from Joseph of Arimathea; continue with his going forth with the blessing of Sir Lancelot and Sir Bors; attend his installation in the Seat (or Siege) Perilous at the Arthurian Round Table; attend the benediction by King Arthur of the Knights of the Holy Grail; and follow the story through eleven more scenes to its culmination in the appearance of Joseph of Arimathea with the Holy Grail. We illustrate the third scene, one of the largest, *The Round Table and the Siege Perilous*.[28] Sir Galahad, as always in red, is led in by a figure swathed in white (Joseph of Arimathea), as the great hall with its vast company is suddenly suffused with light. In the robed chair, no man, not even King Arthur, has "sat with safety"; "it awaits only a blameless occupant."

It seems gratuitous to point out the superiority of Puvis de Chavannes as a composer-designer, but Abbey portrays the great theme in all its glamour, and his colors—the deep reds dominating the creamy whites and yellows—have a strong appeal. Apart from such mural achievements, Abbey is best studied at the Yale University Art Gallery, with its large collection of his drawings (some for the Boston murals), sketches, and oils, including a large one devoted to another of Abbey's major concerns, the works of William Shakespeare. The collection came to Yale in 1937.

27

28

A third series of murals, by John Singer Sargent (1856–1925), is reached by narrow stairs from the top landing of the Main Staircase. Here again, the artist had full control of the whole area, but for Sargent it was a long corridor-hall. He began work in his London studio in 1893 and the last canvas was installed in 1919. There are many lunettes, two wall panels over the staircase, and a frieze at either end below elaborate retables. The theme is *Judaism and Christianity*. We reproduce a section of the north frieze, devoted to the Hebraic Prophets, showing *Zephaniah, Joel, the Seated Obadiah, and the White-robed Hosea*.[29] (A full description of the project is available on request.) The lighting here is murky, and the first impression is of glinting gold, in an almost Byzantine splendor. The Prophets, in their splendid contrasts of black and white, are the most memorable figures in this sometimes overelaborate ensemble. A quarter-century ago, E. P. Richardson (*Painting in America*; New York: Crowell, 1956), compared Sargent's achievement favorably with Puvis de Chavannes's and Abbey's: "But for an interior space, conceived as a decorative unity and given a powerful, dramatic atmosphere by means of wall paintings, I find to my surprise that Sargent's much criticized and highly unpopular room must be given honors that our period may be reluctant to grant." Subsequent opinion has generally supported this estimate.

An attractive handbook, published in 1977, gives an excellent summary of the library and its artistic contents. In addition to works already discussed, there are many oil portraits, busts, and other marble sculptures. The Albert H. Wiggins collection of nineteenth- and twentieth-century prints is both vast and important, and the same is true for the photograph collection, of which a mimeographed summary was issued in 1977. Another survey lists the extensive holdings of Boston architectural drawings and photographs. Last, but not least, are the rare books and manuscripts preserved with loving care in a special section of this great treasure house.

29

Isabella Stewart Gardner Museum

Location: 280 The Fenway

Telephone: (617) 734-1359

Hours: September through June: Tues. 1-9:30 P.M., Wed.-Sun. 1-5:30; July and August: Tues.-Sun. 1-5:30. Free concerts September through June, Tues. at 8, Thurs. and Sun. at 4 (phone for information)

Admission: Charged. Ⓗ

The celebrated collection of Isabella Stewart Gardner (1840–1924), incorporated as a museum in 1900, was opened to the public in the year following her death. Housed in her Fenway Court residence, a palace in the Venetian style completed in 1903, it comprises the results of a lifetime of acquiring works of art. Among many expert advisers, Bernard Berenson was most active in Mrs. Gardner's behalf. An endowment provides for flowers in the Great Court, and for regularly scheduled concerts. A brief guide to the collection was published in 1976, and in 1974 the second edition of the catalogue of paintings. Catalogues of Oriental and Islamic art, drawings, sculpture, textiles, and books and manuscripts are also available. The list of publications gives some indication of the range of artistic treasures here to be seen.

While an itinerary from one floor to the next would be convenient to the visitor, a roughly chronological sequence will make much more sense to the reader—who, as visitor, can readily find the objects in the following discussion, as they come into view, by quick reference to the illustrations.

Our first two examples will be found among the many sculptures that adorn the court. The headless *Draped Female Figure*,[30] known as the *Peplophoros* (peplos wearer), is a Graeco-Roman copy of a superb Greek work of about 455–450 B.C. Of Greek marble, probably from the islands, it stands about 5 feet in height. The missing head and neck were carved separately and adjusted to the cavity at the top of the torso.

30

Whether seen from front or back, the figure is almost columnar, with that restrained grace that marks such figures of the same mid-fifth-century period as those of the Temple of Zeus at Olympia, or the famous bronze *Charioteer* of Delphi. The weight shifts as the right knee bends, just enough to define the form of the body beneath these virtual Doric flutings. At once static and energized, this lady, perhaps Persephone, achieves the timelessness of Euclidean geometry; indeed, the purity of geometric form is everywhere apparent, not least in the rectangular shape described by the chiton as it falls from the breasts. What nobility!

Our second selection, in the opposite corner of the court, represents *Odysseus Creeping Forward during the Theft of the Palladium*.[31] Like the *Peplophoros*, it is Graeco-Roman (c. 50 B.C.), but this time in an archaizing style in the manner of Greek art of c. 490 B.C. Neo-Archaic sculpture could achieve grace and refinement (as in the lovely relief discussed at Yale, CT 63), but not here. This figure fitted into the left-hand angle of a pedimental composition, and as such was visible only from the front. The drapery, in almost comical contrast with Odysseus's brutish anatomy, is pure rhythm, swinging the figure along toward its appointed mission. The contoured pose adapts well to the claims of the frontal plane of the pediment, and the design is remarkable for its repeated and interlocked triangles.

A superb *Stained Glass Window*,[32] French Gothic of the thirteenth century, may have come from Soissons. The design and draftsmanship are similar to those of the windows at Chartres, and one would like to believe, as seems possible, that Henry Adams advised its purchase. Like many such windows, its pieces have largely been renewed through the centuries, for the erosive effect of wind and rain is very great. In its original state the window seems to have depicted the martyrdom of Saints Nicaise and Eutropie. There were probably fewer colors and an even greater dominance of reds and blues. The window is best seen in the afternoon light.

A little gold-ground panel, *The Presentation of the Christ-Child in the Temple*[33] by Giotto (1267–1337), will be found on a stand not far from Sargent's strange portrait of Mrs. Gardner. The attribution to the

31

32

founder of Florentine art and herald of the Renaissance is based on style and quality: no document proves that Giotto painted it, and many consider it the work of an able follower. The arrangement is close to one of Giotto's famous frescoes in the Arena Chapel at Padua, and, as in other works by Giotto in egg tempera on panel, the effect strongly suggests the rugged simplicity of his murals. Note the forceful concentration on the Child by slow curves of drapery upward from the left, and the closing of the composition at the right by the slow spiral movement about the solemn apple-green figure of the prophetess. Contrast Giotto's sparing use of ornament with that of the Sienese painter Lippo Memmi in a little *Madonna* of similar date, nearby.

Few intercity rivalries were more intense than that between Florence and Siena, whether on the field of battle or in the production of religious art. The latter is easily seen in a comparison between Giotto—whose *St. Francis Receiving the Stigmata* at the Fogg Art Museum (MA 114) again more likely by a close follower, gives a stronger impression of his power —and the two great founders of Sienese painting, Duccio and Simone Martini. If Giotto's scenes are enacted by simple peasants or villagers of a stamp not unlike Cézanne's *Card Players*, Duccio's and especially Simone's take us to the world of Byzantine icons and the courtly elegance of Gothic Paris. Simone Martini (1285–1344) is unquestionably the author of the five-panel altarpiece representing the *Madonna with Saints Paul, Lucy, Catherine, and John the Baptist*,[34] although his co-worker Lippo Memmi may have assisted. Comparison with the seven-part altarpiece in Williamstown, by a close follower of Duccio (MA 248), will clarify the grace of Simone's aristocratic style; both polyptychs date from the 1320s. At the same time as these airless gold and bronze-toned images were fashioned in Siena, Giotto in Florence was exploring the space and substance of the world we live in.

33

34

A similar tale of two cities (only fifty miles apart) may be carried into the fifteenth century if we confront the exquisite little tempera panel *The Child Jesus Disputing in the Temple*[35] by Giovanni di Paolo (1402?–82) with a fresco fragment representing *Hercules*[36] by Piero della Francesca (c. 1410–92). Though Piero's major work was done at Arezzo and Urbino, he was trained in Florence and his artistic bent was decidedly Florentine. The *Hercules* displays the grave mien and the anatomical knowledge of the Renaissance, together with its disciplined energy. Giovanni di Paolo, on the contrary, deliberately continued to work in the style of Simone and Duccio. If the setting avows the new (Renaissance) architecture, it is only in superficial details. But there is a disturbing new emotionalism, as of a proto–van Gogh. One feels the strain involved in turning the back on one's own time, while yet achieving an original statement.

It is not certain that Paolo Uccello (1397–1475) painted the incisive profile *Portrait of a Young Lady*,[37] for such representations were common in mid-fifteenth-century Florence. Most critics today doubt such an exalted attribution. Like Uccello's work, however, is the sure sense of pattern (possibly reflecting his early training in mosaic and stained glass), as well as the force of the drawing and the observation unaffected by any desire to flatter. It is curious that Uccello, one of the leading exponents of Renaissance perspective and massive form, increasingly

35

36

37

reverted in the latter half of his career to the flat spaces and the heraldic profiles (as here) of Gothic tapestries. This enchanting silhouette may be described as a strict side view of a Renaissance portrait bust, steam-rolled into a calligraphic arabesque. The lady's ponytail is fashionable once again.

Among many fine examples of Florentine Renaissance painting, the *Madonna with the Eucharist*[38] by Sandro Botticelli (1444–1510) is the outstanding masterpiece. It once belonged to the Chigi family of Rome, and it was acquired for Mrs. Gardner by Bernard Berenson. An early work with echoes of Botticelli's master, Fra Filippo Lippi, it already conveys the haunting, wistful nostalgia of which that worldly monk had no conception. Seldom was Botticelli's hand surer in the swinging quality of the line, the crisp detail, and the gently pervasive light. The wheat and grapes symbolize, of course, the Bread and the Wine. This meaning helps explain the gently troubled smiles of Angel and Virgin. The picture has suffered damages, for example in the far eye of the Virgin.

Botticelli's *Madonna* dates from the early 1470s, and we turn now to two of his near contemporaries, both non-Florentine, who found new possibilities for expression in the verticality and curvilinear interlacement of late Gothic art. Carlo Crivelli (c. 1430–95), who worked in the area around Venice, was influenced by the great Andrea Mantegna (represented in the museum by a somewhat placid *Holy Conversation*), but eschewed that master's astringent formalism as well as his bold adventures into illusionary space. In Crivelli's *St. George and the Dragon*[39] the vertical format virtually eliminates the possibility of a deeply receding continuum. Instead, we have a tapestrylike fairyland, with warped perspectives in the small, but not far distant, towers and spires. The dragon, the horse's tail, and the little landscape at the right all wind *up*, rather than back. St. George and his horse occupy most of the picture space, and Crivelli has loaded them with embossed and gilded detail. A violence, charmingly unconvincing as befits a fable, takes over; and there are interesting similarities to the forms and facial expressions of Giovanni

38

39

di Paolo's picture, already discussed. It is made very clear that the help-less and diminutive little lady will be rescued.

Even more narrowly vertical is the highly ornamented panel repre-senting *St. Engracia*,[40] by Bartolomé Bermejo, a native of Cordova who was active in Valencia, Barcelona, and in Aragon, where St. Engracia was especially revered. Bermejo's technique is clearly indebted to the great Flemish master, Jan van Eyck. This comes as no surprise, since Flemish painting was greatly prized in fifteenth-century Spain; but in the *St. Engracia* there is none of van Eyck's Luminism. Instead, the harsh, incisive line and the loaded ornamentation have such similarities with the art of Crivelli as to suggest—as indeed happened—that all across northern Italy, southern France, and into Spain the discoveries of the Florentine Renaissance met with grudging acceptance. One of Bermejo's finest works, the *St. Engracia* dates from about 1477. The artist died just before the end of the century, and little is known about his be-ginnings.

Soon after 1500 in Florence, Renaissance style developed a broader and grander phase under the influence of Leonardo da Vinci and Michelangelo and their prodigious younger rival Raphael (1483–1520), and just at this time the artistic center of gravity moved to Rome. Raphael's own development into a High Renaissance master is mar-velously illustrated at the Gardner Museum itself; we need only compare his early little *Pietà* of c. 1504 with his *Portrait of Count Tommaso Inghirami*[41] of about 1513, painted in Rome, where the subject was secretary of the Lateran Council.

In the *Pietà*, part of the predella (or foot-piece) of the large altar-piece of the *Madonna* in the Metropolitan Museum of Art, New York, the twenty-year-old painter has softened the lines, broadened the forms, and filled the scene with luminous atmosphere. In the portrait the scale (not the size) is enormous, in keeping with the new Roman culture dominated by Pope Julius II. The shapes, greatly simplified, and with sparing description of detail, are—so to speak—as globular and capa-cious as the Roman Pantheon. First of all there is the spherical shape of

41

40

the body, defined by sloping shoulders, inward-curving arms, and fat, cigarlike fingers. The great girth at the waist is ringed by the sash, and echoed at the neck by the collar band. But the purest globe is, of course, the head; and within the head are smaller globes: an earlobe and two bulging eyeballs. Observe these eyes closely. A subtle extra turn of the right one, giving a slightly walleyed effect, splits the focus of the count's gaze. He looks *up*, presumably toward a speaker, but not precisely *at* him. By this small but telling detail, Raphael avoids the illusionary suggestion of a psychological moment and shifts the emphasis beyond the passage of time. He uses it in other portraits as well, and we find it repeatedly employed by such sixteenth-century masters as Bronzino and Holbein, and in the nineteenth century by Ingres. By contrast, seventeenth- and eighteenth-century portraits, with their Baroque concern for catching the moment on the fly, focus the eyes sharply—often on the spectator—as in the portraits of Rubens, Hals, and Rembrandt and in the busts of Bernini and Houdon (see CT 67), and in Impressionist portraits by Renoir.

A quick comparison between the Houdon bust just mentioned and the Gardner Museum's superb bronze *Portrait of Bindo Altoviti*[42] by Benvenuto Cellini (1500–71) will again illustrate this basic difference in intentions. Cellini's detachment, what we may call his psychological distance from his subject, is reinforced by a rigidly vertical axis and by the near frontality of the pose.

As for Hans Holbein the Younger (1497–1543), the Museum offers his portraits of *Sir William* and *Lady Butts*.[43] Holbein was trained by his father in Augsburg in the methods of local late Gothic painting, matured at Basel in German Switzerland, and through the influence of the Dutch humanist Erasmus became court portraitist to Henry VIII of England. That his work resembles as much as it does the portraits that Raphael painted in Rome indicates how rapidly the forms of High Renaissance art spread over Europe. Sir William Butts was court physician to Henry VIII; and he appears as a character in the last act of Shakespeare's play. These portraits date from the end of Holbein's career, when his style became more incisively linear and somewhat

43

42

flattened under the influence of English taste—seen at its extreme a generation later in the wallpaper images of Queen Elizabeth. For the close connection with Raphael, such earlier Holbeins as the *Portrait of Georg Gisze* (Berlin, 1532) are clearer examples. No matter at what time we consider Holbein, however, we always find a Northerner's obsession with detail—for instance, in Lady Butts's collar and the ornament at her breast.

We turn now to Venice, where Gentile Bellini (c. 1429–1507) and his more famous brother Giovanni, the master of Titian, settled and spun out their distinguished careers. In 1479 Gentile was sent as portraitist to the court of Mahomet II in Constantinople. The miniature *Portrait of a Turkish Artist*,[44] in watercolor on parchment, seems to have been made there by Gentile, though it is just possibly the work of an Oriental. An argument against such a theory is provided by an undoubtedly Persian copy in the Freer Gallery in Washington, its mass flattened out as we should expect. Returning to Venice, Gentile peopled his great processional panoramas with turbaned Orientals, and this exoticism continued to mark Venetian painting into the time of Titian.

An insistent tradition tells us that Titian died in 1576 at the age of ninety-nine, but modern scholarship has settled on a birth date close to 1490. The Gardner Museum's *Rape of Europa*[45] is often cited as Titian's masterpiece, and I will make bold to declare it the greatest painting in New England, if not in America. Measuring 6 by 7 feet, it was painted in 1559–62 for King Philip II of Spain. For 150 years it hung in the Royal Palace in Madrid, where it was copied full-size by Rubens, and adapted by Velázquez for the background of *The Spinners* (Prado), before it passed into French royal collections and in 1896, via Bernard Berenson, to Mrs. Gardner. Van Dyck, the chief pupil of Rubens in

44

45

Antwerp, made a watercolor sketch from the Rubens copy, and this too can be seen in Fenway Court. Perhaps this extraordinary "pedigree," with its testimony to the admiration of other great artists, speaks more loudly than a verbal appraisal. I shall point out only two details: the way the rose scarf echoes the action of Europa's head and arm, and the vaporous poetry of the distant landscape, where, on a strand set before mountains reminiscent of Titian's own birthplace in the Dolomites, Europa's friends mourn her strange levitation by Zeus disguised.

Some idea of the revolutionary nature of Titian's career may be gained from comparing *The Rape of Europa* to a small panel by a window, *Christ Bearing the Cross.* Once attributed to Giorgione, it has likewise been ascribed to other pupils of the aged Giovanni Bellini. Whoever painted it, this little picture is a replica of a work by Bellini himself. In his youth Titian also painted in this manner. We may assume a gap of fifty years between the two pictures; and it is doubtful that any more far-reaching change in the history of art occurred in so short a time.

Returning to Sir Anthony Van Dyck (1599–1641) and to England, where he attained Holbein's position nearly a century later, we consider his *Portrait of a Lady with a Rose.*[46] Like Holbein a foreigner, he developed at Antwerp in the studio of Rubens. If Holbein can be said to have created the image of the Tudor courtier, Van Dyck established the Stuart aristocrat in a style still influential on today's enfeebled portraiture of British royalty. Van Dyck's final decade of residence in England gradually drew him away from the robust energy of Rubens's art. The present work, silvery in tone, its refinement—especially in the elongated fingers—carried almost to the point of listlessness, is probably of very late date (compare the full-length example at Yale's British Center, CT 53).

How far Van Dyck deviated from his master may be judged by a comparison of the last picture with the *Portrait of Thomas Howard, Earl of Arundel,*[47] by Peter Paul Rubens (1577–1640). The preparatory drawing is in the Clark Art Institute, Williamstown (MA 264). This superb half-length, in full armor, of the Earl Marshal of England and

46   47

patron of the arts, was almost certainly painted in 1629/30 when Rubens was in London on a diplomatic mission to the court of Charles I. During this time he was also occupied with designing the ceiling for the Banqueting Hall of Whitehall Palace (see CT 52). Darkly glowing in its exceptionally deep coloration, its mysterious and cavernous spaces set off the massive forms with more than a foretaste of Rembrandt, who at this time was still in his early twenties. As Baroque art, it is unusually reserved, but all the elements of this style are nonetheless present. The alert gaze, sharply focused on the spectator, is one of these elements; and it is even more strikingly apparent in the Clark Institute's drawing. We sense a psychological connection between sitter and artist, rather than the aloofness, mentioned above, felt in portraits by Raphael, Bronzino, Holbein, and Ingres. Curiously, Van Dyck's *Portrait of a Lady with a Rose*—by a lift of an eyebrow and a slight turn of her left eye—coyly evades us; among seventeenth-century portraits this is something of an exception. The pale gray-silver tones of the armor in Reynolds's 1765 *Portrait of Jeffery, Lord Amherst* (MA 7) tell us much about changing taste from the Baroque century to the Age of Enlightenment. The same may be said for Rubens's claret reds as against Reynolds's lavenderish pink sash.

Our next three pictures, two Rembrandts and a Vermeer, help give the Dutch Room its name. The *Lady and Gentleman in Black*[48] (1633, a year earlier than the large portraits in the Museum of Fine Arts) and the *Landscape with an Obelisk*[49] (1638) are superb examples of Rembrandt's maturing style between the ages of twenty-seven and thirty-two. Of the other two of his works in this room, *The Storm on the Sea of Galilee* (1633) is unusually coarse and melodramatic, while the *Self-Portrait at Twenty-three* (1629) is already well along the road to his youthful arrival. The famous *Anatomy Lesson of Dr. Tulp* (Amsterdam) came only three years later. At this period Rembrandt was under the strong influence of the Baroque style—more so in his religious works than in his portraits—with its strong contrasts of lighting, and its forms

48

49

receding from the picture surface. Later he muted these dramatic effects and eliminated such sharp edge and detail as we find in the double portrait. (Contrast the Fogg Museum's *Head of Christ*, c. 1648, MA 124.)

A special article by John Walsh, Jr., "Child's Play in Rembrandt's *A Lady and Gentleman in Black*," appears in the museum's annual bulletin for 1976. A recent cleaning and relining had made this picture more wonderful than ever. During that process X-rays showed many small changes made by Rembrandt as the picture progressed, and two major ones. Instead of the chair at the lower left, there was an amorphous black shape, perhaps a cloth; and between the husband and wife there was a young boy, right arm raised and holding a stick, or perhaps a whip. This surprising revelation leads to speculation. Did the child die? Or did Rembrandt (and/or his patrons) decide on a different kind of picture? What was the child (who seems never to have been more than roughly blocked out) doing? Perhaps he was using a whip to spin a top, but unfortunately there is no sign of any top to prove it. The lady originally looked askance at the child, around to her right and somewhat behind; now she gazes past the mysterious, but compositionally indispensable, chair—its rich red cushion accented by a shaft of light in an otherwise black-and-white and deeply shadowed picture. Although nothing happens, the figures are charged with psychological energy. It is not enough to say they are preparing to stroll outdoors. One senses without being able to explain further that Rembrandt, as he did so often, took a thoroughly conventional theme and gave it new significance.

However that may be, Rembrandt has made the two heads stand out from the minutely detailed ruffs by the most subtle modeling; and the same can be said for the modeling of the lady's black skirt. How do you model in pure black on black?

The careful observer will discover Rembrandt's signature and the date, 1633, in a place where it would seem to belong.

Mystery is further heightened in the *Landscape with an Obelisk*, painted in 1638. Rembrandt often drew and made etchings of landscape, stormy or otherwise; but there are less than twenty oils. Note how the forms have become blurred since 1633, how the light is more evenly distributed and its contrasts reduced, how the cool blues, greens, and mauves are played against the earth tones. Mystery and wonder ride triumphant. Why an obelisk set so close to an ordinary rustic mill? To ask the question is almost to answer it: this is no ordinary landscape, but a vision. Once again, Rembrandt has transformed the expected, and in so doing he was unique among his contemporaries. In his provocative and authoritative study, *Rembrandt, Life and Work* (London: Phaidon Press, 1964), Jakob Rosenberg points out that the master's interest in landscape, which began about the time of the Gardner example, ended around 1645. The reason for this leads to "the problem of Rembrandt's humanity." He found that human content was essential to his own self-expression.

Jan Vermeer of Delft (1632–75), a younger contemporary of Rembrandt, was the most gifted of many Dutch interior painters. Of those who were not primarily storytellers, most were attracted by the magic of light caught on surfaces (Ter Borch), or by the poetic silences of a sequence of rooms (de Hooch). Vermeer suspended all these elements in exquisite aesthetic balance, and still found a place for oblique allusion to human interest. *The Concert*[50] is a superb example. His art bespeaks the prosperity of the Dutch republic after the middle of the century. But it stands far above the status of a mere economic document. Leeuwenhoek, inventor of the microscope and also a native of Delft, was one of Vermeer's friends. There is no necessary artistic significance in this, but Vermeer's paintings do have a strikingly vitreous surface. Visitors to the Museum of Fine Arts will recall the original of the van Baburen *Procuress* hanging on the wall at the right in *The Concert*.

Off the main court, in a Spanish gallery especially arranged for it, is *El Jaleo*,[51] by John Singer Sargent (1856–1925). Dramatically lit from below, the flamenco dancer and her musicians seem to be actually performing. All that is lacking is a sound track, punctuated with cries of *jaleo!*—the flamenco equivalent of the bullfight's *olé*. At the Paris Salon of 1882 it was a sensation. Bought by a New York dealer, it was acquired by the Boston collector T. Jefferson Coolidge. After many attempts, Mrs. Gardner persuaded him to part with it; thereupon began a long association between Mrs. Gardner and the artist. Sargent had made many sketches on a trip to Spain, and from these he developed his big composition in his Paris studio. However imposing, *El Jaleo* seems external by comparison with the psychological bite of dance hall scenes by Degas and Toulouse-Lautrec. It is the Salon piece *par excellence*, not a personal revelation. A quick look at the Clark Institute's small *Venetian*

50

51

Interior (MA 260), painted in the same year, will convince you that when Sargent protested less he was indeed a very fine painter. Showy pictures are unfortunately like performances by brilliant piano technicians: the performance can run away with the music.

Unlike most collectors of the Old Masters, Mrs. Gardner had a lively interest in the art of her own time. Several small galleries on the ground floor demonstrate her ability to discover quality in contemporary work. They contain fine Whistlers, and several masterpieces by the French Impressionists. Totally unexpected, however, is an early oil of the best quality by Henri Matisse (1869–1954). There are surprisingly few paintings by this artist in New England, and a large proportion of them are from his rather easy, agreeable phase of about 1920. *The Terrace: St. Tropez,*[52] however, dates from 1904, when his style first crystallized. Though based on Impressionist art and the dotted color spots of Georges Seurat and Paul Signac, its range of color was, and still seems, daring, as does its use of bold patterns. The house shown here belonged to Signac, and Mme. Matisse posed for the figure in Japanese kimono, seated against the wall. Thomas Whittemore, who restored the mosaics of Hagia Sofia, acquired the picture from the artist, and gave it to Mrs. Gardner about 1910.

Mrs. Gardner was seventy then and Bernard Berenson, her onetime protégé and subsequent agent, had just passed the age of forty. How did he compare with her in his response to contemporary art? Note, to begin with, that Berenson was born in the same year as Matisse. In 1958, he published *Essays in Appreciation*, containing estimates of Matisse and Picasso written when he was in his eighties. The tone is infuriatingly condescending, yet it should be pointed out that Berenson recalls writing a letter to the New York *Nation*, about 1910, defending Matisse from an attack by its Paris correspondent. Appealed to by the Steins in Paris to help the struggling Matisse, whom they so greatly admired, Berenson had bought what he calls "a rather rough painting of a forest clearing." The illustration states that it is in the Belgrade Museum, "formerly in the Berenson Collection." The picture is clearly not up to the standard of Mrs. Gardner's example of about the same period, but Berenson chose it and Berenson disposed of it. In 1950 he called on Matisse, then busily engaged on the Vence Chapel. The essay ends with a querulous complaint: Matisse did not "refer in the slightest to what I had done for him forty years ago."

52

Museum of Fine Arts

Location: 465 Huntington Avenue

Hours: Tues. 10-5, Wed. 10-10, Thurs.-Sun. 10-5 (entire museum including West Wing); Thurs.-Fri. 5-10 (West Wing only); closed Mon. and major holidays

Admission: Charged; free Sat. 10-12. Ⓗ

New England's greatest art museum is surpassed in the United States only by the Metropolitan Museum of Art in New York. While other great American museums may surpass it in certain departments, the overall range and depth of the Boston collections continue to keep the Museum of Fine Arts in this exalted rank—a fact the more remarkable in view of the purely private status of the museum. There are nine departments: American decorative arts and sculpture, Asiatic art, classical art, contemporary art, Egyptian art, European decorative arts and sculpture, paintings, prints and drawings, and textiles. In addition, there are major collections of photographs and of musical instruments, and a vast art library.

The Asiatic collections are recognized as the finest in the world in a single institution. The collections of Egyptian and classical art are rivaled in America only by those in New York. The print collection is one of the seven most important in the world. The celebrated collection of paintings is especially strong in French art of the nineteenth century. Near Eastern and medieval and Renaissance decorative arts are superbly represented, and the textile collection (including tapestries and costumes) is world famous. Those of Early American silver (especially Paul Revere), furniture, and painting (over sixty works by John Singleton Copley) are unrivaled; the additional Karolik collection of painting and furniture is especially noteworthy.

It should be clear from the above that any survey of these riches on a scale comparable to our discussion of other New England museums would require a separate volume. My selection of under fifty masterpieces merely skims off some of the cream. It is designed primarily to fill in gaps in this book in an overview of world art from early antiquity to the present. The reader should assume that for most works discussed elsewhere an example of equal or superior quality is in the Museum of Fine Arts. My selections, however, give a fair impression of the range of riches here to be seen, and some inkling of their grandeur. Catalogues both general and particular are of course available; and the museum's illustrated handbook, revised from time to time, is an indispensable supplement to what is discussed in these pages.

The Museum of Fine Arts was the first in the United States to be incorporated (1870). In 1876 it opened to the public in a Victorian Gothic structure on Copley Square. At this time many of the paintings owned by the Boston Athenaeum—including Stuart's oil studies of George and Martha Washington—were transferred here on indefinite loan. The present building, which opened in 1909, has been greatly expanded by additions through the years. In the summer of 1981, the impressive West Wing, designed by I. M. Pei, was opened to the public. Capped by an Italian-inspired glass-roofed "galleria" over two hundred feet long, it provides superb space for temporary exhibitions, an auditorium, and services for a fast-growing attendance; and it frees the original building for more complete display of the permanent collections. In 1921–25 the upper hall and staircase rotunda at the Huntington Avenue entrance were decorated with allegorical paintings by John Singer Sargent. In 1979 an imaginative decision was fulfilled by the opening of the museum at Faneuil Hall Marketplace (open free of charge Tues.-Sun. 11-6, closed Mon.). This downtown extension, with its entrance at Number One, Old South Market Building, offers changing selections from the museum's collections to the millions who visit the historic market on Boston's waterfront. In this connection, the visitor to the main museum should not miss Gilbert Stuart's *Portrait of Joseph Quincy* (1772–1864), founder of the chief structure of the marketplace and later president of Harvard. The portrait, one of Stuart's most incisive and painted in 1824, shows the Quincy Market in the background. A visit is warmly recommended, both for itself and because something you could not find at Huntington Avenue may well be on view, temporarily, Avenue may well be on view, temporarily, here.

In the particular field of Old Kingdom Egyptian sculpture the Museum of Fine Arts is second only to Cairo among museums the world over. This happy condition is the result of excavations sponsored since 1905 by the museum and directed by the late George A. Reisener. The third of the Great Pyramids and its valley temple, at Gizeh, yielded rich finds, none more remarkable than the schist effigy of its builder, the *Pharaoh Mycerinus and Queen Chamerernebti*.[53] The rigidly frontal pose, with the left leg ceremonially advanced, gives a powerful expression of absolutism; the durability of the stone is fully exploited to accomplish it. Nevertheless, a degree of resilience at the joints and subtle differences of facial expression indicate the sculptor's own sense of vitality. The figures emerge as from a stone shroud.

Further evidence for this statement is provided by the unforgettable *Head of Prince Ankh-haf*,[54] the son-in-law of Cheops, builder of the

53

54

Great Pyramid. Found in the chapel of his tomb, this portrait shows how the sculptor, freed from traditional demands for representation of the pharaoh, could explore the individual personality. Here the limestone has been faced with stucco and painted a rich reddish brown. Like much great sculpture, this piece has a quality of compactness; the skin is stretched taut over bone and muscle.

Both of these masterpieces come from the Fourth Dynasty (2723–2563 B.C.), the head of the prince just before 2600, and Mycerinus and his queen—perhaps the first couple in the history of art—within the next quarter century.

After these sublime echoes of Egypt's greatest age, the small wooden model of *Four Offering Bearers*[55] strikes a note of intimacy. They were made some seven hundred years later, in the Middle Kingdom, when the monarchy was again centralized following a long period of political chaos. Though such figures were also carved in the Old Kingdom in the attempt to perpetuate in the tombs all facets of earthly life, here the proportions are markedly slenderer. Refinement attenuates the older strength. If we ponder, however, all that has happened to our Western world since the age of the Gothic cathedrals, we shall soon understand how sluggish was the velocity of change in Egypt.

At a height of 44 inches, the marble *Cycladic Idol*[56] is one of the largest known examples of its kind. Such figures, presumably representing the deceased or a deity of the dead, were produced in quantity in the Cyclades group of the Aegean Islands in the early Bronze Age during the period 2700–2300 B.C., known as Early Cycladic II. Small examples are so numerous that even today islanders use them as dolls. But a figure of the size of the Boston example is exceedingly rare. Compared with the example discussed at Amherst College, it is markedly elegant, and the iron component in the marble gives it an especially lovely rust-red tinge. Such art might easily have inspired Constantin Brancusi in his polished simplifications of natural form, and, through his influence, the sculptures and paintings of Amedeo Modigliani. Certain late abstractions of heads by the Russian-born German Expressionist painter Jawlensky, come even closer to Cycladic heads. Such twentieth-century enthusiasm for Cycladic art signals the waning influence of the high idealism of fifth-century Greek art; at the same time it serves to

55   56

remind us that "primitive" is perhaps a misnomer when used in the English sense and that it should be used to mean "early," as in the Romance languages.

Artistically as well as chronologically, Cycladic art is early Greek art. Note that it is roughly contemporary with Egyptian art of the Fourth Dynasty, and that already it has broken away from its stone shroud to explore tension and resilience in the human figure.

The museum's celebrated little *Snake Goddess*, in ivory and gold, distantly resembles the ceramic examples from the Palace of Knossos, now in the Herakleion Museum. These date from c. 1600 B.C.—some hundred years before the gigantic eruption of the volcano on Santorini Island, sixty miles to the north, produced a tidal wave that destroyed the Cretan fleet—and Knossos itself—and rendered Crete defenseless to the invasion of the Mycenaeans from the Peloponnesus. The Minoan Cretans worked in ivory and in gold, but no other example of work in ivory with gold is known. The unique Boston example has a surprisingly Victorian air.

The collection of Greek and Roman art is unquestionably the finest in New England, but in order to leave room for discussion of the excellent examples at Worcester, Providence, and Brunswick, only a minimum has been selected here. Although Boston's collection of Greek vases is considered the greatest in America, our discussion of this field is centered on examples in the college museums of Bowdoin, Smith, and Mount Holyoke. To sharpen your expectation of highest quality, however, you would do well to examine a black-figure amphora (squatter than the example at Worcester, MA 288) representing the *Departure of a Warrior* as he steps into his two-horse chariot, and two red-figure examples: a small two-handled cup, or skyphos, of the early fifth century, with the transparent "wet" draperies of marble sculpture of the time, that tells the story of Helen of Troy; and a krater by the Pan Painter representing the *Death of Actaeon*, considered to be one of the finest Greek vases in America.

The Greeks have been called a nation of art critics, so completely did their sense of artistic values affect all forms of their life. Even their coins show this predilection. To celebrate a victory of the Greek colonists over the Carthaginians in Sicily in 480 B.C., Gelon, the tyrant of Syracuse, issued a *Ten-drachma Silver Piece*.[57] The side shown here contains the profile of his beautiful wife, Daramete, encircled by four dolphins and the name Syracuse (reading counterclockwise from right center). The Boston example, the prize of its large collection of ancient coins, is the finest known impression of this design, which has been hailed as the most beautiful in the history of coinage. Note how finely the noble head is centered, how the several large and small circles echo

57

the shape of the whole coin, and how deftly the dolphins weave their motion around it. One is grateful that such beauty was pressed into silver, not a baser metal.

The collection of Greek and Roman engraved gems at Boston is likewise outstanding. Indeed, it ranks with that of Vienna, one of the great collections in the world.

Greek gold is another area in which the museum is rich. An earring of the mid-fourth century B.C. representing a *Victory Driving a Two-Horse Chariot*[58] is perhaps the greatest of these Boston treasures. Its large size (2 inches high) suggests that it was ordered as a votive offering to a goddess. Here in miniature we have all the fine workmanship, the elegance, and the sophistication of the marble and bronze sculpture that followed upon the Age of Pericles.

The so-called *Bartlett Head of Aphrodite*,[59] named for a former owner, is a superb example of the refinement that marks fourth-century art. It comes closer than anything in America to the style of Praxiteles and may even have been carved in his lifetime. The celebrated *Hermes with the Infant Dionysus* at Olympia, sometimes considered a work of Praxiteles himself, at other times a copy of a bronze by that master, seems by the standard of the *Bartlett Head* slick and disappointing. Here the grain of the Parian marble and its delicate translucence have been exploited to catch a mood of soft reverie, but without loss of strength. As in the work of Leonardo da Vinci, whose *Mona Lisa* this *Aphrodite* foreshadows, and in the highly sensuous art of Correggio, there is a feeling of exaltation, of something beyond the limits of mortal beauty.

The difference between Greek and Roman ideals—that is, apart from Roman imitations of Greek art (see CT 63)—can be seen by contrasting this lovely head with a terra-cotta *Portrait Head* dating from the last century of the Roman republic. This tired Roman might be called an ancient existentialist. Be he senator, banker, or jurist, nothing godly resides in him; yet he has developed, through force of character, his own system of values. The realism is so penetrating that we must suppose the use of a life mask; yet the sculptor truly possessed life-giving powers, for nothing, not even a death mask, is quite so dead as a life mask.

More creative, in the sense of psychological interpretation, is the recently acquired *Portrait Bust of Elagabalus*,[60] Syrian high priest and Roman emperor from the age of thirteen in A.D. 218 to his murder four years later. Cornelius Vermeule, the Curator of Classical Art, has written a fascinating account of this work in *Iconographical Studies*, published by the museum in 1980. Elagabalus was the youth's priestly name, after

58

59

his favorite Syrian deity, and he was falsely reputed to be the son of the Emperor Caracalla; as emperor he took the name of Marcus Aurelius Antoninus, but he became known even in his lifetime as the False Antoninus. In his brief imperial adolescence, he cut a wide swath of bizarre sexual adventures. In this portrait he resembles nothing so much as the street-wise Roman boys painted by Caravaggio. The arrangement of the drapery is standard in busts of this time; it is only in the face that the artist sought individual expression. Such work gives pause to the easy theory that Roman sculpture went progressively downhill after the Age of Augustus.

After the fall of Rome, the arts were patronized primarily by the Church, and with the rise of Romanesque art in the eleventh and twelfth centuries architecture dominated the forms of sculpture and painting to a marked degree. Carved Romanesque capitals abound in our museums, but Boston is still unique in America for owning the wall paintings of an entire apse, though they were acquired some sixty years ago. These paintings from Santa Maria de Mur[61] in Catalonia, northeast Spain, date from the mid-twelfth century. The style derives from Byzantine art, but it is more vehement in its rustic way. Christ in a glory is surrounded by the symbols of the four Evangelists with the twelve Apostles ranged below, while the story of the Nativity (damaged) occupies the lowest register. The white ground acts as a foil for a forceful play of line and sharp angle.

As for Byzantine art proper, the museum owns two frescoed heads from the same series as the example at the Williams College Museum of Art (MA 270). These are exhibited in the medieval galleries. The date is probably seventeenth century, but one six hundred years earlier has also been proposed. Evolution in Byzantine form is not its most interesting aspect.

The *Baptism of Christ*,[62] in gilt copper over a foot high, is an unusually important example of French medieval metalwork. Though it was made in Limoges as late as 1200–1250, its lean forms still echo those of Byzantine art. Like the Catalan frescoes, it has a quality of rustic vigor. The rounded sculptural modeling, however, is related to the Gothic sculpture of that time. The stylized water is gouged out from

60

61

the copper plate and filled with gray enamel by a process called champlevé.

The *Virgin and Child on a Crescent Moon*,[63] lower Austrian, c. 1450–60, in polychromed and gilt poplar wood 70 inches high, superbly represents the deep undercutting and angular tension of late Gothic art. It once formed the center of an elaborate altarpiece for a church near Linz on the Danube. Figure and crown are carved of one piece. Less intimate than the smaller example of c. 1430 in the Busch-Reisinger Museum (MA 99), it has a more majestic air. Both should be contrasted with Boston's statue of *St. John Evangelist*, also of polychromed poplar, Tuscan work of the fourteenth century, which preserves the more static and monumental character of thirteenth-century cathedral sculpture. (The legs and feet of the *Evangelist*—seemingly out of proportion— are modern.)

Dating from about 1400 is a rare wool-and-linen tapestry 16 feet long representing *Wild Men, Animals, and Moors*.[64] German work marked by considerable violence, it may have come from Strasbourg on the upper Rhine, since the coats of arms are those of two families from that city. Its labyrinthine patterns are as abstract as its colors, in which deep reds and cream tones predominate. The meaning is difficult to interpret, but it appears to reflect the strange admixture, current at the time, of love and the macabre. Here the "wild men"—ordinarily but not always symbols of evil—attack the fortress of love defended by black Moors, struggle with animals, and bear gifts to a wild woman and her child. Gertrude Townsend, the museum's former curator of textiles, devoted a long article to this tapestry in the museum's *Bulletin* for spring 1958. Relevant background for the emotional character of such

62   63

64

work is contained in J. Huizinga's classic study, *The Waning of the Middle Ages* (London: Edward Arnold & Co., 1924), in the first chapter, entitled "The Violent Tenor of Life."

A many-crocketed retable from Aragon,[65] in northern Spain, painted by Martín de Soria in the late fifteenth century, tempera on panel and measuring nearly 14 feet in height, combines Italianate forms (and a hesitant use of Italian perspective) with Flemish technique and detail. The central image represents St. Peter, patron of the church or chapel that this multipaneled altar once adorned. Here the art of painting is closely associated with that of church furniture. Bright reds and gold unify the disparate parts of a complex construction, seemingly suspended above its predella of paired Apostles.

Mention of Flemish painting brings us to the outstanding example in New England, one of the masterworks of Roger van der Weyden of Tournai (1399/1400–64). The subject is *St. Luke Painting the Virgin*,[66] a fascinating combination of Gothic religious icon and modern artist-and-model picture. St. Luke (for whom many of the guilds and academies of painting were named) holds a silverpoint, and we may discern here the making of just such a drawing as the Dieric Bouts portrait at Smith College (MA 170). The setting flows easily from indoors out to a balcony overlooking a characteristic Flemish cityscape. An early work of the master from about 1436, it is more than usually influenced by the great Bruges painter Jan van Eyck, whose *Madonna of Chancellor Rolin* (in the Louvre) inspired its main conception. Nevertheless, van der Weyden's picture became famous in its own right: there are three other versions in major European museums, but the Boston example is acknowledged to be the original work. Bought at auction in New York by Henry Lee Higginson in 1889 and given to the museum by him in 1893, it was the earliest major Flemish painting to enter an American public collection. Its subject suggests that it was done for the Painters' Guild in Brussels, where Roger chiefly worked. Contemporary with the activity of the first generation of painters of the Florentine Renaissance, it seems to be indebted to them for its converging perspective, although this new device is not systematically employed here. While van Eyck's detail and something of his limpid atmosphere dominate Roger's art, the figures have much more sculptural volume, but without the anatomical coherence of those in the paintings of Masaccio or the sculptures

65

66

of Donatello (see MA 68). Details not to be missed are the simulated carved group of Adam and Eve and the Tree of Knowledge on an arm of the Virgin's throne, and behind St. Luke his symbol—an ox—in the lower compartment of a bookcase.

Acquired in 1964 as the gift of R. Thornton Wilson in memory of President Kennedy is a magnificent *Portrait Bust*,[67] about 2 feet high, made c. 1500 at Salzburg in Hafner ware—fired earthenware with colored glazes of tin and lead. A century later than the Rhenish tapestry just discussed, it still belongs to a disquieted late Gothic age—paradoxically contemporary with Michelangelo's great marble *David* of 1501–04. Compared with the peaceable art of Roger van der Weyden, the bust expresses emotional tension, in the face, in the tightly clasped arms, and in the jagged folds of the drapery. Roger's simple reds and blues could not be substituted for the dour browns of these glazes. Such inner expressiveness foretells the art of the modern Germans, and of another Austrian, Oskar Kokoschka (see MA 105), whose 1908 polychromed clay *Self-Portrait* (in the contemporary section of the museum) projects similar feelings. Clearly a donor image rather than a purely secular one, the Hafner-ware bust may also be a self-portrait—by a master of the Salzburg Hafner Guild.

After viewing these several expressions of the late Gothic spirit, to come upon Donatello's glistening white marble relief of the *Madonna of the Clouds*[68] is to enter a new world, that of the humanistic Florentine Renaissance. A 13-inch-square plaque in very low relief known as *stiacciato*, it dates from around 1430, well into the long career of Donatello (1386–1466). This is perhaps the only work in America by the hand of the greatest sculptor between Greek antiquity and Michelangelo—some would say the greatest sculptor of all time, and Michelangelo in his own time might have supported such a statement. Experts disagree about Donatello's authorship of a fifteenth-century unfinished *David* in the National Gallery, Washington, but generally agree that the conception of the Boston relief is Donatello's and likewise the carving of the Virgin, while the little background angels may be the

67

68

work of an assistant. The powerful form of the Virgin, at once gracious and sublime, clearly foreshadows the art of Michelangelo. We know that Donatello visited Rome and that he was enthralled by ancient Roman art, but his own work managed to recapture the spirit of a Greek art he could not possibly have seen, and to infuse it with a new emotional warmth and tenderness. We also know that this relief was treasured in Florence after the master's death. A certain Piero del Pugliese had it enshrined in a wooden tabernacle with movable wings painted by Fra Bartolomeo; and in Vasari's time (mid-sixteenth century) it was in the collection of Duke Cosimo de' Medici. The most perceptive account of the *Madonna of the Clouds* is by Sir John Pope-Hennessy in *Essays on Italian Sculpture* (London: Phaidon Press, 1968, pages 54–55).

Boston's representation of fourteenth- and fifteenth-century Italian painting cannot match that of the Gardner Museum or the Fogg Art Museum in Cambridge. Mention should be made, however, of the small gold-ground altarpiece of the *Crucifixion*, with wings representing the bishop saints Nicholas and Gregory, of which the center panel is either by Duccio di Buoninsegna (c. 1255–1319), the founder of Sienese painting, or possibly by a very faithful follower. In the section on the Mount Holyoke Museum of Art we discuss a small panel said to have come from Duccio's great *Maestà*, a multipaneled altarpiece for the high altar of Siena Cathedral (MA 204).

Outstanding among the museum's fifteenth-century Italian paintings is the *Presentation of the Virgin in the Temple*[69] by an anonymous artist known as the Master of the Barberini Panels, who flourished in the 1460s. A companion panel of similar size (height 58 inches), representing the *Visitation*, is in the Metropolitan Museum of Art. Both were acquired in the 1930s from the Barberini Gallery in Rome. Efforts to link them with the work of a known artist have met with little success. Whoever he was, he carried the Florentine passion for architectural perspectives to a kind of Surrealist extreme, and so populated his compositions with incident and extraneous characters (who nevertheless help us measure the planar recession) that it is not easy to find

69

the main subject. All the elements of this fantastic building relate to Renaissance architecture, but such a building clearly could not exist; it is best understood as painter's architecture. The two angels atop the main cornice suggest that the picture may have had a very elaborate frame.

The *Dead Christ with Angels*,[70] signed by the Florentine painter known as Il Rosso Fiorentino (1494–1540) brings us past the High Renaissance art of Raphael into the so-called Mannerist art of about 1525. A large oil on panel over 4 feet high and in superb condition, it is not only the most important work of this master in America but probably our finest Mannerist picture. Inspired by both Leonardo da Vinci and Michelangelo, Il Rosso broke with most of their artistic premises: axial balance is dislocated, space is telescoped into a narrow shelf of recession, light and shade run to violent contrasts, and color turns vivid. The naked body of Christ, neither dead nor alive, is set on an altar attended by angels. Perhaps it is resurrected. Its sensuality seems contradictory to its iconic function. We feel at once a weakening of dogma and a heightening of aestheticism. The message here seems to be a celebration of art itself, tinged with highly equivocal overtones of what it is that these androgynous angels are worshiping. In sum, a picture both shocking and marvelous.

The seventeenth century, like the nineteenth, was a century of great painters, and El Greco (1541–1614) lived long enough to initiate it. The seated portrait of the Trinitarian monk, *Fray Felix Paravicino*,[71] often cited as one of El Greco's masterpieces, dates from 1609. The light and color give the monk a kind of phosphorescent energy. The fluid brushwork helps convey the sense of a moment in time. On all these accounts we approach Baroque art, though the Baroque emphasis on physical bulk is conspicuously absent. This is because Domenico Theotocopoulos, called "The Greek" in Toledo to the end of his life, came from Byzantine Crete. The longer he painted, the more closely he returned to the mystical art of his origins.

That this picture was purchased on the specific recommendation of John Singer Sargent is as astonishing as the date of the purchase itself

70

71

—1904, four years before Manuel Cossio's pioneering biography of
El Greco and six years before Julius Meier-Graefe's *Spanish Journey*
established him as an artist for our time. Sargent's insistence, based on
what the European avant-garde was beginning to say about El Greco, resulted in the first acquisition of his work by an American museum. The
price—seventeen thousand dollars—was not inconsiderable for an "unknown" at the time. All of this made possible by the creator of the
Gardner Museum's *El Jaleo* (MA 51) !

Diego Velázquez (1599–1660), the leading painter of the Spanish
Golden Age, is represented in the museum by superb examples of both
his earlier and his mature work. The *Portrait of Luis de Góngora*,[72] the
poet, painted when Velázquez was twenty-five, is marked by the sharp
line, the bony structure, and the thin proportions of Mannerist art of
the previous century. (These are also found in El Greco.) Very Spanish
are the detachment and pride in this intense personage. The *Don
Baltazar Carlos and His Dwarf* was painted some ten years later, after
Velázquez had toured Italy and returned to Madrid as chief court artist.
Full of enthusiasm for the Italian Renaissance painters, especially Titian
and the Venetians, he now used opulent colors, notably deep reds and
violets. He developed a play of silvery texture over transparent darks,
and generally relaxed the intensity seen in the early Góngora portrait.

In Holland the great figure before Rembrandt was Frans Hals
(c. 1581–1666), and Boston's magnificent *Portrait of a Man*,[73] dating
c. 1664–66, is one of his last surviving works. Thus it should be thought
of in the revolutionary terms of the last water-lily canvases of Claude
Monet (much later than any discussed in this book), for Monet too
lived to the age of eighty-six—or considered with the late Pietàs of
Michelangelo, who died at eighty-nine. The unknown sitter fancied himself. He acquired (or borrowed) a deep rust-red kimono of shot silk,
of the sort first given by the Japanese Shogun to officers of the Dutch
East India Company and later exported to a fast-growing European
market. His extravagantly long brown hair (possibly a wig) awkwardly
apes the style then fashionable at the court of Louis XIV. Accoutred in
these status symbols, he observes us with a rather smug smile (I have

72

73

made it, he seems to say). What a contrast to the usual stark black-and-white images of Dutch burghers and their wives!

So much for the subject, but what of the artist? In the twenty years that elapsed since Hals painted *Mevrouw Bodolphe* (Yale University Art Gallery, CT 73), his brushwork has grown increasingly looser and more transparent, as if to express the disillusionment that has crept into his soul. Our status-hungry sitter thus became an occasion for mordant satire. Note, in contrast to the Yale portrait, the total concentration on the head (but do not miss the expressiveness of the hand), peering out from all this foolish finery. If the kimono is brushed with almost nonchalant speed, it is nevertheless a miracle of execution. Two centuries later, its quality was not lost on Edouard Manet. A fine account of the Boston portrait will be found in Seymour Slive, *Frans Hals* (3 volumes; London: Phaidon Press, 1970, 1974, catalogue number 220).

The museum owns an important pair of full-length portraits of Reverend and Mrs. Johannes Elison, painted in 1634 by Rembrandt van Rijn (1606–69)—a year later than the Gardner Museum's *Lady and Gentleman in Black* (MA 48). Other Dutch pictures of note include the Dirk Baburen *Procuress* that appears on the back wall of the Gardner Museum's *Concert* by Vermeer of Delft (MA 50), a marvelous little *Cavalier in the Saddle* by Gerard Ter Borch (1584–1662), and Jacob van Ruisdael's *A Rough Sea*,[74] which we now consider.

Among the younger contemporaries of Rembrandt who specialized in landscape painting, none was more distinguished than Ruisdael (1628/9–82), a native of Haarlem. Indeed, Rembrandt's own landscapes are so personal and psychological (compare the example in the Gardner Museum (MA 49) that it is doubtful they should be considered as landscape in the usual sense of the term.

Ruisdael excelled in all categories of landscape: sky, land, and water, and in all their combinations. His marines, embodying the Dutch love of the sea and of sailing, are perhaps unequaled in the history of art, though they inspired a rival in the young Turner (an example is at the Malden Library, MA 165) early in the nineteenth century. *A Rough Sea* is considered one of the finest marines of his whole career. Painted about 1670, it shows an estuary outside Amsterdam. The broad expanse of water zigzags back in alternating light and dark triangles, with counter-accents of darks and lights in the foreground pilings and the near

74

and distant sails. The brisk lapping of the waves sets up a nervous tension through its sharp linear rhythms, felt again in the shapes of the clouds. Earlier works by Ruisdael are discussed at Springfield (M A 211) and at Manchester (N H 24).

Because Peter Paul Rubens, Nicolas Poussin, Antoine Watteau, and J. B. S. Chardin—major figures of seventeenth- and eighteenth-century painting—are discussed in other museums, we regretfully pass over fine examples of their work in the Museum of Fine Arts. In connection with a superb Poussin (*Achilles on Skyros*), however, the visitor is fore-warned to look up the story of how Achilles' mother concealed him in woman's attire among the daughters of Lycomedes and how a sword destroyed his cover.

Short of his grandiose ceiling paintings in the palaces of Venice, Würzburg, and Madrid, it would be difficult to cite a more sumptuous example of the art of Giovanni Battista Tiepolo (1696–1770) than *Time Unveiling Truth*,[75] an oil nearly 8 feet high dating from c. 1745, in the full glory of the long career of this Venetian decorator. A pen-and-wash drawing, *Hagar and Ishmael*, in Williamstown (M A 266) sets up expectations of power and energy fulfilled here in the oil medium. Tiepolo provides the essential link between Baroque grandeur and Rococo sensuality. The darkish Baroque color—bronzed greens, deep ochers, and wine reds—sets off the lightly keyed flesh tones and sky blues found in French Rococo painting (as in the museum's *Return from the Market*, 1767, by François Boucher [1703–70]). Note how Time's scythe introduces, as at the beginning of a symphonic movement, two major visual themes: a bold curve and a rapidly receding strong diagonal. As we climb up this complex composition these motifs are intertwined in complicated variations. A fluted column at the rear provides a forceful note of stability.

In the city-dominated eighteenth century, views of natural landscape were in little demand. Views of cities, however, and other sights included on the Grand Tour were extremely popular. Often these pictures were rather small, and more often they were replicas turned out in quantity by some well-organized atelier. Antonio Canale, called Canaletto

75

(1697–1768), the leading Venetian painter of such views, like the slightly later (and, to sharp eyes, very different) Francesco Guardi, ran such an establishment. His large (49 by 60 inches) and superbly painted *Bacino di San Marco*⁷⁶ (c. 1740–45) shows us Canaletto at his best, and the picture is probably entirely by his hand. In mid-distance before the Doges' Palace, amid a vast array of shipping, is the impressive *bucintoro,* the golden, many-oared barge wherein, on great occasions, the Doge was enthroned as the symbol of the Most Serene Republic. The painting was purchased from the artist himself for Castle Howard, in England, whence the museum acquired it in 1939. The view is taken from near the Customs Building at the entrance to the Grand Canal, with the Piazzetta and the Doges' Palace on the left, and the island church of San Giorgio Maggiore on the right. Richard Parkes Bonington's view at the Malden Library (MA 166) looks in exactly the opposite direction.

Far to the north from Tiepolo's and Canaletto's Venice, but hardly sixty miles from the Residenz at Würzburg—with its great Tiepolo ceiling frescoes of c. 1750—the ceramic sculptor Johann Martin Mutschele (1733–1804) may be said to have absorbed and transposed Tiepolo's forms into a new medium. His imposing *Madonna of Victory*,⁷⁷ 4 feet high, in white glazed Schrezheim faience, once adorned the portal niche of the residence of the Teutonic Knights (now the Rathaus) at Wolframs-Eschenbach, in Franconia. A unique creation, it is the most important single work of German faience. The date, 1771, appears with the artist's monogram. The Tiepolo influence, referred to above, was not at the expense of German tradition, for eighteenth-century German piety—so pronounced that it amounted to a virtual medieval revival—is strongly in evidence here. The source of the theme is biblical (Revelation: 12): "And there appeared a great wonder in heaven, a woman clothed with the sun and the moon under her feet and upon her head a crown of twelve stars." The museum's *Bulletin* for 1965 carries a fine article on this piece by the then curator, Hanns Swarzenski. Filled with the Baroque sense of drama, the figure at the same time has the intimacy and refinement of Rococo art, further marked by the emphasis on C-shaped curves originally derived from the forms of the conch shell.

Perhaps the least significant fact about John Singleton Copley (1738–

77

76

1815) is that his celebrated *Portrait of Paul Revere*,[78] painted about 1768–70, was almost exactly contemporary with Mutschele's *Madonna of Victory*. Such gratuitous information nevertheless helps us measure the immense gulf that separated American Colonial culture from that of Rococo Europe. As we have seen in the discussion of the great portraits at Bowdoin College (ME 10–12), Copley was among the first to establish the art of the American colonies as other than a provincial offshoot of British art. Perhaps the same can be said for Paul Revere, Boston's patriot-silversmith. We may take special pride that these two artistic forebears come together in Copley's memorable portrait. Like the painting, the silver teapot (very similar to one by Revere in the same room) shows a high order of craftsmanship, painstaking detail, strongly simplified shapes, avoidance of anything showy or ornate. The Revere portrait was painted several years before Copley settled in London and gradually yielded his American heritage to English tastes. Its informal air is in sharp contrast to the many fashionable images in the museum's collection of more than sixty works by Copley. Here his ever-sharp eye and disciplined hand have caught the subject's physical girth, his intense facial expression, and his blunt fingernails—doubtless worn down in the practice of his craft. For other Boston portraits by Copley, see the examples at Dartmouth and Smith colleges, and for an English one the *Mrs. Seymour Fort* at Hartford (CT 25).

Landscape painting, in contrast to cityscapes so popular in the eighteenth century, became the dominant theme of Romantic art. In the same way, nature dominated poetry in the age of Wordsworth. England took a leading position in both arts. The poetry of nature in oils, as landscape painting might be called, moved in two distinct directions: the serenity of the homeland and the exotic appeal of natural wonders abroad. John Constable (1776–1837) stands for the former and Joseph M. W. Turner (1775–1851) for the latter, though this contrast admits of some exceptions. In any event, the museum's Constable, *Weymouth Bay*, with its cloud-swept coast plunging us miles into untroubled distances, contrasts violently with Turner's huge and crashing *Falls of the Rhine at Schaffhausen*[79] (c. 1806). In the one, a little figure walks the moors while in the distance a farmer—his shirt a miraculous speck of light—con-

78

79

tentedly plows his fields. In the other, a knot of figures, horses, and wagons is dwarfed by nature's wild power. A rainbow arches the spume, and the great rock seems to push like an animate being against the roaring torrent. In both, nature, not man, is the protagonist: nature is space, and air, and moisture, and light, and, above all, weather. Indeed, Constable (see CT 57–58) used to make quick sketches out of doors, and mark them with the location, the date, and the direction of the wind. If he is England's closest parallel to Wordsworth in painting, Turner comes nearest to Byron's great apostrophes to the sea.

Despite its extremely unfinished state, nothing could better demonstrate the mysterious power of Honoré Daumier (1808–79) than the *Man on a Rope*.[80] What is the man doing? Is he a circus acrobat? Is he escaping from prison? Is he, as some have said, merely a house painter? We shall probably never know, and even if we did, it would make little difference. The first explanation seems the most likely. The second is possible. But because Daumier could transform the most insignificant incident into a theme of Michelangelesque grandeur, one is tempted to think the third explanation may lie closest to the truth. Balzac, one of Daumier's admirers and in many ways his equivalent in literature, once said of him: "There is something of Michelangelo in that fellow." The date is probably c. 1858–60, well after Daumier's somewhat Neoclassical forms in his lithograph of 1834, the *Rue Transnonain* (CT 41).

Edouard Manet (1832–83) and Edgar Degas (1834–1917) were both closely associated with the circle of the Impressionists in Paris, yet both remained strangely aloof. Essentially this was caused by their basic temperament. Manet and Degas were much more deeply committed to the traditional values of painting than their somewhat younger colleagues in Impressionism. This becomes especially clear in their early works, of which Boston owns examples of the very first order. *The Street Singer* by Manet dates from 1862, the year of Yale's *Young Woman Reclining* (CT 79) and the year before the famous *Olympia* and the *Déjeuner sur l'herbe* (in the Louvre), and the same model, Victorine Meurend, posed for both of them. Degas's portrait of his sister and her titled husband, *The Duke and Duchess of Morbilli*,[81] was painted in 1867. Both Boston

80

81

pictures are low in color intensity, with restrained grays, browns, and greenish ochers underlining the well-bred reticence of the persons portrayed. Both have an aristocratic air, despite Manet's choice of a rather tawdry subject. While Degas's hauteur was partly a matter of natural inheritance, the solid bourgeois background of Manet did not commit him to accepting its social point of view. At this time he found his inspiration in Velázquez, whether in the few attributed works then available in Paris or in black-and-white reproductions we do not know. Degas's sources were Ingres, Mannerist painters like Bronzino, and the purity of line of some of the fifteenth-century Italians. A drawing of the head of the duchess, also in the Boston Museum, is very close to such a Florentine master as Ghirlandajo.

The *Portrait of Madame Cézanne*[82] was painted by Paul Cézanne (1839–1906) about 1877, several years after he had worked with Camille Pissarro at Pontoise (see MA 255) and absorbed Impressionist technique with its high-intensity palette. Here he unites it with his powerful sense of volumes and replaces the Impressionist sense of a fleeting moment with his characteristic solemnity and timelessness. Long his mistress before becoming Cézanne's wife in 1886, Hortense Fiquet patiently posed for him for some twenty-seven portraits over a period of thirty years. He is said to have preferred her to still life because she did not rot. Much of Cézanne's effect is due to his elimination of the camera's illusion of spatial recession (faithfully adhered to by the Impressionists). Thus the figure resembles relief sculpture against a flat plane. Strokes of paint brushed on in small flat rectangles in a close value range lose their impact in the black-and-white photograph, for the hues differ. You soon learn to "read" a change of color as a shift in direction, so they participate in the rounding of a volume. Characteristically, the eyes are sightless, as in many Greek and Roman heads. There is no psychological focus. Indeed, this is a still-life portrait.

Pierre Auguste Renoir (1841–1919) is the leading figure painter among the true Impressionists, as Claude Monet was the leading landscapist. Both of them were notable painters of still life (for Renoir see MA 128 and MA 256). Boston's *Bal à Bougival*,[83] signed and dated by

82

83

Renoir in 1883 and measuring a generous 71 by 38 inches, is one of his masterpieces from the vintage years of the early 1880s, just before he began to move away from Impressionism toward a style marked by more incisive outline and more substantial modeling. Already in this work the process has begun; it approaches a Rubensesque hymn to joys of the flesh. But the color, soon to become both hotter and drier, retains Impressionism's rainbow palette of unmixed prismatic hues, their sparkle enhanced by deft turns of the brush. The foreground figures are more massive than in earlier Renoirs of this sort, but as we move back into the distance the language of Impressionism gains in purity. For this picture, sometimes called *La Danse à la Campagne*, Suzanne Valadon—painter, model, and the mother of Maurice Utrillo (see ME 40)—posed with Renoir's brother.

Two sides of American life in the later nineteenth century may be observed in *Long Branch, N.J.*, an early landscape by Winslow Homer (1836–1910), and *The Daughters of Edward D. Boit*,[84] painted in 1882 by John Singer Sargent (1856–1925). Homer came from Boston, and though Sargent was born in Florence, Boston was his spiritual home. In later life Homer's genius led him to the solitudes of the New England coasts; Sargent's led him to Europe and a fashionable career as a portraitist. Thus we have a clear opposition between native and expatriate art. Sargent belonged to the world of Henry James, whose castigations of Homer for his "vulgarities" (see CT 80) can only be understood in this context. *Long Branch* (1869) is exactly contemporary with the beginnings of Impressionism in Paris, from which Homer had recently returned after a period of study. His concern with light and his subject are the only connections: all else is as different as a Copley from a Gainsborough portrait in the preceding century. Sargent, too, makes poetry of American innocence; but he has left a telling document of a somewhat inbred society. The picture was painted in the Boits' Paris apartment. The big vases, which made many journeys back and forth from Boston, are important in establishing the size of the little girls, and in completing the blue-and-white scheme that helps unite this 87-inch-square canvas. The picture was called "four corners and a void" by a hostile critic when it was shown at the Paris Salon of 1883; but Henry James, in an essay on Sargent written ten years later, much preferred "The Hall with the Four Children," as he called it, to *El Jaleo* (Gardner Museum, MA 51). "If the picture of the Spanish Dancer illustrates, as

84

it seems to me to do, the latent dangers of the Impressionist practice, so this finer performance shows what victories it may achieve . . . [an] astonishing work on the part of a young man of twenty-six" (Henry James, *The Painter's Eye*, edited by John L. Sweeney; Cambridge: Harvard University Press, 1956, page 223).

In the company of Renoir's *Bal à Bougival*, Sargent seems very conservative, especially in his muted colors in this darkened interior. In his youthful years he was an Impressionist more in the vein of the early work of Degas and Edouard Manet—whom he followed in his enthusiasm for Velázquez's hushed illusionism. Similarly, the early work of Vincent van Gogh (1853–90)—born only three years before Sargent—is marked by the dark tones of Pre-Impressionism, as seen in Boston's *Weaver*,[85] painted in 1884. In January of that year Vincent wrote to his brother Theo: "Soon I hope to start another two of weavers, where the figure comes in quite differently, that is to say, the weaver does not sit behind it, but is arranging the threads of the cloth. I have seen them weaving in the evening by lamplight, which gives very Rembrandtesque effects." A pen drawing for the Boston version of this subject (one of several he painted in 1884) is in the Van Gogh Museum at Amsterdam; it includes a lighted lamp not seen in the painting. In some versions the weaver seems almost imprisoned in a kind of cage; but here the effect is less troubled. If the loom is seen in the pale gray light of a sunless day, the pinks and reds of the woven cloth and the blue of the weaver's coat give out a little warmth. For an actual loom like this one, see the Merrimack Valley Textile Museum, North Andover (page 263).

After these tentative but moving beginnings, van Gogh went on to master Impressionism in Paris and then to his great achievements in Arles (CT 81), Saint-Rémy (ME 27), and Auvers. Boston has the marvelous *Postman Roulin* from the Arles period (1888) and the tumultuous *Ravine*, painted a year later at Saint-Rémy. We discuss his 1888 *Self-Portrait*, dedicated to Paul Gauguin, in the section on the Fogg Art Museum of Harvard University (MA 130). As for Gauguin (1848–1903), Boston has impressive examples of his painted wood sculpture and an unsurpassed oil. Over 12 feet wide, it was painted at Tahiti in 1897 as his final testament.[86] At that time Gauguin had planned to

85

86

commit suicide. Signed and dated at the upper right, the canvas carries its provocative title in the balancing corner at the left: *D'où venons-nous? Que sommes-nous? Où allons-nous?* Gauguin's answer to these eschatological questions is organized in a cycle from right to left (counter to expected Western readings). A running dog somewhat obviously starts us off. We are born, we enjoy the fruits of life, we end grayed and shriveled, accompanied by a symbolic bird, described later by Gauguin in a letter as "a strange white bird, holding a lizard in its claw [*sic*] . . . [It] represents a futility of words." Some may find this—and much additional—symbolism excessive. If you are anthropologically inclined, you will discover that the exotic deities—the one at the left, Gauguin wrote, "seems to indicate the Beyond"—have little or nothing to do with Tahitian religion, but are an admixture of the artist's memories of non-Western arts in the Paris museums. In his obsession with such material, however, Gauguin was far ahead of modern enthusiasms; and his example, not lost on Picasso and the German Expressionists, had a profound influence. Still more important were his sense of flat mural design and his revolutionary color. In these respects Henri Matisse was his true twentieth-century follower. In these, too, Gauguin is most respected today. His high opinion of himself was on a different level: discussing the Boston picture, he wrote, "I have finished a philosophical work on this theme, comparable to the Gospels. I think it is good." The title, he insisted, is "not a title, but a signature."

The acquisition in 1958 of *Standing Figure*[87] by Pablo Picasso (1881–1973) brought the museum's collections abruptly into modern avant-garde art, an area in which it had been sadly deficient. This statement holds true even though the picture, 5 feet high, was painted as early as the spring of 1908, a few months after the completion of the celebrated *Demoiselles d'Avignon* (Museum of Modern Art, New York). In the Boston oil Picasso has narrowed the color range to the warm pinks, orange browns, and sky blues of the *Demoiselles'* more complex palette. *Standing Figure* carries nascent Cubism farther along than in that path-finding earlier work. During 1908 and 1909 Picasso further reduced his color range to warm cinnamon browns and subdued greens; and in the next two years it reached a state of virtual grisaille—pale tans, browns,

87

grays—until around 1912/13, when color made its reappearance (as in Dartmouth College's *Guitar on a Table*, NH 11). A study for the central figure in *Three Women* in the Hermitage, Leningrad, the Boston painting was once owned by Daniel-Henry Kahnweiler, a Paris dealer who wrote important treatises on Cubism and a major book on Juan Gris (see MA 184). Interest in the forms of primitive art, inspired by the example of Paul Gauguin, led Picasso in 1906/7 to find fresh sources of creative energy in ancient Iberian and in African and Oceanian sculpture. Into these forms he injected his own sense of violence through sharp edges and angular collisions. He achieved further aggressiveness in *Standing Figure* by making it occupy the full height of the picture surface (contrast Renoir's *Bal à Bougival*), even to the extent of chopping off the top and bottom extremities.

In 1964 the museum purchased Picasso's large *Rape of the Sabines*, painted the year before as a sort of challenge to Jacques Louis David's painting in the Louvre; and eventually a new department of contemporary art was established. "Contemporary" is a less polarizing word than "modern," but modern is what was intended. The first purchase, in 1971, by the department was Jackson Pollock's *Number 10, 1949*. The collection, now fast growing, includes no fewer than six major paintings by the important "color-field" painter, Morris Louis (1912–62). In modern sculpture, David Smith (1906–65) is strongly represented at the museum by two large works, *Cubi XVIII* (1964) and *Zig VIII*,[88] over 8 feet high and fashioned in 1965 in welded and polychromed steel. The title was suggested both by the zigzag directions of the design and by ancient Babylonian ziggurats—winding pyramidal towers ornamented with glazed brick. Against the perfection of a white-rimmed red circle, the girderlike black arms stretch in diagonal opposition.

A glass lamp of the fourteenth century from Mohammedan Syria[89] must stand as a single example of the museum's remarkable collection of Near Eastern decorative art. The ornament, in colored enamels and gold, has a dedicatory inscription around the body, and on the rim a verse from the Koran: "God is the light of the heavens and the earth; His light is as a niche in which is a lamp, and the lamp is in a glass,

89

88

the glass is as though it were a glittering star." Such intricate repetitions and variations in symbolism closely parallel the complexities of the interlaced design.

Our earliest selection from the museum's fabulous Asiatic collections is a *Yaksi Torso*,[90] sandstone, about 29 inches high, from one of the gateways of the Great Stupa at Sānchī, in central India. A masterwork of Buddhist sculpture of the first century B.C., it formed part of the outdoor complex that celebrated the myriad aspects of the phenomenal world. This figure of a tree-dwelling dryad illustrates perfectly the union of spiritual and sensual abundance that is a constant theme in Indian religious art. We must await the nudes of Correggio and Rubens to find anything comparable in Western expression. This transformation of stone into flesh is achieved by lush contours, swelling interior folds, powerful twists of the body, and by the abrupt contrast of the rigid thrust of the thighs. For a discussion of the Great Stupa, including a plan and an elevation, see Benjamin Rowland, *The Art and Architecture of India*, Pelican History of Art.

While Boston's collection of Indian art is outstanding, and its Indian painting reputed to be greater than any collection in India itself, its Chinese and Japanese art is the finest in the Western world. Among the great masterpieces of early Chinese sculpture may be cited the seated *Bodhisattva Maitreya*[91] of the late fifth century A.D. (northern Wei dynasty), and the dedicatory bronze group of the *Buddha Amitabha Trinity and Attendant Deities*,[92] dated A.D. 593 (Sui dynasty). The re-

90

92

91

semblance of such sculpture, especially in the case of the *Maitreya*, to Romanesque art has often been noted: compare the paintings of Boston's Catalonian chapel and the twelfth-century wooden *Virgin and Child* at Worcester (M A 293). The flat plane dominates. There is a minimum of undercutting and of spatial recession: thus their particular appeal to modern eyes. The connection is, of course, purely coincidental, but it has led, with other evidence of widely differing cultures, to a theory of cultural cycles running from the taut "Archaic" stage (seen here and in Romanesque art) to the serene "Classic," to the freewheeling "Baroque." We should be gravely in error to assume that cultures must evolve in this way, for Egyptian and Byzantine cultures did not. Yet it is interesting to speculate whether modern art has created a new archaic stage after the baroque of the nineteenth century.

Both the *Maitreya* and the Sui dynasty shrine are included by Laurence Sickman in the authoritative Pelican History of Art volume on *The Art and Architecture of China.* Of the former (page 49), Sickman notes its purely frontal character and as well its "serenity of spirit." "An anonymous stone-carver," he continues, "has with some naivety and complete sincerity captured a convincing vision of the great Bodhisattva destined to be the Buddha of the future." The shrine is praised (page 61) as an exceptionally complete example of Chinese Buddhist art "in its most vital creative period, the sixth and seventh centuries." He notes that the Buddha and the two Bodhisattvas have "the benign, tender expressions that mark the best Buddhist concepts from the later sixth century."

For discussion of the high "classic" art of the T'ang dynasty (618–906) the reader is referred to the examples discussed at the Fogg Art Museum (M A 134 and 137) and the great stone head at Worcester (M A 311). By the time of the Southern Sung dynasty (1127–1279) painting had so liberated itself from the limitations of drawing and the effects of modeled sculpture as to reach a stage not unlike that ushered in to Italian painting by the great Venetians. In this period Chinese sculpture became markedly pictorial. The seated *Kuan-yin*,[93] one of the Bodhisattvas, or lesser Buddhist deities, is among the greatest known examples of Chinese sculpture of the Sung dynasty. Carved in wood, it dates from the twelfth century. The typical "royal-ease" position suggests a baroque freedom of movement, though it would certainly be an

93

exaggeration to compare it to anything as extreme as a Rubens or a Bernini. The distance in forms that Chinese art has traveled since the late fifth century may be gauged by a comparison to the *Bodhisattva Maitreya*.

Chinese painting followed roughly the same development that we have traced in the selections of Chinese sculpture. If there is any truth in thinking of Sung art as relatively baroque, the great flowering of painting in this age may be cited in support of such a contention. In a Baroque age, architecture and sculpture generally yield their dominant position to painting, and in turn are marked by a desire to compete with painting on its own ground. However this may be, the *Nine Dragons Scroll*[94] by Ch'ên Jung (c. 1210–c. 1261), nearly 36 feet long and one of the most celebrated of all Chinese paintings, unwinds its mysteries in volutes of mist and water. We can learn to respond to the subtleties of the Chinese mind only by repeated exposure and long contemplation. With the least of means—a few scratches and washes in ink heightened by pale suggestions of color—the artist has achieved, almost five hundred years before Leonardo da Vinci, what Leonardo sought to achieve in his drawings of the waters.

Another scroll from the Sung period, *Ladies Preparing Newly Woven Silk*[95] by Emperor Hui Tsung (1082–1135), will strike the observer as much more restrained and much less atmospheric than the preceding example. An explanation may lie in the fact that a later inscription tells us that the imperial artist copied it from a picture by Chang Hsüan, a court painter of the earlier T'ang dynasty. This much smaller scroll, under 5 feet in length, emphasizes elegance and dainty coloring rather than the unearthly mystery of the *Nine Dragons Scroll*. Our illustrations of both are limited to the final section, that is, the left end of each scroll. In accordance with Far Eastern reading habits, such scrolls are regularly unrolled from right to left. It is, of course, as arbitrary to cut off any section as it would be to do the same to a musical score. In these and other ways Far Eastern art challenges our Western conception of the

94

95

framed picture, and even our assumption of the separate categories of the several arts.

Japanese culture, profoundly influenced by the Chinese, increasingly developed its own inflection and style. If the tenth-century (Fujiwara) *Buddhist Deity* at Yale (CT 65) is a harsher, more earthbound variant of T'ang dynasty sculpture, emphasis on warlike exploits in Japanese art left little opportunity for such cosmic expressions as the *Nine Dragons Scroll*. (The dragon was the ultimate symbol for the *Tao*, the elemental vital force of the universe.) A vast cultural divide separates that Sung dynasty masterpiece of the twelfth century from *The Burning of Sanjo Palace*,[96] a scroll of the thirteenth century (Kamakura period) almost 23 feet long that is said to rival anything even in the imperial collections in Tokyo. There can be no hesitation in calling it one of the great war pictures in the world. Our illustration, from near the central portion of this epic, shows approximately a fifth of the whole. Unrolled from the right, it rises gradually to a great crescendo; then, following the conflagration, the action subsides until at the extreme left a single horseman leads the triumphal procession. An analogy to Western symphonic movement is inescapable. Our segment also exemplifies the Japanese method of describing spatial recession—not by converging parallels, but by parallel diagonals. An advantage of this system over Western one-point perspective is that objects in the distance that we know are the same size as foreground ones appear that way here—and we can see them with equal clarity. Furthermore, no illusionistic "hole" is pierced through the paper ground; thus the medium itself is respected.

Monkeys,[97] a six-fold screen, ink on paper dated 1491, is the work of Sesshū (1420–1506), a leading painter of the Muromachi period. That he was a contemporary of such Western artists as Dieric Bouts (MA 100) merely reinforces the difficulty of adjusting our sights as we approach the art of another world. After we study Sesshū's subtle brushwork and peer through his vapors, it is not surprising to learn that he traveled in China and visited Zen monasteries, nor that at this time the Japanese venerated Sung dynasty painting.

96

97

Brockton Art Museum

Location: Oak St., in D. W. Field Park; take exit 18B from Route 24, west of the city; follow Oak St. (Route 37) east. The museum is on your left
Hours: Open daily except Mon. 1-5; on Thurs. 1-10 P.M. except in July and August
Admission: Charged

Opened in 1969, the museum was made possible by the generosity of Myron Leslie Fuller. In that year the architect, J. Timothy Anderson, received the national blue-ribbon award for excellence from the Society of American Registered Architects. The building was cited as "one of America's finest small museums . . . in a brilliantly achieved environment, growing naturally and gracefully out of its surrounding woods and rocky grounds." I suspect you will have no quarrel with that estimate.

The museum maintains an active program of temporary exhibitions, lectures, and art classes, and its public is both numerous and enthusiastic. While the permanent collection is not large, it has range and it is growing. Two of the finest paintings are on indefinite loan from the Brockton Public Library: the *Portrait of Walter Copeland Bryant*, a late work of 1903 by Thomas Eakins, and that of *Abel Willard Kingman* by the stylish Italian master Giovanni Boldini. Both Bryant and Kingman were distinguished residents of Brockton. Emphasis within the collection as it develops is on contemporary American art of a conservative character.

Busch-Reisinger Museum, Harvard University

Location: 29 Kirkland Street, at Divinity Avenue
Hours: Mon.-Sat. 9-4:45; in July and August Mon.-Fri. 9-4:45
Admission: Free. Ⓗ by arrangement

The museum was founded in 1902 as a center for the study of Germanic culture. A part of Harvard University, it is administered by the Fogg Art Museum. The building, erected in 1921 in a style that visitors to Munich will quickly recognize, contains a large Romanesque hall, with casts of German medieval sculpture, and generous space in smaller galleries. As a result of the rapid growth of the Fogg Art Museum, rich holdings in Netherlandish art have in recent years been moved to the Busch-Reisinger Museum; today it thus offers a superb survey of northern European art, that of France and England excluded. The collection is very strong in modern German art, including study material relating to the famous Bauhaus movement (1919–33) and to the architect Walter Gropius and the painter Lyonel Feininger (see MA 277). Organ concerts are given in the Romanesque hall on an instrument fashioned on authentic Baroque design.

Four colossal sandstone statues of *The Seasons*, of which we reproduce *Summer*,[98] occupy the corners of the great hall. Attributed to Johann Joachim Günther (1717–89), they came from the gardens of the palace at Bruchsal, summer residence of the Prince Bishop of Speyer, and were acquired by the Fogg Museum in 1952. The low bases have appropriate seasonal reliefs with frames of rocaille design marked by the irregular C-shaped element that is so characteristic of the Rococo style. The figures are loaded with allegory, but through their svelte undulation, carried through from top to bottom, and through fluid twists of head, torso, and limbs, they take artistic precedence over these accessories. The German Rococo lilt is heavier than its French counterpart, and the nudity is a bit more self-conscious, but these signs of provincial-

98

ism are surely more engaging than detrimental. The date is about 1760–65.

From the excellent casts, one can study masterpieces of German sculpture from the eleventh-century bronze doors of St. Michael's at Hildesheim to the great stone rood screen of the thirteenth century at Naumburg and the Golden Gate of Freiburg Cathedral. An original unpainted wood statue of *St. John Evangelist*, c. 1490–1500, is close to the art of Tilman Riemenschneider, Germany's most expressive late Gothic sculptor. From the neighboring Austrian Tyrol comes a 5-foot painted wood *Madonna and Child*,[99] c. 1430, standing on a crescent moon and crowned with one of the most elaborate examples you are ever likely to see. Note how the swinging lines of the drapery, beginning at Mary's feet, lead you up to it. The rustic innocence of this version of the theme contrasts greatly with the regal poise of the larger example at the Boston Museum of Fine Arts, dating from c. 1450–60 (MA 63). In the base is a small shelf for exhibiting a relic or an offering.

Outstanding among the many fine early Netherlandish paintings are a *St. Jerome in His Study* by Joos van Cleve, c. 1520, and a white-robed *Angel* against a blue-green landscape by an unidentified artist whose expressive power was considerable. But finest of all is a *Half-length Madonna and Child*,[100] oil on panel, by Dieric Bouts (c. 1420–75), the probable author of a precious silverpoint drawing at Smith College (MA 170). Bouts, born at Haarlem, worked in Louvain after the late 1440s. His early pictures combine the meticulousness of Jan van Eyck with the broader, more sculptural style of Roger van der Weyden; but by the mid-1460s, when he must have painted the *Half-length Madonna and Child*, Roger's influence was much the stronger. Comparison with Roger's *St. Luke Painting the Virgin* at Boston (MA 66) will make that clear, especially in the figure of the Child. Another Bouts *Virgin and Child*, in the London National Gallery, dated about 1465, is nearly a mirror image of the Busch-Reisinger example. There is great sensitivity in Bouts's hands (and feet), but the faces are characteristically impassive. The scale is large and imposing, despite an actual height of only 12 inches. An accentuation of the vertical, crossed by rather rigid diagonals, avoids tenderness in favor of the effect of a spiritual icon.

99

100

Infrared photography has revealed a great rarity beneath the *Madonna and Child*: a study of a full-length female nude. No painting by Bouts of this subject, unaccompanied, is known, and only a couple by other Netherlandish masters of the period. An Eve is immediately suggested, but there is no Adam. We are left with two mysteries: who she is, and why Bouts abandoned his original project.

Impassive is surely the word for the *Portrait of a Lady Holding a Flower*,[101] by Barthel Bruyn the Elder (1493–1555), painter of Cologne. This north German contemporary of Hans Holbein the Younger (see MA 43) was a much less incisive portraitist—though the face has a certain charm in its fugitive expression—but he produced superb ornaments in the guise of portraiture and he seems to have had an obsession about fingers in contorted frozen positions. The wiry activity of crisp line and small detail descend from German late Gothic art; and while there is some evidence of a Renaissance understanding of anatomy, the figure conveys no such sense of ease as do Holbein's.

For the eighteenth century, apart from many fine porcelains, there are two three-dimensional models for altars, a red chalk *Assumption of the Virgin* attributed to the architect-sculptor Egid Qurin Asam; and an upper Austrian *Crucifixion* group, c. 1700–25 in pearwood, with the customarily charming flying *putti* and a Rococo cartouche. Most impressive, however, is a *Return of the Holy Family from Egypt*, in painted and gilded wood some 3 feet high, the work of Meinrad Guggenbichler (1649–1723). This fine sculptor, whom we shall discuss in more detail at Wellesley College (MA 235), flourished in the lovely lake region north and east of Salzburg. The date of the Busch-Reisinger altar group is probably just before 1700.

Emil Nolde (1867–1956) was an early and commanding figure in the development of modern German painting. Born Hansen, he took his artistic name from his birthplace just south of the Danish frontier. Of humble peasant stock, he found little to interest him in the slick productions of the later nineteenth-century German academies. He managed to travel a great deal outside Germany, and he was a pioneer, after Gauguin, in responding enthusiastically to the art of primitive cultures. The *Mulatto*,[102] painted in 1915, has the inner expressiveness

101

102

and the formal simplification of African masks, here accentuated by color of an almost savage brilliance. The composition in concentric circles, like that sometimes used by Vincent van Gogh, has a hypnotic effect. The juxtaposed reds, pinks, oranges, and yellows are inherited from Gauguin, but the strong accents of black are Nolde's own; a headband of green provides exciting contrast. At a size of 30½ by 28¾ inches, this vivid oil is not likely to be missed.

As we consider further Harvard's extraordinary riches in this field, a catalogue by Charles L. Kuhn with an introductory essay by Jakob Rosenberg, *German Expressionism and Abstract Art: the Harvard Collections* (Harvard University Press, 1957), should be mentioned for its fine background coverage as well as its complete listing. As you turn its pages—and study the original works—it is worth remembering that all these artists were declared "degenerate" by the Nazis. All of them proclaim the primacy of the artist's imagination; and in a totalitarian society that cannot be endured. Such artists as were still alive in the 1930s and had not left Germany were deprived of working materials, their market shut off, or were otherwise persecuted. Museums that owned their art were forced to sell it.

As early as 1905 a group of painters born in the 1880s joined together at Dresden, and later in Berlin, under the name of Die Brücke (The Bridge). The name signified their sense of connection with Germany's great medieval past, overarching the worldly extravagance of the Renaissance and Rococo eras and especially the hollow academicism of the nineteenth century. They invited the older Emil Nolde to exhibit with them. He did in 1905–07 but then preferred to pursue his own solitary career. The leading spirit in this movement was Ernst L. Kirchner and his most important associates were Erich Heckel, Karl Schmidt-Rottluff, Max Pechstein, and Otto Müller.

Erich Heckel (1883–1970) painted *To The Convalescent Woman*,[103] a triptych 7 feet long, in 1912/13. Like the sculptor Ernst Barlach, he was deeply influenced by Vincent van Gogh, a variant of whose sunflowers appears in a totally new and sickly color scheme at the right. The nude figure at the left suggests African sculpture, another source of inspiration for these intense and primitive-oriented artists. This is easily the most important German Expressionist painting in New England, and it is Heckel's acknowledged masterpiece. Formerly in the Folkwang Museum at Essen, it was forcibly sold during the Nazi regime as "degenerate" art. Both Heckel and Kirchner produced woodcut variants of the central panel. The museum owns an impression of Heckel's version.

103

Woodcut was as important a medium for the German Expressionists as oil painting, and many critics find in their prints (frequently based on their paintings but even more concentrated and powerful) an even higher degree of expressiveness. They made superb lithographs and etchings; but it was the woodcut process, so closely allied to wood sculpture—with its cracks and splinterings—that had a special affinity with these artists' sense of violence in a soon-to-be-war-torn world. The *Convalescent* surely attains a symbolic significance.

The early paintings of the Bridge Group were marked by the curvilinear forms of Nolde and of other older artists (Toulouse-Lautrec, Matisse); but after 1910 the angularities of Cubist art (and of African sculpture) replaced them. This can be seen not only in the Heckel just discussed but in *Self-Portrait with a Cat*,[104] by Ernst L. Kirchner (1880–1938)—even though the pink-red-orange-green palette of Gauguin-inspired Nolde still remains. The date is 1918. The splintered forms aspire to Gothic verticality in this 4-foot-high image of psychological torment. As almost invariably in modern German art, the blacks thunder ominously.

The pen drawing of *Herwarth Walden*[105] by Oskar Kokoschka (1886–1980) may serve to remind us that great masters of line are not limited to the distant past. Kokoschka, an independent Austrian artist, was especially active in avant-garde circles in Berlin, where Herwarth Walden published *Der Sturm* (The Storm), an influential magazine supportive of modern art. Observe the variety of line here, its range of thickness, its shorthand conventions for indicating projections, hollows, shadow, and even the glint of light on glass. Not a stroke is wasted, and each one is set down with a skilled surgeon's decisiveness. The date is 1910; the world evoked is surely that of Sigmund Freud. When not on exhibition, the drawing is kept at the Fogg Museum.

We continue with two watercolors by painters, neither of them German by birth, who exerted a tremendous influence on modern German art. Wassily Kandinsky (1866–1944) came from Russia; Paul Klee (1879–1940), from German Switzerland. In Munich they formed a

104

105

friendship that was to last throughout their lives. In revolt against the worn-out teachings of academic artists, Kandinsky founded in Munich the so-called Blue Rider group (1911) in association with Klee, Franz Marc, and others. The group took its name from one of Kandinsky's early paintings. Soon after the opening of the Bauhaus at Weimar in 1919, the director, Walter Gropius, called both Kandinsky and Klee to its staff; they taught at the Bauhaus until Nazi pressure forced its dissolution in 1933. (Gropius, who later taught architecture at Harvard, was the chief designer of the Harvard Graduate Center.)

Landscape[106] (1918), by Kandinsky, is a work of his rare "Russian period." He was in Moscow during the war, but few of the works of that time are known outside Russia itself. Perhaps under the influence of currents then prevailing in Russian art, Kandinsky sharpened his lines and reduced the atmospheric effects of his better-known "Blue Rider" works, but their animated movement still prevails. Klee's gentle little fantasy *Magnetic Apparatus for Plant Cultivation*[107] (1921) is almost like a Swiss toy. In its expressive atmosphere and its textures and brooding color, it is thoroughly Germanic. Klee's world of magic is seen as if under a magnifying glass, but the forces he evokes tell us, obliquely or not, of life and death.

Self-Portrait in a Tuxedo[108] (1927) by Max Beckmann (1884–1950) is characteristically German in its inner force, in its acid hues dominated by blacks, whites, and grays, and in its starkly angular shapes. The informality of the pose, including the cigarette, strikes a contemporary

106

108

107

note. Like many German painters from Dürer onward, Beckmann was an important printmaker. A refugee from Nazi tyranny, he became a very influential teacher in America, first in St. Louis and later in Brooklyn. A natural sympathy seems to bring modern German and younger American artists together.

At first glance, one assumes that Beckmann's self-portrait is life-size; but the actual height is 56 inches, and since the figure is cut off well above the knees, that would make him very tall indeed. Actually, Beckmann was under six feet, and of broad, muscular build. Again, German-Gothic verticality carries the day: the rigid axis, the line of the window at the side, the direction of a thumb and of the all-important cigarette, and finally the acute spear-shaped angle between the legs. Furthermore, observe how the starched shirt is divided vertically by gray shadow (its tone repeated in the claustrophobic non-view out the window), the vertical steps of black shadow up the face, modeling it, and two strokes of reddish brown (borrowed from the color of the window frame) in the center of the lower forehead—adding yet another touch of grimness to this severe face. The powerful angular pose of the black arms is echoed in the position of the left hand. And what blacks in this image!

Well represented in this museum are the leading figures in modern German sculpture, for the most part by several works each. Born in the 1870s are Ernst Barlach and Georg Kolbe; in the 1880s, Hans Arp, Rudolf Belling, Wilhelm Lehmbruck, Gerhard Marcks, and Renée Sintenis. Associated with the Bauhaus movement (whether in Germany or in its later manifestation at Chicago) are Josef Albers, Herbert Bayer, and László Moholy-Nagy. Arp is best seen, however, in the Harkness Commons of the Harvard Graduate Center, for which he designed a large plywood screen; and Bayer, in the same location in a mural painting, *Verdure*, and in an unglazed tile mural adjacent to a brick relief by Josef Albers. (The center also boasts an oil mural by Joan Miró and an outdoor metal sculpture by the American sculptor Richard Lippold.) Since the building itself is by Walter Gropius, the Graduate Center may be thought of as an extension of the Busch-Reisinger Museum's coverage of the Bauhaus and its activities.

Gerhard Marcks (born 1889) is the author of *Prometheus*,[109] a bronze of 1948, some 30 inches high. He was strongly influenced by Wilhelm Lehmbruck (see MA 240), whose late masterpiece, the *Seated*

109

Youth (1918) at Duisburg, the *Prometheus* somewhat resembles. Marcks's forms are more angular than Lehmbruck's and thus closer to those of Barlach. Their inner tension is strongly felt. Note how the tied hands of the figure are balanced against the bent head across the void of the torso framed by the arms. As you move around the *Prometheus* the empty spaces take their place as positive elements in the composition.

The 7-foot figure of a *Crippled Beggar*[110] by Ernst Barlach (1870–1938) should be compared in its emaciated forms to the reproduction of the Romanesque bronze Crucifix of the abbey of Werden, in the stairwell off the Romanesque hall. Nothing could better illustrate the dependence of modern German art on its own early medieval traditions. This most important work by Barlach in the United States is a second casting in dark vitreous clay (it may be called clinker) of one of three figures that Barlach completed by 1930 for niches in the facade of the fourteenth-century brick Gothic church of St. Catherine at Lübeck. The extra cast was made to be sold to help defray the expenses of the project. Using a medieval language of expression, Barlach evokes a modern world of sorrow and suffering. Comparison with New London's cast of *Singing Boy* (CT 93), of 1928, will show similar Gothic angularities in a theme of gentler import.

We have left to the end a brief description of Moholy-Nagy's highly complex *Light-Space Modulator*, of 1923–30, exhibited in a special gallery. A photograph would tell you what it looks like, but it could give no idea of what it is meant to be. Its aluminum and chrome-plated surfaces are designed to be activated by an electric motor equipped with chain belts. Lighted by spotlights in the darkened room, and casting moving shadows on walls and ceiling, it echoes the modern cityscape as seen at night.

In closing, mention should be made of Harvard's rich collection of modern German prints, housed with other graphic treasures at the Fogg Art Museum. Some decades ago, Jakob Rosenberg, then the curator of prints, and Charles L. Kuhn, then the curator of the Busch-Reisinger Museum, took advantage of current low prices (which have subsequently skyrocketed) to develop one of the outstanding collections in the modern German and Austrian field. With this superb supplement to its holdings in German painting, drawing, and sculpture, Harvard dominates

110

the German field in this country in much the same way that Yale dominates the British field with its new British Center.

Excellent catalogues of the collection are available, including a selection of one hundred works, each with a full-page illustration, published in 1980. In the summer of that year a selection of the same magnitude was exhibited at the National Gallery in Washington.

Fogg Art Museum, Harvard University

Location: Quincy Street at Broadway
Hours: Mon.-Wed. and Fri. 9-5, Thurs. 9-9, Sat. 10-5, Sun. 2-5
Admission: Free. Ⓗ

The Fogg Art Museum houses the most extensive collection of art owned by any university in the world, England excepted. Founded in 1891 and first housed in the former Hunt Hall (1895), it moved to the present building in 1927. From the earliest days of art-historical studies at Harvard the importance of having original examples at hand was clearly understood. Boston was, of course, not so easily accessible from Cambridge; even today there is no substitute for direct and immediate contact with the original work of art.

The college (or university) museum is little known in Europe outside England. This is partly a matter of geography, for the European universities are situated in great cities with their huge artistic resources, while American colleges and universities are usually to be found in the country or in the smaller towns. Whatever the reason, the early collections at Bowdoin, Yale, and Harvard have led to the founding of so many college museums that they have become a unique feature of American cultural life.

The visitor should realize, therefore, that a museum such as the Fogg has a different function from the city museum. It must play an active part in liberal education at both the undergraduate and the graduate level. Its exhibits must change frequently to satisfy the demands of many departments in the university. The visitor should not expect, therefore, to find all of my selections on view at any one time.

Among the special features of the Fogg Museum is a research laboratory for the preservation and restoration of works of art, a collection of drawings rivaled in America only by those of the Metropolitan Museum and the Morgan Library in New York, a superb collection of European art of the late eighteenth and early nineteenth centuries, and holdings of extraordinary quality in Far Eastern art. The latter were established by the late Langdon Warner, who conducted archaeological expeditions to enrich them, and in 1943 they were vastly enlarged by the Grenville Winthrop bequest, also rich in early nineteenth-century art. Today, with the combined resources of Boston and Harvard University, the area is unsurpassed in the world as a center for Far Eastern studies.

A cooperative lending policy links the important print collection of the Fogg Museum with the superb collections of rare illustrated books and illuminated manuscripts owned by the Widener and Houghton libraries at Harvard. Photography is also included in the Fogg's print department.

Construction of the Carpenter Center, designed by Le Corbusier, on the adjoining Quincy Street property brought the practice of art to a level commensurate with the study of art history. Growth of the Fogg's collections has proceeded at such a rate that, as of this writing, plans are well advanced toward the construction of an extensive addition. When this is completed, Quincy Street will become a kind of Avenue des Arts with its sequence of the Carpenter, the Fogg Art Museum, its new extension, the School of Design, and at the far end the Busch-Reisinger Museum, then beyond it, on Divinity Avenue, the Peabody Museum.

Following its opening in 1927, the Fogg exerted influential leadership in conservation of works of art and in the training of museum personnel. These were the respective fields of the two co-directors, Edward Forbes and Paul Sachs. During the 1930s and until other institutions began to catch up with Harvard, an overwhelming proportion of younger directors of American art museums were Harvard-trained. Mr. Sachs, who was not a tall man, objected to the then current habit of hanging pictures well above his line of vision. His influence in lowering them dominated American museum practice for several decades; but today's growth of collections has often necessitated superimposing them.

The representation of ancient art at the Fogg Museum is not extensive, but there are superb examples. The finest work of Graeco-Roman sculpture is a life-size marble figure of the hunter *Meleager*.[111] In style it is close to what is known of the work of Scopas, a leading artist at the time of Alexander the Great. Like most surviving antique statues, this is a later copy, probably Roman in date, but the copyist was unusually competent and spirited. Best known for the twisted action and inner expressiveness of his figures, Scopas is sometimes referred to as the initiator of the Baroque point of view in Western art. Note how the body contours of the *Meleager* make the eye wind around and behind the figure, and break up the sense of the frontal plane. Note also the expressive use of shadow produced by undercutting at the eyes and mouth.

Warburg Hall, on the ground floor, contains some of the Fogg's important collection of French and Spanish capitals of the Romanesque period. Thirteen of these come from Moûtier-Saint-Jean, in Burgundy (about 1130). The material (limestone) is the same as that from which the church and its monastic cloister were constructed. While this identity

111

of materials also occurred in Greek sculpture and architecture (marble), it was not characteristic of the Romans, who thought of sculpture as a part of a veneer of precious materials to be applied to the entire surface of a core of brick and rubble. Observe how the Romanesque designer adapted the form of the Corinthian capital, inherited from ancient Rome, to the special demands of telling the story of *Cain and Abel*,[112] symbolizing the conflict of good and evil. Necessarily, he departs from Greek canons of proportion, warping the figure to make it fit the architectural shape. Below Cain and Abel, who present offerings under the Hand of God, the base is strengthened by an altar in the form of a symmetrical double-headed eagle—a frequent device inherited from the early Christian Near East and, in turn, all the way back to ancient Mesopotamian art. It makes an interesting comparison with the Toulouse capital at Amherst College (MA 3), where the device shifts to two birds with a single head.

A 4-foot marble statue, *The Angel of the Annunciation*,[113] attributed to Arnolfo di Cambio (1260–1302), is said to have come from the facade of the old Cathedral of Florence. Its rough, plebeian character parallels that of Florence's chief contemporary painter, Giotto. It diverges markedly from the elegance of late thirteenth- and early fourteenth-century French art, favored in Siena. Though the large painting attributed to Giotto's chief pupil and godson, Taddeo Gaddi (active 1334–66), *St. Francis Receiving the Stigmata*,[114] is in very damaged

112

113

114

condition and is at best an echo of a similar picture in the Louvre, a comparison of it with the squat proportions of Arnolfo's angel and the blunt turns of heavy drapery hiding the figure's articulation will be instructive. This very large tempera panel, 7½ feet high, and the small one we have discussed at the Gardner Museum (MA 33), give the best idea of Giotto's art that can be found in American museums. For the study of Giotto himself, so celebrated that Dante praised him, there is no substitute for a journey to Padua and to Florence.

Siena, Florence's great rival in the fourteenth century and only fifty miles away, seems ages apart in basic attitude. Though Sienese painters also worked in fresco, egg tempera on gold-ground panel was their preferred medium. Here the exquisite refinement of color and of the goldworker's craft found freer expression. A small *Crucifixion*[115] by Simone Martini (1285–1344), chief painter of Siena after Duccio and chief rival of Giotto in Italy, is a prime example of Sienese art, despite the much larger size of the stiffly Byzantine polyptych in the Gardner Museum (MA 34). One is reminded of manuscript illumination, in which Simone engaged at the papal court of Avignon, where he may have executed this little panel late in his career, and of the svelte figurines of Parisian ivory carving of the same time, such as the superb example at Worcester (MA 294).

Fra Angelico's *Crucifixion*,[116] one of the major possessions of the Fogg Museum and indeed of any American museum in the field of Early Renaissance painting, displays a Florentine resilience in the figures not to be found in Sienese art. Everything about Fra Angelico (1378–1455) would seem to have turned him away from the secular interests of the Florentine Renaissance. He was a Dominican friar, an extremely pious man, and a pupil of entirely medieval masters. We should note, however, that the *Crucifixion* is a very late work, probably from the time of his frescoes in the chapel of Nicholas V in the Vatican.

116

115

We turn now to one of the master drawings in the Fogg's great collection, the *Portrait of Susanna of Bavaria*[117] by Albrecht Dürer (1471–1528). A late work (1521), it was drawn in indelible silverpoint, or zinc point, on prepared green-tinted paper. On the sleeve there are traces of heightening in white to increase the sculptural modeling. Like most great German artists, including Goethe and Thomas Mann, Dürer felt the pull of the South, and so he became a European artist without forsaking his deep Northern roots. Compared with a High Renaissance work of the time, such as the slightly earlier Raphael at the Gardner Museum (MA 41), this portrait is more individualized, but without any sacrifice in formal clarity and construction.

Orazio Gentileschi (1563–1639), whose *Madonna and the Sleeping Christ Child*[118] we now consider, is usually grouped with the followers of Caravaggio. This is true to the extent that, after arriving in Rome as a teenager from his native Pisa, he was eventually attracted to the early work of that master, as exemplified by Hartford's *Ecstasy of St. Francis* (CT 12); but he did not follow Caravaggio's dramatic and tenebrous later style. What attracted him was the master's new informality and intimacy, and his love of light playing on smooth fabrics. Gentileschi developed a special palette favoring lemon yellows and pale blues, seen in the Fogg's fine example, dating from c. 1610. In 1621 he moved to Genoa, then on to Turin and Paris, and finally to London, where he remained from 1626 to his death. He had apparently met Van Dyck in Genoa, and through him became a court painter for King Charles I. In his excellent survey, *Italian Baroque Painting* (London: Phaidon Press, 1960), Ellis K. Waterhouse aptly summarizes Gentileschi's art as having an "odd combination of naturalism, intimacy, and elegance." His daughter Artemisia became the most important woman artist of her time —and one of the first.

Cutting across time and space, let us compare two magnificent examples of the Baroque style in painting. Small as they are, Rubens's 1635 oil sketch for a composition (now in Dresden, *Quos Ego, Neptune*

117

118

Commanding the Waters[119] (from Virgil's *Aeneid*), and Delacroix's *Giaour and Pasha*[120] of 1856 (from the poem by Byron) surpass many larger works by these masters where the execution was entrusted to assistants or where for other reasons the inspiration faltered. For Delacroix (1798–1863) the Romanticism of the new century implied a return to the vehement art of Peter Paul Rubens (1577–1640). As often happens in the history of Western art, a revolution finds its source by skipping over the previous hundred years. It is worth pointing out that both these masters of Baroque energy were highly disciplined and intellectual men. In both, the heart was subject to the mind. Both moved in complex social circles. Both were inveterate correspondents, and Delacroix kept a journal that rivals Dürer's and Leonardo's in profundity and extensiveness of observation. Both paintings come from the final ten years of the artists' careers. Fundamentally, Delacroix and Rubens are so similar that it is hard to realize the passage of over two hundred years and the shift of taste from classical literature to the exotic Near East.

The Rubens sketch, oil on panel about 20 inches high, dates from 1635. It celebrates allegorically what is described in the full title: *The Happy Voyage of Cardinal Infante Ferdinand of Spain from Barcelona to Genoa*—that is, with Neptune's help, on his way to a triumphal entry into Antwerp as the new governor of the Netherlands. In this sketch, as in another at Yale's British Center (CT 52), we see Rubens at his most spontaneous, his forms at their most fluid.

Similar spontaneity, expressed in the medium of terra-cotta, can be seen in Rubens's alter ego in sculpture, Giovanni Lorenzo Bernini (1598–1680). The life-size *Head of St. Jerome*[121] is one of the most

119

121

120

spectacular in a series of twenty-seven studies (*bozzetti*) owned by the Fogg and designed by Bernini for some of his most important marble sculptures. The marble *St. Jerome* fills a niche in the Chigi Chapel of the Cathedral of Siena. The chapel, designed by Bernini himself, also includes a figure of *St. Mary Magdalen*. The date is 1661–63. The Fogg's head closely resembles the final version, but spontaneity was inevitably lost in the transfer to marble. In the terra-cotta we can almost participate in the action of modeling and scraping. Tool marks are evident, and we half expect to find the master's fingerprints, as we do in Carpeaux's terra-cotta head at Wellesley (MA 237). At the time of the Rubens and Delacroix paintings just discussed the artists were both fifty-eight; Bernini was in his mid-sixties when he molded the *Head of St. Jerome*. All three were at the height of their careers.

Another *St. Jerome*,[122] this time a three-quarters figure in oil 50 inches high, is by Jusepe de Ribera (1588–1656). Signed and dated 1640, it is a first-class example of the work of this Sevillian who moved to Spanish-owned Naples about 1616 and worked there until his death. Deeply influenced by the later art of Caravaggio, he infused it with his Spanish reserve and austerity, and with his intense observation of detail. The subject was a favorite of his, and it afforded him an opportunity to enrich his somber black and brown palette with the deep red of the saint's traditional robe. Perhaps the skull, held in his left hand, is the finest element in this moving picture of quiet meditation.

In the century of the Grand Manner, dominated by Baroque explosions of Rubens and Bernini, we forget too easily the counterforce of Classicism—important for understanding Rubens as well, for he developed an impressive collection of ancient marbles in his great house in Antwerp and many of his painted figures were derived either from them or from celebrated examples he saw in Rome. Nicolas Poussin (1594–1665) is the outstanding Classicist in the Baroque Age. If Rubens was inspired by the late proto-Baroque style of Titian (see MA 45), Poussin reverted to that of Raphael (see MA 41). Arriving from France in his youth, he matured in Rome under the influence of conservative painters like Domenichino. Occasionally, as in the Hartford *Crucifixion* (CT 16), he worked in the dramatic spirit of the era, but more frequently, as in the Fogg's *Holy Family*,[123] c. 1650, his art was as intellectually ordered as the reasoning of Descartes. Note the pyramidal construction capped

122

123

by rectangular solids, and the suggestion of early Corot and Cézanne in the landscape on the right. Yet Poussin's pen-and-wash drawings are strongly Baroque in style. This fact helps us understand that his painting was a process of shaping his initial image to fit a dominant ideal. In a Baroque century, he felt, like Milton, a need for clarity, and achieved it through emulation of classical forms. Visitors should not miss another superb Poussin, *The Birth of Bacchus*, an elegiac, hushed work of 1657. Here he speaks of death as well as of generation. As the infant Bacchus is entrusted to the care of the Nymphs, Echo sorrows for the death of Narcissus—whose passing brings to life a beautiful white flower.

To the superb works of Rembrandt van Rijn (1606–69), painted in the 1630s, which we discussed at the Gardner Museum—and the imposing Elison portraits of 1634 at the Museum of Fine Arts—we now add a modest but magical *Head of Christ*,[124] painted about 1648–52. On an oak panel only 10 inches high, it dominates any gallery in which it is hung. We can quickly orient the reader as to Rembrandt's development by a reminder that *Dr. Tulp's Anatomy Lesson* was painted in 1632, the *Night Watch* in 1642, and *The Syndics* in 1661. The date of the *Head of Christ* can be bounded, so to speak, by the *Supper at Emmaus* (Louvre) of 1648—the two Christ heads have similarities— and *Aristotle Contemplating the Bust of Homer* (Metropolitan Museum of Art, New York) of 1653. From there he moved on to such masterpieces of the final decade as the *Self-Portrait* in the Frick Museum, New York, the *Portrait of Jan Six* (Six House, Amsterdam), and the transcendent *Self-Portrait* of about 1663 at Kenwood, outside London. Of the last-named work, Kenneth Clark, in *Looking at Pictures* (Boston: Beacon Press, paperback, 1968), wrote that "the humility of Rembrandt's colossal genius warns the art historian to shut up." That is what I propose to do about the Fogg's *Head of Christ*.

The museum also owns two early paintings by Rembrandt, one a self-portrait, and a wonderful selection of drawings by the master and his followers; in the print department there is much more. The paintings and drawings are studied in an authoritative article by the director, Seymour Slive, in *Apollo* magazine, June 1978, pages 453–63.

If we skip over the Fogg's riches in eighteenth-century art—drawings

124

by Watteau and the Tiepolos, top-grade portraits by Gainsborough and Copley, and much more—that is only because we discuss these masters elsewhere.

Jacques Louis David (1748–1825) is seen here in one of his finest portraits, of *Emmanuel Sièyes, Aged Sixty-nine*,[125] signed and dated in 1817. It came to Harvard in 1943 in the bequest of Grenville Winthrop. One easily understands that Raphael was David's chief source of inspiration, as he was for Poussin. Never was the French sense of disciplined energy more in evidence than in this portrait of a colleague in the days of the Revolutionary Convention, or in the celebrated *Death of Marat*. David's place in history as the leader of the Neoclassic movement is secure when based on such compositions of Greek and Roman history as *The Death of Socrates* and the *Oath of the Horatii* (painted in Rome in 1784); but his portraits demonstrate that he was more than that. It would not be an exaggeration to call him the Classicist among the Neoclassicists. With the exception of Ingres, his disciples—their name is legion—seem to have been caught up in a fashion rather than to have been great pioneering spirits.

It is now well understood that Neoclassicism was a preliminary form of the Romantic movement; and David must be credited with that development too. One of the most dominating figures of any age, he inspired reaction as well as idolatry. He was Géricault's point of departure, and after Géricault Romanticism reached its highest pitch in Delacroix, whose *Giaour and Pasha*, already discussed, marks its flaming and passionate end.

Jacques Ange Dominique Ingres (1780–1867), the most important pupil of David and his assistant in the execution of the celebrated *Portrait of Madame Récamier* (Louvre, 1800), injected a potent element of sensuality into the forms of David as he developed his own style. While his male portraits have much in common with David's, his female ones, and especially his nudes set in an exotic Oriental harem environment, mark the new and clearly Romantic direction that this irascible pundit of classical theory actually followed in his painting. *Odalisque with Slave*,[126] painted in 1839, could hardly differ more from David's athletic nude Greeks and Romans—males all, with only a few

125

126

exceptions. Never has sinuous line been more sexually evocative; and color, with touches of Leonardesque shadow, runs to oblique, secondary tones (David liked red, white, and blue). Ingres's anatomy is distorted for similar sensual effect. André Lhote, a minor Cubist painter but a major teacher in the Paris of the 1930s, made his models attempt the impossible—to assume Ingres's exact poses—in order to convince his classes that distortion can be artistically indispensable. The stomach of the Slave is a masterpiece of soft sculpture. Like an apple seen from the top, it is observed as a larger breast with an indentation in lieu of a nipple. Followers of Ingres, more faithful than he to Academic rules—like Bouguereau and Gérôme—missed these subtleties.

The formidable drawing of a *Negro Soldier*,[127] in sepia and gray wash over pencil, is a consummate example of the art of Théodore Géricault (1791–1824). In the history of nineteenth-century French painting Géricault stands midway between David and Delacroix. As in David's *Sièyes*, the figure is placed squarely across the picture surface in a formal and geometric arrangement; yet the play of light and dark is as rich as in Goya or Rembrandt, and the subject (Moorish) also opened up new possibilities for Delacroix, who found in Géricault his most immediate inspiration. Note how the grays take on a bluish tinge in the context of the sepia washes, so that the whole range of warm and cool tones is suggested, but with the utmost economy of means. This is one of many master drawings given to the Fogg Art Museum by Paul and Meta Sachs.

That Pierre-Auguste Renoir (1841–1919) was already an accomplished composer and colorist by the age of twenty-five can be seen in *Spring Bouquet*,[128] an oil 3½ feet high, signed and dated 1866. Eight years before the first exhibition of a rebellious, Salon-scorned group called Impressionists (by a caustic critic who applied to them that word in the title of an atmospheric sunrise picture by Claude Monet), Renoir was already well launched in the new direction. The subject, of course,

127

128

was traditional, but Renoir found joy in flower painting to the end of his life—or rather until arthritis in his old age made it impossible for him to hold a brush. In this floral cascade lavender grays and fugitive pinks and yellows linger from the work of earlier masters; but during the 1870s they would be outdazzled by the Impressionist "rainbow" palette, as in the celebrated *Moulin de la Galette* (Louvre). The same sequence has been discussed in connection with Claude Monet's *Boats Leaving the Harbor*, painted very likely in 1865, when Monet too was twenty-five (CT 5). However much we rightly admire the will to develop that kept these masters from settling down into routine production, their Pre-Impressionist works are not necessarily inferior to what followed.

With the bequest of the collection of Maurice Wertheim, the Fogg became rich in both Impressionist and Post-Impressionist painting. The latter term is useful for purposes of chronology but it is otherwise meaningless, and even its chronology is misleading. Cézanne, surely a leading Post-Impressionist, was born a year before Monet and two years before Renoir; and as for Monet—the leading Impressionist of them all —his late work (MA 254 and thereafter) makes him an outstanding Post-Impressionist. Such younger painters, born between 1848 and 1864, as Gauguin, van Gogh, Seurat, and Toulouse-Lautrec have little in common except that they mastered Impressionist techniques and then departed from them.

Paul Cézanne (1839–1906), represented in the Wertheim bequest by a fine *Still Life*[129] of c. 1885, had spent many months with Camille Pissarro painting Impressionist pictures at Auvers-sur-Oise. That was in the mid-1870s, but thereafter he steadily moved away from an attempt to catch fugitive effects of light on objects and toward a world out of time. He wanted, as he said, to make of Impressionism something durable, like the art of the great museums. In this *Still Life*, geometry comes to his aid: solid spheres and flat circles, ovals flattened at their ends toward a circular shape, cylinders, flat rectangular planes. The tablecloth, if observed for itself and out of context, is startlingly similar to the geometric rock formations of his favorite motif, the Mont-Ste.-Victoire. Impressionist space, like that of the camera which influenced it, is seen from a single point of view, and everything happens *behind* the picture surface—or seems to do so. Cézanne has changed all this. He looks down at the tabletop, but straight ahead at the large jar, and again somewhat down at the jar's lip. The tablecloth winds back, but

129

not very far, because its farther white peak, strongly contrasted against the dark red-brown commode, leaps forward toward the picture surface. In other words, Cézanne is sacrificing illusion in order to assert the claims of painting as color applied to a flat canvas. The whole composition is full of adjustments: solid bodies and their relationship to flat shapes, spatial continuum as against rhythmic two-dimensional design. It is through these relationships—often spoken of as inevitable—that a sense of permanence is achieved, and one of solemnity and silence. These modest objects are nowhere and no-when. They endure.

In his *Self-Portrait*[130] of September 1888, Vincent van Gogh (1853–90) is represented at the Fogg by one of his finest pictures. It has the additional interest of an inscription across the top to his friend Paul Gauguin, who was soon to join him at Arles. Van Gogh had just received a self-portrait from Gauguin and so he reciprocated. In a letter to his ever-faithful brother Theo, Vincent describes his own picture, which he considered superior to Gauguin's: "It is all ashen gray against pale malachite (no yellow). The clothes are this brown coat with a blue border, but I have exaggerated the brown into purple, and the width of the blue borders. The head is modeled in light color painted in thick 'pâte' against the light background with hardly any shadows. Only I have made the eyes 'slightly' slanting like the Japanese." In Paris Japanese prints had helped turn van Gogh from Impressionist illusion toward the flat arabesque. As later in Nolde's *Mulatto* (MA 102), concentric strokes radiating from the head give it an almost hypnotic effect.

Yet another masterpiece is *Maternity*,[131] painted in 1901 by Pablo Picasso (1881–1973). A prime example from his "Blue Period," it was painted when he was still nineteen. By age sixteen he had passed the examinations at the Barcelona Academy and had taken prizes in competition with mature artists. A trip to Paris in the fall months of 1900 had exposed him to the later developments of Art Nouveau and to the work of the Intimists, especially Bonnard and Vuillard. But his Spanish heritage was strong, and a return to Barcelona in December, to stay until

130

131

May of 1901, fortified it. A second trip to Paris lasted until the end of the year. Whether *Maternity* was painted in Barcelona or Paris need not concern us, for his Paris pictures of 1901 were as profoundly Spanish as his Barcelona ones. The elongated, emaciated figures echo those of El Greco (but without his flamelike strokes) and behind them Spanish Romanesque frescoes (MA 61) and sculpture. Picasso's choice of a dominant deep blue color may have been suggested by the late works of Cézanne, but he chilled it with suggestions of green. The figure of the mother is a wonderfully interlocked chain of flattened Art Nouveau shapes; but her tight embrace is counteracted by the two impassive faces and by her limp, virtually Byzantine hand. The commonest of themes, perhaps suggested by the images of Jean François Millet, here becomes ennobled. It speaks to us through the language of painting, not through external sentiment. Various stages of Picasso's later career are covered in examples from other museums.

Upper Deck,[132] painted in 1929 by Charles Sheeler (1883–1965), has the look of a photograph—a medium in which the artist excelled, especially in industrial subjects—until you come upon the original oil. Here an extraordinarily subtle range of off-whites delights the eye, and this is strengthened by sharp edges, darkest dark ovals in the ventilator outlets, and by all-important diagonals of guy wires and railings. Such art by Sheeler, Charles Demuth (MA 276), Niles Spencer, and Preston Dickinson earned them the term of "The Immaculates."

Our selections of Far Eastern art can do no more than draw attention to the wealth and high quality of these collections. An unexpected parallel in forms is presented by two of the Fogg's most precious items, a *Ceremonial Bronze Vessel*[133] probably of the Shang dynasty (1700–1050 B.C.) and a glazed terra-cotta *Horse*[134] of the T'ang dynasty (A.D. 618–906). Because the vessel approaches the shape of an animal, the resemblance is perhaps less surprising. Yet, over a gap of two thousand years or more, in different materials, and in objects serving widely varying functions, there are striking similarities: in the rhythmic surge of reverse curves, in sculptural compactness and economy of statement, and in a kind of inner alertness. Note the proud arch of the horse's neck, the circular perfection of the rump, and in sudden contrast to these the vibrant diagonal thrust of the legs. In the Shang vessel, of

132

133

the type known as *kuang*, the advanced skill of bronze casting at several levels of relief—occurring over thirty centuries ago—is something to ponder.

How large are these two objects? Do they not suggest the grandeur of monumental art? The fact is that they are not large; but what is important, aesthetically, is not their *size* but their *scale*. Still, they are not mere decorative trinkets. We should not overlook the high ceremonial purpose of the *kuang*, or the destiny of the horse to be buried with a personage of exalted station. Actual maximum height for the vessel is 9¾ inches; for the horse, 14½ inches.

An elongated limestone *Head of a Bodhisattva*,[135] as strong as it is elegant, comes from the Northern Wei period (A.D. 383–565) and probably dates from the fifth to sixth century. Its superficial resemblance to certain Archaic Greek heads of the sixth century B.C. is purely coincidental, but not entirely without significance. Chinese culture evolved through an Archaic-Classic-Baroque cycle in much the same pattern that we can trace in Greek culture, and in the sequence from Romanesque through late Gothic art, and in Renaissance art from its beginnings in Giotto through the Baroque seventeenth century. Such sweeping overviews of cultures are intellectually stimulating, but they run the danger of dogmatic prediction (Egyptian and Byzantine art went through no such evolution) and of denying to the individual artist the freedom to do the unexpected. In the *Head of a Bodhisattva* the Archaic flavor of rough-hewn strength is apparent in the nameless sculptor's respect for the shape of his original block of stone; yet nothing could be more sophisticated than the elegance of the features, the elongation of the ears, or the Modigliani-like slenderness of the neck. The head is about 1½ feet high.

It is generally accepted that the T'ang dynasty (A.D. 618–906) achieved the classic phase of Chinese culture—roughly comparable, that is, to Greek art of the fifth century B.C., to Gothic cathedral sculpture of the thirteenth century, and to the High Renaissance art of Raphael and Michelangelo. The superb fragment of a wall painting, represent-

134

135

ing a *Bodhisattva*,[136] from the caves of Tun-huang (Kansu Province), supremely exemplifies these qualities. It was brought back in 1923 from a Harvard expedition to these caves. Compared with Raphael's *Portrait of Inghirami* in the Gardner Museum (MA 41), the Bodhisattva similarly emphasizes capacious circular and spherical forms, circular curves used for modeling neck contours, and an overall psychological detachment. If our earlier Northern Wei *Bodhisattva* suggests Greek heads of the Archaic sixth century, this one has something of the timeless impersonality of the fifth-century sculptures of Olympia and the Parthenon. A close equivalent in T'ang stone sculpture will be found in the majestic head at Worcester (MA 311).

The Fogg also offers a fine example of a complete stone figure of the T'ang period, a *Seated Sakyamuni Buddha*[137] 4 feet high, from the caves of T'ien Lung Shan. Here the head is very broad, in greatest contrast to the elegant attenuation of the Northern Wei head. But as in the two other T'ang works just cited—the wall painting and the Worcester head —the circular curve again dominates, here in the drapery and in the articulation of breast and neck. The sophisticated ovoid projections of the knees, however, are in seeming contrast, but they provide a forceful base. As a whole, the figure radiates a sense of command and at the same time one of impenetrable detachment. The circular perfection of the eyebrow lines very likely contributes to this effect. Note, in the earlier Northern Wei head, how the oval lift of the brows and a slight suggestion of a smile about the mouth produce an effect of secret self-awareness.

Comparison of the T'ang statue of the Buddha with the Gandharan example at Yale (CT 64), of the first to third centuries A.D., will show surprising continuities in sculptural tradition across great leaps in time and in space—indeed across much of the Asian continent, Gandhara being in modern Afghanistan. While Buddhism united India and the Far East, there was another common denominator in sculptural traditions: the conquests of Alexander the Great. Gandhara formed part of the Bactrian kingdom at the outer reaches of Alexander's empire. It was

136

137

on a basis of Hellenistic Greek art, therefore, that much of the great sculpture of Central and Eastern Asian art developed. To sense the presence, even in echo, of Greek art in the Fogg's T'ang *Seated Sakyamuni Buddha* quickens the imagination.

Harvard is also rich in the art of the Persian and Moghul miniaturists. In this abbreviated account, a fifteenth-century manuscript illumination, *Giraffe with Its Keeper*, at the Worcester Art Museum (MA 313), must suffice for the former. For the Moghul illuminators of Islamic northern India, inheritors of the great Persian traditions, we have chosen an example from the Fogg: an *Elephant Hunt*.[138] Painted at the beginning of the seventeenth century, it is about 15 inches high. On the reverse is a depiction of a palace courtyard with figures and animals. With little sacrifice of the high quality of Persian design and color, such Moghul painting aimed at, and caught, a more homely realism.

Not surprisingly, Harvard scholars have published a wide range of handbooks, catalogues, and special studies of works in the Fogg collections—works estimated as of this writing to number some thirty thousand. In 1978 the London magazine *Apollo* devoted two of its issues to the Harvard collections; they serve as an excellent introduction with many more works discussed and illustrated than could be included in this book.

138

Peabody Museum of Archaeology and Ethnology, Harvard University

Location: 11 Divinity Avenue
Hours: Mon.-Sat. 9-4:15, Sun. 1-4:15; closed July 4, Thanksgiving, Christmas, and New Year's Day
Admission: Charged. Ⓗ (via the adjacent Tozzer Library)

The Peabody Museum contains one of the great archaeological and ethnological collections of the world. If we add its contents to those of the Fogg Art Museum, the Busch-Reisinger Museum, and the rare books and illuminated manuscripts owned by the Widener and Houghton libraries, the total wealth of Harvard's artistic resources puts it in a class by itself among universities the world over. The collections of the Peabody Museum have been amassed from all quarters of the globe, primarily through expeditions sponsored by the university. Coverage here can be only symbolic. The selections were very kindly made by the museum's director and staff, my own knowledge of these areas of art history being anything but authoritative.

Until recent years the museum was more of a storehouse of magnificent treasure than a display showcase. In 1978, however, under the direction of Professor C. C. Lamberg-Karlovsky, "Masterpieces of the Peabody Museum" were superbly shown in a ground-floor gallery, newly appointed for the occasion. The catalogue, well illustrated and with authoritative comment by twenty-one specialists, covers some sixty examples. It is warmly recommended, and my debt to it is great. In his introduction, the director pointed out that "today it has become universally recognized that the art of the tribal people of Africa, Asia, Oceania, and the New World, far from being 'primitive,' attained levels of aesthetic production at times fully meriting the term 'masterpiece.' . . . It should be remembered, however, that the collections . . . are primarily of scientific value."

The museum was founded in 1866 by the same George Peabody (1795–1869) to whom the Peabody museums of Salem and of Yale University—as well as the original concept of philanthropy that later gave rise to the Carnegie, Rockefeller, Ford and other foundations—owe their existence. It has now embarked on an ambitious program of installing in modern galleries selected examples from its vast collections while still keeping the main body of its possessions available to an interested public.

The stone head of a *Maize God*[139] from the ruins of Copan in Honduras is one of the most famous examples of Maya sculpture in the world. A half-length figure in the British Museum is perhaps its only real competitor in artistic grandeur from this culture. Carved from andesite tufa and about 11 inches high, it is one of several such heads from Temple 22 brought back from the Peabody Museum expedition to Copan in the 1890s. (One of these was acquired from Harvard in 1954 by the Cleveland Museum of Art.) Unlike the rendering of other Maya gods, the Maize God was always shown as a handsome young man. The sprouting vegetation above his head is his special attribute. The date is A.D. C. 700–800, when Europe was still in the pre-Carolingian age, while China was producing the wonders of T'ang dynasty civilization. In the century before its abandonment, which apparently took place about A.D. 800, Copan reached its height. A scientific center, it has been called the Alexandria of the Maya world.

The masterly carving of the Peabody head, with its massive ear spools and rugged strings of hair contrasting with the finely chiseled features, was probably enhanced by the suitability of the local tufa for sculpture. At most other Maya sites, the limestone is much more intractable. The Copan head was originally coated with fine plaster and painted red, with the eyes outlined in black.

The fearsome hammered *Gold Disc*,[140] about 7 inches high and dating from A.D. C. 500–700, comes from Sitio Conte, Cocle, Panama. Probably worn as a breastplate, it may represent a trophy head, since the eyes are closed in death. The gold content is over 97 percent. The technique seen here of working in sheet gold was first developed in the New World in Peru in the first millennium B.C. How different are the gold death masks from Mycenae (c. 1500 B.C.), in the release of eternal slumber, as one sees them in the National Museum of Athens!

Crowned by the brilliant red-and-blue tail feathers of the macaw and circled with a spectrum of other feathers and down—whites, blacks, yellows, greens, and more reds and blues—the *Wayana Headdress*[141] is

139

140

141

surely the Matisse of the Peabody Museum. Nearly 4 feet high, it was collected in 1871 by Louis Agassiz, Harvard's renowned professor of zoology and geology, on one of his trips to the northern coasts of South America. Now reduced to under one thousand souls, the Wayana live in small villages in Surinam and southward into neighboring Brazil. Despite its magnificence, such a headdress is not necessarily reserved for a shaman or chief, for it can be worn by a ritual male dancer. It is made on a plaited basketwork base. While the feathers are collected from specified parts of particular birds, they are sometimes tinted to acquire the exact shade desired. Present knowledge of the Wayana does not allow a satisfactory interpretation of the significance of these head-dresses, but everything about them suggests that it goes deep.

The beautiful *Wooden Bowl*[142] with the head of a loon (?) is the work of a Blackfeet Indian artist. Such bowls were sometimes used to hold medicine water in the Sacred Feast and Mystery Dance of the Dakota Sioux. From bird's head to tail the bowl measures 15 inches; the wood is probably maple. It was acquired by exchange with the Worcester Historical Society in 1928. What a magical achievement, to make a wooden bowl come alive!

One of the most startling facts about this 20-by-15-inch *African Plaque from Benin*[143] is its date, late sixteenth to early seventeenth century. Another is that it is in brass (generally miscalled bronze) cast by the lost-wax process. African wood sculpture is said not to survive much beyond 150 years of the local climate, and bronze (or brass) casting is foreign to African art except in the West African kingdom of Benin, Nigeria, discovered by the Portuguese in 1485, which rapidly grew rich through the resulting trade. European bronze-casting technique was presumably introduced in this way, and the wonder is how thoroughly it was mastered.

Weighing no less than 37 pounds, the plaque represents a spear-bearing chief flanked by two warriors, perhaps on their way to honor the Oba, Benin's absolute monarch. In the upper corners, small in size and in much lower relief, are Portuguese soldiers, recognizable by their

143

142

helmets, curved mustaches, and muskets. They are as ancillary to the main purport of the relief as the little angels in Donatello's marble relief of the *Madonna of the Clouds* in the Boston Museum of Fine Arts (MA 68). Such plaques, of which some nine hundred are known, adorned pillars in passageways in the Oba's palace leading to his chamber.

The head of the Benin chief should be compared with the large memorial bronze heads of royalty of the same period. Examples are owned by the Peabody Museum but we illustrate one at the University of Vermont (VT 2). These outstrip our chief in neck adornment as well as in the sense of regal status. Note in the relief the *horror vacui* apparent in the black plane, completely filled with a repeated floral motif and ubiquitous dottings.

The *Great Scoop*,[144] or ladle of carved wood, about 28 inches long, comes from the agricultural Dan ethnic group of Liberia and the Ivory Coast. Collected in 1927 by Dr. George Schwab, a Presbyterian missionary, it can be attributed to a sculptor known locally as Sra, meaning "god," a name given him because of his beautiful work. As in the case of the Blackfeet Wooden Bowl, an ordinarily simple utilitarian object is brought to life through art that responds to its special ritual function. In Dan society there are competitions for the most honored *wunkirle*, or hospitable woman; and each village entrant is already established as a *wunkirle* through her generosity to all, especially to itinerant troupes of singers and dancers. In the ritual dance, while singing her ritual song, each *wunkirle* swings her spoon—large to symbolize her generosity—and then portions out rice into bowls for the invited families.

The head at the handle symbolizes the Dan canon of female beauty, in which narrow eyes rimmed with paint are an important feature. The elaborate hairstyle ends in plaited fiber edges. The sloping shape of the ladle itself, however, speaks in universal, not local, terms.

The two-faced *Helmet Mask*[145] for the female Bundu Society comes from the Gola tribe of Liberia, and it is closely related to masks of the Mende tribe of Sierra Leone. The Janus type, with faces in opposite directions, is very unusual. Worn by women at their initiation to the

144

145

society, it shows the typical high forehead, high headdress, and crown. Hair and neck folds are stylized in chevronlike sequences with powerful effect.

This mask was collected by George W. Harley, a medical missionary. A word should be added about Harley and George Schwab, the Presbyterian missionary who collected the *Great Scoop*. Both men were made Associates in Anthropology at Harvard in recognition of their services as donor-collectors and researchers for the Peabody Museum. Schwab worked in Cameroon and Liberia from 1897 to 1947, Harley in Liberia from 1926 to 1948. Harley's paper, *Masks as Agents of Social Control in Northeast Liberia*, published by the museum in 1950, points out the difficulty for outsiders to learn the most important things in the lives of these people. It is hard to get beyond such statements as that they are known "only by the old men." Should such a devotee be successful in actually joining one of the secret societies, he would have to swear never to reveal what he had learned. Harley and Schwab, however, managed to learn a great deal as the many masks they collected were brought to them. (One hundred fifty, for example, in eight years.) Harley notes that "a mask is the same word used to designate the human spirit and the spirit of the ancestors"; and his general conclusion is that "the masks are visible manifestations of a type of ancestor worship, debased, perhaps, by the necessity of using the masks as practical implements to guarantee the smooth working of a system of government founded on strict adherence to custom." He became especially interested in the Poro Society in Liberia, donated a large collection of their masks to the Peabody Museum, and in 1941 published brief notes on them in the museum's *Papers*.

Cambridge

Massachusetts Institute of Technology

Hours: Open daily (works are on the grounds and in lobbies of buildings)
Admission: Free. Ⓗ

The institute is assembling a collection of modern art that already makes it the most important center in that field in the immediate Boston area. In modern painting, however, its leadership is challenged by the collection of Brandeis University at Waltham. The well-appointed Hayden Gallery, on Memorial Drive, is used primarily for temporary exhibitions (often of considerable importance); there is the smaller Compton Gallery for exhibitions of lesser magnitude. Visitors are strongly advised to call at the office of the Committee on the Visual Arts, Room 145 in Building 7 (turn left from the main entrance on Massachusetts Avenue, ground floor), and ask for a map and a list of the collection, with location of the whereabouts of the many works that are on public view. The institute has a vast complex of buildings and you will need guidance.

In addition to the works discussed below, you should visit Eliel Saarinen's Chapel (across Massachusetts Avenue from the main entrance), both as a fine modern building and for its steel altarpiece and 45-foot aluminum bell tower by Harry Bertoia (1955). The music library in Hayden Memorial Library (Building 14) has a cast of Emile Antoine Bourdelle's powerful bronze *Tragic Mask of Beethoven* (1901); and in the Hayden Library itself there is Rodin's *Large Head of Iris* (1890/1). Other indoor sculptures worth seeking out are by Varda Chryssa, Nicholas Schöffer, Ernest Trova, and Isaac Witkin.

The Iceberg and Its Shadow,[146] designed in 1975 by Larry Bell (born 1939 in Chicago), is his most ambitious sculpture to that date. It is composed of 56 glass panels, square, triangular, or trapezoidal, each having a common base width of 60 inches but of varying heights. The panes, either clear or gray glass, are vacuum-coated with metallic inconel and quartz. It can be installed in an almost unlimited number of configurations. As of this writing, two of them can be seen in the ground-floor lobbies of the Sloan and the Bush buildings (numbers E52 and 13 on the map). Bell's imaginative title is most appropriate: it describes the jagged profiles of the work as well as suggesting the

146

211 MASSACHUSETTS

substance of the iceberg (clear glass) and its shadows (gray glass).
One wonders what Frederic Church, that painter of icebergs (see CT
102), might have thought of it. Bell is concerned with twentieth-century
phenomena: the dissolution of solid form in light, color, and space; and
the shifting ambiguity of disappearing images of the environment (and
of yourself as viewer), mirrored in the glass panes—something initiated
by Marcel Duchamp in his celebrated *Large Glass* (Philadelphia Museum of Art). As in Duchamp's work, sculpture here departs from its
traditional concerns with mass and weight in discrete, fixed objects.
Instead, it invites us to enter a world of evanescence and illusion.

Outdoor sculpture includes *The Big Sail*, 40 feet high, by Alexander
Calder (1966)—the model for it is in Building 9 Plaza; a bronze by
Dmitri Hadzi; a steel *Cenotaphe* by Jean Ipousteguy (1957); the corten
steel *Dunes I* by Beverly Pepper; and steel sculptures by Tony Smith
and Isaac Witkin (VT 13). In front of the Hermann Building (E53)
is a cast concrete enlargement by Carl Nesjar developed from a wood
maquette of 1958 by Pablo Picasso; the interior engraving was done by
sandblasting.

Transparent Horizon,[147] by Louise Nevelson (born 1899 in Kiev,
emigrated with her family in 1905 to Rockland, Maine), is a painted
corten steel piece dating from 1975 and some 20 feet high. It will be
found in the plaza between the Landau Building (number 66 on the
map) and Buildings 62 and 64. Nevelson's career, New York oriented,
was enriched by travel and study abroad and by her own collecting of
African, American Indian, and Pre-Columbian art. At first she produced
human and animal figures, usually in wood, plaster, or terra-cotta.
During the 1940s she turned to assemblages of found wood objects, and
these grew in the next decade to walls of stacked boxes filled with such
wood forms, painted black, gold, or white. In the 1960s she turned
to other materials, especially welded steel, and gradually perforated
what had been compact massings. Her large outdoor sculptures date
from 1969 and after. *Transparent Horizon*, commissioned by MIT in
1974, is a composition in two related parts, both derived from works of
1972 and 1973. The shorter portion was inspired by the projections of
a tropical tree; the taller one, by floral elements including spiked leaf
forms and a capping of petal shapes. In the ensemble there are suggestions of a gate, and of an enveloping landscape. Nevelson describes
herself as "an architect of shadows."

147

Visible from Memorial Drive is *Three-Piece Reclining Figure, Draped,*[148] a bronze of 1976 reaching a length of over 15 feet and a height and depth of nearly 9 feet. Comparison with Yale University's *Draped Seated Woman* of 1959 (CT 69) will show Henry Moore's extraordinary development from more traditional norms to a split-up abstraction that invites you to reassemble it into a single reclining form. A germ of this idea is already visible in Amherst College's *Stringed Figure* of 1938 (MA 13). Actually, the effort of connecting these split elements is powerfully guided by the artist through the orientation of his massive shapes, by their rhythms, and by the sympathetic correspondence of solid and void. Moore's wide exposure to the art of primitive cultures has been discussed in the examples referred to above. Those who have admired the enormous split figure in Lincoln Center, New York, will respond here to the suggestions of prehistoric majesty that so often mark his work. From the back view, in particular, the great hooded head, the massive shoulders and hips, and the tremendous force of the jutting knees are clearly apparent.

In a book so dominated by painting as this one is, I have taken advantage of the opportunity at MIT to redress the balance somewhat. That is not to say, however, that the painting collection should be overlooked. While some of the examples I shall list are in private offices, most of them can be seen (with the help of MIT's list and map) in public locations. My own selection of artists represented will give some idea of the riches available: Albers, Anuszkiewicz, Bush (a Canadian artist who has also found an enthusiastic reception at the Museum of Fine Arts), Gene Davis, Hans Hofmann, Léger and Lurçat (tapestries woven from their designs), Olitski, Rosenquist, Stamos, Trova, Vasarely, and Youngerman. There is also a small group of paintings by the Hudson River School (Bierstadt, Cole, and Doughty), by Homer and Inness, and a portrait by Charles Willson Peale.

Plans are under way, as of this writing, for a new building to house arts and media facilities, and for a much-needed handbook in the form of a walking tour.

148

In an institution devoted primarily to the sciences, it is a pleasure to record a deep concern for the humanities. This should come as no surprise when we recall that Einstein was a violinist on the side and that one of his greatest friends was the art historian Erwin Panofsky; and that Robert Oppenheimer owned paintings by sublime modern masters, including one of the finest van Goghs. Great scientists, like great artists, venture creatively into uncharted lands.

Historic Deerfield, Inc.

Location: Off Route 5, midway between Greenfield (Route 2) and South Deerfield (Route 116). From I-91, take exit 24 traveling north, or exit 26 traveling south

Hours: Mon.-Sat. 9:30-4:30, Sun. 1-4:30 throughout the year, except Thanksgiving, Christmas Eve, Christmas, and New Year's Day. For hours of specific buildings, inquire at the Information Center. For group tours write ahead (Box 321, Deerfield, MA 01342) since ordinarily house tours are limited to six persons

Admission: Charged (per house visited). Phone for further information

Because the interest here is primarily architectural and historical, as is also true at Old Sturbridge Village, the reader is referred to the companion volume in this series by Margaret Supplee Smith, *Historic Houses of New England.* American decorative arts are here in great abundance, however, and several paintings of importance. These we shall consider briefly.

Historic Deerfield, Inc., was founded in 1952 by Mr. and Mrs. Henry N. Flynt to carry on the tradition of historic preservation initiated by the Pocumtuck Valley Memorial Association (founded in 1870) and Deerfield Academy. It offers ten house museums, including Hall Tavern (c. 1760), where the Information Center is located, a Silver Shop in a restored farmhouse of 1814, and the Helen Geier Flynt Fabric Hall in a refitted barn of 1872. Paintings we shall discuss are located in the Dwight-Barnard House (c. 1725, moved from Springfield) and the Allen House (c. 1720).

According to the diary of the Reverend William Bentley of Salem, who visited Deerfield in 1782, "The Street is one measured mile, running North and South. . . . There is a gate at each end of the Street, & about 60 houses in better style, than in any of the Towns I saw." Such was the rebirth of Deerfield during the eighteenth century, following the burning of half the town by the Indians in 1704 and the tomahawking of over half its inhabitants. In later times many of the houses were moved to other sites in Deerfield, and not a few fell into ruin. The restoration has brought a significant number back to their original sites and four more have been saved by removal from the neighboring area to Deerfield's Street. Today more than fifty houses front it to compose one of the greatest concentrations of fine old houses in any New England town.

Mrs. Flynt's collection of textiles, needlework, and costume is tastefully displayed in Fabric Hall. While the emphasis here is on American work of the eighteenth and early nineteenth centuries, English and European examples are also included, some of them from the seventeenth century. In the superb group of coverlets, a finely quilted *Bedspread*[149] has a bold floral design in green and red worthy of Henri Matisse. This American masterpiece dates from the nineteenth century.

The white background has minute quilting hardly a quarter-inch apart, with seven to ten stitches per linear inch. An inner lining gives the coverlet a triple thickness. It is conjectured that this example may have been for a bride, who for reasons of superstition worked only on the floral design. Friends would have done the quilting of the background; indeed, close inspection shows considerable variation in the workmanship.

Among several paintings in the Dwight-Barnard House is the fine *Portrait of John Barnard*—no relation to the Dr. Ebenezer Barnard who practiced medicine there from 1772 to 1790, but a deacon of Cotton Mather's church in Boston. The artist is Peter Pelham (1697–1751), who arrived in Boston from London in 1726 and thereupon painted Mather's portrait and from it made a mezzotint engraving in 1727—the first known American example. The Barnard portrait is also dated 1727, when the subject was seventy-four. He surveys us with Puritanical mien, but the vigor of the modeling is thoroughly English, in the Baroque manner of Kneller. It contrasts with the puffy forms of Smibert's *Bishop Berkeley and His Entourage* (CT 74), painted in 1729 just after *his* arrival in America. Peter Pelham had some influence on the very young John Singleton Copley, for he married Copley's mother in 1748, when the boy was ten years old. Although Pelham died three years later, his studio equipment—and boyhood memories of him—were benefits that accrued to his stepson. In the Allen House, Copley's *Portrait of Reverend Arthur Browne*, painted in 1757 when Copley was only nineteen, shows him already superior to the best of Smibert.

Also in the Dwight-Barnard House is a pair of portraits by the Connecticut Valley painter William Jennys (see CT 87), known from these very portraits to have been in Deerfield in 1801. The sitters are Dr. William Stoddard Williams and his wife. Jennys received twenty-four dollars for the pair. Another, equally fine pair, of Captain Elijah Arms of Deerfield and his wife, hangs in Memorial Hall.

Memorial Hall is an independent historical museum relating to Deerfield. The exhibits include sturdy pieces of furniture, a rare overmantel painting from Bernardston (near Greenfield) attributed to Jared Jessup about 1810, a fireboard representing the very fireplace it shielded, and

149

the Jennys portraits. The brick building was designed in 1798 by Asher Benjamin as Deerfield Academy's first home. It was acquired in 1878 by the Pocumtuck Valley Memorial Association largely through the efforts of the town historian, George Sheldon, who recorded that in the collection "not a single article here is preserved on account of its artistic qualities. . . . The collection is founded on purely historical lines, and is the direct memorial of the inhabitants of this valley, both Indian and Puritan." Period rooms here shown are believed to be the oldest such displays in the United States. (Closed November to April.)

Adjacent to Memorial Hall is the Henry N. Flynt Library, erected in 1970 and named in memory of Mr. Flynt in 1972. Supplementing the archival resources of Memorial Hall itself, the library is an active research center, and the education offices of Historic Deerfield, Inc., are located here.

Deerfield Academy is the fortunate recipient of the Charles P. Russell collection of European and American Paintings, the gift of his daughters, Mrs. Lucius Potter and Miss Lucia Russell, of Greenfield.

As the paintings are undergoing conservation treatment and scholarly research, they are not currently on view, but they are eventually to be displayed in a special gallery. In date they range from the 17th century to shortly after 1900.

Among the European examples are portraits of high quality by Jacobus Leveck (1634–75), a German pupil of Rembrandt, by Nicholas Maes, and by Sir Joshua Reynolds of *Miss Franks* (1766). An early nude (1846) by J. F. Millet is a precious example of the work of his pre-Barbizon years. Landscapes by Théodore Rousseau, Courbet, and by Pissarro in early career (1859) are memorable.

Not surprisingly, most of the American examples are portraits. Those by John Wollaston, Jeremiah Theus, James Peale, and William Jennys are outstanding both in quality and in condition. There is a fine Eastman Johnson genre scene, *Whittling in the Barn* (1866), and as well a diminutive J. F. Peto *Still Life* painted on a palette. Two rainy urban scenes of 1866 and 1891 by Childe Hassam, providing strong contrast with such late works as the *Isle of Shoals* landscape at Smith College (MA 182), are among the finest pictures in the collection.

A preliminary catalogue was published in 1969.

Duxbury Art Complex

Location: 189 Alden St., off Route 3A (from Boston or Plymouth take exit 33 from Route 3 onto Route 14)
Hours: Fri., Sat., Sun. 2-5
Admission: Free

Opened in 1971 in a rural setting not far from the sea, the Art Complex appears as a delightful surprise. It is a graceful, free-flowing building of wood and glass with an undulating roof and skylights that allow natural north light into two galleries. The architect, Richard Owen Abbott, developed the design from original sketches by the late Ture Bengtz, artist and first director of the museum. Its unusual openness and freedom allow the outdoors to blend naturally with the indoors.

The Art Complex was made possible and is supported by the Carl A. Weyerhaeuser family. It includes the large Weyerhaeuser collection of American painting. From this we select a joyous marine landscape by George Bellows (1882–1925), *Farm of John Tom*,[150] painted in September 1916 on the island of Matinicus in Maine. It measures 21½ by 27½ inches. In contrast with the ominous tone of the Farnsworth Museum's *Boating out to Sea* (ME 32), painted in 1913 on Monhegan Island, it proclaims a sunny optimism in intense blues and greens with the foamy effervescence of the breaking surf. Other painters well represented here include Bengtz, Burchfield, Doughty, Hassam, Inness, Homer Martin, Sargent, and Andrew Wyeth.

Another branch of the collection consists of Shaker furniture and artifacts.

The extensive collections of traditional and modern Japanese art had the advantage of the advice of Kojiro Tomita (1890–1976), curator of the Asiatic department of the Boston Museum of Fine Arts for over thirty years and a longtime friend of the Weyerhaeuser family. He was also instrumental in commissioning the construction of a Japanese Tea House, in which demonstrations of the tea ceremony occasionally take place in the summer season.

150

Fine examples of modern Japanese ceramic art are to be seen here, and among the printmakers color woodcuts signed by Kaoru Kawano (born 1916) are especially sensitive. His *Moonlight Night* (with an Owl) and *Twilight* (with Fish) hold their own in the company of celebrated examples in the same medium by Hiroshige (1797–1858).

Since both galleries are used for temporary exhibitions, much of the permanent collection may not be on view at any given time. Free lectures, concerts, and demonstrations of the tea ceremony are added attractions for the visitor. The large art library is particularly strong in books on Japanese art.

Fall River Historical Society

Location: 451 Rock Street
Hours: March-December, Tues.-Fri. 9-4:30, Sat. 2-4
Admission: Free. Ⓗ partially

Fall River Public Library

Location: 104 North Main Street
Hours: Mon.-Thurs. 9-9, Fri., Sat. 9-5, but closed Sat. in summer
Admission: Free

The two institutions, particularly the Historical Society, offer an opportunity to study the work of a gifted local still-life painter, Robert Spear Dunning (1829–1905). Born in Brunswick, Maine, Dunning came to Fall River at the age of five, studied in New York, and returned to Fall River for the rest of his life. A portraitist and landscape painter at first, he turned to still life in 1865. Many of his works are in local private collections. The Public Library staged a Dunning exhibition in 1911 with forty-six; and in 1970 the Greater Fall River Art Association included twenty examples in an exhibition of the Fall River School, 1853–1932. As a longtime teacher he contributed greatly to the local development. There is a good section on Dunning in Gerdts and Burke, *American Still Life Painting* (New York: Praeger, 1971).

Our selection, in the Historical Society, showing a spill of *Potatoes, Onions, Carrots, and a Turnip*,[151] is signed and dated 1879. It makes an interesting comparison with Renoir's *Onions* (1881) in the Clark Art Institute (MA 256). In their elegant company Dunning's American produce seems modest indeed, as if these homely objects had just come out of the ground. They tumble from the brass pail in no such preordained order as Renoir gave to his onions, and they lack the svelte

151

rhythms and color echoes in the tablecloth that make Renoir's picture so much a work of high art. Yet, like Eakins's portraits and Peto's pile of books (both at Smith College), they have an uncompromising honesty. On occasion, as in the Historical Society's large *Still Life of Fruit*, 1883, Dunning included more luxurious accessories (the Victorian silver pitcher) and—following Dutch practice of the seventeenth century —a self-portrait (here on a support of the carved mahogany table). Dunning enthusiasts tend to pick out our plain fare as their favorite, and on a standard of originality we find no reason to disagree with them.

Thomas Badger's *Still Life with Melons and Fruit* at Colby College (ME 36) belongs to an earlier generation, and it retains much of the polish of Colonial and Federal art. Dunning, at least in the example we have chosen, seems to have had the earthy sensibility of a Jean François Millet, as in the Malden Library's *Woman Churning* (MA 167).

Among other local painters of still life, Bryant Chapin (1859–1927) is well represented at the Historical Society, particularly in his specialty, baskets of strawberries.

The society's granite building, stern and finely proportioned, was formerly the home of the Brayton family. Built in the 1840s, it was moved, block by block by oxen, in 1870 to its present site and reconstructed. The style agrees with that of the scores of magnificent factories that are Fall River's chief claim to architectural splendor, although the many fine houses on Highland Avenue are not far behind in interest. Within, the society's possessions are handsomely displayed.

Elsewhere in the city are the Marine Museum (70 Water Street, admission charged), with ship models, marine paintings, lithographs, and posters relating to the growth of maritime steam power; the U.S.S. *Massachusetts* of Second World War fame (open daily, admission charged); and for the criminologist the Lizzie Borden House (230 Second Street). The great granite and brick factories once made Fall River the largest cloth-manufacturing city in the world.

Fitchburg Art Museum

Location: Merriam Pkwy.; from Main St. (Route 2A) turn east at Upper Common onto Merriam Pkwy. Parking available
Hours: Tues., Wed., Fri., Sat. 10-5, Thurs. 10-9, Sun. 2-5; closed July and August, and Thanksgiving, Christmas, and New Year's Day
Admission: Free

The museum was established in 1925 through the generosity of Eleanor Norcross, daughter of the first mayor of Fitchburg. The original building, opened in 1928, was destroyed by fire in 1933. The present fireproof building was constructed in the following year. It houses the permanent collection and provides space for adult and children's art classes. The museum's annual regional exhibition attracts entries by artists from more than forty neighboring towns.

An active program of temporary exhibitions, on an average of one per month, is supplemented by lectures by visiting artists, scholars, and critics; by crafts demonstrations; and by bus tours to Boston, Worcester, Manchester (N.H.), and other leading centers. A large and enthusiastic membership is evidence that Fitchburg enjoys one of the better small art centers in New England.

The collection, not large but steadily growing, is richest in works on paper. An impressive print collection, maintained in well-designed storage racks, is strongest in Japanese woodblock prints and in work by twentieth-century Americans, but a large example by Joan Miró (see CT 32) should not be missed. There are fine watercolors, too, including a pair by Charles Burchfield, and Edward Hopper's *Two Lights, Maine.* Prints by Mary Cassatt and the German Expressionist Kaethe Kollwitz are of fine quality here.

Among the oil paintings in the permanent collection are a small study for Sargent's *Hosea* in the Boston Public Library (MA 29); *Theophila Palmer Reading "Clarissa,"* by Sir Joshua Reynolds (1771); and *The Wedding* (1903) by Edward Lamson Henry (1841–1919)—that infinitely patient observer of American life.

Set in its magnificent original Chippendale frame, the *Portrait of Mrs. Sarah Clayton of Liverpool,*[152] measuring 50 by 40 inches and painted in 1770 by Joseph Wright of Derby (1734–97), is the outstanding Old Master work in the collection. Mrs. Clayton sits in dignity at a mahogany table holding an architect's plan of the St. Nicholas Church at Liverpool. The subtle color scheme runs from the mauve and lavender of her taffeta dress and bows to the green curtain blown across the inevitable status-column—of the sort that belatedly (and unnecessarily) exalts Thomas Jefferson in the Gilbert Stuart portrait of 1805 at Bowdoin College (ME 13). Apart from a trip to Europe in 1773, Wright spent most of his life in Derby, far removed from the fashionable London of his slightly older contemporaries, Reynolds and Gainsborough. Trained under Thomas Hudson (1701–79), Wright did not venture, as a portraitist, much beyond the models set by his teacher, who was also the master of Reynolds. Of Hudson, Ellis K. Waterhouse, in the Pelican History volume on *Painting in Britain,* has said that for all that he was Reynolds's teacher, his work is "straightforward and solid, with no graces and no nonsense and no poetry about it." (The visitor to the Fleming Museum at the University of Vermont, after seeing Hudson's *Portrait of Miss Ann Isted* (VT 4), may take issue with this judgment.) Despite Wright's clear advance in subtlety and in psychological penetration beyond Hudson's attainment, he seems closer to his Boston contemporary, John Singleton Copley, than to the leading portraitists of London. By London standards, Wright—again as a portraitist—was a provincial, as was Copley; but, as in the case of Copley, these standards are not relevant.

Wright is known today less for his portraits than for his pictures of candlelight scenes of scientific experiments, for moonlight landscapes and scenes of grottoes and caverns, and for views of Mount Vesuvius in eruption. In such works he was among the forerunners of the Romantic movement. There is no hint of any of this in his portrait of Mrs. Clayton, but the lavender-mahogany-green color scheme is similar to that in many of his landscapes.

If the Wright portrait offers us high competence without aesthetic surprises, that cannot be said of our second selection, *Still Life with a Bottle of Olives,*[153] by William M. Harnett (1848–92), signed and dated 1877. This Irish-born Philadelphian supported himself until that year as an engraver of silver in Philadelphia and New York. His first oils date from 1875, and when in the following year a depression in his regular trade cut off his livelihood, he took up painting as his new profession. The surprise offered by Fitchburg's small picture, therefore, is double: that he so quickly achieved competence, and that he initiated a form of still life that would be difficult to parallel in the long-sustained American interest in this theme during the nineteenth century. We can find minutely spotted apples and sharply detailed descriptions of cut melons, but where such a sentinellike bottle of stuffed olives, its contents huddled behind a streak of light on glass? All this before

152

153

Harnett set off in 1880 for a six-year stint of study in Europe, chiefly in Munich. After his return, he went on to such expansive tours de force as Springfield's *Emblems of Peace* (MA 220). In the section on the Smith College Museum of Art (see MA 187), we shall have more to say about this Jan van Eyck of American painting, including some curious developments that took place after his death.

Archaeologically minded visitors to Fitchburg will be interested in a dig on the edge of town, sponsored by the museum and the local Historical Society and conducted by the museum's director. With meticulous care, vestiges of the Spofford Garrison, one of the area's earliest sites, are slowly reemerging into the light of day.

Danforth Museum

Location: 123 Union Ave.; take exit 13 from Mass. Tpke. to enter the city on Route 126; from Route 135 turn north to the business district. Parking available
Hours: Wed.-Sun. 1-4:30; closed major holidays
Admission: Free. Ⓗ

Development of a flourishing art center in Framingham has overcome two great disadvantages: its proximity to the artistic riches of Boston and the fact that the museum opened as recently as 1975. With commendable imagination and initiative, public-spirited citizens took over a vacated school building, renovated it, established an ambitious program of classes in arts and crafts and of lectures, films, and exhibitions, and quietly began assembling a permanent collection. The emphasis here is on prints, including good examples by the great masters and very fine ones by the German Expressionists.

The small collection of oil paintings includes a pair of Gilbert Stuarts and a somewhat simpering, but characteristic, Bouguereau (see M A 257); and excellent examples of the landscape art of Jasper Cropsey (1832–1900), Samuel Gerry (1813–1906), and Frank Shapleigh (1842–1906).

Outstanding is a modest but lovely early work by Albert Bierstadt (1830–1902), *Near North Conway, N.H.,*[154] measuring 18 by 24 inches and painted about 1860. Beyond a screen of dark evergreens a wide prospect opens out under a pale gray sky, climaxed by the silvery sheen of a distant lake. A very different response to Conway scenery is offered by a large Inness at Mount Holyoke College (M A 206). As for Bierstadt, he later expanded onto enormous canvases like *Domes of the Yosemite* (1867) at St. Johnsbury (V T 14), and let himself go in Wagnerian Romantic fervor as in *Seal Rock* (1872) at New Britain (C T 44).

154

Cape Ann Historical Association

Location: 27 Pleasant St. Ask for map and directions at information booth on the waterfront, reached at end of Route 133 from Route 128
Hours: Tues.-Sat. 11-4
Admission: Charged

There is no more attractive small museum in New England than the Cape Ann Scientific, Literary & Historical Association. Housed in sea captain Elias Davis's 1804 home and a tasteful gallery added alongside in 1936, the association dates from 1875. In addition, it owns and maintains two eighteenth-century houses in the town. Apart from a library of historical documents relating to Gloucester's seafaring life, its displays —arranged with impeccable taste—include fine antique furniture, silver (some by Paul Revere), pewter, china, and glass; ship models and ship portraits; and fishing gear. Much care and expert knowledge have been expended on the explanatory labels.

The major attraction is the collection of thirty-two oils and over one hundred drawings by Fitz Hugh Lane (1804–65), born and died at Gloucester, and one of the most precious masters of mid-nineteenth-century America. While examples of his work may be seen in many other museums (notably in the Karolik collection of the Boston Museum of Fine Arts), none comes near to matching what can be seen here. A superbly designed and illustrated catalogue, with text by John Wilmerding, was published for the Historical Association in 1974 by the Stinehour Press. Three oils by Lane were included in the Museum of Modern Art's memorable 1976 exhibition, "The Natural Paradise: Painting in America, 1800–1950." Lane and Martin J. Heade (1819–1904) form a close pair in what is now called American Luminism; the fact that thirteen oils by Heade were shown in the Museum of Modern Art's exhibition should signify no lesser rank for Fitz Hugh Lane, but only that his career as a painter, delayed by a period of earning his living in Boston as a lithographer of town views, hardly spanned a quarter century, whereas Heade's long life made possible a career of over twice that length. While the two have much in common and it would be easy to believe that the older Lane inspired Heade's early development, there is no solid evidence that they ever met, or even that Heade knew Lane's work. For a discussion of both artists, see Barbara Novak, *American Painting of the Nineteenth Century* (2nd edition, New York: Harper and Row, 1979), chapters 5 through 7. For Lane, see the brilliant monograph by John Wilmerding (New York: Praeger, 1971) on which his catalogue for the Cape Ann Association's collection is based.

Partially paralyzed in his legs, Fitz Hugh Lane worked mostly at Gloucester and inland on Cape Ann, but there are memorable paintings of the Maine coast, which he often visited in the company of a younger Gloucester friend, Joseph L. Stevens, Jr. The Stevens family had a house

at Castine, on Penobscot Bay. Arriving there by train and boat, Lane
and his friend cruised the coast, with Rockland a favorite subject for
sketching. Wilmerding suggests that Lane traveled light, making only
pencil sketches and color notes, and that the resulting oils were painted
in Gloucester "with a sense of reverie, now seen to be an enviable
characteristic of the nineteenth century."

Gloucester Harbor from Rocky Neck,[155] signed and dated 1844, is
the earliest oil in this collection and one of Lane's largest pictures
(29½ by 41½ inches). It has the crispness and meticulous detail of his
early lithographs—indeed, he made a lithograph version of it—and of
his pencil sketches. It also achieves a sense of tranquillity extending into
great distances. But it is through a pervasive, limpid light and discreet
spottings of color that he turns description and topography into poetry.
Patience is sometimes the enemy of feeling, but not here.

Riverdale,[156] signed and dated 1863, more concentrated as a composition and ever so slightly looser in technique and richer in color, shows
us how faithful Lane remained to the standard he had set two decades before. Hardly twenty miles to the north by crow's flight from Gloucester,
and at exactly the same time, Heade was painting similar haying scenes
on the salt marshes near Newburyport. We illustrate an example of
c. 1865–70, at Bowdoin College (ME 14). Heade's vision of an
Emersonian harmony between man and nature is gently disturbed by a
passing shower (frequently he introduced ominous storms, as in CT 100,
an oil of 1863). But for Lane, Cape Ann's salt marshes were serene
and untroubled. Wilmerding, who holds out for the likelihood—notwithstanding the lack of evidence—of a connection between the two
artists, suggests that in such late works as *Riverdale* Lane was influenced
by Heade's haying scenes.

However that may be, in Lane's magical idyll, a mushroom-shaped
load of hay has passed by some bread-loaf rocks, and in good time will
reach the gate in a stone wall built by patient hands. The trees do not
stir. In the pale distance a village rests in summer slumber.

155

156

The Hammond Museum

Location: 80 Hesperus Ave., west of the town. Exit from Route 128 onto Route 133 and follow it to the waterfront; at the town's information booth ask for a map and directions
Hours: Open daily 10-4, except in winter; December-March, Tues.-Fri. 10-3, Sat.-Sun. 10-4; closed during January and on Thanksgiving, Christmas, and New Year's Day
Admission: Charged

The home of Mr. and Mrs. John Hays Hammond, Jr., was established as a museum in 1931, soon after its completion. Designed by Allen and Collens, later the architects of the Cloisters in New York, it provides a medieval setting for an extensive collection of architectural fragments, sculpture, painting, furniture, and decorative arts dating from the Roman period to the Renaissance. It is situated picturesquely on the rocky coast somewhat west of Gloucester, not far from the reef of Norman's Woe, celebrated in Longfellow's "Wreck of the Hesperus." Chief element in the design is the Great Hall, which is based on the proportions of the Gothic transept of the church of St. Nazaire at Carcassonne. This contains the largest pipe organ in private possession. Organ recitals, early music concerts, and other musical events are open to the public throughout the year.

Because the guided tour, lasting about an hour, is very competently conducted, only the outstanding exhibits will be mentioned here. The finest architectural elements, incorporated in the conservatory-court, are two timber house fronts of the fifteenth century, one from Amiens and the other from the neighborhood of Tours, and a large flamboyant Gothic portal in limestone from the Loire region. Opposite the fireplace in the Great Hall are three examples of architectural stone carving of Italo-Byzantine provenance: an altar frontal, a round-arched portal, and a bishop's throne. The last-named piece comes from Lecce, near Bari in southern Italy. Late as these examples may be, their style is of the sort that filled the time gap between the fall of Rome and the Romanesque age of the eleventh and twelfth centuries. The emphasis in these carvings is on flat ornament, strongly Eastern in character. They differ from early Byzantine art chiefly in their rugged crudeness.

Over these carvings is a gilt organ screen from the Marienkirche in Lübeck, in northern Germany. Johann Sebastian Bach used to hear Buxtehude play the organ there, and later he became the organist. The screen itself is of late Gothic date. The reverse curves ending in floral finials mark the flamboyant style, of which the French limestone portal in the conservatory-court is an example on a larger scale.

As of this writing, the collections are undergoing scholarly study and attribution. Since they are primarily of architectural or decorative character, they fall outside the scope of this book.

In one wing there is a series of Colonial American rooms with excellent examples of furniture, glass, pewter, a marine painting, and a small bronze statue of Thomas Jefferson.

The museum has an active program of temporary exhibitions, a lecture series, and sponsored trips to other museums. As a whole, it offers a free-ranging early twentieth-century Romantic interpretation of a medieval castle-residence. Unlike some historical reconstructions, it has the good sense not to dress up the guides in historical costume.

An attractive illustrated handbook is available.

Hancock Shaker Village

Location: On Route 20, 5 miles west of Pittsfield and near the New York State line; do not approach via Hancock Center, which is on Route 43. Parking provided
Hours: Open June 1-October 31 only, daily 9:30-5; use of library at other seasons by appointment only
Admission: Charged. Ⓗ within limits

In preparation for a visit, which should be unhurried, to this model preservation of a not quite extinct phenomenon of American culture, you are enthusiastically advised to seek out, in the nearest available library, the December 1966 issue of *Harper's* magazine. There you will find a most engaging account of this enterprise by Russell Lynes. Failing that, all is not lost, since you will receive a well-organized orientation in the attractive Visitors' Center.

On a pasture, woodland, and meadow site are some twenty buildings, several of them dating from as early as the 1790s. From 1779 to 1790 residents of Hancock, Richmond, and Pittsfield heard Shaker testimony and joined together in Hancock. In 1783, the year before her death, the founder, Mother Ann Lee, visited Hancock and Richmond; and by 1786 the Believers had raised a meetinghouse—dismantled in 1938 but replaced in 1962 by a similar building moved from Shirley, Mass. In 1790 Hancock—the "City of Peace"—was formed as the third covenant Shaker community under the leadership of Father Calvin Harlow and Mother Sarah Harrison. The true name for the Shakers is the United Society of Believers in Christ's Second Appearing.

Important construction in the early nineteenth century included the Trustees' House (c. 1800, modernized at the end of the century); the Schoolhouse (c. 1820, reconstructed in 1976 on the original site); the celebrated Round Stone Barn (1826); and the Brick Dwelling House (1830). By the time of the last-named building, the community had reached its numerical peak of 247 members; the Dwelling housed 100 brethren and sisters.

In 1960 Shaker Community, Inc., was formed, under a dedicated board of trustees, to save the buildings and to perpetuate the Shaker traditions. In that year the community had officially closed, and the buildings were threatened with destruction by a neighboring racetrack (which subsequently also closed).

An extensive program of reconstruction and repair was inaugurated immediately after the formation of the corporation, and this was accompanied by major collecting activities geared to illustrating all phases of Shaker life and manufacture. The capacious Brick Dwelling is only the most sizable of the many fascinating exhibition areas to be seen here. A varied sampling of Shaker work greets you in the Visitors' Center, but a vast assemblage of furniture, tools, wooden models for making bonnets (strangely similar to the simplified nature abstractions of Brancusi), and all manner of crafts will be found in the various buildings.

An experimental program of inviting craftsmen to demonstrate the Shaker techniques—on special summer occasions—proved so successful that a second barn, near the Round Barn, has recently been equipped for year-round activity by resident artisans. Their products, made strictly in accordance with Shaker practice, will be sold at the sales shop of the adapted structure.

An extensive library of Shaker materials has been assembled, and a complete Shaker bibliography, by Mary Richmond, published. The library is now actively used by scholars and other specialists in Shaker life. Another branch of Shaker activity, cooking, has also received devoted attention. You can purchase publications of Shaker recipes, and on special occasions you can savor a Shaker repast.

Most precious of Shaker creations are the Inspirational Drawings— divinely inspired visions of the spirit world. A group of forty-two examples formed the centerpiece of a Shaker exhibition, "The Gift of Inspiration," held in 1979 at Hirschl & Adler Galleries, New York; of these, half were lent by Hancock Shaker Village, many of them done at Hancock itself. Well attended and enthusiastically reviewed, the exhibition was a Hancock benefit.

In many instances the author of the drawing is duly inscribed. At Hancock, Hannah Cohoon (1788–1864) appears to have had exceptional talent, or, to speak more reverently, to have been vouchsafed more inspirational revelations. Four of the finest drawings are by her hand. *The Tree of Light or Blazing Tree* is inscribed [*sic*]: "Seen and received by Hannah Cohoon in the City of Peace Sabbath Oct 9th 10th hour A.M. 1845. drawn and painted by the same hand." The three other drawings date from the 1850s—comforting evidence that inspiration was not short-lived. *Tree of Life*,[157] 18 by 23 inches, is inscribed: "City of Peace Monday July, 3rd 1854. Seen and painted by, Hannah Cohoon." And on the back: "Aged 66." We also learn that on October 1 at 4:00 P.M. the design was identified to Hannah Cohoon by Mother Ann, "writing" its title through the hand of a medium. The inscription further reveals that ". . . the spirit shew'd me plainly the branches, leaves and fruit, painted or drawn upon paper. The leaves were check'd or crossed

157

and the same colors you see here." The leaves are green-green; the fruit dark green and vermilion-vermilion. To other Believers the revealed colors were gentler and subtler; many of the drawings feature yellows, pinks, and sky blues.

The activities of the village are strengthened by programs in research and in education. In addition to the work of local and visiting scholars, there are frequent visits by student groups from schools, colleges, and centers of graduate study—some from as far away as Michigan.

Nearby, in New York State off Route 295, is Old Chatham, with a Shaker museum containing another huge collection of Shaker materials. While the range of objects rivals Hancock's, there are no Shaker buildings, for no community was established there.

Fruitlands Museums

Location: Prospect Hill (P.O. address R.R. 2, Box 87); from Route 2, exit
south on Route 110, turn right on Old Shirley Rd. and follow the signs
Hours: Open May 30 to September 30, Tues.-Sun. 1-5; closed Mon. except
when a holiday
Admission: Charged

Founded in 1914 by Clara Endicott Sears, the Fruitlands Museums include an early eighteenth-century farmhouse where in 1843 Bronson
Alcott and other Transcendentalist leaders founded a new social order
known as the Con-Sociate Family; a Shaker house; an American Indian
museum; and a picture gallery. A library is open throughout the year to
qualified research workers. These buildings are situated on a beautiful
two-hundred-acre estate that commands a superb view of Mt. Wachusett
and Mt. Monadnock.

The gallery contains Miss Sears's collection of portraits by itinerant
American painters of the nineteenth century and landscapes by members
of the Hudson River School. In both fields Miss Sears was among the
first collectors.

Mt. Ascutney, Vermont[158] was painted in 1862 by Albert Bierstadt
(1830–1902). Often this master impressed through sheer size or through
the choice of a melodramatic landscape subject (VT 14). While this is
a fairly large picture, about 6 feet in length, the effect could hardly be
more unassuming. Like George Inness in his earlier pictures (see ME
23), Bierstadt simply communicated his own peace of mind as he con-
templated the serenity of a broad New England prospect. He was born
in Düsseldorf, but his family emigrated to New Bedford when he was
only two years old. In 1853 he returned to Germany to study painting
and remained for six years, including travels to Italy, Switzerland, and
the Rhine. Characteristically, he went to the Rocky Mountains in search
of extraordinary scenery. In later life he made three more trips to Europe.
Bierstadt painted this lovely pastoral near Claremont, N.H., looking
across the Connecticut River to Vermont. Note how gently, but firmly,
he leads us down the center of the broad panorama to the elms in the
middle distance, where the river takes us to the farthest mountains.
There is much to be seen at the sides, but our attention is never dis-

158

tracted. While this picture is more ambitious than the lovely small example of 1860 discussed at Framingham (MA 154), it is in a similar spirit.

The *Portrait of a Lady*,[159] from the Walter Perkins House in Brookline, is attributed to Alvan Clark (1804–87). Of the many tightly compressed images that stare out from these walls, this is perhaps the most memorable. Furtive and reclusive, the face is framed in a blue headdress that looks exactly like ribbon candy. The lady has black hair, she is dressed in black velvet, and there is a black ground. A dark red curtain provides a little relief in color, but adds to the feeling of ominous tension. The scale of the figure is enhanced by meticulous dottings on the headdress, at the throat, on the gilt buckle at the waist, and on the wrist and the cuff. The lady may be described as a Puritan Bloody Mary played by Lillian Gish. There are finer portraits here, but none so alarming. What would Dr. Freud have made of it?

Subsequent donations have greatly enriched Miss Sears's collection of nineteenth-century American painting, but within the same scope. Not previously represented is Thomas Chambers, a landscapist who was born in London in 1808, came to America in 1832, and frequented New York, Boston, and Albany during the 1850s and 1860s. His subjects included the Delaware Water Gap, the falls of the Genesee at Rochester, and Niagara, but his favorite was the Hudson River at West Point. One of the last-named, fairly similar to the version at the Albany Institute of History and Art, can be seen here. More characteristic, however, is *View from Mount Holyoke*, showing the Oxbow of the Connecticut River. The setting is nearly identical to one by the French-born Regis Gignoux, who came to America in 1844 and painted in what may be called the normal Hudson River School style, especially that of Frederic Church. Chambers, on the contrary, seems to have based his compositions on popular prints. He gave them a strongly personal stamp, marked by a play of rich oranges, greens, and whites, and by crisp contour lines. Born more than thirty years before the self-taught Henri Rousseau (*le douanier*), he prefigured to a surprising degree Rousseau's fresh and modern point of view.

William Matthew Prior (1806–73), son of a Maine shipmaster and now firmly established as a portraitist of ability, was already represented in Miss Sears's collection by six examples, but many more have now come to Fruitlands, including a large picture of *The Sons of Edwin A. and Sarah R. Hill*.[160] The date of 1853 on the red binding of the half-opened book agrees with the known ages of Edwin Lawton, Augustine Prentice, and John Pierce Hill: one, six, and four respectively—provided that we keep in mind that portrayals of Early American children invariably make them look older than they actually were. The arrangement is not unskillful, and the varying reds, blues, greens, and browns unite its parts successfully. If the bright red cherry and the bright green leaves on the floor, presumably dropped by Edwin, do not match the fruit he holds, they seem appropriate color accents for the bare lower-left corner.

Prior appears to have started out dutifully enough in the prevalent early Romantic manner of portraiture, as in the 1831 example of *H. B.*

Webb of Bath, Maine, and gradually to have turned to the manner seen in the Hill children. Yet as early as 1831 he advertised in the *Maine Enquirer* to the effect that "persons wishing for a flat picture can have a likeness without shade or shadow at one quarter price." An itinerant limner, he traveled as far south as Baltimore, but worked chiefly around Boston. He made a specialty of painting on glass, including copies of Gilbert Stuart's *George Washington*, one of which is in the Fruitlands collection.

Other paintings of note include portraits of a man and a woman of Sturbridge, by an anonymous master of considerable skill, and one of the earliest works of George Inness, *March of the Crusaders* (1824).

In the Tea Room behind the director's office is a photographic exhibit devoted to the founder, Miss Sears, clearly a person of great charm, style, and intelligence. Her vision for Fruitlands has been carried out in a manner that would surely win her approval.

159

160

The Holyoke Museum, Holyoke Public Library

Location: 335 Maple St. Take exit 4 from Mass. Tpke., or exit 16 from I-91
Hours: Mon-Sat. 1-5
Admission: Free

The museum provides an interesting reflection of collecting activities in the nineteenth and early twentieth centuries in this manufacturing city, when its mills were generating much wealth. In many ways it is as impressive as the Greek Ionic portico of the 1902 library building. Both the library and the museum were established in 1870, three years before the incorporation of Holyoke itself as a city.

Made possible by gifts, bequests, and the Joseph Skinner Art Fund, the collections cover American and European painting, decorative arts from the seventeenth through the nineteenth century, ceramics, glass, scrimshaw work, and American Indian basketry. While American paintings dominate, European landscapes, portraits, and genre subjects include examples of quality. American artists of note seen here are Asher Durand, Alfred Bricher, Eastman Johnson, William Merritt Chase, Frank Duveneck, and John Alden Weir.

Particularly sensitive is *Fog on the Cliffs*,[161] an oil measuring 17 by 36 inches, by Alfred Bricher (1837–1908), signed at the lower left. A comparable work, *Beach Scene at Sunset*—with no cliffs but instead a distant sailing vessel—is owned by the New Britain Museum of American Art; and the Wadsworth Atheneum at Hartford has *Fog Clearing: Maillon's Cove, Grand Manan*. Subtly atmospheric pictures like these, painted in the 1870s and conceived in the quiet vein of Fitz Hugh Lane and Martin Heade, add to our understanding of Luminism as a major development in American painting. Two other Bricher landscapes, also in his customary narrow horizontal format, were included in an important exhibition shown in 1976 at the Museum of Modern Art: "The Natural Paradise: Painting in America, 1800–1950."

Eastman Johnson's *The Kite*, with two figures on a hilltop, closely resembles early paintings by Winslow Homer (see CT 80), but at bolder scale and with more brilliant areas of white in strong light. *Young Girl* by William Merritt Chase, an oil in vigorous wide strokes in a deep brown key, reflects his early work in Munich; it contrasts strikingly with the much later oil at Dartmouth College (NH 10). His contemporary

161

—and companion in the Munich years—Frank Duveneck (1848–1919) is well represented by *Portrait of a Woman.*

Decidedly worth the visit in itself is a 50-by-40-inch *Seated Portrait of Sir John Skynner* (1703–1805) by Thomas Gainsborough (1727–88)—one of three ordered in 1785, of which at least two were completed by the following year. The others are at Christ Church College, Oxford, and Lincoln's Inn, London. The Holyoke example, included in the definitive monograph on the painter by Ellis K. Waterhouse, was given by bequest in 1975 from the estate of William Skinner II. Heavily bewigged and clad in a scarlet gown, the subject wears a long chain of elaborate goldwork, with a Tudor rose suspended from it. This insigne connotes no special order, but was awarded for service to the king (Henry VII had added the Tudor rose to such traditional chains). An identical chain is worn by Sir Thomas More in Holbein's celebrated portrait in the Frick Collection, New York. There is some probability of work in this picture by assistants, but on the whole—and in particular in the rich landscape detail at the left—it is a most impressive Gainsborough. See also CT 54 and MA 306.

The painting collection is well displayed on the second floor of the library in the Donald R. Taber Gallery.

De Cordova Museum

Location: Sandy Pond Rd., ½ mile from the village center; parking available
Hours: Tues., Thurs., Fri. 10-5, Wed. 10-9:30, Sat. 12-5, Sun. 1:30-5
Admission: Charged, except Wed. evenings 5-9:30

Opened in 1951 as the De Cordova and Dana Museum and Park, this is among the most firmly established and flourishing art centers in New England. Set in extensive grounds on a hilltop not far from Walden Pond, it is housed in a Rhenish-looking brick *schloss* converted in 1910 from the former residence of Thomas Dana by his son-in-law and law partner, Julian De Cordova (1851–1945). After a lifetime of amassing a miscellaneous collection of art objects, De Cordova gave the estate to the town of Lincoln in 1930; eight years later the house was opened to the public as a museum and that summer drew fourteen hundred visitors.

As of 1951, the focus here was placed on the creation of a community art center for direct participation in the arts. It has maintained ever since an active program of temporary exhibitions (such as the memorable and highly important one on the China Trade in 1979), lectures, and concerts; and now offers over three hundred classes in painting, drawing, printmaking, design, pottery, and jewelry. An amphitheater and workshop building have been added to the facilities, and large sculptures dot the nearby grounds.

Given the proximity of Lincoln to the great museums of the Boston area, and given the artistic value of what Mr. De Cordova collected, it was a wise decision on the part of the trustees to preserve his Thoreau-inspired dreams of the estate as a whole, but to transform entirely the character and the use of the house itself.

As for the permanent collection, the original intention was modest. The plan was to encourage local talent by occasional acquisitions from exhibitions held at the museum. Gradually the scope was extended to include contemporary New England artists, and ultimately contemporary American artists and a few European ones. Since the available exhibition space is completely taken up when major exhibitions are staged, the visitor will normally find it difficult to get much idea of the very large collection that now exists. A catalogue listing, which can be consulted at the entrance desk, is the best way to find out what is here; and you may be lucky enough to find a large selection on display. On my visit I listed a score of impressive works, and selected two for reproduction and illustration. The earliest examples on my list are *Thistles*, an oil of 1945 by the English artist Graham Sutherland, and *Cape Split*, a watercolor of 1949 by John Marin. It also includes works by Aaronson, Baskin, Frasconi, Georg Grosz, Hans Hofmann, Kepes, Levine, Liberman (*Cardinal Points*, a large steel sculpture of 1965 in the gardens), Maurer, Henry Moore (a large linen wall-panel representing two figures), Ohashi, Sheeler (*Hex Signs*, a small tempera of 1958), and an untitled gouache of 1954 by the German painter Fritz Winter (honored internationally but too little in this country, although Harvard owns a fine large oil).

Figure,[162] an oil of 1956 about 6 feet high by the New York Abstract Expressionist Franz Kline (1910–62), is perhaps the outstanding large painting in the collection. Characteristically rough-brushed in dense black strokes on a disturbed white ground, it exemplifies John W. McCoubrey's penetrating comment in his fine book, *American Tradition in Painting* (New York: Braziller, 1963, page 10). Contrasting another large Kline with a superficially similar work by the French painter Pierre Soulages, he writes: ". . . the American painting appears raw and violent, without any pretention to small imperfections. . . . The brush strokes reach to the very edge of the canvas and seem hardly contained by the frame. . . . It cannot be read, as can Soulages' painting, as a material object—or figure—against a ground." In short, we are faced with a brash New World, with all its energies and dislocations.

Among the outdoor sculptures, *Three Lines,*[163] by George Rickey (born 1907), offers the spectacle of three slim spears of stainless steel, 18 feet high, moving rhythmically with every passing breeze. Rickey's kinetic art is based on considerable engineering knowledge. It differs from Calder's mobiles (see N H 2), limited to movement in horizontal planes, in the introduction of action along vertical axes. This is achieved by carefully calculated counterweights clustered at the base. The approach of sculpture to the delights of ballet is thus closer than in the work of any previous sculptor; but Rickey's steel ballets are inspired by nature, by the movement of trees and grasses in the wind.

162

163

Malden Public Library

Location: 36 Salem Street (Route 60)

Hours: Mon.-Thurs. 9-9, Fri.-Sat. 9-6; closed Sun. and holidays; closed Saturdays June through Labor Day. But see last paragraph, below

Admission: Free

The library building, opened in 1885, is one of the masterpieces of the Boston architect Henry Hobson Richardson (1838–86). Designed in Romanesque style with a brown sandstone exterior and an oak interior featuring an impressive barrel vault over the main hall, it has the powerful massing, the spaciousness, and the richness of materials and ornament that characterize his work.

Since 1892 the library has been acquiring a small but fine collection of European and American paintings purchased from the Elisha S. and Mary D. Converse art funds. An illustrated brochure, *Thirty Paintings in the Malden Collection*, was published in 1976. In addition to the five examples discussed below, attention is called to excellent works by Albert André, George Loring Brown, John Singleton Copley (*General Picton*), Charles H. Davis (1856–1933, a Boston Constable follower whose skies are memorable), Jean Léon Gérôme, Francesco Guardi, Winslow Homer (*The Whittling Boy,* 1873), George Inness (*In the Berkshires,* c. 1878), Martin Lewis (*The Flatiron Building—Madison Square*), Anthonie Palamedesz (*Boy with Dogs,* 1656), Hubert Robert, and Constant Troyon.

The so-called *Armorer,*[164] by Nicolaes Maes (1634–93), a pupil of Rembrandt in Amsterdam, is no armorer, but a military or paramilitary person dressed up in a late seventeenth-century Dutchman's idea of classical garb—a reflection of the revival of interest in classicism that began in Holland in the 1660s. Maes's early work (such as *An Old Woman at Prayer* in the Worcester Museum) developed from Rembrandt's later style toward an unaffected, compassionate sentiment rich

164

in effects of color and shadow. In the 1660s, however, he went to Antwerp, where he fell under the sway of the fashionable Baroque school of Rubens. The *"Armorer"* clearly shows this influence. It should be compared with the great Rubens portrait of the Earl of Arundel in the Gardner Museum (MA 47). Though it will not hold up in such company, we may nevertheless admire the vigor of its modeling, and its honest middle-class look.

Seascape with Squall Coming Up[165] is considered one of the finest early Turners in America. The arrangement is generally similar to Turner's most famous work of this time, the *Calais Pier* in the National Gallery of London (1803). All these works were strongly influenced by such seventeenth-century Dutch marine painters as Jacob van Ruisdael (see MA 74). Turner, however, stepped up the value range, enriched the color intensities, and increased the sense of struggle between man and the waters. Note the dramatic opposition of light on dark at the left against dark on light at the right. Already Turner has sounded the basic theme of Romanticism: nature wild and untamed. He then went on to such feats as *The Falls of the Rhine at Schaffhausen* (MA 79) and later (1840) to *Rockets and Blue Lights* (MA 253), but his theme remained constant.

Doges' Palace,[166] by Richard Parkes Bonington (1801–28), measuring 64 by 45 inches, is one of his largest paintings and among his most important in America. The Fogg Art Museum owns a small variant or sketch for it. Guided by the perspective lines, our eye travels rapidly along the Riva degli Schiavoni, past the great pink Gothic marvel and Sansovino's Renaissance Library, and on to the far distance. The rich colors run to high intensities in the shadows. The effect is at once powerful and sensuous; it is an Englishman's Romantic reaction to a fabulous

165

166

world. We share the young bargeman's fascination in a passing religious procession. Just as Turner deepened the space of Dutch marines of the seventeenth century and stepped up their value contrasts, so did Bonington in comparison with eighteenth-century Venetian artists' views of their city. Malden has a shimmering little example: *View of San Giorgio Maggiore*, by Francesco Guardi—with which Bonington's should be compared. Note too how Bonington has enriched the colors as against the blond palette of Guardi's Rococo statement. One may admire Bonington's intimate little English scene at Yale (CT 59) even more than his more ambitious record of Venice, but the latter brings him closer to his Romantic French contemporaries, Baron Gros and Delacroix, who saw his work at the Paris Salons and were influenced by them. *Doges' Palace* dates from c. 1826, just before Bonington's death at the age of twenty-seven.

Woman Churning,[167] by Jean François Millet (1814–75), was exhibited at the Salon of 1870, where it was well received. Of Norman peasant origin, Millet studied in Paris and was enthralled by the work of Michelangelo and of Poussin (see MA 123). Like Daumier, his near contemporary, he adapted the grandiose forms of great past masters to a deeply felt interpretation of the life he knew so well. The churn is a powerful truncated cone, its axis reinforced by the instrument the woman handles so confidently. Her figure has the stability and the density of a limestone Gothic portal statue. The cat huddles against her. A deep space, defined by the paving stones and the rough oak beams, provides an ample continuum for this transformation of a moment in daily life into something majestic and monumental. The many objects in the back plane are appropriately subdued, but they run to stable geometric forms: squares, globes, cylinders. Color is likewise subdued in this serious, hushed world.

What a contrast in Frank Benson's *Hilltop*,[168] a big (71 by 51 inches) variant of French Impressionist art! Born in 1862, some twenty years

167

168

later than Claude Monet (who often painted the same theme in the 1880s but without the prettiness or the sentimental appeal of the small boy), Benson brushed this picture of sunny innocence in 1903. He outlived Monet by a quarter century, but never ventured into the complex and daring directions of Monet's later years (see MA 254). Despite the intrusion of "story" interest (what are the children seeing in the distance?), Benson's picture can be enjoyed as exhilarating painting, notably in the freshness of his whites and bright blues, and in the flutter of drapery and scarf. While the girl's figure has no sense of Millet's substance, the foamy billows of her dress can excite you.

Visitors should take into account that the library hours given above do not apply literally to the special gallery where the paintings are exhibited. Libraries are notoriously understaffed and underendowed. Plan your visit accordingly.

Museum of the American China Trade

Location: 215 Adams St. Follow Route 28 (Randolph Ave.) northerly from Route 128, turn right on Adams St.; from Boston, follow S.E. Expressway (Route 3) to exit 22, turn right
Hours: Tues.-Sat. 1-4; closed holidays
Admission: Charged

The museum is housed in the Captain Robert Bennet Forbes mansion, a sturdy edifice of 1833 overlooking Quincy Bay. The style might be called modified Greek Revival with an Oriental flavor.

The collection is a gem of its kind. If this were a book on the decorative arts, our account would be a long one and it would be generously illustrated. The focus here is on one of the most exciting and important developments of the post-Colonial age of sailing. Far Eastern wealth was vital to American maritime and industrial growth. When the United States entered the China Trade soon after the Revolution, it was not with government backing, as with the Dutch and English companies, but through the enterprise of individuals at their own risk. Smaller and swifter than those of their competitors, American ships were able to deliver cargoes at a lower price. Trade was limited to Canton, where foreigners were restricted to a section of hongs (factories) on the waterfront.

Fine China export is often to be seen in other museums, but the displays here are dazzling. Cases of rare porcelain—green, blue, apricot, and occasionally yellow—make the visitor wish he could finger their subtle glazes. Ship portraits and views of the teeming Canton waterfront bring this faraway world vividly to life. Fantastically ornate Chinese Chippendale furniture, sometimes more interesting than inviting, attracted a new American taste emerging from its Puritan bonds. Not to be overlooked is a vitrine on the upper floor filled with diminutive samples of wares offered by the hongs to prospective buyers. Fine textiles and rugs will also whet your appetite.

Virtually all American households on the eastern seaboard that could afford them coveted these luxury items. Backing up the displays are some seventy-five thousand documents of the China Trade. Throughout the year lectures and programs for all ages and interests related to this great American venture are available.

Whaling Museum

Location: 18 Johnny Cake Hill (just south of Route 6 near the harbor)
Hours: Mon-Sat. 9-5, Sun. 1-5; closed Thanksgiving, Christmas, New Year's Day
Admission: Charged

Among the attractions offered in New Bedford are the Sandwich Glass Museum, the Seaman's Bethel, and the Whaling Museum. The first-named is unfortunately beyond the scope of this book. The second, administered by the New Bedford Port Society and located opposite the Whaling Museum, was dedicated in 1832 to the moral and spiritual improvement of seamen. The shoreside early portion of Melville's *Moby Dick* surely memorializes it, along with the oratorical sermon preached from its nautical pulpit.

The Whaling Museum was established in 1907 by the Old Dartmouth Historical Society, named for the Colonial township that included what is now greater New Bedford. Substantial additions have been made to the original building, given by the family of Jonathan Bourne, along with a sixty-foot model of his whaling ship, the *Bark Lagoda.* This is said to be the largest ship model in the world. Boardable, it is a complete and accurate reduced version of the typical sort of whaleship that set forth from New Bedford around the middle of the nineteenth century.

A full and enthralling account of the whaling industry can be obtained here, including paintings of the sea giants and their intrepid hunters. Figureheads and stern boards, of the kind visible at Mystic Seaport (CT 42) and the Peabody Museum at Salem, Mass., are much in evidence, as well as the expected array of scrimshaw work. A "jagging wheel," or pie crimper, is an especially elegant example, with its handle in the form of a unicorn. There is a large collection of marines and ship portraits.

The museum is also concerned with local history and the work of New Bedford artists. Albert Bierstadt and Albert Pinkham Ryder both grew up in New Bedford, and of lesser note are William Bradford, R. Swain Gifford, William Allen Wall, and Clifford W. Ashley. The museum owns a single Bierstadt and no Ryder, but of the others listed it has the largest existing collections. There are also portraits by Gilbert Stuart, Rembrandt Peale, and Chester Harding.

Bierstadt's *Gosnold at Cuttyhunk* (one of the Elizabeth Islands due south of New Bedford) is a precious record of his early years. Dating from 1859, it immediately precedes the lovely example discussed at Framingham (MA 154). R. Swain Gifford (1840–1905), too easily confused with his distant cousin Sanford Robinson Gifford (1823–80; see VT 16), will also enchant you. While the Giffords owed much to the older painters of the Hudson River School, their feeling for light and their delicacy of touch relate them to such Luminists as Fitz Hugh Lane and Martin Johnson Heade.

The New Bedford Free Public Library owns three more paintings by Bierstadt and several by Bradford. While not all of its paintings are on view, a visit is recommended.

Smith College Museum of Art

Location: Elm Street
Hours: Tues.-Sat. 11-4:30, Sun. 2-4:30; closed academic holidays; in June open by appointment only; in July and August, Tues.-Sat. 1-4
Admission: Free. Ⓗ

Smith College is fortunate in possessing one of the two most important college art museums in the United States. It shares this distinction with Oberlin College, and the two collections are surpassed only by those of such major universities as Harvard and Yale. Founded in 1881 as the Hillyer Gallery, in 1926 it received attractive new quarters by bequest from Dwight W. Tryon, an Impressionist painter of reputation who directed the gallery from 1886 to 1920. Steady growth of the collections and of the art enterprise at Smith forced a decision to build a whole new complex, involving the destruction of both the Hillyer and the Tryon facilities. During the period of new construction, fifty-eight of the Museum's finest nineteenth- and twentieth-century paintings were circulated by the American Federation of Arts to ten American museums, from Washington, D.C., to Seattle, from Texas to Ohio, and from Richmond to Utica, N.Y. Designed by John Andrews of Toronto, the new complex houses the collections, studios, lecture and seminar rooms, and the art library. It opened in 1973, the new museum building being named Tryon Hall.

Thanks to a generous endowment, the museum has assembled excellent works of sculpture and an impressive selection of prints, drawings, and photographs. It is chiefly known, however, for its paintings, particularly by nineteenth- and twentieth-century French masters. Many of these were acquired through the perspicacity and daring of its directors in the years 1920 to 1946, Alfred Vance Churchill and Jere Abbott; the collection continues to expand in this field. It also includes Dutch and English landscapes; French and Italian paintings of the eighteenth century; American painting in its entire development; and modern European painting.

To the discussion of Greek vases at Bowdoin College (ME 1-3) we happily add an *Archaic Red-figure Kylix*,[169] or drinking cup, dating from c. 520 B.C., about 5 inches high and with a diameter of 13 inches. Of exceptionally fine quality, it is attributed to the Nikosthenes Painter. The date places it at the earliest appearance of the red-figure technique

169

—discussed in the Bowdoin entry—and some thirty years before Bowdoin's *Black-figure Lekythos.* In other words, the transition from the
earlier and more difficult black-figure technique to the more manageable
red-figure method took place only gradually. (It took a comparable time
for automobiles to cease looking like carriages.) The drawing style is
remarkably free for its, or indeed for any, time. Satyrs and symposiasts
ornament the outer rim; in the center a discus thrower bends in harmony
with the surrounding circular frame, and the discus provides an echoing
circle. Our illustration, however, is focused on the profile of this elegant
vessel. The wide shape of its gently upcurved bowl is similar to the form
of the bearing member (*echinus*) of Archaic Doric capitals of the same
period. An authoritative study of this lovely possession, by Phyllis
Lehmann, appeared in the 1957 issue of the museum's *Bulletin.*

Greek and Roman marble sculpture is well represented here, especially
by a *Head of an Athlete,* from the fourth century B.C., powerful despite
its damages and abrasions. There is a fine small mosaic, and from
Easternized Roman antiquity comes a *Mummy Portrait* from Fayum,
Egypt, of the first or second century A.D.—a starkly impressive foretaste of Byzantine art.

A small gold-ground wooden *Processional Cross,* painted in tempera
on both sides, gives a fine impression of Italian painting of the thirteenth
century as it infused Gothic feeling into Byzantine traditional forms.

In the large city museum, the public generally overlooks drawings,
and it tends to forget that a painting is (or used to be) the end of a
long creative process. The smaller, informal gallery, which can escape
departmentalization, has a great educational advantage, and this has not
been overlooked here. Perhaps the museum's most precious possession
is an early Netherlandish drawing, *Portrait of a Young Man,*[170] attributed to Dieric Bouts (c. 1420–75). Such studies for small oil paintings on wooden panel are exceedingly rare. Here the delicacy of touch
matches the fugitive beauty of the medium, silverpoint. The metal point
leaves an indelible trace on the prepared paper, and thus the most
disciplined skill is called for. This drawing is widely considered one of
the masterpieces of its kind and few have hesitated to accept it as the
work of the Haarlem-born master of Louvain, who painted the *Half-
length Madonna and Child* in the Busch-Reisinger Museum (MA 100).
But Erwin Panofsky, in his monumental and authoritative *Early Netherlandish Painting,* argued that while the tall cap was in vogue in the
1470s, everything about the drawing suggests that it is a self-portrait, and

170

thus much too young to be Bouts himself, who was at least fifty by 1470. Anyone who disputes Dr. Panofsky on Early Netherlandish matters does so at his peril.

Another drawing of prime quality and significance is a black chalk *Study of Drapery*[171] by Mathis Gothardt-Niethart, called Grünewald (1465–1528). This is presumably a study for the lost *Transfiguration of Christ*, once in the Dominican Church of Frankfurt-am-Main, dating from about 1512. The corner inscription, "A. Dürer"—a brave guess of long ago—can be discounted. Born about the same time as Dürer (1471–1528) and dying in the same year, Grünewald worked primarily in the Rhenish area of Mainz, but his masterpiece is the great multi-paneled altarpiece, completed in 1515, for the monastery of Isenheim, near Colmar, where it is preserved in that city's museum. The Smith College drawing is so close to the drapery of the Madonna in the Incarnation panel that it might have been a study for that figure. The Isenheim Altar, or rather, certain sections of it, inspired Paul Hindemith's Expressionist opera, *Mathis der Maler*. Expressionism is a modern term, but its extension backward to include such masters as El Greco and Grünewald is now accepted. The hypernervous wiggles of outline in the drawing, the sudden breaks, the cavernous recessions, the strangely fleshy appearance of the right knee despite the fact that it is covered with drapery—all these indicate the tumultuous spirit that produced the wild *Temptation of St. Anthony* and the agonized, even gangrenous *Crucified Christ* of the Isenheim Altar.

Among several fine Dutch seventeenth-century paintings, the *View of Rijnland*,[172] signed and dated in 1647 by Jan van Goyen (1596–1656), is outstanding. An oil on hardwood panel, only 16 inches high, it presents a vast panorama of the Dutch flatlands reduced to a 4-inch horizontal strip under a densely clouded, lowering sky. Gray and olive-brown tones set the mood of this restless image of infinity. A group of cows and a few figures establish the foreground—all very diminutive, but nonetheless telling—and a horseman starts us off on our long journey. Such views resemble less Rembrandt's *Landscape with an Obelisk* (1638, in the Gardner Museum, MA 49) than Vincent van Gogh's Dutch drawings of the years before he moved to Paris and then on to Provence.

171

172

We turn now to a series of portraits spanning time from the Age of Louis XIV to the beginning of our century. An oil sketch, 20½ inches high, of the great naval commander *Victor Marie, Marquis de Coeuvres, Duc d'Estrées*,[173] by Hyacinthe Rigaud (1659–1743) served for a full-dress, "paraphernalia" portrait in the grand manner of Rigaud's celebrated image of the Sun King himself (Louvre, 1701). Interestingly enough, in that portrayal the head of the monarch is painted on a separate canvas affixed to the main one. Louis, of course, sat for the head alone, and a retainer stood for the figure—as also occurred when Goya painted the Spanish royal family in 1800 (Prado).

Like Edouard Manet, in Smith College's fine *Portrait of Marguérite de Conflans* (1873), Rigaud worked rapidly and with confidence. Both artists observed their subjects and then set about ordering the features in a pictorial style. Both were excited by the medium itself, Rigaud in the shape of the shadow cast by the chin, the sensual bow of the upper lip, the liquid surface of the eyes—each with its spot of highlight—and the furry texture of the brows. Manet's subtle play of greens and black is matched by Rigaud's pink-orange flesh tones, the black wig, the natty little dabs of mustache, and the deep shadow of the chin.

Such continuities in the French approach to painting stand in contrast to the American one, as seen in portraits by McIlworth, Copley, and Eakins. Thomas McIlworth (active 1758–69), in his *Portrait of Dr. William Samuel Johnson*,[174] painted in 1761, strikes for the elegance of an ivorylike finish, long and lean features, and shoulders sloping to form an oval related to the inner oval framing the figure. There being no evidence of the flurry of brush strokes, we sense a personage taken out of time, rigidly posed, and set for long painting sessions. Rigaud captures the moment; his subject almost seems to be breathing, as in portraits by the Impressionists. While Dr. Johnson is forcefully characterized, our remarks about his physique apply to a whole range of McIlworth's portraits, and thus it may or may not have corresponded to the truth.

About the same time that McIlworth was painting in New York City

173

174

and the Albany region, John Singleton Copley (1738–1815) was at the top of his form in Boston, before he left for London (and forever) in 1774. His magnificent *Seated Portrait of John Erving*,[175] c. 1772, over 4 feet high, is much more deeply observed than McIlworth's *Dr. Johnson*; it is less rigid, and it has the peculiarity of a somewhat stunted physique. Nevertheless, it too has a high sheen; nothing moves; and the figure is approached in exactly the same painstaking and objective spirit as the inkstand and letter, the side chair, and Erving's cuffs, buttons, and wig. In short, it is a still-life portrait. In quality it matches Bowdoin College's *Thomas Flucker* of c. 1770 (ME 12).

Thomas Eakins (1844–1916) painted *Mrs. Edith Mahon*[176] in 1904. Allowance made for the passage of more than 125 years, we might almost be in the presence of another Copley image, for the subject has been observed with the same hard, uncompromising honesty. Eakins's picture came late in his career, almost thirty years after *Elizabeth at the Piano*, that dark masterwork at Andover (MA 17). The light is stronger, and details of the face thereby limned more clearly; but the expressive gaze is as fixed in reverie as John Erving's is riveted upon the spectator. Eakins has no interest in Edouard Manet's worldly sophistication, nor in the subtle evocations of Degas's portraits, but rather in the physical presence of a personality. Mrs. Mahon was an English pianist —yet another case of Eakins's obsession with music and musicians.

Of several paintings by J. B. C. Corot (1796–1875) in the collection, a small *View of the Romanesque Abbey of Jumièges*[177] is perhaps the finest. Painted about 1830, it shows the remains of now-vanished wall paintings in the central tower. This early work has a directness, to which the simple geometric forms no doubt contribute. Such works were far ahead of their time, though there is precedent for them in earlier French painters like Poussin. (Compare the landscape background of the *Holy Family* at the Fogg Museum, MA 123). Until Corot altered his style to

176

175

177

a softer, more ingratiating manner, which is shown in the museum's
Dubuisson's Grove (1868), he was virtually unrecognized. After 1900
his early work was admired by the Cubists, but by that time it had become clear that Paul Cézanne had already brought fresh vision to Corot's
discovery of durable forms beneath the shifting appearances and magical
lights of nature. Smith was fortunate in acquiring the *Jumièges* in
1924, long before prices for early Corots ballooned. It has been widely
exhibited and universally admired.

Alfred Vance Churchill, the director who enriched the Smith collections in these early years with so many French nineteenth-century
masterpieces, produced his own in 1929 with the acquisition of a major
work, measuring over 6 by 8 feet, by Gustave Courbet (1819–77).[178]
Known as *La Toilette de la Mariée* until recently, it has now become
La Toilette de la Morte. No Village Bride here, but the preparation of
a dead girl's body for burial. X-ray, ultraviolet, and infra-red examination produced surprising revelations: the "bride" was originally nude,
her head sagged toward her left shoulder, the left arm of the attendant
(not of the bride) held the mirror, and the bride's arm lay limply across
her lap. It was clear from the fumbling character of the alterations that
Courbet did not make them; furthermore, the position of the mirror so
close to the bride makes no sense unless it is held by the attendant for
her own use. Off to the right, young friends recite prayers for the departed; any other interpretation is senseless. Ensuing research revealed
that Courbet did indeed paint a *Toilette de la Morte* (not surprising in
view of his 1849/50 *Funeral at Ornans,* in the Louvre), but there is no
record of a *Toilette de la Mariée.* The alterations were made long after
Courbet's death (for it never left his studio) in order to make it more
salable, since morbid pictures do not ordinarily attract buyers. All this
was duly recounted in the catalogue of the great 1978 Paris retrospective
of Courbet's work.

No action has been taken by the museum to bring the picture back to
its original appearance, partly because the picture itself is not finished
(the upper left and right corners are by no means resolved) and partly
out of respect for its actual history. As to its date, some time between
1850 and 1855 is generally agreed upon.

Despite these problems, the picture has enormous power. As a dark
poem of village life it rivals the works of Emile Zola, Courbet's alter
ego in literature. The rough brushwork gives many of the figures,

178

notably the central one leaning forward, the impact of French Gothic limestone sculpture. A dominant grayness underscores the stonelike character, as does the composition, with its strong rectangles and its many globular shapes. From this work we can understand why Courbet was criticized for painting "as if with a trowel."

Jephtha's Daughter,[179] 1858–60, is the largest and one of the finest of the early figure compositions of Edgar Degas (1834–1917). It measures 6½ by 10 feet. In a superbly fashioned circular design bracketed at the sides by standing men, the conquering Jephtha enters— to make the agonizing discovery that it is his daughter and only child who comes forth to greet him, across an expressively void space. (See Judges 11:30–40.) While the figure style emphasizes outline drawing, as instilled in Degas by his admiration for Ingres (see M A 126) and his own study of the Early Renaissance masters in Florence, the color has a range and a subtlety unknown to these precursors. The brushwork, though subdued, is as sensitive as Titian's. Observe, for example, the orange bandeau around Jephtha's head. From the point of view of compositional progression, circular and oval elements announce the advancing procession and prepare you for the oval plateau on which the daughter stands with her distraught companions. Right of center, the impressive figure of a foot soldier serves two artistic functions: he turns the action toward the daughter, but his curved sword (which helps to fill a nearby vacant upper corner) disguises by its counteraction what would otherwise be a too obvious hubless wheel in the composition as a whole. In Handel's late oratorio *Jephtha*, one finds similarly restrained passion, similar use of convention to reinforce clarity, and musical subtleties to be discovered only in repeated hearings. Unhurried study of Degas's great composition is likewise recommended.

If we were discussing a museum of lesser consequence, we should now consider paintings by Ingres (and a wonderful double portrait in pencil), two more masterworks by Degas, the Manet portrait already mentioned, two Monets, a portrait of an invalid woman by Renoir, and other Impressionist works. There is even an early Gauguin of a Paris suburb, signed and dated 1879, when he studied with the Impressionists —well before his characteristic Breton and Tahitian pictures.

179

We cannot fail, however, to consider *La Route Tournante à La Roche-Guyon*,[180] by Paul Cézanne (1839–1906). The date is 1885, when Cézanne spent some summer weeks with Renoir in this village not far from Giverny, where, the year before, Claude Monet had begun his visits and would later buy a house and develop his famous garden and lily-pad pool. La Roche-Guyon has a magnificent medieval donjon, but Cézanne paid no attention to it; his interests were not archaeological. *La Route Tournante* was acquired by Mr. Churchill in 1932—his last purchase. A certificate signed by Cézanne's son states that it was painted by his father and given to Renoir. For its mid-1880s date it is more loosely and thinly brushed than usual (compare the Fogg Art Museum's *Still Life*, MA 129). We may hazard a guess that Cézanne's momentary partial return to his Impressionist technique of the previous decade was, if not influenced by Renoir's art, intended as an oblique compliment to him. In every other respect, however, the picture is a denial of Impressionist premises. The camera's single point of view has given way to a multiple one (a photograph of the motif shows the hillside masonry at the left canted inward); the road curves upward rather than back (thus reinforcing the plane of the canvas itself); the high horizon brings the hill forward and effectively reduces what Cézanne called negative space—something to be avoided in the interests of making all parts of the picture function actively in an organic whole. As a result, Impressionism's single-instant image seen from a fixed position has been lifted out of the passage of time; Cézanne's view is not how "it looked," but how it will always be. We may argue that the work is unfinished; but to see a Cézanne in process, developing evenly in all its parts, is a precious experience.

In a memorable book, *Characteristics of French Art*, Roger Fry discussed the special French combination of a sense of actuality with a feeling for broad, monumental forms. Nowhere is this better seen than in the work of Georges Seurat (1859–91), whose masterpiece, *Sunday Afternoon on La Grande Jatte*, is a major possession of the Art Institute of Chicago. Smith College owns three studies for this work: a small oil of a woman with a monkey and two Conté crayon drawings. *Three Women*,[181] c. 1885/6, shares Cézanne's sense of permanence. The

180

181

wonderfully observed shapes are entities in themselves, their spatial position established merely by size and by the degree of pressure on the black crayon. The rough grain of the paper is not disguised; indeed, it may have suggested to Seurat the minutely dotted touches with which he laboriously executed his 8-by-10-foot canvas. Notice that in the drawing, as in the final painting, the overall texture supports the reality of a picture as a flat surface to which medium is applied. Note also that in the small oil sketch, painted quickly on the spot in Impressionist technique, both shapes and texture receive less attention. That will come later, in the studio, under no summer Sunday illumination, but, as Seurat preferred, by gaslight.

We have discussed Childe Hassam (1859–1935), the leading American Impressionist, in a stylish Parisian picture of 1888 at New Britain (CT 46). Eleven years later he painted *White Island Light, Isles of Shoals, at Sundown*.[182] This strong and brilliantly colored marine (for water is the main subject once you clear the great cliffs) has the high horizon of Claude Monet's *Rocks at Belle-Ile* and his *Haystack* series of the late 1880s and early 1890s, but the brush strokes are more regularized. While it would be a mistake to call them Pointillist, in the manner of Seurat, their ordered parallels do manage to achieve something of the same mosaic effect. A fascinating exhibition organized in 1978 by the Art Galleries of the University of New Hampshire, with text by Susan Faxon and others, included sixteen Childe Hassams painted on the Isles of Shoals between 1886 and 1912. Smith College's example was one of them. For its title, "A Stern and Lovely Scene: A Visual History of the Isles of Shoals," the exhibition borrowed a phrase from Nathaniel Hawthorne's description in *American Notebooks*, 1852. These rugged islands, some ten miles off Portsmouth, N.H., attracted many summer residents, and the list of painters included Olaf Brauner, William Morris Hunt, and William Trost Richards as well as Childe Hassam.

The briefest glance at *The Suitor*[183] (also called *The Workshop*), an oil of 1893 only a foot high by Edouard Vuillard (1868–1940), will indicate that Seurat's Pointillist technique had a following in France. In Vuillard, however, it served a different purpose. Although he painted

182

183

some large canvases, his work at the turn of the century favored the intimacy of a small format, and he crowded it with pattern upon pattern with an almost claustrophobic effect. The introduction of "story" interest here, in the peeping suitor, is unusual. Vuillard's interiors, into which natural light penetrates with difficulty, are frequently uninhabited; when people are present they sit in silence, or bend in total concentration on their household duties. The household, indeed, is Vuillard's chief subject. Its décor is out of fashion in today's antiseptic arrangements, but readers old enough to recall elderly hotels in France will understand what Vuillard was responding to. He lived quietly in Paris with his mother and did his work in their small apartment. Familiar with the painting theories of Maurice Denis, he emphasized the picture's flat surface. The Symbolist theories of the poet Mallarmé also attracted him. Like Mallarmé, who opposed "naming" an object in favor of an appeal to the reader's imagination through evoking and suggesting it, Vuillard knits his objects into a complex tapestry. Writing of the Smith picture in the catalogue for the Museum of Modern Art's retrospective in 1954, Andrew Ritchie observed: "By a process of telescoping planes in a picture . . . the foreground, middleground and background overlap and fuse into a pulsating space that bears a kind of relation to the fusion of imagery in a poem by Mallarmé." Echoes of Vuillard's strong influence on the young Matisse in the 1890s linger in the latter's painting of 1904 in the Gardner Museum (MA 52).

The developing theory of painting as first of all a flat surface, promulgated as the nineteenth century came to a close, and the influence of Cézanne's painting by flat planes that marked his mature and late work, led to the rise of Cubism in Paris. The seminal figures here were the Spaniard Picasso and the Frenchman Georges Braque, in their work of c. 1908–12. In general, Picasso was the daring pathfinder, Braque the more cautious creator of fine paintings. A younger Spanish friend of Picasso who took the name of Juan Gris (1887–1927, real name González) quickly followed their lead into collage, that is, the use of pasted papers as an additional element in what was to be applied to the canvas. Nothing could be flatter than these snippets of newsprint or wallpaper. If they happened to carry a printed message or to represent something, such meanings were rarely relevant to what the artist intended to convey; they were to be regarded as patterns, elements of scale in an organized design. With photographic illusion now left entirely to the photographers, the artist was free to make his statement without recourse to it. *Glasses and Newspaper*,[184] a Gris collage of 1913/14 some 2 feet high, remains true to Picasso's and Braque's "Spanish" grisaille scheme of tans, grays, blacks, and whites—current in their Cubist paintings and collages of c. 1910–12. If Gris's newsprint has browned with time, we may welcome this alteration on the same basis that weathering enriches medieval stained glass. The Cubists' subject was essentially the Montmartre bistro: a table with or without a cloth; glasses, bottles, carafes, siphons; playing cards, the game of chess; the day's newspaper, the guitar of a strolling musician. Gris's collage contains some of these elements of the new iconography. In line with Mallarmé's appeal to suggest rather than to name an object, none is completely represented.

All are fragmented (including the masthead of *Le Journal*). Such fragmentation implies multiple observation of the object from shifting points of view. Semitransparent and interpenetrating planes assist in the formation of a shallow space. You are looking *down* at the table instead of looking at objects *on* a table from the traditional viewpoint (as in ME 36). Cézanne's desire to make all parts function actively in the design is fully achieved here. Note, for example, the large glass at the upper left, in what would traditionally be an empty corner.

Jere Abbot's purchase of *La Table*,[185] an oil of 1919/20 by Pablo Picasso (1881–1973), did not make all Smithies happy even though the date of acquisition was 1932. Today, few would deny that it is a masterpiece of later Cubism; and none that the eye that chose it—and chose Degas's *Jephtha*, and Degas's portrait of his young brother René, and the superb *Blonde Gasconne* by Corot, and Seurat's oil sketch for *La Grande Jatte*, and Monet's *Seine à Bougival*; and the previously discussed van Goyen landscape, the silverpoint drawing by Bouts (*pace* Dr. Panofsky), and *The Suitor* by Vuillard—that this eye was anything less than sensitive.

By 1913 (as in the still life at Dartmouth College, NH 11) color returned to brighten Picasso's grisaille Cubist palette of the years just preceding, and his collages from that time on followed suit. From the beginning, collages had involved a witty give-and-take between reality and illusion: the illusionary representations on the *papiers collés* and the illusionary newsprint messages played second fiddle to the reality of the artist's abstract statement. Such oils as Smith's *Table* may be thought of as illusions of collages, since they contain no collage whatever. However that may be, it is fair to say that at his best Picasso expresses himself through sharp and angular patterns full of knife-blade shapes evocative of the nervous tensions of our age. All of this has its roots in the art of Picasso's Spain; and the trend was apparently set by the effects of seven centuries of Moorish impact on Spanish culture. Central to Picasso's art is the piling up of a construction rickety as a house of cards. Here as always his invention surpasses the apparent possibilities of the

184

185

subject: in this instance a table, a tablecloth, and a guitar. For the visitor who desires to arrive at an understanding of Cubism, prolonged study of this masterpiece cannot be recommended too highly.

Goat,[186] a drawing in pen and colored inks of 1925 by Paul Klee (1879–1940), was the gift of Jere Abbot in 1976; it had long been a treasured item on indefinite loan. We have discussed other small Klees of the same period at Colby College (ME 41) and the Busch-Reisinger Museum (MA 107); but this one attains a larger scale and greater mysteriousness, no doubt from the impact of the horns and the eyes. Note that only the right eye is a full circle; the other, bisected, suggests a turn back into space. Like the Chinese and the Japanese, Klee manipulates a few well-defined abstract notations through what we may call musical variations to describe only what is essential. One of these variations is in the color of the ink chosen.

Discarded Treasures,[187] oil on canvas about 19 by 29 inches, was purchased in 1929 as a work of William M. Harnett (1848–92), whom we discuss in a very early example at Fitchburg (MA 153) and a characteristic late one at Springfield (MA 220). Signed "W. M. Harnett" at the lower right, the Smith painting seemed authentic, though the signature did not have the customary dating, and the style was somewhat softer than usual. During the 1940s the San Francisco critic Alfred Frankenstein noted that a large group of supposed Harnetts had the same peculiarities, and this launched him on a voyage of fruitful research. Proof positive that something was awry came when he found that minutely painted postmarks on a letter and a postcard in one of these "soft" Harnetts (*Old Scraps*, purchased by Nelson A. Rockefeller and later given to the Museum of Modern Art) bore the date 1894—two years after Harnett's death. Further exploration, with all the twists and turns of a detective story, led to the discovery that some twenty of these pictures were the work of John Frederick Peto (1854–1907)—

186

187

and a trip to Island Heights, New Jersey, where the artist's daughter still lived, surrounded by his pictures and the very objects shown in many of the paintings under discussion. Peto was, at the time, little known except as one of many modest competitors of Harnett in fool-the-eye painting and influenced by him. Harnett, highly successful in his day with a clientele that paid high prices for his expensive-looking assemblages, was enthusiastically "resurrected" and sought after by museums and collectors in the late 1920s and 1930s, having earlier been edged into oblivion by the rise of modern art. Whether Peto's pictures were turned into Harnetts soon after Harnett's death or more recently is uncertain, but in either case it is clear that Peto was entirely innocent of the falsification. All of this is recounted in Frankenstein's *After the Hunt* (Berkeley: University of California Press, revised edition, 1969).

In 1950, forty-three years after Peto's death, the first one-man exhibition of his work—including Smith's picture—opened at the Smith College Museum of Art, and then traveled to the Brooklyn Museum and to San Francisco. On this occasion I bought *Pipe and Church Sconce* for Williams College, and learned that on Frankenstein's suggestion the staff at Smith had taken their "Harnett" out of its frame, discovered about an inch of additional painted canvas turned under at the base, and that on this strip the word EACH completed the simulated sticker, "10 cents"—and that at the far right there was a clear indication of an erased signature under the Harnett one.

Subsequently, Peto—sometimes called the poor man's Harnett because of the relative plainness of the objects he portrayed—has been reinstated as indeed a worthy competitor. Some who have compared Harnett with Jan van Eyck because of his extreme precision have been reminded of Vermeer of Delft by Peto's painterly touch and less petrified vision. When the Smith College picture changed authors the event was a bit of a shock, but all's well that ends well.

Our next selection, a small watercolor of *Freight Cars*[188] by Charles Burchfield (1893–1967), differs so greatly from the jumbo-sized example discussed at New Britain (CT 49) that at first glance it appears to be the work of another artist. But the Smith watercolor dates from 1919, whereas *Lavender and Old Lace* was not begun until 1939 and not completed until 1947. A closer look at the weathered surface of the freight cars and the painting of their undercarriages will indicate similarities of touch—for example, compare the trees above the old house in the New Britain example. Burchfield's mastery of his medium, achieved by his mid-twenties, is everywhere apparent here. The subtlety

188

of his range of reds, heightened by a daring use of black, is exemplary. It would be easy, but unfortunate, to pass by this small gem, which came to Smith in 1970 from most knowledgeable donors—Mr. and Mrs. Alfred Barr, Jr.—to honor Jere Abbot.

Our lengthy discussion of Smith's paintings and its drawings (fine ones by Tintoretto and Daumier not even mentioned) should not distract attention from the collection of sculpture. Leaving to the sections on other museums discussion of ancient, medieval, African, and Pre-Columbian examples, we turn to works by two major French sculptors. Claude Michel Clodion (1738–1814), the sculptural counterpart of such Rococo painters as François Boucher and Jean Honoré Fragonard (see MA 252), is the highly talented author of a pair of terra-cotta groups, each a foot high above the handsome red marble base. A luscious *Nymph*, prefiguring Renoir but with more style and spirit, looks across at a Nijinsky-like *Satyr*.[189] Both are accompanied by playful or sleeping infants. They are among the finest acquisitions of the museum in the 1970s; and it is doubtful that they are surpassed by anything comparable, even in the Louvre. Their fluid modeling and varied textures rival any painter's brushwork; yet they retain, a century later, much of the strength of Bernini's marbles. As sometimes happens, but not very often, these terra-cottas expand beyond their small size through the bold scale of their design and the authority of their idea. We can easily imagine them executed at monumental size in stone, as in the contemporary German statues of the *Seasons* in the Busch-Reisinger Museum that once decorated the palace gardens at Bruchsal (MA 98). Discussions of Clodion's work too frequently miss his power. A definitive after-the-fact argument for it exists in the considerable influence Clodion had on the greatest French sculptors of the next century: Jean-Baptiste Carpeaux (see MA 237) and Auguste Rodin.

Both Carpeaux and Rodin broke with Academic insistence on smooth finish and general prettiness; and they were abused for it. The detailed textures of Clodion were a natural point of departure for them as they turned toward greater realism and deeper emotional expression. In Rodin's case the Clodion connection was limited to his youthful work, as in several enchanting plaster busts of young women modeled around 1865–70. Another point of contact was Rodin's training with the

189

sculptor Carrier-Belleuse, known as "the Clodion of the Second Empire," and work with him during this period at the Sèvres porcelain factory.

But Rodin's *Walking Man*,[190] a headless bronze 7½ feet high, is another matter. A late work of 1906, it immediately justifies its large size, even though it evolved as the enlargement of a much smaller study, executed almost thirty years earlier for the *St. John Baptist Preaching*, completed by 1880. First cast in 1907, the enlargement seen here is the ninth cast of an edition of 1965 from the celebrated Rudier foundry in Paris. *Man Walking* differs profoundly from the *St. John Baptist*. Minus head and arms, it avoids the overt moral message of a subject; its pocked and scarified surfaces are totally at variance with the relatively smooth torso and limbs of the *St. John*. If at first the Smith figure seems a mechanical expansion of a 3-foot-high study (which was also headless, armless and scarified), closer inspection reveals many changes, of which the most significant is the position of the right shoulder, which is shoved farther forward to increase the figure's driving force. *Walking Man* attains much of the grandeur of Michelangelo and Bernini, both of whom Rodin adored, but never imitated. A cast was offered in 1912 by some friends of Rodin to the French embassy in Rome and set up in the courtyard of the Farnese Palace. The ambassador rejected it: no headless statue to act as diplomatic agent for *his* country, even in a Rome full of beheaded antiques! As for Rodin, a pioneer in what was to become a dominant twentieth-century motif—the fragmented figure—he insisted that the body itself could express the noblest ideals. And even more than in the *St. John Baptist Preaching*, he achieved the nearly impossible: a walking figure that does not walk off its base. The more you study it the more you will discover departures from what would happen if a cast were taken from a living figure in this position. For a fuller account of this major work, the relevant pages of Albert E. Elsen, *Rodin* (New York: The Museum of Modern Art, 1963), are recommended.

Since the Baroque era of Bernini, no one had commanded the field of sculpture as Rodin did. An army of followers imitated him and many original talents who turned in new directions began their careers under his inspiration, among them Aristide Maillol and Constantin Brancusi (see CT 68). A brilliant younger German, Wilhelm Lehmbruck (1881–1919), arriving in Paris in 1910 for what turned out to be a four-year

190

stay, found the anti-Rodin movement toward greater simplification well under way. He was greatly attracted to Maillol (1861–1944), a painter who had turned to sculpture around 1900 and by 1905 had produced *La Méditerranée* (Paris, Tuileries Gardens), a masterpiece of serenity. Lehmbruck introduced a poignant inner feeling in his variations on Maillol's earthy classical nudes. Smith College's *Torso of the 'Pensive Woman,'*[191] cast in stone and reworked by the artist in 1913/14, superbly exemplifies Lehmbruck's early achievement. While the emphatic division of the body at the waist and the regularity of spherical and ovoid solids follow Maillol's lead, there is a new tenderness here, as well as an almost Gothic sense of vertical thrust. Note the hypersensitive flow of outline from thigh to waist. In sculpture, such an effect from one angle can result only from what, at another angle, is seen to be modeling. As you pass around the figure you will find that Lehmbruck's subtly molded surfaces produce similarly sensitive outlines from all views. The *Torso* was purchased in 1922, long before Lehmbruck became accepted in the United States, and, still more surprisingly, by that ardent Francophile, Alfred Vance Churchill.

Much attention in the foregoing has been paid to the two early directors of Smith College's museum. I am happy to add that succeeding ones have held to the high standard already set. Subsequent purchases already discussed include the Rodin, the Clodion, the Hassam, the McIlworth, the Rigaud, and the Greek *kylix*. There are many more for the visitor to discover.

191

Merrimack Valley Textile Museum

Location: 800 Massachusetts Ave., at exit 43 from Route 495
Hours: Tues.-Fri. 10-5; Sat., Sun. 1-5; closed New Year's Day, Easter, Thanksgiving, and Christmas
Admission: Charged, except on Sat. Ⓗ

This attractive and well-appointed museum developed from the energies of Samuel Dale Stevens (1859–1922), a wool manufacturer of North Andover who successfully promoted the establishment of the North Andover Historical Society in 1913. At his death he left a large collection of spinning wheels, reels, hand looms, warping frames, combs, tape looms, niddy noddies, and swifts. For readers needing further enlightenment on these terms, see Dr. Horatio Rogers's account of Stevens and his collection, published in January 1969 in the Essex Institute Historical Collections. Dr. Rogers, a retired surgeon, was the husband of Stevens's only daughter, who was determined to bring to fruition the original hopes of her father. In 1958, when Mrs. Rogers became president of the Historical Society, his collection was stored in a barn. With the enthusiastic support of Walter Muir Whitehill, director of the Boston Athenaeum, she laid plans to have the collection find its place in a museum that would give an account of the role of wool manufacturing in American history; and in 1959 a professional director was appointed. By this time some thousand cubic feet of the business records of M. T. Stevens & Sons Company had been added to her father's collection. With admirable vision the trustees decided against limiting the activities of the proposed museum by any regional or chronological restrictions. In 1964 the present building opened to the public; its eighteen thousand square feet of interior space was almost evenly divided among the exhibition area, the study collection, and administrative areas.

The exhibition, supplemented by photographic blowups, covers the development of American wool manufacturing from the seventeenth century to its modern industrialization, as well as the various processes required—from raw wool to finished product. Much of the time you may watch skilled craftspeople card, spin, and weave. Meanwhile, modern power machines hum and clatter. Examples of textiles are featured throughout.

A Conservation Center has also been added to the museum's facilities. Its extensive library is in constant use by scholars and other interested persons.

While this museum lies beyond the scope of the present book, a visit is such a delight that I have gladly made an exception. Furthermore, one of the exhibits, a loom of the type used in Holland since about 1700, brings a note of actuality to the Dutch Period painting of Vincent van Gogh discussed in the section on the Boston Museum of Fine Arts (MA 85).

Watson Gallery, Wheaton College

Location: Routes 123 and 140
Telephone: (617) 285-7722
Hours: Tues.-Sun. 1-5, Mon. 10-12 and 2-4; during summer and college vacations by appointment (phone ext. 428)
Admission: Free

The Watson Gallery, the gift of Mrs. Thomas J. Watson, is an attractively appointed modern space in the Fine Arts Center usually occupied by changing exhibitions organized by the gallery itself. An excellent reputation has been established for these exhibitions and their well-designed catalogues: a model for how to accomplish much on a very limited budget.

The permanent collection consists of the College Portraits, usually displayed in other buildings, and the gallery's modest but growing holdings. For the location of the portraits, inquire at the gallery. They include a series, painted mid-nineteenth century by Eunice M. Towle, of the Wheaton family. Judge Laban Wheaton (1754–1846) founded the college as a seminary for women in 1853 in memory of his daughter Eliza. He received the strong support of his wife and his daughter-in-law, Mrs. Laban Morey Wheaton. The last-named (1809–1905) appears, bespectacled, in a Towle portrait in her early maturity, and again, at the age of ninety-five, in a penetrating interpretation by John W. Alexander.

Among alumnae donors of art to the college was Eleanor Norcross (class of 1872), who founded the Fitchburg Art Museum. From c. 1890 to 1923 she was an expatriate artist living in Paris; there, at the height of enthusiasm for Japanese prints, she chose the fine collection given to the college by Mrs. Laban Morey Wheaton. They span the best period of such work, from Harunobu (1725–70) to Hiroshige (1797–1858).

The college's representation of nineteenth- and twentieth-century European and American prints is a good one, as is its collection of glass —from ancient examples to early and more recent American work. Among the paintings is *Audrey, the Shepherd Lass*, painted c. 1886/7 by Gari Melchers (1860–1932)—once owned by Potter Palmer of Chicago and before that widely exhibited in European cities. A George Inness, *Montclair: Meadow Scene*, dating from c. 1885, is in the misty late manner of this artist, whose stronger early work is discussed in examples at Orono (University of Maine), Andover, and Mount Holyoke College (MA 206). A strange but fetching little oil, *The Motherless*, painted c. 1865 by Elihu Vedder (1836–1923)—long before he turned muralist in Art Nouveau style—has a Dickensian sympathy for the orphaned.

The Berkshire Museum

Location: South Street (Route 7)
Hours: Tues.-Sat. 10-5, Sun. 2-5
Admission: Free. *For the Hancock Shaker Village (5 miles west on Route 20) see Hancock*

Founded in 1903 by Zenas Crane, the museum combines the functions of a museum of science and an art museum. The art collections are installed on the upper floor; in the basement is an interesting Historical Room with items of Berkshire interest. While two of the upstairs galleries are often occupied by temporary exhibitions, there are permanent installations of Old Master paintings, ancient decorative arts (fortified by a number of excellent plaster casts of major works of sculpture), and Far Eastern art. The Crane Room, at the head of the stairs, usually displays a very important group of large paintings by the Hudson River School.

The *Half-length Figure of a Priest*[192] is one of a series of six limestone sculptures from ancient Palmyra, an outpost of the Roman Empire in the Syrian desert. The date is about A.D. 150. These examples, particularly the one shown here, are among the finest in America of this phase of art history. Long before the formation of the Byzantine Empire, the elements of its art were so well established in Near Eastern art that it would be easy to imagine such a figure transformed into a gold-ground mosaic and looking very much like the representation of Justinian and his court at Ravenna. The priest, who holds an oil jar and incense bowl, is stiffly frontal, but by no means devoid of vitality. There is a wonderful play of three-dimensional forms, as in the chin, against the incised flat lines and ornaments. The eyes stare outward. Note that Boston's bust of the Emperor Elagabalus (MA 60), A.D. 219, though later and also Syrian, is much less Easternized; it originated in no desert outpost.

192

Two late medieval paintings in this museum are masterworks in any company of their peers. The first is an *Adoration of the Magi*[193] dated 1477 and signed in Latin by the north Spanish painter Juan Pons. It was presented to the museum in 1913, well in advance of the growth of interest in medieval Spanish art. (Mrs. Gardner, however, acquired the *St. Engracia* by Bermejo, MA 40, in 1904.) The life-size figures are compressed into the shallowest space, from which the only release is provided by a small marine landscape at the upper right. The painter combines a native delight in rich brocades, gold and Burgundy red, with a Flemish-inspired insistence on realistic detail. He leaves no doubt, for example, that Joseph was a carpenter. Joseph's halo, incidentally, is scalloped to indicate his lesser station in relation to the divine Virgin and Child. The ox and the ass are crammed into a sort of niche whose bow-shaped edge helps to centralize the action and unite the figures in this politely enacted scene.

Joachim Patinir (c. 1485–1524) is one of the links between Hieronymus Bosch and Pieter Brueghel in Flemish painting. In a later age he would have been a pure landscape painter; in his own day he selected religious themes, which gave him the greatest opportunity to exercise his remarkable gifts. Sometimes another painter executed his foreground figures. *The Flight to Egypt*,[194] and the related theme of the Rest on the Flight to Egypt, became one of his favorite subjects. It was also popular with Patinir's followers, of whom one of the most important was Adriaen Isenbrant, a Bruges master in the circle of Gerard David. Heartless recent connoisseurship has assigned the Pittsfield picture to Isenbrant rather than to Patinir himself. The distinction is a subtle one, but we must respect it. Beyond the foreground group, with their emphatic reds, we wind slowly toward the ice-blue distances of this landscape in much the same way that a Chinese painter invites us to join him in a contemplative journey through nature. Thus the element of time is added to visual art, as in a musical experience. For a total contrast, compare Hartford's *Return from the Flight to Egypt*, painted a century later at Antwerp by Peter Paul Rubens (CT 15).

193

194

A fine *Vision of St. Ignatius*, long attributed to Rubens, is now securely assessed as a school piece, though the design is possibly by Rubens. The forms are softer than those of the master and there is a greater sweetness in gesture and facial expression. Some Dutch pictures are under study to determine if they are replicas or variants by assistants. Several British portraits give a thoroughly autograph impression. A bust-length *Portrait of John Newton*, surveyor of His Majesty's Customs for Nova Scotia, is a work of John Singleton Copley not inferior to the great *Portrait of Thomas Flucker* at Bowdoin College (ME 12); it is on indefinite loan from the Berkshire Atheneum. The museum also owns one of many replicas of the bust of Hiram Powers's celebrated *Greek Slave* (see VT 9).

Valley of the Santa Ysabel,[195] an oil 40 by 60½ inches, is signed and dated 1875 (at the lower left) by Frederic E. Church (1826–1900). Discussing it in that year, Henry James wrote: ". . . a large and elaborate landscape at Goupil's—a certain 'Valley of Santa Isabel,' in New Granada. We know of nothing that is a better proof of the essential impotence of criticism, in the last resort, than Mr. Church's pictures. . . . If you praise them very highly, you say more than you mean; if you denounce them, if, in vulgar parlance, you sniff at them, you say less. . . . Why not accept this lovely tropic scene as a very pretty picture, and have done with it? A very pretty picture, surely, it was, and a very skilful, and laborious, and effective one . . . his brush is an extremely accomplished one, and we should be poorly set to work to quarrel with the very numerous persons who admire its brilliant feats" (*The Painter's Eye*, edited by John L. Sweeney; Cambridge: Harvard University Press, 1956, page 101).

Not my favorite art critic, but always provocative and interesting— even infuriating when he discusses Winslow Homer—James scored a near miss on Church's impressive panorama. What he missed, though he saw the "softest violet glow" and the level rays of the "yellow tropic sun" as they "come wandering forward down the mile-long gorges," was the poetic spell of the Luminism that connects Church with such earlier masters as Fitz Hugh Lane and Martin Johnson Heade. Such exotic visions as *Valley of the Santa Ysabel* are a very long way from Church's modest beginnings in New Haven a quarter-century before (CT 43). The road to New Granada began, soon after, in the Catskills section of the Hudson River. (See MA 210.)

195

The early residence of Alexander Calder, creator of mobile sculpture and later of "stabiles" (see CT 35), at Richmond, near Pittsfield, is signaled by works in the Berkshire Museum. Two small pre-mobile mechanisms, one worked by a hand crank, are in the starkly geometric vocabulary of the Bauhaus School. In the auditorium are two "mobiles," designed to flutter when the ventilation system is turned on; their gaily colored forms have the free shapes of the painting of Joan Miró (see CT 32) in the 1930s.

Pilgrim Hall

Location: 75 Court St. (take exit 38 from Route 3) ; Court St. is on
Route 3A
Hours: 9:30-4:30 daily
Admission: Charged

Built in 1824 by the Pilgrim Society, Pilgrim Hall contains a library and
collection of material bearing on the history of Plymouth Colony. In
addition to architectural fragments, furniture, pewter, silver, and arms
and armor, the collection contains several paintings of the seventeenth
century.

Pilgrim Hall also contains a plaster death mask of Oliver Cromwell,
whose connection with Pilgrim history came through his employment of
Edward Winslow, governor of Plymouth Colony, on two diplomatic
missions. Furthermore, Governor William Bradford hailed the English
Commonwealth as establishing in England the principles for which the
Pilgrims had been exiled.

As American painting prior to 1700 is exceedingly rare, almost any
surviving example is worthy of note. While the three Winslow portraits
(1651) seem to have been painted in London by Robert Walker, the
Portrait of Elizabeth Paddy Wensley (1641–c. 1713), whose daughter
married Isaac Winslow, is almost certainly an American work of about
1675. The painter is unknown, and any attribution is made more difficult by the poor condition of the picture. The colors run to a rather rich
red-orange to brown scheme. The flat geometrical design with its tight
details takes us back to traditional English painting of the Elizabethan
era—here in a provincial echo. There are superficial resemblances to
two works at the Worcester Art Museum (MA 303, 304) : the *Self-
Portrait* by Thomas Smith (c. 1680), and the highly accomplished *Elizabeth Freake and Baby Mary*, painted c. 1674 by an artist unknown, but
not the same as the painter of Elizabeth Paddy Wensley.

Near Plymouth Rock a replica of the *Mayflower* is moored; and two
miles south on Route 3A is Plimoth Plantation, a replica of the Pilgrim
Colony (open daily mid-April through November; admission charged).

Essex Institute

Location: 132-134 Essex Street (parking garage on Liberty St. around the corner)
Hours: Tues.-Sat. 9-4:30, Sun. and holidays 1-5; open Mon. June 1-October 15; closed Thanksgiving, Christmas, New Year's Day
Admission: Charged

The institute was organized in 1848 by union of the Essex Historical Society and the Essex County Natural History Society. It operates some of Salem's most notable historic houses, including the John Ward House (seventeenth century, in the garden of the institute); the Gardner-Pingree House, designed in 1804 by Samuel McIntire (adjoining the institute at 128 Essex Street); and the Peirce-Nichols House, an earlier work of McIntire (at 80 Federal Street). The library of the institute is considered one of the finest in New England for historical research.

The museum, on the upper floor of the institute, contains a recently reconditioned picture gallery and a large collection of furniture, decorative arts, and miscellaneous historical items. The paintings, principally portraits of persons important in the life of Salem, include works by such leading artists as Badger, Greenwood, Smibert, Blackburn, Copley, Trumbull, Stuart, and Harding. Perhaps the most important example is Smibert's life-size *Sir William Pepperrell*,[196] inscribed "Lt. Gen. Sir Wm. Pepperrell, Bart. / The Victor of Louisbourg A.D. 1745." The portly hero indicated in no subtle manner the scene of his victory over the French land forces on Cape Breton Island. He was the first American to be created a baronet. Silver presented to him by the British is displayed at Saco, Maine (see page 455). His portrait, which came to the Essex Institute in 1821, must have been painted soon after Sir William (already knighted in 1745) returned in triumph in 1746, for Peter Pelham made a mezzotint of it in the following year. In style the paint-

196

ing contrasts considerably with the imported English fluency of Smibert's *Bishop Berkeley* group at Yale (CT 74), dating from more than fifteen years earlier. If the style is now "Americanized," it hardly rivals Robert Feke's attainments of about the same time (ME 10). The eighteen buttons down Sir William's endless scarlet coat exhibit patience, but not much painterly flair. Two cannon balls on their way to the French forces —with trajectory duly marked—hardly suggest imaginative subtlety. Some authorities have suggested the help of shop assistants, but there is little evidence in the artist's work of any real command of the human figure. For all that, the picture manages to convey an impressive physical presence.

Of the other portraits in this important collection, those by Joseph Blackburn and John Greenwood are especially memorable, and Trumbull's *Alexander Hamilton* is superb. An appealing *Nathaniel Hawthorne*, by Charles Osgood (1809–90), shows him young and handsome, with a kind of Byronic mien.

The startling scene of *Salem Common on Training Day, 1808*[197] is the work of George Ropes (1788–1819), a local Salem painter of marines, landscapes, signs, and carriages. If there is another instance of an artist who was deaf and dumb from birth, I am not aware of it. Ropes also painted a portrait of the fabulous *Cleopatra's Barge*, the personal yacht of Captain George Crowninshield (the picture privately owned, but published in *Antiques* for January 1930, together with an account of the splendid furniture with which the ship was equipped). *Salem Common* shows us the militia in formation before a considerable crowd of onlookers. Crowned by an arc of very tall and very stiff poplars, it is strangely similar to certain Paris scenes of Henri Rousseau (*le douanier*), and it could keep company with the finest Karolik-collection pictures by American primitives in the Boston Museum of Fine Arts. The former, however, were painted around 1900, while the Karolik pictures generally run toward the mid-nineteenth century.

A second Ropes painting in the institute, *Launching of the Ship "Fame" in Salem Harbor, 1802*, is enlivened by as many standees— ashore and aboard ship—as *Training Day*. If the enormous flags don't sink it, *Fame* will not founder. To whet the reader's appetite for the art of George Ropes, I suggest consulting the color plate of this picture in Priscilla Lord and Daniel Foley, *The Folk Arts and Crafts of New*

197

England (Radnor, Pa.: Chilton Book Co., 1975). Ropes should be much better known than he is at present. He should not be confused with Joseph Ropes (1812–85), also of Salem, whose four panoramic views of Hartford, each 18 by 62 inches and painted in 1855, describe the city's appearance from north, south, east, and west. They are owned by the Wadsworth Atheneum, Hartford.

Peabody Museum

Location: East India Square, 161 Essex Street (parking garage nearby on Liberty St.)
Hours: Mon.-Sat. 9-5, Sun. and holidays 1-5; closed Thanksgiving, Christmas, and New Year's Day
Admission: Charged. Ⓗ

East India Square, turned into a mall with attractive walkways, planting, and restored fine buildings, must rank as one of the most successful examples of urban redevelopment. The Peabody Museum is at its entrance from the end of Essex Street. A superb modern addition, providing a corner entrance, has more than doubled the exhibition space. Built in 1976, it is sensitively related to the original building (facing the square), erected in 1824 by the East India Marine Society. The society was founded in 1799. The ground floor of the old building was once occupied by the Asiatic Bank, the Oriental Insurance Office, and the U.S. Post Office, while the large hall above was devoted to the museum and to the meetings of the society. At the dedication exercises President John Quincy Adams delivered the main address. Apart from the recent expansion, additions were built in 1885, 1906, and 1952 to provide for the growing collections amassed by the society in its worldwide activities.

This museum is of unique importance in America, for its collections long predated the modern interest in primitive art and anthropological research. As a historical display of American maritime commerce it is unrivaled. Its name comes from George Peabody, born near Salem in 1795, died in London in 1869, who in 1867 gave funds to combine the museum of the society with the natural-history collections of the Essex Institute for the promotion of "Science and Useful Knowledge in the County of Essex." Membership in the society was open to "any persons who shall have navigated the seas near the Cape of Good Hope or Cape Horn, either as Masters or Commanders or (being of the age of twenty-one years) as Factors or Supercargoes of any vessels belonging to Salem."

Comment on the fine assortment of ships' figureheads in the Marine Hall is reluctantly omitted, and the reader is referred to the discussion of similar work at Mystic Seaport (p. 00). Our illustrations of the ethnological collections can give only the merest suggestion of the fabulous wealth of material on display. Although the Peabody Museum was never intended to be an art museum, its contents often command respect on aesthetic grounds. There are many thousands of exhibits, covering all the non-European world, with emphasis on the Pacific Islands and Japan. Catalogues and a useful *Visitor's Guide to Salem* are available.

East Hall, entered from the Marine Hall, is dominated by a 6-foot *Wooden Idol*[198] from the Hawaiian Islands. Coming from a *morai*, or cemetery, it was given to the society in 1846. It is thought to have been the temporary resting place of a particular god during ceremonies at a temple, and not an actual object of worship. The powerful forms speak their own language of warlike grandeur. One cannot help wondering what the outcome would have been if the accidents of history had brought such "idols" to the attention of Picasso and other modern artists instead of those much tamer African Negro sculptures which they "discovered" in Paris art shops about 1905.

The Maori civilization of New Zealand is abundantly represented in the same gallery. The so-called *Short Club*[199] (Number 144) was used as a thrusting weapon somewhat in the manner of fencing, not as a club. It is beautifully ornamented with curvilinear interlacement, a more elaborate example of which may be seen on a *Door Lintel* (Number 559).[200] If such ornament reminds us of Scandinavian woodcarving of the ninth century (the Osberg Ship at Oslo) and later, or of Irish manuscript illumination, or of very ancient Chinese bronzes, we should not be altogether surprised. While the explanation may lie purely in the realm of coincidence, there is much credibility in the theory of the migration of cultures.

The visitor interested in the art of the Pacific Islands should consult the books of Hooper, Borland, Tichnor, and Linton. The ethnological background is covered in Elsdon Best, *The Maori as He Was*, in Sir Peter Buck, *The Coming of the Maori*, and in David Malo, *Hawaiian Antiquities*.

198

199

200

The representation of objects brought in through the China Trade (discussed in the section on the museum devoted to that field at Milton, page 244) is one of the most important in existence; and the same can be said of the scrimshaw collection, which has unusually large examples. Ship models trace the full range from the age of sailing to the present, including the *Bremen,* the *Queen Mary*, and the *Queen Elizabeth II*. Ship paintings, also in abundance, include several by Fitz Hugh Lane (see M A ₸55), one of them the *Brittania* in a bad storm. Ships' figure-heads include a surprise: the *Rembrandt* (built in Kennebunkport, 1876), showing the artist young, in a red tam-o'-shanter and a red cape falling all the way to his feet. This figure is nearly twice life-size. It is so memorable that I gladly contradict an earlier statement that comment on these carvings would be omitted.

Heritage Plantation of Sandwich

Location: Pine St., 1 mile from the center of the village. From Sagamore Bridge follow Route 6A; from the village center take Route 130 *north* for ½ mile, turn left on Pine St. and follow it to the plantation
Hours: 10-5 daily from mid-May to mid-October
Admission: Charged. Ⓗ

Located outside Cape Cod's oldest town, the plantation consists of seventy-six acres of gardens and woodlands—a delight in their own right—and several museums of Americana. Flatcar buses take you easily from spot to spot.

The ensemble was founded in 1969 by Mr. and Mrs. J. K. Lilly, in memory of Mr. Lilly's father, an enthusiastic collector of many phases of popular and utilitarian American art, including automobiles. These are superbly shown on two levels of a replica of the celebrated Shaker Round Barn at Hancock (see page 230). The 1912 *Mercer Raceabout*,[201] gleaming yellow and black, and in perfect condition, is one of the most spectacular of these machines. Its four-cylinder, fifty-eight-horsepower engine drove it slightly faster than its legendary competitor, the Stutz Bearcat (also seen here in yellow and black). A small circular windshield provided the only protection; goggles, caps, veils, and dusters were *de rigueur*. The 1912 cost was twenty-five hundred dollars. The svelte lines and shapes proclaim this two-seater a work of art appropriate for inclusion in this book. On a plane of high luxury, however, consider the thirty-eight-hundred-dollar red Oldsmobile of 1912, with its brasses and mahogany floorboards, and the forty-thousand-dollar Duesenberg touring car built in the 1930s for Gary Cooper. A 1906 Stanley Steamer like the 1911 example here had the distinction of achieving a speed of 197 miles per hour—before it became airborne and disintegrated.

The Military Museum houses firearms—including a model of the great German gun that bombarded Paris in the First World War from a distance of seventy-five miles—and some two thousand hand-painted military miniature figures arranged in historical settings. Attached to the Arts and Crafts Museum is a complete and functioning carousel (with

201

calliope) built about 1912 in Riverside, R.I. Within are extensive collections of Currier & Ives lithographs, early American tools (the fish
spears are of especially beautiful design), and American folk art. Here
you may see a smaller variant of the *Grasshopper Weather Vane* that
surmounts Boston's Faneuil Hall (see page 133), made of copper about
1882, probably at Waltham, Mass. Note the spikes on the back legs,
and note too how the designer has given this creature a sense of potential
speed. Up to life-size painted wood figures, not all of them commercial,
attain a considerable degree of vitality. I particularly enjoyed a batsman,
rather like the figure in Eakins's *Baseball Players* at Providence (RI 17).
Much more sophisticated, but overloaded with descriptive detail, is the
bronze *Mountain Man* by Frederic Remington (1861–1909) of 1902/3,
with the horse inclined downhill at a dizzying angle. The small but
choice scrimshaw collection includes finely designed knitting needles and
swifts (to hold yarn). The paintings are best described as good period
pieces. There is some artistic merit, as well as accuracy, in the collection
of carved and painted birds, many of them by Anthony Elmer Crowell
(1862–1951) of East Harwich.

A leisurely visit to the Heritage Plantation, especially on a fine day,
will be well rewarded.

Art Museum, Mount Holyoke College

Location: Route 116, near the intersection of Route 47
Hours: Academic year: Mon.-Fri. 11-5, Sat., Sun. 1-5; closed academic holidays. Summer: Mon.-Fri. 1-4. Parking provided
Admission: Free. Ⓗ

In 1976 the museum celebrated with an exhibition the one-hundredth anniversary of the housing of the college's art collection in a permanent home on the campus. "College Collections, 1776–1876" traced the history of art collecting by American colleges in that period. As the list is both short and of some interest, we mention the colleges included: Amherst, Bowdoin, Dartmouth, United States Military Academy, Vassar, and Mount Holyoke. Not included, but listed with a historical summary, were: University of Michigan, University of Notre Dame, University of Vermont, Syracuse University, Harvard University (but the collections were for the most part kept at the Boston Athenaeum and the Museum of Fine Arts until 1895), and Cornell University (a hope at its founding in 1865, but not fulfilled until 1953).

The present building, which opened in 1971, provides well-appointed facilities for the art department, its library, and the collections—now fast growing since their move from the rugged old Dwight Art Memorial of 1902. Extension of the museum space is already anticipated. Modest purchase funds were augmented by gifts and by an unusually dedicated and active Friends of Art organization; special funds donated by Mrs. John M. Warbeke in memory of her husband have made possible the acquisition of an impressive Far Eastern collection. Continued interest of the department of classics, especially in excavations, has made possible a fine small collection of Greek and Roman art. The print collection is large, broadly ranged, and well selected. A special bequest brought in a small group of early Italian paintings of quality. In the contemporary field, acquisitions have emphasized, but not excessively, work by women artists.

To our survey of Greek vase painting, notably in the entry on Bowdoin College (ME 1–3), we now add a fine example of the Geometric Period, eighth century B.C. This *Low-handled Bowl*,**202** or *skyphos*, is covered with abstract motifs typical in such ware. The repetitive figures of women spinning, like the ornament, are applied flat on the surface.

202

Unlike sixth-century black-figure ware, these have no engraved interior lines. The shape of the vase, squat but capacious, suggests utility without concern for elegance.

The prize of the Classical collection is a Greek bronze statuette, under 9 inches high, of a *Standing Youth with Right Arm Extended*,[203] closely related in style to the famous *Charioteer* of Delphi (c. 475 B.C.). From every angle, but especially from the back, this small masterpiece conveys the sense of excitement that the sculptor must have felt in liberating the human body, as he surely did, from the confines of inorganic material. In this unique gift of the Greeks to human self-understanding, bronze led monumental sculpture; thus not even the magnificent marble sculptures of the Temple of Zeus at Olympia, dating from c. 460, match the little bronze in resilience and freedom of movement. (That is no criticism of the Olympia sculptures, for their more rigid and formal character is exactly right in their architectural context.) In the Mount Holyoke bronze, acquired near Athens in 1926 by Professor Caroline Galt of the classics department, there is prodigious energy in the rounded planes and contours; prodigious too is the inner restraint. An article in the fall 1977 issue of the museum's *Newsletter* reported on a thorough laboratory examination of the *Standing Youth*. If you have been disturbed by the right arm, you will be glad to learn that it has been bent. (Much of the hand is obviously missing.) Less disturbing is the right leg, newly bent from the knee down, with resulting displacement of the foot. The nipples have been gouged, perhaps to extract small gold inlays. The head has fortunately escaped the breaks and patchings apparent in the neck area. Fears that these might mean the head did not belong to the body were allayed when radiography demonstrated that the two were never completely separated. Possibly the original casting was defective in this area. Very likely the youth was shown pouring a libation from a cup of gold; and there is some slight evidence that the whole figure was gilded. My unusually detailed discussion of this marvelous piece is surely appropriate to its quality and importance in Greek sculpture of perhaps its greatest period.

In the exquisite field of fourteenth-century Sienese painting, Mount Holyoke boasts a small panel from the great *Maestà* painted in 1308–11 by Duccio di Buoninsegna (active 1278–1315). The *Bust of an Angel*[204] served as one of the small pinnacle elements atop the frame

204

203

of the elaborate altarpiece, painted for the high altar of Siena Cathedral, and now shown in the adjacent Opera del Duomo. In a work of such complexity and magnitude, it is not unlikely that auxiliary parts like this were assigned to an assistant, but if so the painter worked faithfully in the master's style. The *Angel* was once in the collection of the Kaiser Friedrich Museum in Berlin. It was acquired by gift to Mount Holyoke in 1965. Panels from the predella below the central Madonna and Saints are in the Frick Collection, New York, and the National Gallery, Washington.

A pen drawing of *Christ among the Doctors*[205] is attributed to the Italian Baroque painter Guercino (1591–1666). This master worked primarily in the region of Bologna, but in the early 1620s he was in Rome, where he painted his famous *Aurora* for the ceiling of the Casino Ludovisi (not to be confused with Guido Reni's tamer version of the same subject in the Casino Rospigliosi). This drawing seems to have been made during Guercino's stay in Rome. While it is more conservative than the art of Bernini, its Baroque character is clear. Observe the breadth of Guercino's forms, and the freedom of their diagonal movement forward and back in space. For Guercino, line was movement, texture, shadow, and volume, all merged inseparably. On the reverse, a slightly later drawing by Guercino in a tamer technique, representing *Christ among the Doctors*, shows us, first, that paper was expensive and, second, that Guercino was not always at top form.

Acquired in 1981 is an impressive oil, nearly six feet high, *St. Sebastian Attended by St. Irene*, Italian work of the later seventeenth century. The artist, not as yet identified, is clearly one of consequence.

Not illustrated here—only because of generous coverage of the artist in other museums—is a fine landscape by Albert Bierstadt (1830–1902), *Hetch Hetchy Canyon* (some fifty miles from the Yosemite). It was painted in 1875 and the following year purchased from Bierstadt himself and presented to the college on the opening of its first museum building. (See VT 14.)

The Conway Meadows,[206] an oil more than 3 by 5 feet, is a brilliant example of the work of George Inness (1825–94). Painted in the White Mountains in 1876, it departs significantly from Hudson River School approaches to landscape, to which Inness twelve years earlier, in *The Elm* (ME 23), had been so faithful. It is equally different from his brooding, perhaps symbolic *White Monk* of 1873 (MA 16), painted

206

205

during his four-year stay in Europe. On his return, in 1875, he developed from sketches made on the spot the brightly luminous *Etretat* (Wadsworth Atheneum, Hartford) in a style clearly affected by the work of the Impressionists. Yet the texture, even on these great white cliffs of the Normandy seacoast, is furry rather than dappled, and the color is more local than broken up into prismatic glints. *The Conway Meadows* came in the following year. It carries still further, into a composition of size, the freedom of Inness's oil sketches. With extraordinary consistency it maintains the broad sweep of cloud-covered land while at the same time all the details sparkle as in an early morning dew. The greens are wonderfully varied and fresh. In all respects the picture surpasses the oil study of the same subject owned by the Fort Worth Art Association. Late in his life Inness moved into an atmospheric-mystical vein based on the late phases of Whistler and Corot. (Two examples from 1891/2 are in the Clark Art Institute, Williamstown.) His earlier work seems much more inspired, perhaps because in the nineteenth century the American imagination functioned best on a basis of meticulous observation, whether in painting or in literature.

The *Portrait of Annie Lavelle*,[207] by Robert Henri (1865–1929), the leading figure in the so-called Ashcan School of the early 1900s, indicates his winning informality, sharp eye, and deft brushwork. Henri's portraits should be contrasted with the more elegant and much more thoughtful ones of his exact contemporary, John Singer Sargent (CT 45 and MA 84). In his reaction against Sargent's high-toned posture, Henri sought out the life of city streets, and he resisted European influences. Nevertheless, his technique owed something to that of Edouard Manet, but coarsened to a point just short of commercial painting. This charming study of a child, however, rings true, and the range of reds and pinks produces its own visual delight.

From the college's Far Eastern collection we have selected a Chinese hand scroll, here illustrated by a detail. *Spring Morning at Yen-Chi*,[208] in ink and colors on silk, is the work of Wang Hui (1632–1717), a major painter of the Ch'ing dynasty. To judge from Laurence Sickman's account of him in the Pelican History of Art volume (*The Art and Architecture of China*, pages 191–92), he had such varied talent that he

208

207

could "paint successfully in a number of different ways and yet assert his own individuality." The Mount Holyoke scroll strongly resembles an album leaf, dated 1677, in the Musée Guimet, Paris; thus, it appears to be a personal variant of the style of Wang Mên (died 1385), an outstanding artist of the Yüan dynasty (1260–1368). Worthy of note in the Mount Holyoke scroll are the tender washes laid in strips horizontally across the top, where mists cut off the summits of the highest hills.

Had there been more space in this limited survey of an excellent small museum, I should like to have discussed a superb Maurice Prendergast watercolor, *Festival, St. Mark's Venice,* c. 1898/9; *Lurid Sky,* an oil of 1929 by Yves Tanguy (see MA 227); Dmitri Hadzi's *Floating Helmets,* a bronze study for the large version of 1965 at Yale University; and a precious late Gothic statuette of polychromed wood representing *St. Anne with the Virgin and Child.*

On the Quadrangle

Location: For directions, see Museum of Fine Arts, Springfield

Before or after visiting Springfield's two art museums, which we are about to discuss, be sure not to miss the monumental bronze figure of *The Puritan*[209] by Augustus Saint-Gaudens (1848–1907), which commands the slope at the open northern angle of the Quadrangle—on which both museums face. Saint-Gaudens was the leading American sculptor of the nineteenth century. Erected in 1899 on a well-designed circular granite base, it is a theoretical portrait of Deacon William Chapin, one of the founders of Springfield. A variant, with a different base, is in Fairmount Park, Philadelphia; and small castings of this variant exist in some quantity (examples are at the Addison Gallery, Andover, Mass.; the Williams College Museum of Art; and at the Saint-Gaudens Memorial, Cornish, N.H.). The rear view is especially powerful, with the flowing cape masking what may seem excessive detail from the front. At his best, Saint-Gaudens achieved much of the breadth and energy we find in the architecture of his great contemporary H. H. Richardson.

The Puritan was presented to the city of Springfield by Chester William Chapin, banker, railroad president, and descendant of Deacon Samuel Chapin (1595–1675), one of the city's founders. No visual record of the deacon being available, Saint-Gaudens modeled the head from the donor's son, whom he had met in Paris. He theorized that the deacon must have had the same square jaw and beetling brows. The statue, 12 feet high, was unveiled in Sterns Park in 1887, but in 1899 it was moved to its present position.

For further discussion of the artist, see the entry on the Saint-Gaudens National Historic Site, Cornish, N.H.

209

George Walter Vincent Smith
Art Museum

Location: On the Quadrangle. For directions, see Museum of Fine Arts, Springfield
Hours: Tues. 12-9, Wed.-Sun. 12-5; closed New Year's Day, July 4, Thanksgiving, and Christmas
Admission: Free

The George Walter Vincent and Belle Townsley Smith collections were installed in an Italianate villa designed by the firm of Renwick, Aspinwall and Renwick, and Walter Tallant Owen of that firm, in the year 1890, opened to the public in 1895 and deeded to the city of Springfield in 1914. This is the oldest of the four museums on the Quadrangle and was originally called the Springfield Art Museum, although it then also housed the Museum of Natural History.

There had been a Museum of Natural Science, Art, and Curiosities established in 1859, which shared with the city library two small rooms in the old city hall. By 1889 a number of prominent citizens began plans to move the museum to its present location. The property was secured through the bequest of Horace Smith, and many other Springfielders contributed to the building fund.

The architecture and collections of the museum have remained intact since the death of the Smiths, George Walter in 1923 and Belle Townsley in 1928, giving the historian and the museum visitor a clear picture of the tastes and aesthetic sensibilities of a bygone era. Nine elegantly arranged galleries present a treasure trove of decorative arts and paintings from Europe, Asia, and America. The Oriental collections of jade, cloisonné, ceramics, armor, and rugs are among the finest in America. There is a large collection of plaster casts of famous sculpture and a gallery devoted to changing exhibitions in which the work of many artists and craftsmen have received their first public exposure. The museum's lively program of classes for children and adults makes it one of the region's leading centers for the study of the visual arts.

The collection of American paintings is strong in its representation of artists of the Hudson River School, especially Sanford R. Gifford (see VT 16) and Frederic E. Church (1825-75), whose *Scene in the Catskills*,[210] some 3 by 4½ feet in size, dominates one of the galleries. Painted in 1851, it greatly expands the scope of Church's modest but winsome beginnings seen in the New Britain Museum's *Haying near New Haven* (CT 43), painted two years earlier. Indeed, the Catskills picture may be taken as an absolutely typical Hudson River landscape, and one of highest quality. Later, Church was to venture afar in search of more spectacular subjects, as in *Icebergs*, in the museum at Waterbury (CT 102), and the *Valley of the Santa Ysabel*, at Pittsfield (MA 195).

Other memorable paintings are by George Inness and by Alfred Bricher, whom we discuss in the entry on the Holyoke Public Library (MA 161). The stained-glass window at the head of the stairs was made by Louis Tiffany Studios from a design by Edward Simmons.

The collection of casts, recently refreshed and now superbly exhibited, rivals that at Norwich (CT 94). An attractive illustrated brochure is available. As with the Norwich collection, Ancient Greek and Roman and Italian Renaissance examples are included—nearly fifty of them— but the Middle Ages are skipped. Such was the force of classical taste prevalent around 1900. Greek works seen here in replica begin with Myron's *Discobolus* (Roman copy) and the lovely fifth-century Eleusinian relief; and Hellenistic ones include the *Laocöon* and the *Venus of Melos. Hermes Resting* is a notable Roman bronze. From the Florentine Renaissance are major works by Donatello, Luca della Robbia, and Jacopo della Quercia; and Michelangelo dominates with the Louvre's *Bound Slave* and three figures from the *Tomb of Lorenzo, Duke of Urbino*, in the Medici Chapel, Florence.

210

Museum of Fine Arts

Location: 49 Chestnut St. Follow these directions carefully! Take Springfield
Center exit from I-91; turn east onto State St. Continue on State St. for two
blocks; turn right onto Dwight St. Extension. Follow arrows and bear left
onto Chestnut St. Entrance to the Quadrangle is the first driveway on right
Hours: Tues. 12-9, Wed.-Sun. 12-5; closed New Year's Day, July 4, Thanksgiving, and Christmas
Admission: Free. Ⓗ by prior arrangement

The Springfield Museum of Fine Arts was founded in 1933, when the
present building was constructed. Growth of the collections has been
rapid, thanks especially to an endowment by James Philip Gray for the
purchase of paintings. Dutch paintings of the seventeenth century,
French and Italian of the eighteenth, French of the nineteenth, and
American paintings form the main strength of the museum's holdings.
There is also an extensive collection of Far Eastern art, including more
than three thousand Japanese prints, and Western printmaking is well
represented. The museum is rich in decorative arts, and there is a special
collection of "Art Deco." An excellent handbook is available.

An adroit system of labeling has been initiated here. Happily, the museum believes in giving the visitor background information about the
works of art on display. This function is accomplished by an illustrated
leaflet available in each of several galleries. The leaflets are well written
and no charge is made. The usual solution—extensive labels attached to
the wall—can interfere with the visual effect of a gallery, and they are
hard to read with any comfort.

Outstanding among the fine Dutch pictures here is a foot-high
Landscape near Dordrecht[211] by Jacob van Ruisdael (1628/9–1682),
the leading figure among many Dutch specialists in this field. It is signed
and dated 1649, a year later than the *View of Egmond* at the Currier
Gallery of Art, Manchester (NH 24). This "little giant of a picture" (a
phrase reserved for such occasions by Professor Frank J. Mather, Jr.)
manages to embrace most of what is important in Dutch painting of
this sort: land, sea, clouds, trees, human interest, all constituting a
voyage into infinite distances. This effect, achieved by diagonal and
serpentine movement and by rich contrasts of dark and light, connects
Dutch landscape painting with the prevailing trends of seventeenth-

211

century Baroque art. Ruisdael was probably influenced by Rembrandt's famous etching *The Three Trees* (1643), which it superficially resembles.

Ruisdel painted a number of superb marines (for example, MA 74) in addition to his landscapes, but Willem van de Velde the Younger (1633–1707) devoted a career to them. *Fishing Boats Offshore in a Calm*[212] (28 by 34 inches) is a typical example. Employing a horizon line hardly a seventh of the height of the whole composition, he enveloped the scene in a vast space flooded with light. Working first in Amsterdam, he spent the last thirty years of his life in London and Greenwich. The National Maritime Museum at Greenwich preserves his many pen drawings and grisaille studies of English ships, which set high standards for later ship painting in England and America. The Springfield picture, monogrammed at the lower left, is not dated; it appears to have been painted c. 1690, and thus during his English period. It passed through several distinguished English collections and was exhibited at the Royal Academy in 1871.

Alessandro Magnasco (1677–1749) was a prolific Genoese painter whose mannerisms and bravura often became a substitute for artistic creativeness. His forms stand midway between Baroque drama and the more intimate and small-scale art of the Rococo. *Monastery Interior,*[213] an oil more than 3 feet high, shows him at his best and in his specially favored subject. This is certainly no scene of cloistered medieval piety; indeed, these frantic monks seem attacked by St. Vitus's dance. In an

212

213

interesting article in *Apollo* magazine (1938, pages 69ff.) E. Scheyer dates the picture about 1712 and discusses it in connection with the monastic decline of the time in Italy. The possibility of satire in Magnasco's paintings of this sort should not be discounted. His technical procedure consisted of first painting the canvas a rich dark brown and then brushing on warm and cool bluish tones for a nearly monochromatic effect.

The Arch of Titus[214] gives us an impression of the art of Giovanni Paolo Panini (1691–1764) very different from his vast *Interior of St. Peter's* at the Boston Athenaeum (MA 26). Signed and dated 1754, and only 29 inches high, it appears to have been made on order for the two English students who take in the spectacle of past Roman glory under the guidance of their dark-garbed tutor. Note the picturesque condition of the Roman Forum as it existed over two centuries ago. While many works of this Venetian-born painter who made a career of view painting in Rome run to archaeological tedium, here a limpid light envelops the scene and little vignettes of contemporary Roman life enliven it—while at the same time helping establish the measured recession toward the Colosseum in the far distance.

The Fortress Königstein, near Pirna[215] is a masterwork of an itinerant Venetian landscapist named Bernardo Bellotto (c. 1720–80). The nephew and pupil of Canaletto (see MA 76), he is also known by his uncle's name. He worked in Germany—Pirna lies on the Elbe not far from Dresden—Austria, Poland, and Russia. While his art followed eighteenth-century fashion in its small scale and animated surfaces, Bellotto displays his Baroque inheritance in his dark foreground and in the forceful way he pulls us down this serpentining prospect. His detail is both painstaking and insistent, but everything falls magically into place in this highly ordered design.

In the memorable 1979 retrospective exhibition of the work of Jean Baptiste Siméon Chardin (1699–1779) held at the Boston Museum of

214

215

Fine Arts, Springfield's oval still life, subtitled *Rafraîchissements*,[216] held its own in competition with celebrated works lent by the Louvre and other great museums of the world. Many thought it one of the finest pictures on display. The oval format, popular in eighteenth-century portraits and other compositions, is unusual in Chardin, but the design sensitively accords with it, and the position of Chardin's dated signature (1764) helps confirm the impossibility that the picture was cut from an originally rectangular frame. Its 5-foot height is also unusual in the work of this modest master, but since even his smallest works have a way of seeming much bigger than they are, it is not surprising that he could manage the large canvas as well. In an age of Rococo frivolity in court circles, Chardin stands out as a disciplined forebear of the still-life paintings of Paul Cézanne. To their credit, Rococo patrons recognized his merit. It seems fortunate that Chardin died before the Revolution. There would have been no place for him in a world dominated by the marbleized art of Neoclassicism.

Judge Suetonius Grant Heatly with His Sister, Temperance[217] is the hefty title of a charming "conversation piece" by the German-born English painter Johann Zoffany (1735–1810). Approximately 40 inches high, it was painted in India during the 1780s. Exquisite in color and workmanship, its crisp outlines and smooth surfaces echo the gradual shift that was taking place in European art from the painterly Rococo style (as in the museum's *Journey to Market* by François Boucher) toward Neoclassicism. Zoffany's meticulous detail, however, is part of his German inheritance that in turn runs all the way back to the Flemish fifteenth-century masters. The relaxed atmosphere of the conversation piece—of which Zoffany is one of the acknowledged masters —is indicative of eighteenth-century reaction against the stiff etiquette and high ceremony of the Baroque courts. Zoffany visited India from 1783 to 1789, but it would be pointless to look for overtones of Indian art in his work of those years. He was as much the Britisher abroad as Judge Heatly and his sister—and as satisfied about it. Nevertheless, the

216

217

Indian at the left caught his interest, even to the extent of unbalancing a rather sloppily composed arrangement.

Although the large white-gowned portrait of *Madame de Servan* (not illustrated) is no longer considered to be the work of Jacques Louis David, but of a follower, it is a fine period piece, c. 1800; and it well exemplifies what has been said above about Neoclassicism. More than period interest, however, can be gained from the *Portrait Head of a Young Man*, formerly attributed to Eugène Delacroix. The intense, brooding gaze, reinforced by a smashing contrast of black hair and yellow coat, are Romantic to the core—a Heathcliff, as it were, out of *Wuthering Heights*.

When we come to the *Madman-Kidnaper*,[218] we are confronted by an authentic work of that inspirer of Delacroix, Théodore Géricault (1791–1824). This great initiator of French Romanticism not only unleashed the passions but he literally carried these forces beyond reason's control. One of Géricault's intimates, a doctor turned psychiatrist, commissioned him to make a series of portraits of mad persons, of which the *Kidnaper* is one. It rivals the most famous of them all, the old woman known as *The Hyena* (in the Lyons Museum). Both in subject and in painterly technique Géricault broke with David, as we have seen before in the Fogg Museum's wash drawing of a *Negro Soldier* (MA 127) and Hartford's watercolor of *The Coal Wagon* (CT 19). In so doing he managed to usher in both of the main streams of French nineteenth-century painting before the Impressionists: Romanticism and Realism. All of this, and dead at thirty-three!

Other French pictures not to be missed are Jean François Millet's sketch for the celebrated *Gleaners* (in the Louvre) and his sensitive early *Portrait of Virginie Roumy*, and Gustave Courbet's *Château de Chillon*, painted in Switzerland in 1873, when he was in exile for his participation in the pulling down of the Vendôme Column in Paris, during the Commune. The rise of Impressionism can be traced in the sequence from Eugène Boudin's three small landscapes to Gustave Caillebotte's *Game Birds and Lemons* (1883). Boudin was Claude Monet's mentor at Honfleur. Caillebotte, a member of the Impressionist circle, has received critical attention for his innovative treatment of space (see the catalogue of a major retrospective at the Brooklyn Museum, organized in 1976/7 by J. Kirk T. Varnedoe).

Early American painting is well represented at the museum by

218

Raphaelle Peale's *Still Life with Watermelon* and by a glossy *Portrait of Nymphas Marston*, a Boston work of John Singleton Copley. The latter somewhat resembles the magnificent *John Erving* at Smith College (MA 175), but without its intensity or flair.

The American gallery is dominated by an enormous canvas, *Historical Monument of the American Republic*,[219] 9 by 13 feet, painted c. 1876 by Erastus Salisbury Field (1805–1900). Field, who had studied with Samuel F. B. Morse (see CT 6), painted adequate portraits for some thirty years before suddenly launching into this strange, but impressive, manifestation. In his excellent *American Painting: History and Interpretation* (New York: Bonanza Books, 1960, page 571), Virgil Barker introduces Field with the following comment: ". . . a workman in possession of a technique adequate for his ordinary purposes may venture into unfamiliar territory of the mind with a bland unawareness that he needs a different technique. He may be ignorant of what he needs, but his self-forgetful confidence in what he wants to say transforms his ignorance into an innocence fresh enough to bring him easily through." What a Babel of towered fantasy Field has given us! I shall not try to compete with Barker's description: ". . . multiplied masses of Sumerian ziggurats rounded into dwindling Tombs of Hadrian and walled with Romanesque arched galleries so maze-like that the total effect approaches the Gothic."

We return abruptly to reality with *Emblems of Peace*,[220] an unusually large and sumptuous fool-the-eye composition by William M. Harnett (1848–92). Measuring 28 by 34 inches, it is signed and dated 1890 at the lower left. Reference to Harnett's *Still Life with a Bottle of Olives* at Fitchburg Museum (MA 153), painted in 1877, will quickly indicate his extraordinary development—without, however, denigrating the

219

220

quality of the earlier work. In discussing J. F. Peto's *Discarded Treasures* at Smith College (MA 187) we have rehearsed the story of how some of Peto's work was, for a time, sold with forged Harnett signatures. Comparison with the Springfield picture will immediately show how different they were. The museum acquired its Harnett from a Springfield hotel owner-manager who had bought it from a Springfield dealer for ten thousand dollars in the year after Harnett's death—well before the twentieth-century revival of interest in such pictures sparked the forging activity.

Harnett, a Philadelphia painter, was an ardent student of Dutch art, but his infinitely painstaking detail puts us more in mind of Flemish art in the tradition of Jan van Eyck. *Emblems of Peace* is perhaps more like the skin of a van Eyck than its substance, because there is no hidden significance in this patient inventory. Unlike Chardin (see MA 216), Harnett is not concerned with formal relations between objects in space. Every inch of his surfaces claims the same attention, and their accentuation denies all consideration of spatial position. When the picture was once exhibited at Smith College, a professor of music had a moment of triumph on discovering that Harnett had omitted the dot of a quarter-note on the score.

Like several other New England museums, Springfield is fortunate in possessing a pair of portraits by William Jennys (active 1795–1805), whose work we have discussed at New London (CT 87). Its oil by Winslow Homer, *Promenade on the Beach*, is one of only two known works of his in this medium from the year 1880—a year of great progress in his watercolors toward his later style, darker and soberer than before (see the example at Rockland, ME 31).

We conclude this too brief survey of a fine collection of paintings with two large twentieth-century canvases. George Bellows (1882–1925) painted *Edith Cavell*[221] in 1918, three years after the English nurse was shot as a spy by a German firing squad. It is worth remembering that Goya's great picture of the *Massacre of Madrileños* on May 3, 1808, was not painted until 1815. Like Goya, Bellows had time to contemplate—and to raise propaganda to the level of considered artistic expression. Perhaps, in Bellows's case, the picture was a bit too carefully planned as a composition and too much loaded with ancillary detail to achieve Goya's shock impact. However that may be, the light is eerie, the darks portend the coming tragedy, and the white figure of Edith Cavell stands out effectively. Personally, I could do without the stacked

221

rifles and spiked helmet, though it was necessary to emphasize the foreground plane at that point and lead the spectator's attention to the firing squad, dimly suggested at the extreme right.

Helen Frankenthaler (born 1928) is the author of an abstract image, 10 feet high, painted in acrylic in 1969. It bears the mysterious title *Cave*.[222] This afterthought may have been a purely associative reminiscence, but as a cave the picture could be read as either looking in or looking out. Such ambiguity is intrinsic to Surrealism, and as well to such older masters as Paul Klee and Pablo Picasso; but Frankenthaler's connection with these currents of modern art is at best tenuous. What counts here is the impact of pure shape and of pure color: from left to right, olive green, raw canvas, cinnamon orange, deep purple, and sky blue. It is remarkable how well these colors carry in the black-and-white photograph. That suggests a rare perception of color value, of the sort that is so extraordinary in the painting of Edouard Manet (for example, in Hartford's *Beach at Berck*, CT 23). As for shape, observe the power of the dominant purple area, forming a kind of 7; and observe, too, how the other colors set it off. The effect is of something colossal; thereby, it seems to me, the great size of the picture is justified. At such a scale straight edges and flat painting would produce boredom: hence the careful modulations of texture through brushwork, particularly in the purple and "orange" areas; and hence the ragged edges, as of torn papers, suggesting a collage that does not exist. Finally, a strange light seems to seep forward through the screen of purple. This picture can be passed by as formalism without content—or in Mark Rothko's phrase ("a painting does not *represent* an experience, it *is* an experience") it can be an experience of envelopment, as in a dream.

222

Chesterwood, the Studio
of Daniel Chester French

Location: Two miles west of Stockbridge, off Route 183; follow the signs at Glendale. If arriving by the Mass. Tpke., use exit 1
Hours: 10-5 daily, from May 1 to October 31 or early November
Admission: Charged

Owned and operated by the National Trust for Historic Preservation in the United States, Chesterwood, with the Saint-Gaudens National Historic Site at Cornish, N.H., makes available to the public the life and work of one of New England's—and America's—two most prominent sculptors of the late nineteenth and early twentieth centuries. They were almost exact contemporaries: Augustus Saint-Gaudens (1848–1907) and Daniel Chester French (1850–1931).

Chesterwood opened in 1955. It contains models, casts, and photographs of the work of a prolific career, and a large collection of personal mementos. In the studio itself the most important piece is the 6-foot-high *Plaster Study*[223] for the 20-foot marble statue of *Abraham Lincoln* in the Lincoln Memorial, Washington, D.C. This commission came near the end of French's career, almost fifty years after his figure of the *Minute Man* was unveiled by Ralph Waldo Emerson at Concord, Mass., in 1875. The Concord commission had come to him when he was only twenty-two, and it was his first statue. Other notable works by French include the *Alma Mater* for Low Library at Columbia University, *John Harvard* in Harvard Yard, the equestrian *George Washington* in the Place d'Iéna, Paris, and the standing *Lincoln* for the statehouse at Lincoln, Nebraska. To this list of widely familiar monuments I would add one admired locally, but too little recognized for its surpassing quality, the *General Oglethorpe*, on one of the main downtown squares of Savannah, Georgia.

In *Memories of a Sculptor's Wife*, Mrs. Daniel Chester French describes the difficulties encountered in erecting the huge marble *Lincoln* within the Lincoln Memorial. When it was finished in 1920, the architect, Henry Bacon, French's close friend, had died and his original plan for a glass ceiling had been changed to one of translucent marble. Though the interior had a beautiful glow, the lighting of the statue was disastrous. French had, of course, expected a lighting identical to that in the Chesterwood studio. Eventually Congress appropriated the money required to effect the present system of indirect lighting in the memorial. An interesting comparison of two photographs of the face (page 262 in Mrs. French's account), one lighted from above, as intended by the artist, the other from the front and below, graphically illustrates what is perhaps sculpture's most crucial problem. Today in Washington as well as at Chesterwood this noble image achieves the effect its maker desired.

In addition to the studio, one may visit the adjacent house and the Barn Gallery, which is attractively appointed to serve permanent and temporary exhibitions dealing with French's life and career, the Berkshire milieu, historic preservation, and local history. You will also enjoy walking through the beautiful wooded areas of the 120-acre estate, with their fine views of the surrounding Berkshires.

Until 1969, when Chesterwood passed to the National Trust by gift of French's daughter, Margaret French Cresson, Mrs. Cresson devoted over thirty years to preserving the estate with its studio, working toward opening it to the public and (after 1955, when this was accomplished) to presiding over its activities. The remodeling of the barn in 1962 was designed by Helen D. French, A.I.A., and the grounds were landscaped by her husband, Prentiss French, F.A.S.L.A., newphew of the sculptor.

223

The Old Corner House

Location: Main Street (Route 7), corner of Elm Street
Hours: Open daily 10–5, except Tues.; closed Thanksgiving, Christmas, New Year's Day, and the latter two weeks of January
Admission: Charged

Since this book is not concerned with architecture, we pass over the beautiful house itself, of late eighteenth-century design and formerly the home of James Fowler Dwight, a descendant of Joseph Dwight of Stockbridge, a general in the French and Indian War. Saved from demolition in 1967 by the activity of concerned Stockbridgians, it was restored and soon put to use as a home for the works of the town's most famous citizen.

This display is the only significant collection of paintings by Norman Rockwell (1894–1978) in existence. Most of these are owned by the Norman Rockwell Foundation, on loan as long as the Corner House shall exist, but some are borrowed from private collections, and others have been acquired as permanent possessions by the museum itself. Since we have discussed and illustrated at the New Britain Museum of American Art one of Rockwell's finest humorous illustrations (*Weighing In,* CT 51, for which the redoubtable Eddie Arcaro posed), our selection from the Old Corner House collection presents Rockwell's serious side. *The Problem We All Live With,*[224] an oil 36 by 58 inches, was painted on commission for *Look* magazine, which reproduced it in the issue of January 14, 1964. Centered between the towering legs of two pairs of U.S. marshals, a little black girl neatly dressed in purest white marches bravely forward. A ripe tomato, smashed against the leaden gray wall, lies on the ground. Graffiti on the wall tell the rest of the terrible story. Norman Rockwell invariably insisted, with characteristic modesty, that he was an illustrator, not an artist. This painting, however, rivets the attention not only by its message, nor even only by its realism, but by its shapes *as such,* by its sequence of darks and lights, and by the dread rhythm of its march.

224

Old Sturbridge Village

Location: On Route 20, ½ mile west of junction of Mass. Tpke. (exit 9) and I-86 (exit 3). Parking provided
Hours: April-October: 9:30-5:30 daily; November-March: 10-4 daily, except closed Mon. December-March; closed Christmas and New Year's Day
Admission: Charged. Ⓗ

One of our largest "outdoor" museums, Old Sturbridge Village tells the story of inland New England life during the eighteenth century and up to about 1840. On a two-hundred-acre tract bordering the Quinebaug River, the more than thirty buildings brought from nearby towns in Massachusetts and Connecticut have been sited to form a typical village and neighboring farm area. A separate formal-exhibits and demonstration area concentrates on the vast collections of arts and crafts and offers living demonstrations of the processes and techniques involved. Entrance is through the well-appointed modern Visitor Center.

Except for its many paintings and occasional examples of sculpture, Old Sturbridge Village lies outside the scope of this book. For further information see the forthcoming volume on *Historic Houses of New England* (in the David Godine series) by Margaret Supplee Smith.

Like the other collections here, the paintings owned by the village are generally limited to the cutoff date of 1840 and to what might have been seen in village establishments of the period. As of this writing, there is no special building for their display, and for security reasons the most valuable ones cannot be shown as incidental ornaments in the various houses. The Visitor Center, however, mounts changing exhibitions that often include selections of them. Visitors who have a particular interest in works and artists in the following list should make special arrangements in order to be sure to see them. Artists of unusual quality represented here are Mrs. Shute, Ethan Allen Greenwood, Erasmus Salisbury Field, and Matthew Prior. Most of the artists are anonymous. One of them painted a terrifying child in blue with a woolly dog; this picture reminded me of the rubbery, inflated humans of the contemporary Colombian painter Fernando Botero.

A rare example of wall painting will be found in the large room upstairs in the Salem Towne residence. These decorations (c. 1796), probably representing cedars of Lebanon, are original with the house, and were moved with it. In that year the Fayette Lodge of the Masonic Order was founded in the Charlton-Dudley-Sturbridge area, and for the first ten years of its existence it met in this room. The lodge was named for General Lafayette. Some of the paintings have been restored.

Overmantel paintings are an especially interesting branch of Early American art. The format calls for decoration on a wood panel and it offers an opportunity for a background of landscape. The village owns an unusual example depicting Moses Marcy of Sturbridge. As Marcy died in 1777, the painting is presumably pre-Revolutionary and thus one of the earliest such panels in existence. The subject was a merchant. In eternally fixed pose he invites us to survey his world. His house, rather startlingly located in this strange scene, is not unlike Publick House, a famous coaching inn built in 1771 in Sturbridge itself, about a mile from Old Sturbridge Village.

Rose Art Museum, Brandeis University

Location: From the Mass. Tpke. take exit 14 (coming from the west) or exit 15 (from Boston), onto Route 128 North; exit on Route 30 West, turn right (just before the stoplight) onto South St., which leads to the campus. The university is located east of Route 128 midway between Routes 30 and 20. Parking nearby

Telephone: (617) 647-2402

Hours: Tues.-Sun. 1-5; closed holidays

Admission: Free

The gift of Mr. and Mrs. Edward Rose of Boston, the well-designed building by Max Abramovitz dates from 1961, only thirteen years after the establishment of the university. A major addition was completed in 1974. The museum specializes in American and European art of the twentieth century. In the field of painting and sculpture since the Second World War it shares leadership in the Boston area with the Massachusetts Institute of Technology. The print collection, both in this field and in Japanese Ukiyo-e prints, is large; and the photograph collection is fast growing. Other collections include Tibetan, Oceanic, American Indian, and Pre-Columbian art, and the Rose collection of ceramics.

Because much of the available space is often filled by temporary exhibitions, it is advisable to call ahead about seeing the permanent collections. When you arrive at the university's information booth, ask directions to the museum and follow them carefully!

While the collection of modern art well represents the Post-Impressionists, the School of Paris, the Cubists, and early twentieth-century Americans, it is strongest in Abstract Expressionism, Pop Art, Color Field painting, and more recent developments.

Suspended appropriately in a network of rods set in the center of a reflecting pool is *Figure in Space*[225] (1958/9, total height 56 inches), a bronze by the English sculptor Reg Butler (born 1913). If you are familiar with the paintings of the same decade by Butler's compatriot

225

and contemporary Francis Bacon—smeared figures similarly imprisoned
—you will sense a mutual affinity. Expressive of the tenuousness of the
human condition, Bacon's figures are regularly detached from earthly
support. Like many modern sculptors, Butler evades gravity, traditionally
respected since Graeco-Roman times in the sitting, kneeling, standing,
or walking figure. The tensile properties of metal, rather than the static
ones of stone, are exploited to make this departure possible. It was a
brilliant idea to set Butler's piece over water; the reflection accentuates
its lift.

A remarkable oil by the Belgian Surrealist René Magritte (born
1898), provides an earlier analogy for Butler's topsy-turvy world.
L'Atlantide[226] (also called *The Reflection*), 40 inches high, was painted
in 1927. This was the year of his first exhibition, at Brussels; and the
unfavorable response stimulated a move to Paris, where Magritte was
quickly taken up by the newly founded Surrealist group. Against a black
so deep as to suggest the space of a dream, a masonry-veneered tub
establishes an abrupt and stark foreground. At its left end what seems
like a curtain rises diagonally to top center—a curtain until you discover
the upside-down corridor leading up a flight of stairs to a closed chapel
in a rocky cliff. In the following year, 1928, Magritte painted a kind of
manifesto: a meticulous fool-the-eye smoking-pipe. But under it he
carefully lettered the following inscription: *Ceci n'est pas une pipe.*
Not a pipe, that is, but a painting. Reality, as certain of the ancients
insisted, lies not in appearance.

Another Surrealist painter of the dream world represented here is
Yves Tanguy (1900–55), who lived and worked in Connecticut after
leaving Paris in 1940. He married the American Surrealist painter Kay
Sage (see CT 103), and it was from her estate that *Terre des
Dormeuses*[227] came to the Rose Museum. All Tanguys evoke dreams,

226

227

and their titles—often more oblique than this one—direct us to the subconscious. While Magritte exploits the paradox of realism transformed, Tanguy fills his dream space with bonelike shapes, some soft, some brittle and piercing, and with Miró-like shadows cast by yet others not seen. The Brandeis example was painted in the same year, 1927, as Magritte's *L'Atlantide*.

Still Life: Radio Tube,[228] by Stuart Davis (1894–1964), is a companion piece to *Salt Shaker* (1931) in the Museum of Modern Art, New York. These and the work of the same year discussed at the Portland Museum of Art (*New York–Paris Number 2*, ME 25) are the fruit of an eighteen-month exposure to Cubist art in Paris. It is true that Davis had already worked out of illustrative painting into Cubist forms prior to his Paris sojourn, but that experience gave him the confidence he needed to move ahead in a direction that culminated in his magnificent canvases of the 1950s and early 1960s. At the ambitious size (for Davis at the time) of 50 by 32 inches, *Radio Tube* combines abstract Cubist forms with Fernand Léger's interest in those of modern industrial machinery; and in a characteristically brusque American way it adapts the amalgam to a specifically American subject, diminutive by the tape measure, explored and then enlarged. Through the art of Stuart Davis a radio tube and a saltshaker somehow become symbols of the American scene. Not surprisingly, he later influenced the development of Pop Art in the United States. In *Radio Tube* the restricted color—cleanly defined small areas of intense red, yellow, blue, and green spotted against much larger areas of black and white—indicates that the work of Piet Mondrian was yet another ingredient in the Davis mix. For this American, however, it was impossible to stay within Mondrian's ascetic limits, or within Léger's formal language of planes and cylinders. Furthermore, his American pragmatism barred Davis from Picasso's wild flights of imagination. He had permanently eliminated the human figure as his vehicle of expression. From now on he would find human interest in the colors, rhythms, half-read advertising slogans, and the overall excitement of life in a modern American city.

The inspiration for *Elegy to the Spanish Republic, Number 58,*[229] measuring 7 by 9 feet, by Robert Motherwell (born 1915) may date

228

229

from 1937, when the very young art student, graduated only a year before from Stanford University with a bachelor's degree in philosophy, heard André Malraux speak on the Spanish civil war at a San Francisco rally. Such a statement is simplistic, for it skips eleven formative years of Motherwell's artistic and intellectual life. However that may be, the motif first emerged in 1948; *Number 34* of 1953/4 is a major masterpiece of Abstract Expressionist painting (Albright-Knox Gallery, Buffalo: see my *Art Tours and Detours in New York State*; New York: Random House, 1964, page 23); *Number 54* (Museum of Modern Art) differs greatly from the Rose Museum's *Number 58* of the same period, 1957–61; and as late as 1978, in *Reconciliation Elegy*, the motif finds a tenuous resolution in stability in an enormous friezelike canvas in the new East Wing of the National Gallery of Art, Washington. Motherwell has said that his Elegies are not specifically political, but are "general metaphors of the contrast between life and death, and their interrelation." They are his personal *Guernica*. Many of them, including the Brandeis example, were shown in a major retrospective exhibition of the artist's work at the Museum of Modern Art in 1965, and illustrated in the catalogue. Such a decades-long series, always varied, always evolving, is a sure sign of a talent in depth. It is a modern equivalent of Cézanne's Mont-Ste-Victoires, of Monet's Water Lilies, and—to take the artist above all revered by Motherwell—of the Bathers of Matisse.

In the Buffalo *Elegy* of 1953/4, the motif is a relatively clean "7070" hanging free at the base, the menacing black 7's crushing the o's into vertical ovals held precariously; and the dominating blacks are relieved by small touches of intense color. By the time of the Brandeis example, black and ashen white bring the tonality closer to that of Picasso's *Guernica*, and the forms are looser. The direction of change is much like that which led to the latest Mont-Ste-Victoires of Cézanne and to Matisse's murals of cutout papers. A final suggestion to the reader: turn our illustration upside down and note how much is lost when the forms are no longer in suspension; note too that the deceptively slipshod drips and the downward pulls of the brush no longer have a gravitational reference.

The expressiveness and power of our next painting, appropriately titled *Untitled*,[230] cannot begin to be conveyed in a black-and-white

230

photograph. The picture itself makes its statement exclusively through color and brushwork. Willem de Kooning (born 1904) is a leading figure in the first generation of Abstract Expressionist painters that emerged—one might say exploded—on the New York scene in the 1940s and 1950s, soon to be joined by such younger artists as Jackson Pollock and Robert Motherwell. The Rose Museum's *Untitled* (80 by 70 inches) dates from 1961, and is thus a latish example of de Kooning's vigorous shorthand transcription of landscape. (The pictures in his celebrated Woman series of the 1950s—for all their savage reference to billboard sex symbols—have been described as female landscapes.) If *Untitled* moves you, dear reader, skip to the next paragraph. If it does not, look through Thomas Hess's catalogue for the Museum of Modern Art's major retrospective (1968). The following quotation from the artist may be obliquely helpful. It comes from the year of *Untitled*, when the artist found his image not in the clamorous metropolis but in farthest east Long Island. "I am very happy to see that grass is green. At one time, it was very daring to make a figure red or blue—I think now that it is just as daring to make it flesh-colored." Flesh-color finds its way into this landscape too, in a heady admixture with the greens, yellows, blues, and earth browns that animate it.

Just as post–Second World War Abstract Expressionism (also called, perhaps preferably, Action Painting) was a revolt against the meticulous detail and the storytelling art of the Regionalist painters of the 1930s (see Grant Wood's drawing in the Rose Museum for his well-known *American Gothic*), so Action Painting gave rise to a countermovement in the early 1960s. Pop Art was no return to the art of Wood, Benton, and Curry; but it did involve a return to elements of everyday life, and it eschewed the deeply personal flavor of the frenetic brushwork of de Kooning, Kline, and Pollock. Andy Warhol and Roy Lichtenstein are the most prominent names here, but in my opinion James Rosenquist (born 1933) is the major talent. The museum's *Two People*[231] (also called *Fishpole*) was purchased in the year of its execution, 1963. An oil and assemblage on canvas measuring 72 by 93 inches, it compacts disassociated fragments of leering billboards, food, common textiles, a license plate (full of nothings), and come-ons for a summer vacation into a closely knit, powerful design. Rosenquist's paintings have been described as floating like giant clouds. Cacophonous and disquieting, their impact is ironically not unrelated to that of the very art the Pop artists rejected: the harsh clang of a Franz Kline (MA 162) and the wild frenzy of a late Pollock (CT 34).

231

Wellesley College Museum

Location: In the Jewett Arts Center, between Routes 16 and 135; from Route 128 take exit 54 onto Route 16. Parking available
Hours: Mon.-Sat. 10-5, Sun. 2-5; closed Easter Sunday, mid-June through August, Thanksgiving, December 24, 25, and 26, New Year's Day
Admission: Free. Ⓗ

A brilliant new chapter opened for the museum in 1958, when it moved from a venerable building given by Isaac Farnsworth in 1883. Nevertheless, the old quarters had hospitably housed a long-distinguished art-history department and a collection that took on new life in 1944 with the appointment of Professor John McAndrew as its director. Sophisticated, scholarly, and endowed with taste and enormous enthusiasm, McAndrew quietly performed a miracle in the years of his stewardship. When the collection was unveiled in its wing of the spacious new Jewett Arts Center, it was quickly recognized as one of the best in the nation's smaller colleges. In the year following McAndrew's retirement from teaching in 1968, the museum mounted an exhibition of some forty works selected from the great many more that he had given, or persuaded others to give (in his time there were no purchase funds of consequence), as well as other works presented for the occasion in his honor. Few directors have done so much with so little.

Sad to relate, the construction of the new museum was accompanied by McAndrew's resignation as its director. Opposition by the administration on certain critical issues produced a deadlock; but the museum's loss was teaching's gain for another decade. McAndrew's final years were devoted to Venice, where he died, much honored for his untiring efforts in organizing support for conservation of Venice's deteriorating buildings and works of art.

John McAndrew's interests were wide-ranging. He took advantage of the then low prices for sculpture (which is particularly difficult to teach through slides and photographs). He assembled a rich array of Baroque painting and of modern art in all media—areas that had been sadly neglected. Virtually every important twentieth-century artist is represented in at least one medium.

Today, the collections, enriched by further gifts and purchases, are extensive in sculpture, painting, drawings, and prints. Since 1971, with the gift of twenty examples of the work of Eugène Atget (1857–1927), the photograph collection has also forged ahead. Attention is currently being paid to developing the representation of nineteenth-century American art.

An active Friends of Art organization issues a *Newsletter*, but no catalogue has appeared since *European and American Sculpture, Paintings, and Drawings*, published on the occasion of the opening of the new museum in 1958. A new catalogue, however, is projected.

The Jewett Arts Center, the gift of the family of George Frederick

Jewett, was designed by Paul Rudolph. Elaborate and interesting in plan, elevation, and interior spaces, and fitting harmoniously with the brick-and-stone College Gothic of the surrounding buildings, it received considerable critical acclaim; but there are some who wish it had the simplicity of a Mies van der Rohe design or the substance of one by Louis Kahn. As you arrive you are confronted by a handsome bridge connecting two major wings set at a comfortably enclosing angle. The left wing provides facilities for music and drama; the right one contains the museum, the art department, and its fine library; and the bridge, under which you pass, is the main gallery of the museum—also serving as the foyer for concerts and theater productions.

Although our first piece, the life-size marble *Torso of an Athlete*,[232] is an ancient Roman copy of an original work by Polykleitos, it gives an excellent impression of later fifth-century Greek sculpture. Comparison with the contemporary grave stele of a *Warrior* at Worcester (MA 289) is helpful, both to complete the action of the Wellesley figure and to clarify the original strength of the badly eroded surfaces of the Worcester example. While the body twists freely on its axis, the frontal plane is strongly emphasized, and a similar planar effect will be gained from observing the magnificent back. Thus Polykleitos tempered his daring innovations with the discipline of earlier Greek tradition. How taut this figure is may be quickly discovered by comparing it with the *Meleager* at the Fogg Museum (MA III), a work marked by the Baroque trends of the next century. The Wellesley statue is the finest of some nine known copies of Polykleitos's *Discophoros* (the figure once held a discus in his left hand; the right arm was extended). It long stood in the Palazzo Odescalchi in Rome, embellished by fanciful restorations that were removed when it was sold and soon afterward given to Wellesley in 1905. It is not at all certain that the head belongs to the torso. What is very certain, however, is that it was attached erroneously—the two breaks do not coincide and a neck connection was invented—with the result that the head does not have its proper downward turn to the right, visible in other copies. This has the further disadvantage of disrupting the rhythmic curve from bottom to top in the otherwise superb rear view.

232

Not a capital like the somewhat related Burgundian example in the Fogg Art Museum (MA 112), but a corbel support, is the late twelfth-century Romanesque *Musician Playing a Viol*.[233] This sensitive carving in limestone, a foot high, comes from Provence; and because of its close similarity to a corbel in the Cloisters, New York, showing a dancer or acrobat, it appears to have come from the neighborhood of Saint-Gilles, not far from Arles.

The profile *Portrait of Estienne Menessarre*, a 5-inch roundel relief of sparkling marble, is a superb example of French sculpture of c. 1500, subtly balancing late Gothic realism with Italianate formal clarity. It was acquired in 1980.

The polychromed terra-cotta statue of the *Madonna and Child*,[234] 3 feet high, is attributed to Jacopo Sansovino (1486–1570) because of its relationship to his bronze figures and his terra-cotta *Madonna and Child* on the Loggetta in Venice, at the base of the great bell tower of the Piazza San Marco. The possibility of an atelier variant is not eliminated, but the piece is faithful to the master's subtle style of the 1540s. Trained in Florence in the purest traditions of ancient art then known to the Western world, Sansovino moved to Venice in 1527. Because of the higher polish of the Wellesley statue near its base, it is thought that the figure was designed to be seen high up, and presumably in a niche, since the rear is unfinished. Despite its Mannerist elongation, it preserves something of the sturdiness of Donatello (for example, in the pressure exerted by the Virgin's hands) and of the vigor of Michelangelo, who was only ten years Sansovino's senior. Purchased for a former owner by Wilhelm von Bode, the great German connoisseur of Renaissance sculpture, it was for some time on loan to the Kaiser Friedrich Museum in Berlin. Sansovino's sweetness and serenity require no special comment.

Wellesley owns a 2-foot bronze version of the famous marble of *The Rape of the Sabine Women* by Giovanni Bologna (1529–1608) in the Loggia dei Lanzi, Florence. Bologna's marble (1579–83) won him such fame that there developed a wide demand for small bronze replicas, turned out by highly trained assistants. Whoever made this

233

234

one—not excluding Giovanni Bologna himself—it is of very high quality. The whirling action is contained within an invisible cylinder, and only to this extent is it more restrained than the fully centrifugal explosions of Baroque sculpture of the seventeenth century.

An *Angel*,[235] only a foot high but seemingly larger, of gilded and polychromed wood, is the work of Meinrad Guggenbichler (1649–1723). It came from a side altar erected in 1706 in the celebrated little parish church in St. Wolfgang, on a beautiful lake in the mountains east of Salzburg. Wonderfully tender in feeling, somehow floating instead of standing on its pedestal, and with outstretched arms that once held a swinging censer, it is typical of those Austrian and German variations on Italian Baroque forms—Bernini's Angels on the bridge leading to the Castel Sant'Angelo in Rome may be a source of inspiration here—that marked the first half of the eighteenth century. Where Bernini is heroic and operatic, the Austro-German sculptors are spiritual and tremulous. Bernini is grandiloquent like Rubens; Guggenbichler, lyrical like Botticelli. The fluttering wing of the *Angel* is as expressive as the face and hands. Such works are rare outside the region of their origin. They are as much beloved by Austrians and Germans today as when they were made. In our discussion of the Busch-Reisinger Museum at Cambridge, we mentioned a larger group of Guggenbichler's, *The Return from the Flight to Egypt*. A delicate little half-length *St. Joachim*, perhaps by his school, is in the Williams College Museum of Art.

Only in Austria and Germany, and in Spain, did the medieval tradition of polychromed and gilded wood sculpture continue in popularity through the Baroque era. This reflects the deep piety of those Catholic areas—a piety not notable in eighteenth-century Italy. One of the most remarkable Spanish sculptors of the time was Francisco Antonio Salzillo (or Zarcillo), whose career was restricted to the provincial region of Murcia, back from Spain's southeast coast. He lived from 1707 to 1783. The attribution to him of Wellesley's *St. Teresa of Avila*[236] has strong scholarly support. Salzillo's reputation is based primarily on his painted wooden *pasos*: life-size scenes from the Passion wheeled through the streets in Holy Week. In his lifetime they were thought to have been

235

236

made with divine assistance. The *St. Teresa*, about 2 feet high, may well be the work of assistants, at least in part, because Salzillo employed a great many, apportioning them specialized tasks, such as flesh painting and drapery painting. With some eighteen hundred works assigned to him, caution must be one's guide. However that may be, the combination of strong sentiment and intense realism comes through here as profoundly Spanish. That and, as well, great reserve: the most fleeting memory of Bernini's ecstatic marble altar of St. Teresa in Rome will indicate how far Salzillo's art strayed from normal Baroque canons of religious representation. Bernini, the pure sculptor, got his color from concealed amber glass lights; Salzillo liked the contrast between a black robe and a flowered silk cape, and between highly polished flesh tones and eyes of glass. A folk-art votive element here is a panel in the drapery that opens to reveal a startling illusion of the saint's heart.

We continue our selections from Wellesley's sculpture with two very different heads of women by French contemporaries active during the second half of the nineteenth century. The terra-cotta *Head of Anne Foucart at Age Sixteen*[237] was modeled by Jean-Baptiste Carpeaux (1827–75); that of *Diana Huntress*,[238] carved in marble, is a replica of the full-length nude figure by Jean-Alexandre-Joseph Falguière (1831–1900). The contrast is absolute. The Carpeaux shows painterly modeling in the tradition of Bernini (see MA 121) and Houdon (see CT 67): animated psychology, flying hair, a twisting neck, a deftly raised shoulder. The Falguière has the process of carving concealed under a veneer of pure white surfaces, a minimum of light and shade oppositions, a closed psychology, smoothed hair, a little animation suggested

237

238

by a turn of the head and the stump of a raised arm. The lives of the two sculptors differed in ways we should expect. Carpeaux's beginnings were marked by suffering and discouragement until at age twenty-seven he won the Prix de Rome; yet there was the fond memory of having been received at age eighteen by the great François Rude (see VT 10) and instructed by him for a year and a half. Important commissions came his way during the Second Empire (pediments of the Louvre, *La Danse* for the facade of the Opéra), but always marked by bitter controversy. Carpeaux died in his late forties at the height of his powers. Falguière had, on the other hand, favorable acceptance at the Ecole des Beaux-Arts; dutiful Academic training; the Prix de Rome and eventually the medal of the Légion d'Honneur; a long and untroubled life. In painting, the best parallel for Carpeaux is Gustave Courbet (that is, in Courbet's frank nudes and vigorous portraits). It would be unfair to call Falguière the Bouguereau of sculpture (see MA 257), for his *Diana* exudes a purity that Bouguereau never expressed. Furthermore, it should be said that Falguière transcended the limitations of those pale remnants of Neoclassicism that many other Academic sculptors clung to. The reader will easily guess how my choice lies, but I urge a careful look at the *Diana* for its lack of affectation and its very high order of craftsmanship. As for the *Anne Foucart*, I reproduce the back view[237A] as well as the front, to show how the movement is generated at the lower left and never loses its momentum. You can see the mark of the tools on it, and may even expect to find the sculptor's fingerprints, so much are you caught up (I hope) in the excitement of witnessing the creative act. Many Carpeaux heads exist in terra-cotta replicas, but they generally lack the all-important personal touch of a sculptor whom Rodin was proud to call his master.

The work of the somewhat younger Aimé-Jules Dalou (1838–1900), who studied for a time with Carpeaux, has received considerable critical notice in recent years. Like Gustave Courbet, he became involved with the Commune in 1870/1 and was forced into exile. Unlike Courbet, he later returned to Paris, received major commissions for bronze monuments, and was awarded the exalted title of Officer of the Légion d'Honneur. It is his smaller works and studies that are especially admired today. Those familiar with Dalou's vast, heaving *Triumph of the Republic*, in the Place de la Nation, may be surprised by the poignant realism of his bronze *Lavoisier*[239] and its compact design. This fine piece,

239

acquired by purchase in 1977, is a reduction of Dalou's 1892 monument (in the Sorbonne) to the great scientist who was guillotined in the Revolution. At a height of only 20 inches it suggests much larger forms. The rare malachite green patina is only one of many indications of refinement in this penetrating work. The original plaster is in the Petit Palais, Paris.

Other fine bronzes in the collection are by Giuseppe Piemonte (1664–1742) and Renoir in his final years.

Two superb heads, by the German Wilhelm Lehmbruck (1881–1919) and by Marcel Duchamp's brother, Raymond Duchamp-Villon (1876–1918), take us into the twentieth century. Both works date from 1911 and both loom large in the artists' careers. Lehmbruck's *Head of the Kneeling Woman*,[240] 20 inches high, is a cast stone replica, patinated by the master himself to resemble terra-cotta, of the upper part of his celebrated 70-inch 1911 figure in the Museum of Modern Art. A second cast stone version of the *Kneeling Woman*, purchased in 1938 by the Albright-Knox Gallery, Buffalo, was exhibited at the famous Armory Show in New York, in 1913. Buffalo already owned the Wellesley head (a gift in 1927), but the acquisition of the complete figure resulted in the sale of the head, which Wellesley was most fortunate in acquiring through a generous gift. For further discussion of Lehmbruck, a suicide at thirty-eight and generally acclaimed as Germany's finest twentieth-century sculptor, see the entry on his *Torso of the "Pensive Woman"* at Smith College (MA 191). Although it is two or three years later than the *Kneeling Woman*, the Smith example is more conservative and less typical of the artist's expressive attenuation of forms.

Duchamp-Villon's *Bust of Baudelaire*[241] is a painted plaster version of a work ordinarily seen in bronze. This somber head, with its haunting eyeless gaze, became the subject of two Cubist etchings by Jacques Villon, the artist's older brother. Such a development is of itself evidence of the formal purity of the work. (One can hardly imagine a Cubist version of a Rodin.) Duchamp-Villon was a leader in the reaction against Rodin's scarified and deeply penetrated surfaces. As a characterization, the head has little of the morbid overtones of Baude-

240

241

laire's nineteenth-century verse; but it conveys much about his great critical intelligence and perceptiveness.

A fine selection of African sculpture includes a superb Benin bronze *Warrior* of the seventeenth century (compare MA 143) once owned by the painter André Derain, a leader in the modern interest in "primitive" art. It is one of many gifts from Mr. McAndrew. Of the ten sculptures already illustrated and two others mentioned, eight came to the museum through the generosity or the persuasiveness of the former director.

The oldest painting in the museum is also one of its earliest acquisitions. Purchased in 1905 from a fund given by President Hazard, *Christ Mounting the Cross and the Burial of St. Clara*, tempera on panel 31 by 21 inches, is the work of a follower of Guido da Siena, the late thirteenth-century initiator of Sienese painting and predecessor of the great Duccio (see MA 204). Strongly influenced by Byzantine traditions, it breaks with them in its linear swing, an element fundamental to the art of Duccio and Simone Martini (see MA 115).

The *Holy Family with Saints Francis and John the Baptist*,[242] by the Florentine painter and biographer Giorgio Vasari (1511–74), is the museum's most impressive pre-Baroque painting. Oil on panel 41 inches high, it is in mint condition, and its harsh pink reds, ice blues, greens, and apricot oranges make a strong foil for the enameled flesh tones. The date is c. 1544, soon after the artist received his first important commissions. Other versions of this work exist in the museums of Bordeaux and San Francisco (De Young Museum), but Wellesley's is the finest. Vasari drew from many sources, and never managed to achieve a unique style; but his sources were admirable and he combined them with great skill. Echoes of Andrea del Sarto appear in the elderly saints, of Michelangelo in the heroic Madonna, and of Parmigianino in her long neck and attenuated right hand. The hardness that gave a nickname to the painter Bronzino (1503–72) is also in evidence here. The general format, with its vertical axes climbing up symmetrically across a central one, and the twisting of forms to bring them parallel to the picture plane, suggests Il Rosso's *Dead Christ with Angels* (c. 1525/6) in the Boston Museum of Fine Arts (MA 70).

Limitations of space and the discussion of many fine examples in other museums force me to summarize Wellesley's fine display of seventeenth-century painting. Not to be missed are a *Youth in a Plumed Hat* by a

242

follower of Caravaggio, *Christ and the Woman of Samaria* by Domenichino (with an early appearance of modern landscape), and religious
paintings by Crespi, Dolci, Furini, Giordano, and especially the *St.
Francis in Ecstasy* by Bernardo Strozzi (see CT 14). Many of these
Italian pictures were the gift of Dr. and Mrs. Arthur K. Solomon, of
Cambridge, as was a large, Italian-inspired mythological picture by the
Flemish painter Abraham Janssens the Elder (c. 1574–1632), a contemporary of Rubens. Dutch marine painting is well represented in a
battle piece by Willem van de Velde the Younger (see MA 212); Dutch
church interiors in an example by Emanuel de Witte; and Dutch genre
painting in the remarkable *Soldiers Playing Cards*, by Gerard Ter Borch
(1617–81), of which other versions exist.

    Landscape with Approaching Storm, by the Venetian Marco Ricci
(1676–1729), takes us into the early eighteenth century. A similar verve
animates the brush of the Genoese painter Alessandro Magnasco, whose
small *St. Bruno in Ecstasy* recalls the agitated monks in his painting at
Springfield (MA 213). Evidence of the spread of Parisian Rococo style
is seen in the fresh and charming *Perseus and Andromeda* by the Venetian-born Jacopo Amigoni (1675–1752), who worked in Bavaria, England, and Spain, as well as in his native city.

    During the 1970s two important gifts from alumnae strengthened the
representation of American painting: J. S. Copley's Boston-period *Portrait of Mrs. Roland Cotton* (c. 1763) and a 40-by-60-inch canvas, *The
White Mountains: Mt. Washington*, by John Frederick Kensett (1816–
72).[243] The latter is an absolutely superb example of art in the Hudson
Riven vein, comparable to such works we have discussed as the early
Bierstadts at Framingham and the Fruitlands Museums at Harvard,
and Frederic Church's *Scene in the Catskills* (1851) in the George
Walter Vincent Smith Museum at Springfield. The Kensett panorama
dates from toward the end of the 1860s. It has his typical low-intensity
colors. He once explained that "bright colors are sparingly distributed
throughout the natural world . . . the main masses are made up of cool
greens, grays, drabs and browns intermingled, and are always harmonious and agreeable."

    An unexpected introduction to the modern movement in painting is
provided by a brashly stroked, primarily black-and-white *Portrait Roman-
tique*[244] of c. 1868–70. I suspect you will have trouble guessing which

244

243

celebrated artist painted it, even after being told that it is an early work. Early works can be deceptive, and this one is further offbeat because the artist was not often given to Romantic overtones—though there are other examples of the same period. His technical source here is the "black" works of Edouard Manet of the 1860s with their revolutionary emphasis on painting by flat tones; but this artist laid them on heavily in a near frenzy, that is, in a spirit totally different from Manet's judicious strokes. Instead of Manet's elegant aloofness we find here a devil-may-care explosion of energy. Should you need further identification, illustration MA 82 will show you a portrait of 1877, and illustration RI 21 another of c. 1890–92—by the same master.

Head of a Man by Pablo Picasso is only a small gouache sketch, but it has the force and the nascent Cubist character of his large *Standing Figure* of the same year (1908) in Boston (MA 87). It is thought that the relative calm seen in Picasso's work of 1908, following the violence of his 1907 *Demoiselles d'Avignon*, resulted from the influence of the memorial exhibition in Paris of the work of Paul Cézanne, who had died in 1906.

Mother and Child,[245] a Cubist composition measuring 26 by 21 inches, was painted in 1921 by Fernand Léger (1881–1955). It was given in honor of Alfred H. Barr, who introduced at Wellesley the first course in America on contemporary painting. Léger's cylindrical and spherical forms have been called "Tubist." Set against an emphatic vertical and horizontal grid in a compressed space, they give a feeling of three-dimensional sculpture. Color, which runs to primaries and high intensities, adds another note of formal purity. The restraint and equilibrium of Léger's geometric world is thoroughly French, in the tradition of Seurat and Cézanne. An affinity with the Classicism of Poussin (1594–1665) becomes most striking when the picture is compared with Poussin's *Holy Family* at the Fogg Museum (MA 123). A sharp contrast, however, emerges on comparison with Picasso's *Table* of 1919/20 at Smith College (MA 185), even though the two artists were born in the same year and Léger's Cubism owed its origin to Picasso's pioneering inventions. Neither picture makes much of its apparent subject.

245

Both depart from it to achieve other artistic goals. Picasso sought a symbol of modern anxiety; Léger, a symbol of the power of modern machinery.

Noir et Rouge,[246] a collage of cutout colored papers by Henri Matisse (1869–1954), measures only 17 by 21 inches, but it could easily be enlarged to mural dimensions. The date is 1950, before Matisse did in fact expand his new technique into vast decorative schemes such as the *Swimming Pool* (Museum of Modern Art, 1952). Beset by infirmities of old age, the great painter could no longer manipulate a brush. With a long stick he traced these biomorphic shapes on sheets of paper already colored in gouache and on contrasting black ones. Assistants performed the cutting operation for him. "To cut to the quick in color," he once said, "reminds me of direct cutting in sculpture." Reference to the bronze nude *Seated Woman* at Manchester (N H 30)—fashioned, of course, in clay before it was cast—will not only clarify Matisse's statement; it will suggest that his collage shapes are not as flat as they at first appear to be.

We have discussed in some detail an untitled composition of 1961 by Willem de Kooning (born 1904) at the Rose Museum in Waltham (M A 230). Wellesley's *Woman Springs*,[247] painted on a door panel 80 by 36 inches, is signed and dated 1966. It was given in 1978 in memory of Professor McAndrew. The title may well have a double meaning. This woman indeed springs, as in a wild dance; but Springs is the name of the eastern Long Island village where de Kooning and other artists of his circle have enjoyed a retreat from New York City. This sea of flesh-colored oil is a kind of Soutine landscape or marine extracted from the woman subject that has appeared intermittently in de Kooning's work since he introduced it in the early 1950s. In a decade dominated by earthworks, curtained natural scenery, conceptual art, and various manifestos of anti-art, it is gratifying to find an "old master" evolving in the tempo of his own style—just as Edward Hopper did—and, for that matter, Matisse, Claude Monet, Frans Hals, Titian, and Botticelli. All these "old masters" in their literally old age remained true to themselves. Excitement about the latest novelties—particularly rife and even destructive today—could not touch them.

246

247

Sterling and Francine Clark Art Institute

Location: South Street
Hours: Tues.-Sun. 10-5, throughout the year, and 10-5 on Memorial Day, Labor Day, and Columbus Day; closed New Year's Day, Thanksgiving, and Christmas
Admission: Free

Open to the public since 1955, the institute houses the impressive art collection formed by Mr. and Mrs. Robert Sterling Clark. Born in New York City in 1877, the grandson of a partner of Isaac Singer, inventor of the Singer sewing machine, Mr. Clark graduated from Yale in 1899 as an engineer and entered the army, serving in the Philippines and in China during the Boxer Rebellion. After leading a scientific expedition into the remote areas of northern China, he settled in Paris in 1912 and began acquiring works of art.

Collecting was an interest that ran in the family, and both Sterling and his brother Stephen undertook art-buying sprees in Europe, some with the guidance of the American sculptor George Grey Barnard. Initially, Clark focused his attention on Old Masters, particularly Italian, Dutch, and Flemish artists. Then, in the 1920s and 1930s, encouraged by his French-born wife, he concentrated on French nineteenth-century painting, examples of which now dominate the collection. His interests did not extend to twentieth-century modern art.

Just before the Second World War, the Clarks, who had previously divided their residence between the United States and France, returned to New York and drew up plans to make their collection—nearly three hundred works (not counting drawings, prints, or the extensive collection of silver and porcelain)—available for educational purposes. In 1950, they selected Williamstown for its natural beauty and associated cultural advantages, and five years later dedicated their Neo-Classical building of white Vermont marble. In 1964, a service building was added behind the original edifice to house a regional conservation laboratory and the institute's workshop. A red granite building designed by Pietro Belluschi and the Architects Collaborative of Cambridge, Mass., to the south of the original complex, was opened to the public in 1973. The new structure provides exhibition galleries, offices, an auditorium, and an art library, as well as a locale for a two-year graduate program leading to an M.A. degree from Williams College.

Since the deaths of Mr. and Mrs. Clark (in 1956 and 1960 respectively), the institute has grown slowly with deliberate restraint. A dozen major painting acquisitions have been made by the trustees, from interest on the endowment, along with many additions to the drawings and print collections. The first purchase, made in 1962, secured for the museum its oldest work, a seven-part polyptych over 11 feet long: *Virgin and Child surrounded by Saints, Old Testament Prophets, and*

Angels.[248] This tempera panel painting is attributed to Ugolino da
Siena, active from 1317 and one of the more distinguished followers
of the great Trecento master Duccio, painter of the *Maestà* for the Siena
Cathedral (MA 204).

Ugolino's altarpiece reflects the conventions of an earlier, hieratic
tradition. The rigidity and frontality of the figures, the richly ornamented background of gold leaf, and the ensemble's overall iconic di-
dacticism perpetuate aspects of late Byzantine style, modified by a
suggestion of the linear rhythms of Gothic art. The work is in a good
state of preservation; the materials used (cobalt, lapis lazuli, violet),
bound to their support by the classic egg-yolk emulsion, have retained
much of their original luster. In terms of quality, size, and completeness,
the painting is matched in New England only by the five-panel altarpiece by Simone Martini in the Gardner Museum, Boston (MA 34).

Another devotional altarpiece, *The Madonna and Child with Four
Angels,*[249] assigned on the basis of style to the Renaissance master Piero
della Francesca (c. 1410–92), almost begs for comparison with the
earlier Sienese example. Certain pictorial conventions have been adhered
to: again, Mary and the Christ Child are the center of attention, but how
differently the two artists have rendered them! Where Ugolino promotes
ethereal/mystical sensations, Piero emphasizes physical presence (the
qualities of weight, solidity, and mass) and intellectual clarity. The
cessation of all movement, supported by Piero's blue-gray tonality into
which even his reds are absorbed, projects an intense calm into the work.
Swags stretch across two marble panels, one black with deep red vein-
ings, the other the color of porphyry. The columns have some of the re-

248

249

silience of living figures, yet the figures themselves seem to vie with them in immobility. The artist's skillful handling of line and of soft light, blond and fresh, has enabled him to impart depth and form to every element of the composition. Contrast the four silent, full-modeled angels, standing firmly on the ground in a defined space, with the seraphs hovering restlessly in the spandrels of Ugolino's altarpiece. Working approximately 150 years later, Piero has imbued his design with an intense interest in the theoretical studies of perspective and geometry. His work is marked by deep understanding of the revolution in thought implicit in the Italian Renaissance.

No documents exist to uphold the panel's attribution to Piero, and it may not be entirely autographic. Moreover, while the picture seems to be complete in other respects, it may have been the central panel of a triptych. A shadow at bottom center, possibly cast by another column outside and to the left of the existing composition, supports this theory. An examination of the panel's edges might help solve the mystery, but this is not possible because the original poplar support was replaced by a composite panel in 1957.

Pietro Vannucci (1445–1523), called Perugino from the principal city of Umbria, was separated from Piero by a full generation. Though both were Umbrian by birth, Piero went to Florence for his training before returning to work in Arezzo and Urbino. These facts account for some of the differences evident in their work, but we may also assume a fundamental difference of temperament. Perugino was typically Umbrian in his gentleness. There is no hint of Piero's cool rigidity in the *Sepulcrum Christi* (inscribed with Perugino's name, but not otherwise documented as his work).[250] What predominates is delicacy of sentiment and lusciousness of soft color. The iconography of this picture is unusual. Placed upright on a stone parapet or sepulcher cover and attended by young Nicodemus and the bearded Joseph of Arimathea, the dead Christ is the focus of attention. No ancillary figures complicate the scene; no outward movements distract the eye from the limp body. The subtle but engaging look of Nicodemus is enough to establish a psychological link with Joseph, and to invite the spectator to meditate on the

250

image of Christ as Redeemer. Thus, the sepulcher seems to become an altar with Christ offering the Eucharist. Quiet and contemplative, the privacy of the scene is accentuated by the placement of the figures close to the picture plane; its serenity is sustained by the artist's evocation of atmosphere more than by the rendering of sculptural form.

Such warm and suffused light and such softened contours and muted detail are salient aspects of Perugino's art, but here they somehow transcend the character of Perugino's known work (see page 381). Was his art ever so accomplished? We know that he was the chief master of Raphael (1483–1520). But what of the possible impact of a gifted pupil on his less-talented master? This phase in the careers of the two artists has been left in considerable shadow. The *Sepulcrum Christi* also clearly bears a close affinity to certain inventions of the Venetian Giovanni Bellini (c. 1430–1516)—the composition of the group, the quiet dignity of the figures, the soft modeling of the flesh, the poetic quality of the colors. Perugino is believed to have made a trip to Venice in 1494; some scholars list Venice as the actual provenance of the Clark painting. Could it represent Perugino's response to Bellini's types and forms? Surely, such mysteries add to the picture's allure.

Among the Flemish paintings here is the small *Portrait of Canon Gilles Joye*[251] by Hans Memling (c. 1430–94). It is only 15 inches high, including the engaged painted frame. Memling came from the Rhineland and studied in Brussels, perhaps with Roger van der Weyden. Settling in Bruges in 1466, he continued the tradition of Jan van Eyck to the end of the fifteenth century. One of the most admired portraitists of his day, his popularity was due to his ability to render physical likenesses and to capture something of the intellectual and spiritual character of his subjects. Though portrait panels like this were originally intended as covers or wings for small private altarpieces, during the second half of the fifteenth century the demand for portraits as independent works rapidly increased. It is likely that the portrait of Joye, an important prelate and musician at the court of Philip the Good, Duke of Burgundy, was commissioned for itself alone. The name of the sitter was established with the help of a small label discovered on the reverse of the panel, written in Latin and visible only with special photographic equipment. Though not contemporary with the portrait, the label and other related bits of information enabled scholars to trace the insigne

251

on the frame and the matching crest on one of the two rings on the canon's finger to make a positive identification.

If the impression of calm, cool piety in the Memling portrait is reinforced by the artist's highly controlled treatment of the painted surface, what a contrast this makes with the surface of our next painting! The *Portrait of a Man*,[252] traditionally called the Warrior, by Jean Honoré Fragonard (1732–1806), sparkles with the fast-moving rhythms associated with Rococo painting—and music. A strong and important work, 32 inches high, it is thought to be one of fourteen *têtes de fantaisie* completed c. 1764–69. A favorite of Louis XV and the French court, much in demand for his delightful vignettes of dalliance, his pastoral subjects, and his landscapes, Fragonard here proves himself capable of portraying powerful character. The high cheekbones, the angular face, the lips pursed pessimistically, the eyes gazing off into the distance, the hand extended to rest on the stone parapet, the flamboyant costume, the torso twisted arrogantly to one side—all these details would seem to indicate a specific person. Portrait or not, it is a masterpiece.

Color is of paramount importance here. Note how in the face, pure tones have been juxtaposed without transition, and how, when combined with Fragonard's virtuoso brushwork, a whole symphony of yellow, white, red, and orange is developed. Witness too the Hals-like square strokes that model the tip of the nose and the fingers—can one deny a premonition of what was still considered audacious in late nineteenth-century French painting?

The Clark Institute is fortunate in possessing a very fine example of the sort of English landscape painting that cast a spell on the French Impressionists during their formative years. Its full title is *Rockets and Blue Lights (Close at Hand) to Warn Steamboats of Shoal Waters*, and the artist is Joseph Mallord William Turner (1775–1851).[253] A late work of 1840, it stands in extreme contrast to his Dutch-inspired beginnings. Even at its size of 3 by 4 feet, it seems more daring than his enormous *Falls of the Rhine at Schaffhausen* of 1806, now in the Boston Museum of Fine Arts (MA 79). An artist of immense range, Turner often ran afoul of the arbiters of taste, producing works the nineteenth

252

253

century was not conditioned to accept or readily appreciate. Here his extraordinary imagination transforms a scene of storm-tossed ships into an abstraction of filmy shapes and glowing colors. Turner completed many such canvases, attempting to render in oil the same brilliance he achieved in watercolor. A contemporary, John Constable, described such works as "airy visions painted with tinted steam." Turner becomes virtually Expressionist in his vehemence of effect as he appeals straight to the viewer's sensibilities, setting them on edge.

Another picture whose composition and treatment point to the future is *Rouen Cathedral, the Facade in Sunlight*,[254] by Claude Monet (1840–1926). One of a series of twenty or more canvases completed between 1892 and 1894, it offers a view of the cathedral's west facade from a second-story shop window across the square. Notice the effects of cropping the motif at the top and both sides, and even at the bottom; witness the tensions that arise through the elimination of both sky and ground. Also, note the fusion of subject and art object, that is, the linkage between the complicated, shifting planes of the building's stone surface and its elaborate Gothic tracery and sculpture, and the thick layers of paint applied to the canvas. The paint itself collects light, reflects it, and casts small shadows.

The institute owns six other Monets, dating from five to thirty years earlier, all representative of the artist's Impressionist technique. But it is with the Rouen Cathedral series that Monet made his great breakthrough from Impressionist recording of visible nature to the transformation of objects into symbols of images of personal consciousness. To quote George Heard Hamilton, Director Emeritus of the institute, "Twenty moments represented by twenty views of Rouen are less views of the cathedral (one would have been sufficient for that), less even twenty moments in the going and coming of the light (which is an insignificant situation), than twenty episodes in Monet's private, perceptual life. They are twenty episodes in the history of his consciousness, and reveal a new psychic, rather than physical, reality."

Camille Pissarro's *River Oise near Pontoise*,[255] an early work of 1873, is charming in its simplicity and subtle in its combination of form and

254

255

atmosphere. Pissarro (1830–1903) was a much more traditional artist than Monet, his younger fellow Impressionist; yet under his brush the unromantic industrial outskirts of Paris become magical. This picture clearly reveals Pissarro's indebtedness to the landscapes of Corot, especially in the use of grays and gentle greens, in the relatively unbroken patches of color, and in the overall quiet modesty. The arrangement of small geometric units parallel to the picture plane, however, may herald the influence of Paul Cézanne, with whom Pissarro often painted at Pontoise in the 1870s.

Pierre August Renoir (1841–1919) began his career as a painter of porcelain in Limoges, a training that may have inclined him toward his light palette. He then studied with the Academician Gleyre in Paris. He exhibited in the Salon of 1864, but ten years later was among those organizing the rebellious first Impressionist exhibition. After trips to Algeria and Italy in 1881, his work began to diverge from that of his colleagues; his drawing became firmer and less spontaneous, his color more directed toward the creation of solid structure and form.

The institute is particularly rich in Renoirs, as the Clarks began to purchase his work while the artist was still unappreciated in Europe, and in one instance even before his death. From the thirty-seven paintings they collected we have selected a still life of onions on a table, painted in Naples in 1881. Though of small size, it manages to become the grand composition Renoir's later pearly-fleshed nudes merely aspire to. *Onions*[256] is a supreme example of the artist's gift as a colorist. All his joyous abandon, his subtlety in texture and movement, appear in this little masterpiece. Note how the pure reds and blues at the edge of the tablecloth are taken through myriad variations, even to form the dry, flaky skins of the vegetables. Such a work is a triumph of the human mind. As Walter Pater once said, the greatest painting aspires to music. Here the least promising of themes has become a symphonic tone poem. *Onions* was one of the first three Renoir purchases made by Mr. Clark and remained one of his favorites.

At one point Renoir, on being fitted with a new pair of glasses to correct his myopia, threw them to the floor and exclaimed: "Bon Dieu! Je vois comme Bouguereau!" Alas, the Academicians, notably William Adolphe Bouguereau (1825–1905), whom we next discuss, were the successful artists of their era, esteemed and at the height of their careers in the mid-to-late 1800s. Their Impressionist rivals, insisting on painting how and what they liked, were the butt of public scorn. Today the tables

256

are turned. Artists once admired are often later maligned, their work ironically eclipsed by what had been considered a sign of barbarism. The climate of opinion is changing again, but on the whole, previously valued Academic qualities are still scorned.

Representative Academic works obediently cater to pre-established theories of beauty, reality, composition, and color; their execution bears witness to endless training in the fields of historical research, anatomy, costume, and drawing from the nude. The original basis of the Academic system was sound; but for various reasons the program degenerated to a level of reducing painting to sterile repetition of formulae. With the onset of the twentieth century, it began to suffer a barrage of criticism, and works by the likes of Bouguereau, despite the fact that during the artists' lifetimes they were snapped up with enthusiasm, were dismissed as fit only for storage or barrooms—that is, until recent years.

No one genuinely interested in painting can deny admiration for such artists' technical aplomb. Their performance was truly staggering. Bouguereau was among the ablest practitioners of his craft; so clever, in fact, that his dexterity gained for him membership in what was dubbed "The School of the Invisible Brush-stroke." He had an avid interest in formal values. The composition of the Clark's notorious *Nymphs and Satyr*[257] (1873), nearly 9 feet high within its huge frame, is elaborately synthesized, all its elements tightly coordinated and yet stated with almost photographic precision. Color verges on the eerie as the whites of the flesh glimmer against the dark greenish shadows. It is hard indeed to accuse Bouguereau of having created something with merely the outer skin of art and none of its deeper qualities. Yet Pissarro, painting on the banks of the Oise in the same year, 1873, was light-years ahead of him artistically.

The Women of Amphissa[258] (1887) by Sir Lawrence Alma-Tadema (1836–1912) is another excellent example of the kind of large narrative pieces and scenes of exotic splendor or debauchery that were calculated both to satisfy the Academy's requirements and to titillate the bourgeois consumer. Drawing on Plutarch for his source material, Alma-Tadema painstakingly researched story and period detail to assure representational

257

authenticity. With all its Victorian histrionics, this work is a fetching depiction of the waking debauchees from Phocis encountering the kindness of the Amphissan women. The effects of light on marble and drapery are marvelous. Nevertheless, we have the jarring feeling that we are watching the artist's contemporaries posturing in togas. At the same time, we enjoy Alma-Tadema's joy in *painting.* Unlike Bouguereau, he did not hide his own process.

Winslow Homer (1836–1910) began his career in the heyday of huge landscape panoramas of the Hudson River School; while many of his contemporaries fled America for the Continent, searching for less "provincial" inspiration, he draw his material from the domestic American scene (CT 80). There is something astonishingly modern in Homer's work. Witness his *Sleigh Ride,*[259] a mysterious little picture of 1893 just over a foot high, similar in style to the great *West Wind* of 1891 at Andover (MA 18). Here we are aware of the artist's belief that lines, shapes, and colors can represent reality and at the same time convey meanings on their own. Homer's painting is wonderfully understated and reserved. His composition testifies to extremely careful planning; an effort to simplify, eliminate, and concentrate on large forms and movements is clear. There is an exquisite sense of balance—note how the diagonal of the snowbank forms a solid base for the entire design, how this playing-up of the great mound makes for a forceful statement about man, the elements, and nature. Unusual here is the accent on blues. The institute owns ten Homer oils (and many watercolors, too), but though *Sleigh Ride* is one of the few small ones, it is surely the most poetic of them all.

John Singer Sargent (1856–1925) was an international figure. He commuted constantly across the Atlantic, painting portraits of the rich

258

259

and influential in a manner reminiscent of Velázquez peppered with the brio of a Sir Thomas Lawrence (see CT 56). As much at home in Paris, London, or Florence as in Boston, Sargent, like many artists before him, harbored a weakness for the magic city of Venice. He was forever fascinated by its unique combination of water and architecture and its endless subtleties of light. The actual location of his gemlike *Venetian Interior*[260] is unknown; the dim hall could be the loggia of many a shabby Renaissance palazzo. A spear of light cuts in to warm the bleak dampness. In the foreground, girls gossip. It is a quiet, mundane scene; but the occasional red accents enliven an overall somberness. The sharply receding perspective lends the picture an evocative air of mystery. Sargent was only twenty-six when he painted it in 1882, but it is in his finest vein, without the showiness of *El Jaleo* (MA 51), of the same year.

We turn now to two of the institute's most outstanding portraits. Hilaire-Germain-Edgar Degas (1834–1917) was an artist of varied subjects. His motifs, drawn largely from urban life, included ballet dancers, women bathing, and racehorses; but it was as a portraitist that he reached his greatest heights. The sitter in *Portrait of a Man*[261] has not been identified, but the date of the painting is roughly 1881–85. The beauty of the work lies first of all in the drawing, as seen, for example, in the crisp linear accents about the eyes and at the neck. The girth of the figure and the forceful structure of the skull are established with a minimum of effort. The man's bulk is bolstered comfortably at the right, and as our eye travels to the left, the broadly curved forms gradually give way to angular ones. Especially remarkable is the painting of the hands. A subtle pink at the far left lends its echoes to the flesh tones and the background. Degas has not sought to flatter his subject; his aim was not to provide a pretty picture, but to render the truth as he saw it.

The institute is rich in Degas works: oils, drawings, pastels, and bronze casts made after his death from wax figures of dancers and horses, used by him in developing his compositions on these themes. In addition, there is his celebrated *Little Dancer, Age Fourteen*, 39 inches

261

260

high, of which there are several casts. We reproduce and discuss the one at the Shelburne Museum, Vermont (VT 23).

Henri de Toulouse-Lautrec's *Portrait of Dr. Jules-Emile Péan*[262] (1891) provides us with another occasion where the artist has turned in unexpected directions for his inspiration. Best known for his vivid portrayals of Parisian nightlife—for cabaret performers, dance hall habitués, nudes, ladies of the evening—Toulouse-Lautrec (1864–1901) has selected as his subject an outstanding Paris surgeon performing an operation (a resection of the maxilla). Péan, who scorned the usual clinical attire, is shown with a napkin tied about his neck. A versatile man, he was one of the founders of modern gynecological surgery, and he designed the arterial clamp being used in our picture. At the right an assistant administers ether. Painted on paperboard in oil mixed with turpentine, this apparent sketch projects enormous power. We find an almost Expressionist violence here, a totally new use of the broken colors of Impressionism; but these only accentuate the drawing, which closely resembles some of the most advanced work of Daumier. Note how a few flourishes suggest the existence of a background.

Like Vincent van Gogh, Toulouse-Lautrec went to Paris to study with the Impressionists, became their apt pupil, and then found his own artistic direction. Of his four splendid paintings in the institute, two are "early" (c. 1885)—but at sixteen he was already well launched—and two come from the final decade of his meteoric career. We may contrast the early half-length *Carmen* with *Jane Avril*, or *The Studio* with the Péan portrait just discussed. Within each pair the composition is almost identical, but the scale, the handling of the paint, and the controlling conception are vastly different.

The Clarks were avid collectors of master drawings, but until the publication of a superb two-volume catalogue, under the direction of Professor Havercamp-Begemann of Yale University (Yale University Press, 1964), the extent and quality of the collection were little known. Among the earlier examples, consider a page of *Sketches of Animals and Landscapes*[263] by Albrecht Dürer (1471–1528), in pen and ink

262

263

and colored washes. Six animals and two landscapes fill the sheet, vying for our attention. The identification of the landscapes is uncertain, but it is thought that Dürer drew the lynx, the chamois, the baboon, and the three lions at the zoological gardens in Brussels on a visit there in 1521. The grouping of the figures is unusual and would have resulted in a confusing page had not the artist anchored each image to its own ground plane and viewed each from different levels and distances. The crisp quality of Dürer's line also lends clarity. Its range is amazing: from the lion's rippling mane to the lynx's dagger-pointed ears.

In 1926, Mr. Clark purchased a superb drawing by Peter Paul Rubens (1577–1640), a brown ink-brush *Study of Thomas Howard, Earl of Arundel*,[264] for the portrait now in the Gardner Museum, Boston (MA 47). While its main purpose was apparently to fix the composition of the final oil, what strikes us is the spirited description of this eminent connoisseur and antiquarian. Working quickly from life, Rubens made summary use of his medium. A few strokes sufficed to outline costume and suggest surroundings; a slight turn of the body was enough to energize it. Our attention is riveted by the face, where the artist has detailed an imposing demeanor, accentuating the unruly curl of the mustache, the flare of the nostrils, and the penetrating stare. It is interesting to compare the Clark drawing with the finished portrait, where we see a more introverted man whose features and expression are less subjected to Rubens's modifications. Both versions almost certainly date from 1629, when Rubens was in London designing the Whitehall Palace ceiling (CT 52). According to the eminent Rubens scholar Professor Julius S. Held, the drawing is a rarity in the artist's oeuvre; such elaborate retouching in ink is most unusual.

Rubens exerted a strong influence on our next master draftsman, Antoine Watteau (1684–1721), especially in his facility for capturing gesture and attitude with the merest suggestion of line. In Watteau's *Studies of a Flutist and Two Women*,[265] quick delicate strokes, not long contours, build up the images of the flutist (dressed in what resembles the sixteenth-century costume of the Comédie Italienne) and two women. The profile of the older one is set against the three-quarter view of her lovely young companion. Such drawings combine two major themes in Watteau's art—modest femininity and music. We quickly recognize the

264

265

hand of the painter of the celebrated *fêtes galantes*, dreamworlds replete with the pleasures of the theater, music, dance, and a life of elegance. Watteau's extreme sensitivity to pose and his feeling for textures are everywhere in evidence in the Clark drawing. He used only red, black, and white chalks here, but the colorism he created almost rivals that of a Degas pastel.

In *Hagar and Ishmael in the Wilderness*,[266] by Giovanni Battista Tiepolo (1696–1770), swift and bold pen lines are applied over an extremely summary chalk underdrawing and touched lightly with dark and paler brown wash. All these magical marks combine with large areas of blank paper to strike a sensitive balance between the suggestion and the full realization of form. Tiepolo manages to introduce here some of the delicate luminosity and airy perspectives of his great ceiling decorations and allegorical compositions (see MA 75). This sketch has not been connected with any known painting, but the theme is a favorite one in Tiepolo's vast oeuvre.

Our last selection, *Study for "La Source,"*[267] in black-and-white chalk on blue-gray paper, is by Pierre Paul Prud'hon (1758–1823). While it may seem related to those Academic nineteenth-century paintings we have already discussed, it truly reflects the tenets espoused by the academies before their takeover by the bourgeoisie. We sense here that Prud'hon has achieved much more than a faithful copy of a female nude. The purpose of the study may have been a preparation for an official commission involving a monumental column with allegorical figures of the rivers Rhine, Po, Nile, and Danube at its foot. The nude is appropriately statuesque. Prud'hon's expert use of his medium, with the blue-gray paper becoming the middle value of the modeling from light to dark, imparts a softness to the figure, reminiscent of Correggio. The result is a suggestion of not-so-innocent sensuality.

An introduction to the Clark Art Institute should not conclude without mention of its very distinguished collection of silver. Spanning nearly five centuries, it includes examples by many world-renowned metalsmiths, with English artisans predominating. Paul de Lamerie (1688–1751) heads the list. Apparently, the Clarks were as fond of his work as they were of Renoir's.

266

267

Williams College Museum of Art

Location: Opposite the college chapel on Main St. (Route 2)

Hours: Academic year, Mon.-Fri. 9-5, Sat., Sun. 1-5; summer, 1-5 daily; closed legal and college holidays

Admission: Free

The museum was founded in 1926 by Karl E. Weston, first chairman of the Williams College department of art. On his initiative Lawrence Hall, the former college library, was renovated for its new function, and classrooms and additional gallery space were provided in a new rear wing. The original building, designed in 1846 by Thomas Tefft of Providence, is a brick octagon containing on its upper floor a handsome Ionic rotunda in Greek Revival style. This was the gift, at a cost of nine thousand dollars, of Amos Lawrence, Boston manufacturer, founder of Lawrence, Mass., and a major benefactor of the college through his great friendship with President Mark Hopkins. His full-length portrait, in Paisley dressing gown, was delivered to the college in 1846. Painted by Chester Harding (1792–1866), it is an exact replica of the portrait now in the National Gallery, Washington—although the unlikely possibility exists that the Williams version came first.

Wings along the Main Street front were added in 1890, and in 1938 an addition on the west side provided two large galleries, the Edwin Howland Blashfield Room (the gift of his heirs along with examples of the artist's work) and the George Alfred Cluett Room (the gift of an alumnus-collector of Spanish painting and furniture). Plans for extensive further additions and renovations are well advanced as of this writing.

Like other college museums, Williams's is an indispensable asset to instruction in art history and the practice of art. During the college year there are frequently changing temporary exhibitions. The permanent collection, including some one thousand prints and a growing corpus of photographs by outstanding masters, is being developed to provide a broad coverage of world art in original examples. Since the impressive holdings of the Clark Art Institute are for the most part limited to European and American art and to the period 1300–1900, the college's collections of Ancient, medieval, contemporary, and non-Western art provide an important complement to them.

Sculpture is especially well represented in the Williams museum. In addition to the examples discussed below there are Greek and Roman terra-cottas, bronzes, and small marbles (primarily the gift of the family of Charles B. Bolles-Rogers); important examples of Romanesque and Gothic stone sculpture and silversmith work; a life-size fifteenth-century Italian *Madonna* in polychromed wood; Baroque and Rococo bronzes and wood sculpture; nineteenth-century bronzes by Barye (see VT 1), Meunier, Rodin (head of the *Naked Balzac*, RI 23), and Saint-Gaudens (small replica of *The Puritan* at Springfield [MA 209]); and twentieth-century examples by Bourdelle, Maillol, Duchamp-Villon, David Smith, Ferber, and Rickey. A selection from the museum's non-Western sculpture is discussed below.

Among the first works of art given to the college are two large Assyrian reliefs from the Palace of Ashurnazirpal II, near Nineveh. These were shipped by camelback in the 1850s to a Mediterranean port and thence by sea to Boston—and thence across the state of Massachusetts long before the construction of the Hoosac Tunnel. They were the gift of a missionary alumnus of the college, the Reverend Dwight W. Marsh, who wrote of his hopes that "students who look upon the relics of the past may think wisely of time & be led to take a deeper interest in the efforts to rescue the degraded from the beastliness of their present life. . . . May they remember that God is older than the ages— that the glorious future of America is not eternity." The reliefs are similar to those received at the same time by other New England colleges; our discussion of them will be found in the entry for Amherst College (MA 1).

The primary examples of Greek and Roman marble sculpture at Williams are a *Hellenistic Head*,[268] presumably of Zeus, dating from about 50 B.C., and a headless Roman male, clad in toga, tunic, ankle gear, and boots, probably from the first century A.D. The bearded Greek head, probably originating from the Syro-Phoenician coast, reflects the style and workmanship characteristic of a very late phase of Hellenistic art. The deep undercutting and fluidity of forms of such examples have been called Baroque because of their similarity to the works of seventeenth-century sculptors like Bernini (see MA 121). Indeed, it is possible that there was some recutting about the mouth in Bernini's own time.

268

Two more heads, an ancient *Roman Mosaic*[269] and a *Byzantine Fresco*,[270] provide an unusual opportunity to contrast Western and Near Eastern traditions of representation. The mosaic, probably of an enemy warrior from the North (note his blond hair), is executed in a manner strongly influenced by the illusionist tendencies of Roman painting. Its relatively late date of c. A.D. 300 is suggested by the rather large stones with which it is composed (Pompeiian mosaic tesserae are extremely small). The image is strongly sculptural in effect: the three-quarters pose and the modulations of shadow seem to mold space behind the head. The diagonal tilt, the flying hair, the set of the eyes, and the curve of the mouth all suggest action, and thereby the sense of a moment in time. The concern for physical mass, for the pull of gravity, and for the organic resilience of the human figure is evident—nearly a thousand years after its inception in ancient Greece.

The Byzantine fresco fragment, which includes a small portion of the Saint's halo at the right, comes from a church in Jerusalem and may date from as late as the 1640s. Here an austere frontality rules, held fast by the perpendicular axis. There is a small amount of modeling by shading, but thick dark outlines—all in the same plane—dominate. Shadows under the eyes are stark flat triangles, and the whites are perfect circles. Such simplification of forms accounts for the work's special appeal to twentieth-century taste. (Three other heads from the same source are in America: two in the Museum of Fine Arts, Boston, and one in the California Palace of the Legion of Honor, San Francisco.)

On a basis of quality, the fifteenth-century Franco-Flemish alabaster figure of *St. John Evangelist*[271] is surely one of the museum's finest treasures. Brownish-warm in tone, elegant in shape, fluid in cascades of soft drapery, the Saint projects an intense spirituality as he gazes up-

269

271

270

ward. The throat with its prominent Adam's apple framed by a *V* of straining muscles is remarkably expressive; in profile, the sequence from chest to chin develops a powerful rhythm. From the rear, all is columnar grace and peace save for the hunched shoulders and the turn of the head. While the sculptor was not unaware of classical understanding of organic anatomy as retrieved from antiquity by the Italian Renaissance, he clearly thought in terms of a limited frontal view. The rear view, however beautiful, may never have been intended to be seen; the figure probably formed part of a Crucifixion assemblage placed against a back plane of stone. For a contrast in sculptural intention, note in the draped Roman statue, mentioned above, how the folds wind around to the front, making the figure an organic whole. A large group of alabaster sculptures, generally similar in style to our *St. John Evangelist* and found in museums around the Western world, is often assigned to an itinerant artist known as the Rimini Master because of a Crucifixion altar originating in that Italian town and now in the sculpture museum of Frankfurt-am-Main. Since this altar is missing its required St. John, some scholars have suggested that our figure actually belonged to it. Experts who have seen the original in the Williams Museum, however, agree that its quality is much superior. Thus the hypersensitive Master of the Williams College *St. John Evangelist* still lacks a more definitive name. His style is clearly not Italianate; analogous works suggest an origin in the lower Rhenish region of France or Flanders, and a date c. 1430. Comparison with the Busch-Reisinger Museum's Austrian *Madonna and Child on a Crescent Moon* (MA 99), also c. 1430, indicates that our sculptor was more attuned to the influence of the Italian Renaissance.

Williams's representation of Florentine and Roman Renaissance art cannot match that of the Clark Art Institute, but two prints of exceptional importance offer a most useful complement: the great engraving of *The Entombment* by Andrea Mantegna (strongly influenced by Donatello's sculpture at Padua and subsequently influencing both Raphael and Rembrandt), and Ugo da Carpi's chiaroscuro woodcut of *Diogenes* (after a lost drawing by Parmigianino inspired by the art of Michelangelo).

A *Millefleurs Tapestry* measuring about 8 by 7 feet, replete with falcons, rabbits, a lion, a stag, and a unicorn, appears to be the work of Flemish craftsmen working in the Loire Valley area. Its date of c. 1510–25 reminds us that in the "Gothick North" the incursions of the Italian Renaissance were both gradual and sporadic.

The gift of George Alfred Cluett included fine paintings and furniture from Spain and Spanish-owned Naples. Further acquisitions have resulted in the museum's owning the leading collection of Spanish art before Goya in New England outside the major cities.

Francisco Pacheco, the master and father-in-law of Velázquez, proves himself a true Spaniard with his portrait, signed and dated 1626, of an unidentified *Knight of the Order of Santiago*.[272] Adjectives that come to mind to describe its Spanish character include austere, precise, reserved, astringent, and above all dignified. Much of this flavor passed on to the young Velázquez, as seen in his *Portrait of Luis de Góngora*, in the Boston Museum of Fine Arts (MA 72). Note how Pacheco has focused attention on the knight's face by the accent of the white collar, and on his bleak gaze through a calculated emphasis on his eyeglasses.

Though no document supports a traditional attribution to Juan de Valdés Leal (1622–90), a chief painter at Seville during Spain's Golden Age, the large *Annunciation*,[273] an oil nearly 6 feet high, reflects his masterly blend of the Baroque action of Rubens and Bernini with the Venetian technique of Titian and Tintoretto. It is not often in New England that we can experience so completely the spirit of the Baroque as here through the dark colors, dramatic lighting, plunging diagonals, and energetic action of this picture.

Two other Baroque painters in the museum's collection, both active in Naples and both influenced by Caravaggio (see CT 12), offer an opportunity to contrast differing cultural heritages: Jusepe de Ribera (1591–1652) and Massimo Stanzione (1585–1656). Archrivals and almost exact contemporaries, Ribera (*The Executioner*) came from Spain, worked for the local viceroys, and was twice visited by Velázquez, while the Italian Stanzione (*St. John Evangelist Exorcising a Demon from the Cup*) trained in Rome under the strong influence of the Carracci and Guido Reni. We find tautly restrained violence in the former, operatic sentiment in the latter.

Our final selection from the Spanish pictures is an impressive *Still Life*[274] of c. 1626 measuring 32½ by 50½ inches. It is signed by a leading master of this genre, Juan van der Hamen y León (1591–1631). Born of Flemish parents in Madrid, he spent his life there and became a painter at the court as well as a member of the palace bodyguard. Although he resented being praised only for his still lifes, they were, and continue to be, in great demand. Flemish still lifes (such as Frans

273

272

274

Snyders's at Amherst College, MA 6) are earthier and more festive than Spanish ones, which tend to be somber in tone and, despite their intense realism, as abstract in form as Picasso's of 1908/09. Van der Hamen lit his compositions theatrically from the left side into a black depth. Those of the early 1620s have a less cohesive arrangement than the later ones, such as the Williams example. Here much of the weight is shifted to one side with the balance redressed by placing the elements on large gray plinths. All of them cast a spell of silence.

Through the bequest of Charles M. Davenport, of Boston, the museum acquired an extensive collection of Early American furniture and British and American portraits. Other acquisitions make it possible to compare in fine examples of almost the same year the Englishness of Thomas Gainsborough (*Robert Butcher*, variant in the Prado) with the Colonial stamp of John Singleton Copley (*Reverend Samuel Cooper*, c. 1770, earlier variant in the Emerson House, Concord), and to compare Copley with the itinerant Connecticut painter William Jennys (*Colonel Benjamin Simonds* of Williamstown, signed and dated 1796—see the discussion of this artist in the sections on the Connecticut Historical Society at Hartford and the Lyman Allyn Museum at New London, CT 87). Reynolds, Romney, Raeburn, and Gilbert Stuart are also well represented.

Nineteenth-century paintings seen here include Kensett's *View of Lake George*, two watercolors by Homer, one from the key year 1880 (see ME 31), an Eakins portrait of the music critic *John Neil Fort*, several landscapes by George Inness, fool-the-eye still lifes by Harnett and Peto, a huge *Niagara Falls* by William Morris Hunt, and an 1877 *Pontoise, on the Banks of the Oise*, by Camille Pissarro (see MA 255). Among twentieth-century American watercolorists, the museum boasts three by Maurice Prendergast, four by John Marin, and six by Charles Demuth.

Off York Island, Maine[275] is a powerful and explosive work of Marin's maturity (1922). A certain viscosity pervades it, suggesting an intention to carry the liquid medium into the more symphonic effects of oil painting. This example stands in greatest contrast to Colby College's *Brooklyn Bridge*, of 1912 (ME 38).

"John Marin and I drew our inspiration from the same source, French Modernism. He brought his up in buckets and spilt much along the way. I dipped mine out with a teaspoon, but I never spilled a drop."

275

That this oft-quoted statement was actually made by Charles Demuth (1883–1935) has been questioned; but authentic or not, it is apposite. It has the stamp of Demuth's own art: crisp, elegant, cool. His variant of Cubism, developed from study in Paris in the crucial years 1912–14, departed widely from the somber tone of the formal discipline invented by Picasso and Braque. The museum's six watercolors range in date from 1914 to Demuth's last years. *Trees and Barns, Bermuda*[276] (1917) marks the artist at the height of his powers, and is radically different from the loose fluid handling of the medium that typified the preceding years. Note the precision of the finely penciled contours, over which the thin washes of watercolor were laid, then touched with blotting paper to absorb the moisture and to produce Demuth's special delicacy of texture in a fragile tracery.

Cubist vocabulary is also evident in Lyonel Feininger's oil painting *Mill in Autumn*[277] (1932). Feininger's style evolved during visits to Paris between 1906 and 1911 from exposure to emergent Cubism, which he tempered with the Orphist color of Robert Delaunay and the angularities of Italian Futurist painting. Connections with the tradition of German Romantic landscape painting have also been proposed. In *Mill in Autumn*, the accent is less upon forms or motifs than upon a subtle, poetic, very personal depiction of a season. Rich browns, ashen whites, and muted bluish greens pervade the work, lending it a melancholy grace accentuated by the rhythmic sweep of the mill vanes.

Mill in Autumn came to the museum in 1977 with the bequest of a large number of American paintings, drawings, and sculptures from Lawrence H. Bloedel, whose collection was divided equally between Williams College and the Whitney Museum of American Art, New York. Another masterwork in the Bloedel bequest is *Morning in a City*,[278] by Edward Hopper (1882–1967). Signed in 1944 and measuring 4 by 5 feet, it has been widely exhibited in the United States as well as at the Ninth Bienal at São Paolo, Brazil; and it is generally acknowledged as one of Hopper's major paintings. Here we find his poetic realism expressed through a remarkable economy of statement. His detached view of a woman facing another day captures the loneliness

276

277

of the person in a city of anonymous millions; and it imparts much of the artist's own vision of the American environment. Plain and nude, the woman stands solid and silent in a cramped bare room. The black windows opposite reveal no inhabitant. Stark planes, sunlight cutting into the room to mold shapes with strong color value—everything is calculated to transform the facts of routine existence into something universal.

Modern art is well represented in the museum, not only by the work of sculptors already mentioned, but by drawings and prints and by the paintings of such leading figures as de Chirico, Léger, Miró, Tanguy, and Matta, and by a series of boxes and collages by Joseph Cornell, the gift of his sister, Mrs. John A. Benton. One of the finest examples of post–Second World War Abstract Expressionism is *Black and White*,[279] a collage and oil by Franz Kline (1910–62). Concentrated on a sheet of paper less than a foot high, this work of c. 1958 can stand comparison with the artist's best large canvases (see MA 162). *Black and White* projects a sense of vast scale and an almost brutal power. Note the force of the black diagonals, the drag and sputter of paint from a dry brush, the range of textures in the sparingly applied collage of papers—torn edges, a sparkle from grains of sand—and the un-expected touches of color that energize the whole surface.

As in Kline's collage, much of the appeal of *Valor*,[280] an elegant sculpture by the Japanese Masayuki Nagare (born 1923) hinges on the

278

279

280

artist's sensitivity to his chosen medium. Carefully polishing Swedish black granite to a high sheen, leaving only a few areas roughly chiseled —as if eroded—Nagare created surface contrasts that manage to invest the piece with a living presence. The unfinished look also injects an element of tension in this age of machine tooling and plastics. The date is 1967. At the base a human face is suggested clearly enough to transform the major element above into a black headdress like those worn by Japanese heroes of long ago (see MA 96). Our first impression of this element is also relevant: that it suggests the blade of a ritual sword. As in the work of Isamu Noguchi (see ME 45), the influence of Brancusi (see CT 68) is strong here.

The collection of Oriental art, while small, has distinguished examples of Indian sculpture, Moghul painting, a superb Buddha head in stone from the T'ang dynasty (on indefinite loan from the Clark Art Institute), and a rare gilt-bronze *Seated Vairocana* (the central principle of later Buddhist cosmology) from the Yüan dynasty (1279–1368) of the Mongol Kingdom. This piece, only a foot high, is another example —with Kline's collage—of majestic power achieved in a small compass. The Williams bronze makes an interesting comparison with the colossal *Japanese Sun Buddha* at Providence (RI 28). It was shown at Cleveland and at Asia House, New York, in the exhibition "Chinese Art under the Mongols" (Cleveland: Cleveland Museum of Art, 1968, number 13 of the catalogue).

Perhaps the finest of the museum's Far Eastern works is the sandstone *Female Divinity*[281] from Koh-Ker, Cambodia, early tenth century, some three centuries before the celebrated sculptures of Angkor Wat. Three feet high, the headless figure is wonderfully restrained and simplified, as in the subtlest columnar draped figures of early Archaic Greece. It differs strikingly from Indian images, with their full sensuous forms, deeply convex surfaces, and often provocative postures (see MA 90). In the same way it contrasts with the work of Gaston Lachaise (1882– 1935), who was inspired by the lush female images of prehistory and by Indian temple sculpture as well. The museum's bronze *Torso*,[282]

281

282

from the Bloedel bequest, is a relatively early work derived from Lachaise's first life-size female figure, *Elevation* (a cast in the Whitney Museum, New York). There is nothing titillating or lascivious here, only an earthy fervor steeped in the exaggerations and distortions of the art of bygone ages. Observe the flowing rhythms evident throughout, the upward lift that starts from the knees, whether from front or back view, and the solidity of the modeling. One's first impression that the woman is fat is quickly dispelled; on the contrary, she is abundant. The breasts are full but firm, the buttocks narrow and spare. How powerful are the empty shapes between each upper arm and swelling hip!

For further information on works in the museum, see my *Handbook to the Collection*, published by Williams College in 1978, with over seventy discussed and illustrated.

In addition to the Clark Art Institute and the Williams College Museum of Art, Williamstown is blessed with the leading collection of rare books and manuscripts in any *college* in the nation. The Chapin collection is housed in Stetson Hall, once the college library and now a branch of the new Sawyer Library. The manuscripts range from Egyptian papyri to illuminated medieval and Renaissance volumes. The collection of incunabula is extensive, and it includes a fifteenth-century block book and the complete woodcut *Apocalypse* by Albrecht Dürer. There is also the complete *Book of Job*, as engraved by William Blake. Modern typography and book illustration are well represented through recent gifts. As in most libraries of this kind, Piranesi is in abundance, but not all of them have Audubon's elephant portfolios, or the great series of reproductions of Holbein drawings at Windsor Castle.

American Antiquarian Society

Location: 185 Salisbury Street
Hours: Mon.-Fri. 9-5, except on legal holidays
Admission: Free. Ⓗ

Founded in 1812 by Isaiah Thomas, this was the first national historical society to be established in the United States. It owns the largest collection of printed materials relating to American history and culture up to the year 1877. This cutoff date also applies to its art collections, which include some ten thousand prints, thirty-five thousand book plates, a few very impressive pieces of furniture, and—within the purview of this book—over 150 oil portraits and miniatures. An illustrated brochure published by the society in 1970 on the portraits and furniture, written by two experts, Louissa Dresser and Wendell Garrett, is highly recommended. Visitors interested in early American music may wish to know that the society also owns sixty-five thousand examples of sheet music.

The *Portrait of Hannah Bush*,[283] signed "M'Kay" and dated 1791, measuring 36 by 30 inches, will not soon be forgotten. While the portrait of her husband, John, likewise signed and dated, has no such monumental construction to fill the top of the composition, it is equally intense. Little is known about M'Kay or MacKay (for *both* versions appear in signatures on the husband's portrait). The only other surviving work of this rugged artist is a portrait (signed "MacKay" and dated 1791—it would be hazardous to call that his vintage year) in the Garbisch collection at the National Gallery, Washington. All three portraits were presumably painted in New York, where John Bush had moved from Worcester at an early age, to become a broker. There, a certain John M'Kay, "painter and glazier, 10 Warren" appears in the city directory for 1795; but this M'Kay is not necessarily the painter of the Bush portraits. The meticulous detail and sharp observation seen in Hannah's portrait are so much in the tradition of the anonymous Freake

283

portraits in the Worcester Art Museum (MA 303) that it is hard to believe a gap of some 120 years separates them. Like Mrs. Freake, Hannah Bush manages to emerge as a personality from the multiple details that encase her. Despite such attractions as her vast white bonnet with its bows and loops and its clawlike termination, and the long journey of the black ribbon that holds a miniature of her husband, her emergence is something of a triumph. The whole picture is a symphony of salmon reds, pinks, and grays. As to Hannah's age, in Early American portraiture one soon gets used to surprises, forgetting that life was hard: she was twenty-six. When her portrait was shown at the Metropolitan Museum of Art in 1939 ("Life in America," number 44 of the catalogue), it was accompanied by the following verses, published in *The Universal Magazine* in 1768—not entirely appropriate, but surely worth reproducing:

> When he views your tresses thin
> Tortured by some French *friseur*,
> Horsehair, hemp and wool within
> Garnished with a di'mond skewer,
>
> When he scents the mingled steam
> Which your plaster'd heads are rich in,
> Lard and meal and clouted cream,
> Can he love a walking-kitchen?

The stern *Portrait of Isaiah Thomas*[284] was painted in 1818 by Ethan Allen Greenwood (1779–1856). It was bequeathed by Thomas himself, who not only founded the society but was its first president, from 1812 to his death in 1831. The portrait, in oil on wood panel 32 by 26 inches, shows him at the age of sixty-nine. Printer, publisher, and bookseller, Isaiah Thomas played an important role in the American Revolution. In its early stages he made his newspaper, the *Massachusetts Spy*, the voice of the Whig party. Couriers of the Committee on Correspondence distributed it from Quebec to Savannah. Just before the battles of Lexington and Concord he managed to move his press from Boston to Worcester—and the Antiquarian Society still preserves it. His desire to keep a record of the Revolution for posterity led to his founding of the society. His portrait is in the tradition of Gilbert Stuart's *Thomas Jefferson* (ME 13), with the obligatory column and red curtain, but the

284

sharp delineation of the strong features has a more incisive American flavor.

Among other portraits are examples by Thomas Smith (see MA 304), *Peter Pelham* (the master of Copley), Copley himself, and Winthrop Chandler.

The present building, dating from 1909, is by Winslow, Bigelow, Wadsworth and (Richard Clipston) Sturgis of Boston, with a 1972 addition by Shepley, Bulfinch, Richardson, and Abbot. (How the great Boston names perpetuate themselves!). The spacious Antiquarian Hall, with its surrounding balcony, is a handsome setting for the varied historical and artistic exhibits.

The John Woodman Higgins Armory

Location: 100 Barber Ave. (off Route 12, north of the city, east of the north end of Indian Lake)
Hours: Tues.-Fri. 9-4, Sat. 10-3, Sun. 1-5; closed national holidays
Admission: Charged. Ⓗ

This museum of metal craftsmanship opened to the public in 1931. It was founded by John Woodman Higgins, chairman of the Worcester Pressed Steel Company, who served as its president from 1910 to 1950. Chartered as a nonprofit educational institution, it is devoted to the history of the world's steel industry from its origins in the Bronze and Iron ages to modern times. The building itself is of open steel and glass construction.

Its collection of medieval armor has earned the museum worldwide fame. The exhibits also contain armor of all periods, and, more generally, fine metalwork from earliest times. In addition, there are a library, an armorer's workshop, a display of stained glass contemporary with the great age of armor making, and a number of paintings and tapestries with related subjects. One of the paintings, *The Forge of Vulcan*, is by Jan Brueghel (1568–1625), one of the sons of Pieter Brueghel the Elder (see ME 8).

The magnificent array of suits of armor occupies a hall of Gothic style hung with appropriate banners and weapons.[285] An armored dog guards the central passage. Throughout, the emphasis naturally falls on functional beauty. While any beautiful object may be said to serve a function —to refresh the spirit and to stimulate the imagination—there is no necessary conflict between such an intention and that of serving a more practical end. Anyone who has visited Carcassonne or a modern warship will have already discovered this truth.

One of the rarest and most beautifully fashioned suits of armor in the

285

collection is of Nuremberg make, about 1520. It is of the type associated with the Emperor Maximilian I. The flutings, or corrugations, add to the strength of the armor without adding to its weight. At the time this was a very practical consideration, because as firearms improved, armor had to become heavier. Carried at several points of the body, the weight is well distributed. The lance rest appears by the right arm. The back plate, gauntlets, and elbows are stamped with the mark of the Nuremberg guild. The suit is etched with birds and rustic persons in contemporary costume. The process of etching designs on armor led to printmaking, first from an iron plate, and later from a copper one. Albrecht Dürer of Nuremberg, one of the first etchers, made a few prints from iron plates early in the sixteenth century.

Maximilian was a great exponent of the joust. While this suit was designed primarily for such a purpose, it could also be used in unmounted battle. The square toes were much better for walking than the long pointed ones of earlier Gothic suits.

Worcester Art Museum

Location: 55 Salisbury Street. Parking nearby
Telephone: (617) 752-4678
Hours: Tues.-Sat. 10-5, Sun. 2-5; closed July 4, Thanksgiving, Christmas, and New Year's Day
Admission: Charged, except Wed. Ⓗ but phone ahead

The Worcester Art Museum has long enjoyed the reputation of being one of the finest small museums in America. The visitor will soon discover, however, that "small" is a relative term, for the Worcester Museum is small only in comparison to the great metropolitan treasure houses. After the Boston Museum of Fine Arts, its position as the second largest art museum in New England is challenged only by those of Hartford, Providence, and of Harvard and Yale universities. The Gardner Museum in Boston has a greater concentration of masterpieces, but its range is much more limited.

Founded by Stephen Salisbury III in 1896, the museum opened its original building two years later. Major additions were constructed in 1921, 1933, and 1970. The latest of these includes facilities for the museum's professional art school and studio areas for art classes for all ages. The collections span fifty centuries of world art, and works in all media. The museum issues a bulletin and an illustrated handbook is available.

From the many fine examples of ancient art at Worcester exhibited on the ground floor to the right of the Salisbury Street entrance I have selected two limestone figures, a life-size *Female Torso*[286] of the Egyptian Fifth Dynasty, c. 2440 B.C., and a foot-high *Male Statuette*[287] of the early dynastic period of Sumerian civilization (3000–2500 B.C.).

286

287

The latter was found at Khafaje, northeast of Baghdad, by an expedition from the University of Pennsylvania. The two make an interesting comparison, particularly when we realize that they may have been carved —in the very round numbers of ancient history—at about the same time. Both are "Archaic" in their rigid frontality and their minimal undercutting. But here the similarity ends, and one quickly learns that general terms like "Archaic" can be very misleading. In the company of the dwarflike Sumerian deity, the Egyptian torso looks almost Greek in the push of the forms through the sheath of clothing, and in the subtle transitions of modeling. It must be pointed out, however, that if the head and feet were not missing the whole effect of the statue would be more rigid than it is now. Furthermore, the Egyptian carver was less bound by convention in representing the female figure than the male, that is, when he represented, as here, a person of high station. (Compare the Boston group, MA 53; the Worcester figure undoubtedly belonged to a similar one.) To give the face of his statuette a more striking expression, the Sumerian artist carved the eyeballs separately and fixed them into the sockets. One is missing.

These two figures should also be compared with a small (6-inch) marble fertility figure from the Cycladic Islands, dating from c. 2000 B.C. We have discussed this aboriginal Greek art in the large (4-foot) example at Boston (MA 56), which is much more boyish in form than Worcester's and more svelte in execution. Such figures, almost on tiptoe with knees slightly bent and arms tightly clasped, convey a feeling of resilience that brings the stone to life, however schematic the anatomy. The Egyptian and Sumerian examples cannot match them in vitality.

From the field of ancient Classical art, a wine container and a gravestone of a warrior have been selected. Because of its quality, preservation, and large size, this painted clay *Amphora*[288] is an outstanding example of Greek ceramic art. The frieze represents Leto mounting a chariot, with her children Apollo and Artemis. At the right is Hermes with his winged sandals, herald of the gods. On the other side is a standard image of Dionysus flanked by Maenads and Satyrs. By its style this vase can be dated in the late sixth century B.C. Like the first two selections, it may be called Archaic. A similar insistence on profile and frontal views leaves the picture surface unbroken by movement into depth. Space is suggested merely by overlapping areas, as at the base.

288

The artist, known as the Rycroft Painter, was particularly skilled in representing the anatomy of humans and horses. The process used here is called black-figure because the lacquer is applied flat within the silhouettes, while interior lines are incised with a stylus to expose the red clay beneath. (See the discussion in the entry for Bowdoin College, ME 1–3.)

Except for temple sculpture and grave reliefs, original marble sculpture from fifth-century Greece is rare. Most freestanding figures are copies made in Hellenistic or Roman times. The life-size *Gravestone of a Warrior,*[289] despite its evident damages, is therefore a precious possession. That its quality is of a high order may be seen by comparing it with a much coarser stele fragment in the same gallery, representing an old man. The Warrior could almost be placed beside the metope sculptures of the Parthenon, and is of slightly later date (420–410 B.C.). It is carved from the same Pentelic marble. The position of the figure approximates that of the famous *Spear Bearer* (known only in debased copies) by Polykleitos. The modeling of the exposed shoulder is especially vigorous, and the circular curve of the shield closes the easy upward swing of the limbs from the base at our left. Note how the modeling guides our eye around and across the torso, breaking up any sense of Archaic frontality and achieving a new sense of classic ease and repose.

Another much-damaged fragment from a fifth-century grave stele, a *Woman with a Jewel Box*, combines the columnar severity of drapery and the sense of human anatomy with much of the success of the Erechtheum Maidens on the Athenian Acropolis. In this figure the marble has a lovely reddish cast, resulting from its iron content.

The bronze *Bust of a Lady of the Antonine Period,*[290] 2 feet high, is an unusually refined example of Roman portraiture of the second century A.D., but without the energy of the *Bust of Elagabalus*, from the next century, at Boston (MA 60). Said to have been found in Anatolia, in Roman Asia Minor, it may represent a person of such high

289

290

station as one of the daughters of Marcus Aurelius. For such an image
of high society normal Roman realism is here softened. An extreme contrast is provided by Worcester's scowling and bloated figure of a man,
recumbent atop his clay cinerary urn, an Etruscan work of the second
century B.C. Such unflattering observation passed on to the Roman
artists of the Republic and continued into the Empire, despite a counter-
trend to imitate the high nobility of Greek art (see MA 232 and CT
63).

We skip some 350 years to consider the huge *Floor Mosaic from Antioch*291 (about A.D. 500), in the entrance court, a prize from an expedition sponsored in part by the Worcester Museum. Here the illusionism of earlier Roman mosaic (MA 269) has broken down into isolated
fragments of pink and greenish stones set against a flat light ground.
The forms of Byzantine art are already at hand, though as yet the intention is purely secular. This "carpet" style has practical advantages:
we may approach the mosaic from any direction, and we do not seem
to be stepping into a hole. Note how the pomegranate trees, set at
diagonals in the four corners, give structure to the composition.

The large bronze *Buckle*,292 engraved and silvered (7 by 3¼ inches),
is characteristic of the art of the Merovingians, who ruled France before the time of Charlemagne. It dates from the seventh century. Although such objects are rare today, they were produced in quantity for
the luxury trade. This example was found near Toulouse, in southern
France. The patterned and dotted ornament on the shaft is curiously
similar to that on the seventeenth-century African plaque from Benin,
in the Peabody Museum, Cambridge (MA 143)—indicating, of course,
no connection or influence, but the universal language of certain forms
of art.

As for the nomadic peoples who swept over Europe at the fall of the
Roman Empire, their art should caution us about calling them "barbarians," and even about using the term "Dark Ages" except in a very
relative sense. Art history is full of terms that originated in opprobrium
to express one culture's opinion of its superiority over another. For the
Greeks the Persians were also barbarians; the Italian Renaissance, look-

291

292

ing back to Classical Antiquity, regarded the intervening centuries as a lowly midway station between two pinnacles of enlightenment; Gothic, Baroque, Impressionist, Fauvist, and Cubist all were originally terms signifying inferiority; while "primitive," as we have suggested before, is best left to denote merely "early." However that may be, the art of the barbarian invaders, seen in a very fine belated example in Worcester's Merovingian buckle, passed on as a formative influence to the Irish metalworkers and manuscript illuminators, and to Spain.

Outside the Metropolitan Museum of Art and the Cloisters in New York and Harvard's Fogg Museum, Romanesque figure sculpture is by no means plentiful in the United States. Worcester has a superb polychromed wood *Virgin and Child*,[293] 3 feet high, of the late twelfth century from Autun, Burgundy, one of the greatest centers of Romanesque stone sculpture. As she appears in the photograph, the Autun Virgin seems precariously unbalanced, not entirely because part of the throne is missing. This fact serves to demonstrate how completely the carver thought of his image in frontal terms, though one must admit that the head expresses a wonderful roundness through the soft modeling of the cheeks.

Nearby, a gallery off the entrance court was remodeled in 1932 to contain an entire Romanesque chapter house reconstructed after its removal from the former Benedictine priory of LeBas-Neuil, near Poitiers in west central France. Dating like the Autun *Virgin* from the later twelfth century, it shows the intrusion of the new Gothic method of ribbed vault construction in an otherwise pure example of Romanesque building.

The ivory relief (height 8 inches) of the *Virgin and Child*[294] is a supreme example of the elegance and sophistication that marked Paris of the fourteenth century. If it was not made there, we can be certain that the craftsman was a close student of the fashions of Paris, where a whole industry of ivory carving developed at this time. We may be shocked to learn that this ivory was once gilded, though probably with

293

294

discretion. Today we enjoy the beauty of its texture, aged to the tone of natural wood. For a comparison to other ages, one must go to Praxiteles (see MA 59), to Leonardo da Vinci, and to Chinese sculpture of the Sung dynasty (MA 93). It would be difficult to find a better illustration of the change in European culture that occurred from about 1175 to 1325 than in a comparison between the wood Virgin and this exquisite Gothic masterpiece.

Similar elegance in fourteenth-century Italian panel painting, which was probably influenced by such portable Parisian art as the ivory just discussed, is seen in the art of Simone Martini of Siena (see MA 34) and in Worcester's 30-by-18-inch panel of *St. Agnes* with her symbolic Lamb of Purity, painted by a gifted follower. As courtly life grew more and more elaborate toward 1400 (after recovery, that is, from the ravages of the Black Plague of 1348), an art of almost unparalleled delicacy and grace became its natural expression. The ingredients of the style were Parisian and Sienese—their early union marked by the appearance of Simone Martini at the court of the Popes-in-exile at Avignon—plus an admixture of Flemish realism.

We see the end result in Worcester's superb little *Madonna of Humility in a Rose Garden*,[295] attributed safely to the Veronese painter Stefano da Verona (c. 1374–1438 or later). In this so-called International Gothic Style, which spread from Spain to Hungary, languid reverse curves, brilliant high-keyed color, boneless figures, buttery surfaces, and a tapestrylike profusion of ornament make up an enchanted world. The date of Stefano's painting is toward the middle of the fifteenth century, when the style was rapidly falling victim to the Florentine Renaissance, and had done so in centers more progressive than Verona. Renaissance Madonnas, like those of Masaccio and Donatello, are full-bodied humans enthroned in high majesty.

One can argue *ad nauseam* whether such late fifteenth-century Northern Madonnas as Worcester's superb example by the anonymous Master of the St. Ursula Legend[296] are "Renaissance" or "late Gothic." There are excellent claims for both sides of the controversy. Clearly the International Gothic Style is here only a distant memory and the knowledge

295

296

of anatomy owes much to the Florentines. Yet the space is ambiguous, lacking the measured depth of Renaissance perspective, and the drapery develops wayward rhythms independent of the forms beneath. The Virgin's sweetness is not worldly, but filled with medieval piety. This master, who owed much to Roger van der Weyden (see MA 66) and Dieric Bouts (see MA 100), seems to have worked mainly at Bruges, but appears to have had connections with Cologne as well. His name comes from an altarpiece at Bruges. In this painting the pale blue crown-bearing angels are set against a cinnamon ground and the cloth behind the Virgin is a deep yellow-green with violet edging. The Child holds an apple; he is thus the Second Adam, marking a new beginning for a sinful world.

The Miracle of St. Sylvester,[297] by Pesellino (c. 1422–57), whose real name was Francesco di Stefano, is a fully developed example of Florentine Renaissance art, albeit in relatively informal vein. Painted in tempera (the powdered colors were mixed with egg yolk) on a panel 12 by 31 inches, it formed (with two other panels now in the Doria Pamphili collection in Rome) the predella-base of an altarpiece. The sainted Pope, kneeling in prayer, brings a bull to life in the enthroned presence of the Emperor Constantine and his mother, St. Helena. Other witnesses to this proof of the power of the Christian God are representatives of pagan and Jewish religions. Above the slowly rising bull, the Jewish magician who had caused its death acknowledges his own defeat. The figures are methodically placed in a converging space laid out on the Florentine system of one-point perspective, invented in or about 1425, reputedly by the architect Filippo Brunelleschi. Pesellino once collaborated with the better-known Fra Filippo Lippi, and seems to have been greatly influenced by him. As the dress shown here is contemporary and Pesellino had a sharp eye, his paintings are an important source for the study of mid-fifteenth-century Florentine costume.

The Discovery of Honey by Bacchus,[298] a tempera panel 32 by 51 inches painted by the Florentine Piero di Cosimo (c. 1462– after 1515), takes us into a world of playful fantasy. Here the artist, described by

297

298

Vasari as a mad genius, has taken the story from Ovid. Bacchus stands at the right, nude and very self-satisfied, beside a richly dressed Ariadne. Beyond them a boisterous Silenus rides in on his donkey. A motley crew of satyrs and humans bang on pots and kettles to make the bees settle in a hollow tree, which looks strangely like a standing bear. Even the landscape seems to oscillate between the everyday reality of the hill town at the left and the almost sinister fantasy of the rock formations at the right. Another fine work by Piero di Cosimo, *The Discovery of Wine*, in Harvard's Fogg Art Museum, makes a pair with this one, commissioned for the house of Giovanni Vespucci in Florence. Still another, at the Wadsworth Atheneum in Hartford, perhaps representing *Hylas and the Nymphs*, is one of a group of six scenes of primitive man—as imagined by an unfettered spirit.

It is hard to believe that the great Flemish tapestry of *The Last Judgment*, which hangs in the entrance court, was made at about the same time as Piero di Cosimo's painting. Such was the force of medieval tradition in the European North, particularly in the decorative arts. Our discussion of the tapestry art, however, is centered on another magnificent example at Manchester, N.H. (NH 19).

Portrait of a Man,[299] painted about 1555 by the Bergamask master Giovanni Battista Moroni (active 1546/7–78), brings us to mid-century Mannerist art as seen in the bronze sculpture of Benvenuto Cellini (MA 42). In this large canvas, 3 feet high, the nervous contours flow with great confidence, while the abstraction of the design is sealed at the corner by a plain rectangular window frame. Note the clever counterplay of minor diagonals in collar and cuffs, edged in coral. Degas would have admired such a design had he known it. He too found delight in small diagonal projections—the point of an umbrella, a cigar at a saucy angle, the brim of a top hat—just as Moroni found it in the end of a sword and its scabbard.

We pass by a fine Bernardo Strozzi (see CT 14), the *Calling of Matthew*, and an adequate early Rembrandt, *St. Bartholomew*, to consider two paintings by lesser Dutch masters of the seventeenth century among many fine examples from this school owned at Worcester. Pieter Saenredam (1597–1665), who specialized in church interiors, is seen in the superb *St. Bavo Church, Haarlem*,[300] an oil on oak panel 28 by

299

300

22 inches, completed in 1660. Like Vermeer of Delft (MA 50), who was born thirty-five years later, Saenredam worked so slowly and pain-stakingly that scarcely fifty works are known by his (or by Vermeer's) hand. These masters, whom we may think of as progenitors of the twen-tieth-century Piet Mondrian (see CT 85), are at the opposite pole from prolific and rapid painters like Frans Hals and Rembrandt. Everything depends in their work on exact adjustments and balances. Less con-cerned with the play of light on surfaces than Vermeer, Saenredam in his austere compositions came closer than anything before Mondrian to approximating that ideal of orderliness which we associate with Dutch life—Hals, Rembrandt, and Vincent van Gogh to the contrary notwith-standing.

Gerrit Heda (active 1640–67), like his father Willem Claesz Heda, specialized in still-life painting at Haarlem. Worcester has a fine ex-ample[301] by Gerrit, an oil 31 by 25 inches, in which glassware, silver, pewter, and cloth are rendered with refinement and precision. Although such painting lies behind the art of Chardin (see MA 216) and the American William M. Harnett (see MA 220)—both discussed at the Springfield Museum of Fine Arts—Chardin arranged his forms more compactly and employed a fatter, more succulent medium, while Harnett insisted on such microscopic detail as to invite inspection rather than contemplation. Unlike Harnett, however, Heda does not crowd his canvas. There is space to breathe in, and room to savor the wonderful shapes of his glasses, as well as the subtle tones of olive, olive green, nut brown, and dark tan.

In Spanish painting at Worcester, Ribera, Alonso Cano, and Murillo are well represented, but the *Repentant Magdalene*[302] by El Greco (1541–1614) is so fine that, in its different way, it rivals Boston's *Fray Felix Paravicino* (MA 71). Blue is the dominant color of the Magdalen —a blue that reappears in Picasso's emaciated figures of the first years of the twentieth century; whereas Paravicino is seen in ashen grays, deep reds, and with skin tones like old parchment. The Magdalen's symbols, a skull and an ointment vase, exist in an unearthly light. The whole picture has a glow that requires an adjective that all writers use—no

301

302

other will do—phosphorescent. It was painted about 1577–80, not long after El Greco arrived in Toledo and some thirty years before the Paravicino portrait.

A happy outcome for the 1963 purchase of a freshly and vigorously painted *Head of a Girl*, attributed to Peter Paul Rubens, followed doubts about its authorship. It is now accepted as a superb example of Rubens's earthier assistant and pupil, Jacob Jordaens (1599–1678), from about 1615–20. Far better a fine Jordaens (who is otherwise not well represented in New England) than a not-quite Rubens!

Acquisition in 1963, after a long-term loan, of the portraits of Mr. and Mrs. John Freake gave Worcester the finest known examples of American painting in the 1670s. There are advantages to considering them now, in their seventeenth-century context, rather than as the beginning of a new line of development. We shall concentrate on the *Elizabeth Freake and Baby Mary*[303] because the portrait of the husband gave the anonymous artist less opportunity to show his mettle. In the absence of any evidence to demonstrate that such art evolved from prior work in the American settlements, we are forced to suppose that the Freake Painter was born in England and that he had some impression of provincial English painting of around 1620 and even of outmoded Elizabethan work. Obviously, the elegant imagery of Sir Anthony Van Dyck (1599–1641), court painter to Charles I, was no part of his experience. Yet the dimly seen red curtain echoes Baroque tradition even if nothing else does so. A date of c. 1674 is proposed from the fact that the marriage of the Freakes, in Boston, took place in 1661, and that Mary was the youngest of their eight children. If our painter inherited his passionate obsession with ornamental detail from English sources, it is still true that his sharp eye set a standard for realism that was to become the most basic characteristic of American painting until modern times. Miniature in appearance through its microscopic scale, the picture nevertheless measures 43 by 37 inches. Its airless rigidity (as later seen in Harnett, MA 220) by no means precludes sensitivity in two-dimensional design. Any doubt you may have on this score should be quickly dispelled by turning the illustration upside down and observing the interlocked rhythms.

303

It is generally agreed that the *Self-Portrait*[304] by Thomas Smith, a mariner who came to America around the middle of the century, is the earliest painting done in New England by a known painter. The naval battle, seen in the same position as landscape views in early Flemish portraits, involved English and Dutch forces, as the flags tell us, but it has not been identified. The annals of Harvard University's Corporation tell us that one Thomas Smith was paid four guineas in 1680 "for drawing Dr. Ames effigies." The Worcester portrait is usually dated c. 1690; that it is a self-portrait is demonstrated not only by the naval reference but also by the skull and the poem below it—in part, the poem reads, "Why why should I the World be minding / therein a World of Evils Finding. / Then Farewell World . . ." Other works by Captain Smith include the *Portrait of Captain George Curwin*, c. 1680, at the Essex Institute, Salem. Smith's bulky forms, including a more massive version of the Baroque curtain than in the Freake portrait, suggest a Dutch rather than an English origin, or at least that sort of Dutch painting brought to England in the early seventeenth century by such artists as Daniel Mytens, favored by James I and Prince Charles before the arrival of Van Dyck.

It is not often that we can compare artists of major importance in works of first quality in a museum of Worcester's relatively moderate size. In the field of British painting of the eighteenth century, however, the *Portrait of William James*[305] by William Hogarth (1697–1764) and the *Portrait of the Artist's Daughters*[306] by Thomas Gains-

304

305

306

borough (1727–88) give us such an opportunity. Furthermore, they allow us to compare England's two most original painters of the Century of the Enlightenment. Both were influenced by Rococo trends in French art. Hogarth limited the connection to a method of painting, while insisting on the virtues of middle-class English life. Gainsborough, equally chary of the boudoir overtones of the Louis XV style, created an image of diaphanous elegance that approached the earlier effects of Watteau (see M A 265). Indeed, Watteau and Gainsborough at his best may be called the most lyrical poets of eighteenth-century art.

William James, whose subject served as High Sheriff of Kent, characterizes the substantial country squire whom we meet in the pages of Henry Fielding. Hogarth painted him in 1744 at the age of forty. Undercutting the easy flattery that marred much of the portraiture of the day, Hogarth stressed his subject's moral integrity despite a good-humored suggestion of self-importance. The companion portrait of his wife, Elizabeth, is competent, but more standard fare. At a measurement of 30 by 25 inches they are of what was called "cabinet size," as are the general run of portraits of lesser personages in British and American art of the time. The internal painted oval frame is also standard.

When Gainsborough painted his daughters, about 1770, he was well established at the fashionable resort of Bath. Note the moist sparkle of highlights in the eye of the standing girl, and along the drawing instrument held by her older sister. The cool tones of their white and blue dresses suit the mood of quiet reverie. Hogarth, on the contrary, used bright colors in his forthright statement. For a double portrait the cabinet-size format was not appropriate, and Gainsborough has given us a full-dress performance on a canvas measuring 50 by 40 inches. Mary and Margaret, here aged about twenty-two and eighteen, were among his favorite subjects. Much has happened to him since the early 1750s, when he painted *Girl Seated in a Park*, already discussed at Yale (CT 54). Now silvery and fluid, his art has a languidness that approaches sadness. Attenuated forms—the statue, Mary's left hand—are especially close to Watteau, as are the complex rhythms and textures of the drapery. Even the bow that ties the picture-album in Margaret's lap seems to droop in sympathy with these frail creatures. Still faintly visible at the left is the original position of the older sister, facing in the opposite direction. Gainsborough's revised composition is surely a great improvement.

By the 1770s Gainsborough was independent enough to indulge his passion for landscape painting, for which there was little demand on the English market. Worcester owns a superb large example, 58 by 63 inches, of slightly earlier date, c. 1765. Later ones are more vaporous and the tones move away from browns and greens toward low-keyed lavenders.

Nineteenth-century painting and sculpture in Europe is not Worcester's strongest field, but two examples of highest quality demand inclusion here. *The Brooding Woman*,[307] painted in 1891 in Tahiti by Paul Gauguin (1848–1903), is unusually sculptural in the work of this master of flat decoration. (Compare the large picture in Boston's Museum of Fine Arts, M A 86.) Gauguin tended to oscillate between these poles, occasionally combining them, as here, in a wonderful synthesis.

The apricot, blue-violet, and yellow-green tones of this painting implied a voyage of discovery into uncharted seas of color. The sculptural aspect of Gauguin's art derived from two sources: his study of Far Eastern and primitive sculptures in the Paris museums and a deep appreciation of the art of Cézanne, by whom the Worcester Museum owns a superb oil sketch for the central figure in the *Card Players* (in the Barnes Foundation, Merion, Pa.). For a brilliant study of Gauguin's often bizarre responses to primitive and exotic arts, and his preparation in Paris and Brittany for the Tahitian adventure, I strongly recommend an essay in Robert Goldwater, *Primitivism in Modern Art* (revised edition, New York: Vintage Books, 1967, pages 63ff.).

Auguste Rodin (1840–1917) was a contemporary of the Impressionists—Claude Monet was born in the same year and Renoir a year later —and while it is easy to find connections between their fluid surfaces and Rodin's ever-fluctuating effects of light and shade, to call him an Impressionist sculptor would be an egregious error. It is helpful to remember that Rodin was only eight years older than Paul Gauguin, who, trained by Pissarro in Impressionist technique, quickly veered off to his own exotic version of the newly emerging Symbolism. Rodin avoided the exotic, but he carried Symbolism to the level of Michelangelesque Expressionism. Stated with fewer "isms," this means that Rodin has much more in common with Daumier (see MA 80) before him and later with Edward Munch (see CT 29) and Wilhelm Lehmbruck (see MA 240) than with his own contemporaries. It was with Daumier alone, however, that he shared a passion for the grandeur of Michelangelo.

Head of Sorrow: Portrait of Eleanora Duse[308] is in many ways a summation of Rodin's career. The double title is appropriate (but not always given), for the head had emerged by 1882 on two figures for the *Gates of Hell*, a gigantic undertaking that spanned most of Rodin's working years. In simplified form it is seen there as the head of the *Prodigal Son* (the whole figure is remarkably prophetic of Lehmbruck's art) and of Paolo in the group of *Paolo and Francesca*. Toward the end of his life Rodin planned to use the head in a monument to Joan of Arc for New York City, but the project was never carried out. In 1905, how-

307

308

ever, he reworked it into a portrait of the great Italian actress Eleanora Duse. Thus he combined the sublime universal—human anguish—with the particular, much as in Michelangelo's Medici Tomb effigies. As we have seen more than once in these pages, the continuity of an image, ever evolving, is one mark of genius. We think of Leonardo da Vinci's *Mona Lisa*, whose face appeared years before he met her and continued, androgynously, ever afterward, or of Cézanne's Mont-Ste-Victoire. Illuminating discussion of this and other facets of Rodin's art will be found in Albert Elsen, *Rodin* (New York: Museum of Modern Art, 1963).

American painting at Worcester starts out with the Freake portraits and Thomas Smith's self-portrait, already discussed. We pass over many superb eighteenth- and nineteenth-century examples only because the artists concerned have been studied in other museums. Do not miss, however, John Singleton Copley's *Portrait of John Bours*, c. 1761, with its brilliant sheen and elegant pose; or Ralph Earl's *William Carpenter*, 1779, a twelve-year-old in a bright red suit, painted in England not long after Yale's *Roger Sherman* (CT 75); or Gilbert Stuart's virtuoso oil sketch of *Mrs. Perez Morton*, c. 1802; or John F. Kensett's *Conway Valley, N.H.*, 1854; or Thomas Eakins's oil study for the head of *Dr. Gross* (the *Gross Clinic*, in Philadelphia, 1875, is his masterpiece); or Marsden Hartley's *Wave*, 1940, perhaps *his* masterpiece, at least among the later works.

Although the oil painting of John Singer Sargent (1856–1925) has been discussed on several occasions, to omit his brilliant watercolors would be unfortunate. Worcester owns one of the most spectacular, *Muddy Alligators*,[309] signed and dated 1917. Painted in Florida, it is unsurpassed in sheer virtuosity in this medium. Note how Sargent utilizes the white of the paper to achieve his sparkling effect. The alligators may be muddy, but Sargent's color certainly is not.

Worcester's collection of modern art is not large, but it contains good examples of oils by Kandinsky, Rouault, and Kline, and an impressive cast bronze by the Italian Arnaldo Pomodoro (born 1926). A sphere entitled *Rotante dal Foro Centrale* (1966), 7 feet in diameter, interrupts the perfection of a geometric form by signs of erosion and decay, as in the cylindrical *Ruota* at Ridgefield (CT 96), of five years earlier.

Pre-Columbian art at the museum is spectacular, especially as it is shown in a special modern gallery. Our single example, while only a sample of these riches, is only a bit over 4 inches high. Nevertheless, the

309

veined onyx *Pendant in the Form of a Mask*,[310] of classic Teotihuacán style, A.D. c. 500–700, rivals the grandeur of Old Kingdom Egyptian sculpture and that of the T'ang dynasty of China, which we now consider.

Worcester's Far Eastern section is also distinguished. Among its Chinese objects the over life-size *Head of the Buddha*,[311] carved in gray limestone, is considered one of the great examples of T'ang sculpture anywhere in the world. It came from the famous caves at Lung Mên. The reader may wish to review the discussion of Chinese art at the Boston Museum of Fine Arts and at the Fogg in Cambridge in order to clarify the position of this head as a masterwork of the "Classic" phase of Chinese culture. Comparison with the contemporary painted head from Tun-huang at the Fogg Museum (MA 136) will show how strong a connection existed between sculpture and painting during this period (A.D. 618–906).

In the Sung dynasty (960–1280) Chinese art became freer and less austere. Sculpture seems to have followed painting in striving for movement and more complex light and shade. The delightful little green bronze *Incense Burner*,[312] perhaps representing Lao-tzu, the founder of Taoism, on a water buffalo, perfectly exemplifies these trends. A most dangerous beast, the buffalo is tamed by the philosopher's exalted detachment from the unruly aspects of nature.

We conclude our long, but much too brief, survey of this outstanding museum with a small masterpiece, only 10 inches high, a Persian manu-

310

312

311

script illumination of the fifteenth century representing a *Giraffe with Its Keeper*.[313] It comes from a history of Tamerlane (1307–1404) and seems to have been executed at the beginning of the century. The strange beast was presented by the Sultan of Egypt to the ruler of Persia. The lavender background against a sky of gold sets the scene in hilly country. Such art became a major source of inspiration to Matisse, early in our century, and thus it lies behind the modern liberation of color as flat tone. It also became, more immediately, the basis for the manuscript art of Moslem India, of which we have discussed a fine example at the Fogg Museum (MA 138).

313

New Hampshire

New Hampshire

• Hanover

•
Cornish

• Concord

Manchester •

New Hampshire Historical Society

Location: 30 Park Street at State Street (near the state capitol)
Hours: Mon., Tues., Thurs., Fri. 9-4:30, Wed. 9-8 P.M.
Admission: Free

Centered under the elaborate marble entrance-rotunda is a superb example of Concord's famed product, the *Concord Coach*.[1] I hope no one will object to my including it as a work of art—or to my making an exception in its favor in a book that does not cover crafts or manufactured objects. Such coaches were first built by Abbot and Downing, of Concord, from 1827. The example seen here dates from 1852 and was acquired by the Historical Society just over a century later. It was built by J. S. and E. A. Abbot; as the inscription makes clear, it was used by the U.S. Mail. Concord coaches ran in regular service as late as 1910. Up to twelve passengers could be carried inside (in the large models) and as many more seated on the roof. They were also used on the Wells-Fargo routes in the Old West. The society owns a painting showing thirty of them on flatcars being shipped by rail to Omaha, Nebraska, on April 15, 1868. This fascinating picture is by John Burgum (1826–1907), better known as Abbot and Downing's most renowned painter of the coaches themselves.

The society's collection of furniture and paintings (primarily portraits) is important, as are its historical prints and photographs and its research library. Temporary exhibitions are shown in a large gallery to the right of the rotunda. Upstairs is a series of period rooms covering New England life primarily from 1700 to 1750. While there are some historical discrepancies, the representation of household articles and decorative arts is extensive. Painted floors often substituted for carpets, and the black-and-white diamond pattern seen here—imitating marble floors of more affluent homes—was especially popular.

The furniture collection is celebrated among connoisseurs. Among the prize pieces is a high chest of drawers attributed to John Dunlap of New Hampshire, c. 1780. On the grand staircase you cannot miss the full-length *Portrait of Benning Wentworth* by Joseph Blackburn, painted in Portsmouth in 1760. We have discussed a work of this master in a

1

very different vein at Bowdoin College (ME 11). A replica of the portly Governor Wentworth (1696–1770) hangs in the nearby state capitol among its array of gubernatorial images. A companion portrait by Blackburn, also painted in 1760, of *Lieutenant Governor John Wentworth*, who died in 1730, likewise confronts you on the staircase of the Historical Society.

Of wider-ranging historical interest is the *Portrait of Benjamin Thompson, Count Rumford* (1753–1814), in the officer's uniform of the King's American Dragoons, c. 1782. The former attribution of this picture to Thomas Gainsborough has not stood up to modern connoisseurship, particularly when it is compared with the Fogg Art Museum's sparkling image of him (in red coat), unquestionably by that great English master. A Tory sympathizer, Thompson departed from America in 1776 to join the British forces, leaving his wife and an infant daughter. A brilliant scientist, he soon became a member of the Royal Society in London. He commanded British troops in Charleston and on Long Island. After the defeat of the British, in 1783 he traveled to Munich, where he was welcomed by Charles Theodore, Elector of Bavaria. Here he laid out the now famous English Garden, in 1790. Already knighted by King George III, he was now made a Count of the Holy Roman Empire. For his personal title Thompson took the old name of Concord (Rumford), where he had been married. In the following year his wife died in America and by 1796 his daughter Sarah, now twenty-two, had joined him. She so charmed the Elector that he received her as Countess of the Empire, and she was known thereafter as Countess Rumford. It is recorded that, noticing her father's attentions to the young daughter of Countess Baumgarten, and further noticing Sophy's "striking resemblance" to her father, she became aware for the first time that "I was no longer to consider myself an only child." Back in London, Rumford busied himself with a variety of scientific inventions. Settling in Paris in 1803, he courted and married the widow of the guillotined Lavoisier (see MA 239), but the union proved unhappy. His daughter Sarah, who died in 1852, spent her last years at Concord in the home of her birth. Her possessions came to the Historical Society in 1978 through the will of a collateral member of her mother's family. So ends the extraordinary Rumford saga. An exhibition utilizing these memorabilia was organized by the society in 1979; the notes that accompanied it make fascinating reading.

St. Paul's School

Location: Follow Pleasant St. (Route 103) for about 3 miles west of the center of Concord; look for sign on the left for entrance to the school
Hours: Tues.-Sat. 10-4:30 except during school holidays
Admission: Free. Ⓗ

Visible on the grounds near Memorial Hall from April through October, but dismantled and stored during the winter months for safety's sake, is a fine mobile-on-stabile by Alexander Calder (1898–1976). Its playful title, *Iguana*,[2] stretches the imagination a bit, but humor is no stranger to Calder's art, as visitors to the Whitney Museum in New York discover daily in observing the antics of his many-peopled *Circus*. An early mobile of Calder's, rather shrublike in shape, bears the title *Calderberry Bush*. From our visit to Hartford (CT 35) we know that he could rise to the occasion of inventing his own gigantic, but engaging, horse to suit the requirements of a much earlier bequest. In *Iguana*, made in 1968 of aluminum and steel and reaching a height of over 6 feet, the forms and their gay colors relate, as so often, to those of the paintings of Joan Miró (see CT 32). A smaller Calder mobile can be seen in Memorial Hall itself, suspended from the lobby ceiling.

For a good many generations in the history of this distinguished academy, interest in art was restricted to fine buildings (the chapel is an example) and to memorials. One of the latter, in a small oratory to the left of the chapel's entrance, is especially interesting. It is a carefully made replica of the great fresco by Pietro Lorenzetti (Sienese, active 1320–48) in the Lower Church of San Francesco at Assisi, representing the *Madonna and Child with Saints Francis and John the Evangelist.* Commissioned from Nicholas Lochoff, a specialist in this kind of reproduction, it is painted in true fourteenth-century fresco technique (with the gold leaf and certain colors and details added after the plaster had dried). What we see here is a scholarly craftsman's estimate of the appearance of this marvelously expressive work when it was new. Lochoff received another commission, from the Frick Art Reference Library,

2

New York, to make a replica of the same fresco in its modern damaged state. It adorns the main reading room of that institution. To make it, Lochoff produced a work similar to the fresco at St. Paul's and then painstakingly destroyed it to match its twentieth-century condition. Since fresco is made by layers—dry painting atop pigments that have sunk into the wet plaster—you cannot make a satisfactory replica by imitating surfaces in a single medium.

With the considerable growth of concern for art at St. Paul's in the past twenty years, Hargate Hall has been adapted to serve as what is known as The Art Center in Hargate. Excellent exhibitions have been organized, and visits by leading artists, such as Robert Motherwell (see MA 229) in 1970. A taped record of his remarks has been published by the school under the title *On the Humanism of Abstraction.* It is an important statement. A small permanent collection, primarily of American art, is being developed.

Saint-Gaudens National Historic Site

Location: On Route 12A (N.H. side of the Connecticut River), 2 miles north
of the covered bridge from Windsor, Vt.; follow the sign up the hill. From
Route 91 use exit 8 or 9 toward Windsor
Hours: 8:30-5 daily from the last weekend in May to October 15
Admission: Charged (sixteen years and older)

Operated since 1964 by the National Park Service, the former home and
Little Studio of Augustus Saint-Gaudens (1848–1907) have been supplemented by a well-designed gallery and sculpture court where much
of his work is shown in originals, models, or casts. The house was once
a tavern, built in 1800. The Little Studio was Saint-Gaudens's workshop.
A Large Studio, where major works were built to full scale, formerly
occupied the site of the gallery, but it burned in 1904 with the loss of
Saint-Gaudens's correspondence, sketchbooks, records of commissions,
and numerous works in progress. Reconstructed in the following year,
it burned again in 1944.

Since American sculpture lagged well behind European work until
the late nineteenth century, it may be significant that our greatest sculptor
prior to the advent of modern art was born in Dublin of Irish and
French parents. He arrived in this country when they emigrated. Like
the painter William Michael Harnett (see M A 220), also born in 1848,
he was trained at the Cooper Union and the National Academy of Design in New York. For both artists study in Europe was of the highest
importance, but there all similarity ends.

The *Diana*,[3] shown in our illustration in its central position in the
commodious Little Studio, is a bronze cast of the half-size model for a
13-foot figure that once topped Stanford White's Madison Square Garden in New York (at Fifth Avenue and Twenty-sixth Street, destroyed
1925). The figure itself, installed in 1893 and once gilded, is now at the
head of the main staircase of the Philadelphia Museum of Art. Small
bronze replicas, with a much less elaborate bow, were sold in some

3

quantity, and may be seen at the Currier Gallery of Art in Manchester, the Williams College Museum of Art, and elsewhere. The half-size bronze at Cornish is actually a cast made in 1972 from the plaster, still preserved at Cornish and the only piece salvaged from the fire of 1944. An earlier bronze cast is in the Metropolitan Museum of Art, New York. A cement cast was presented to Stanford White in 1894, and is now privately owned in New Mexico. In a newspaper interview of 1897 with the young woman who posed for the *Diana*, it was revealed that the pose was so difficult that she had to be propped up by ladders, but the sculptor was so impatient that he made a casting directly from her body. We are not to suppose, however, that he did not make his own alterations and refinements. Saint-Gaudens's cast of a fifth-century B.C. Greek stele, hung in his studio, suggests his concern with Greek idealization at its noblest period rather than with the prevalent taste for smoothed-out Neo-Classicism that had so long held American sculpture in its chill grasp.

Saint-Gaudens's first major commission, which assured his future, came in 1876, for the monument to Admiral David G. Farragut in New York's Madison Square. The plaster for the figure was exhibited in Paris in 1880, where it received an honorable mention, and was cast there in bronze. Erected the following year, it was set on a Hudson River bluestone base. This *Base*,[4] removed in 1934 because of erosion, was replaced by a simple black granite one; it is now a major possession of the Cornish Site. Measuring 7 feet in height by more than 8 in width, it was almost certainly cut by the artist himself, the budget being a tight one and Saint-Gaudens not yet in a position to surround himself with assistants. It is remarkable for a flowing design that can without exaggeration be called Art Nouveau before its time. The long inscription commemorating Farragut is noteworthy for its innovative lettering. A symbolic sword plunges through the central panel of waves, flanked by allegorical figures of Courage (on the right) and Loyalty. These are already marked by a surprising break with Neo-Classical formulae. The whole base forms a semicircular exedra, or seat—again a radical departure from the normal conception of such supports. It is known that Stanford White had much to do with this design; indeed, White signed the base as architect after Saint-Gaudens's signature as sculptor.

Important commissions that followed the enthusiastic reception of the Farragut Monument included *The Puritan* for Springfield, Mass. (MA 209), the Adams Memorial in Rock Creek Cemetery, Washington, D.C.

4

(bronze replica in the garden near the Little Studio), the monument to Colonel Robert G. Shaw (Boston Common opposite the statehouse, earlier full-size design in plaster at Cornish), the General Sherman Monument in New York's Fifty-ninth Street Plaza, and the *Diana* for Madison Square Garden.

Saint-Gaudens settled in Cornish in 1885. Many other artists joined him in the area, including such painters as George de Forest Brush, Thomas Dewing, Kenyon Cox (page 429), Charles Platt (also a distinguished architect), Stephen Parrish, and Stephen's enormously popular son, Maxfield Parrish. Thus the Cornish Colony came into being. It also attracted poets (Witter Bynner), novelists (Winston Churchill), editors, actors, and musicians. The artistic impact of summers at Cornish was great, but it inevitably fell victim to the rising tide of modern art.

We should append to this list of Eminent Victorians (and Edwardians) the sculptor Daniel Chester French (1850–1931), established luxuriously on his own estate at Stockbridge, Mass. (see MA 223). The current revival of all these artists has restored them to their rightful and prestigious place in American art.

Hood Museum of Art, Dartmouth College

Hours: Galleries in the Hopkins Center: Mon.-Fri. 10-4, Sat., Sun. 2-4; Carpenter Hall: Mon.-Fri. 11-4, Sat., Sun. 12-4; Wilson Hall: Mon.-Fri. 9-5, Sat., Sun. 12-4. Holiday hours usually follow Sun. hours, and all galleries closed Christmas and New Year's Day
Admission: Free.

The art collections of Dartmouth College are extensive, but until present hopes for an adequate museum are fulfilled, it is difficult to see them with any completeness. The Hood Museum is scheduled to open in 1984, in a location near the Hopkins Center.

As of this writing, the greater part of the collection is kept in the excellent storage facilities in the basement of Hopkins Center, where the museum offices are also located. Changing selections are shown in two galleries in the center (when they are not occupied by temporary exhibitions) and in Carpenter Hall, a wing off the Baker and Sherman libraries. The archaeological and ethnological collections are displayed in Wilson Hall, across the street left of the main entrance to Hopkins Center. Orozco's impressive fresco cycle fills the walls of a study area below the main floor of the Baker Library. Modern sculptures are placed on the college grounds, in the lobby of Hopkins Center, and in a small court at the center. Carpenter Hall is the home of art history; Wilson Hall, of anthropology; and Hopkins Center, of studio instruction. A college map is available, and most helpful.

Apart from the examples we discuss or mention, Dartmouth owns fine collections of photographs, prints of all periods (especially rich in Piranesi, nineteenth-century masters, and among the very few American museums to own the complete Vollard suite of 100 etchings by Picasso), posters from both world wars, and Chinese porcelains. There are also collections of coins and medals, and of costumes.

Among New England colleges that received Assyrian reliefs during the mid-nineteenth century through the interest of missionary alumni, Dartmouth and Amherst received the lion's share. These reliefs are discussed in the entry for Amherst College (MA 1), but to Dartmouth belongs the credit for a publication of its group (in relation to the more than seventy in American museums) in a brochure by John B. Stearns and Donald P. Hanson, *The Assyrian Reliefs at Dartmouth* (1953).

Art collecting at Dartmouth began in 1771 with the presentation of a silver bowl of "monteith" type by Colonial Governor John Wentworth, a trustee of the institution. It was made in Boston by Daniel Henchman and Nathaniel Hurd, two of Paul Revere's most highly considered competitors. Dartmouth's first painting, which hangs in the Baker Library, is a full-length *Portrait of Eleazar Wheelock III* (1711–79), the college's first president, commissioned in 1793 from Joseph Steward. Later portraits with Dartmouth connections include works by Chester Harding and Thomas Sully. An important gift of over one hundred paintings and including bronze sculptures by Georg Kolbe and Charles Despiau was received from Mrs. John D. Rockefeller, Jr., in 1935. Primarily by living American painters, the works also included Thomas Eakins's *Portrait of the Architect John Joseph Borie.*

In addition to its exhibition galleries on the top floor, Carpenter Hall contains in the library a large Renaissance mantelpiece from the Château of Chenonceaux, near Tours, brilliantly designed and bearing the initials and the salamander symbol of Francis I and Queen Claude. It makes an interesting comparison with the English example, of nearly a century later, at Amherst College.

From the Roman Empire, second to third century A.D., is an important sarcophagus panel, marble 19 by 47 inches, representing *Eros with Nereids, Tritons, and Seahorses.*[5] It was formerly in Wilton House, near Salisbury, the seat of the Earl of Pembroke. Finely chiseled and polished, it is filled with figures enacting themes with Eastern as well as classical connections. These are interestingly discussed in Octavio Alvarez, *The Celestial Brides: A Study in Mythology and Archaeology* (Stockbridge, Mass.: Herbert Reichner, 1978, number 143), where the Dartmouth relief is described as a Romanized version of the ancient and exotic love story between the soul and celestial females. Exceptional in reliefs of this kind is the intensity of the embrace of the female at the extreme left. The central Nereid approached by a Cupid bearing the wedding band appears on other sarcophagi; here her incipient captivation of the sea god is contested, or perhaps assisted, by a third female, who struggles with a rearing horse, another symbol of masculinity.

A flattening process, observable in the difference between the Williams College example of c. A.D. 300 and the Antioch mosaic of c. 500 at Worcester (MA 269 and MA 291), that effectively altered the style of late Roman mosaic is carried still further in Dartmouth's *Dog Ram-*

5

6

pant in Flying Gallop.[6] This panel is one of four fragments of a floor
mosaic representing a hunt. It comes from Roman Syria, fifth to sixth
century, and measures about 4 by 6 feet. Such scenes are closely related,
in theme and design, to the art of neighboring Sassanian Persia. It is
worth keeping in mind that the Justinian mosaics of Constantinople and
Ravenna are little more than a century distant in the future, for Roman
illusionism has all but completely disappeared here. A "carpet" effect
now being desired, there is no longer a need for the minute tesserae
that made such illusionism possible, nor for the wide range of colors
that in Pompeiian times supported it. Nevertheless, the broad outlines
manage to suggest rotundity, as does the circular arrangement of the
tesserae themselves in the neck and chest areas of this alert animal.

Italian Renaissance painting is represented by an early *Madonna and
Child with Saints Sebastian and Roch,*[7] by Marco Palmezzano (1459–
c. 1545), who worked at Forli, across the Apennines northeast of Florence in the region known as Romagna. Painted in tempera on a panel
67 by 63 inches, it combines a Peruginesque quietude (see MA 250)
with the somewhat dry manner that was in vogue in both Florence and
Rome at the end of the fifteenth century. Distant connections with the
Venetian art of Giovanni Bellini are also observable. Color is relatively
subdued, but a lovely light suffuses the landscape background. The picture has suffered considerable damage. It dates from about 1490.

A Baroque oil representing *St. Paul Hermit and the Raven,* attributed
to Giacinto Brandi (1621–91) has much of the dramatic force of the
Currier Gallery's *Martyrdom of St. Bartholomew,* at Manchester (NH
23). It is fully discussed in an article in Dartmouth's well-illustrated
publication, *Acquisitions, 1974–1978.*

A good color plate in the publication just cited records the startling
beauty of Dartmouth's finest portrait, the *Governor John Wentworth,*[8]
a pastel (now mounted on canvas) by John Singleton Copley (1738–

7

8

1815). Given to the college in 1977 by a collateral of the Wentworth family, it has been widely exhibited and published, notably in Jules Prown's definitive monograph on the painter (Cambridge: Harvard University Press, 1966). Smaller than Copley's "cabinet size" half-length oils, it nevertheless reaches a height of 2 feet. Copley's monogram and the date, 1769, appear at center right. Copley's forty known pastel portraits (as against the hundreds of oils he painted) were almost all executed prior to his departure for England in 1774, and there is none finer than his image of the last royal governor of New Hamphire. These pastels rival Europe's best, by Rosalba Carriera (1675–1757), Chardin (1699–1779), and Maurice Quentin de LaTour (1704–88). Such a feat is the more remarkable because Copley taught himself the technique, receiving some instruction only through correspondence with a talented Swiss practitioner of the medium who was living in London, Jean-Etienne Liotard (1702–89). The governor is shown at the age of thirty-two in a pale dove-gray silk coat flecked with rust red against the brown-gray tone of the background. His powdered hair strikes an exact balance between the tone of his coat and the whites about his neck. The ruddy flesh tones relate to the russet hues on his coat. The hair is presumably a wig, but Copley has made it appear to be a natural growth. Silvery, as in Gainsborough (see MA 306), is the word for the general effect—from hair to the silver buttons at the base of this masterpiece. Copley painted the governor in Portsmouth, then the provincial capital of New Hampshire. Many copies of the portrait were made by other painters, including one of 1878 in oils by Ulysses Dow Tenney that is owned by Dartmouth. Copley himself made a replica in pastel for John Hurd of Portsmouth—apparently commissioned because the original was about to be shipped to Paul Wentworth in London. A tradition that the beautiful frame was made by Paul Revere is unsubstantiated. (Further information will be found in articles in *Acquisitions, 1974–1978* and in *Portraits at Dartmouth*, by the curator, Arthur R. Blumenthal, 1978).

Like Thomas Cole, eight years his junior, Thomas Doughty (1793–1856) was a pioneer in the development of the Hudson River School of landscape painting. Dartmouth's *Rowing on a Mountain Lake*,[9] 17 by

9

44 inches, was painted about 1835. Its fine quality is such that it was included in "The Natural Paradise," an important exhibition staged in 1976 by the Museum of Modern Art that traced the continuity of American Romanticism in nature-painting from 1800 to 1950. Accompanying the illustration in the catalogue is a quotation from Ralph Waldo Emerson (1836): "The world proceeds from the same spirit as the body of man. It is a remoter and inferior incarnation of God, a projection of God in the unconscious. But it differs from the body in one important respect. It is not, like that, now subjected to the human will. Its serene order is inviolable to us." Born in Philadelphia and self-trained, Doughty settled in New York in 1838 following a brief trip to England. In New York he died, impoverished and little appreciated, though he had had considerable success in his most productive years. In *Painting in America* (New York: Crowell, 1956, page 157), E. P. Richardson suggests that a comparable Doughty of 1835 in Detroit "has something of the quality of Bryant's poem, *To a Waterfowl*, and Doughty, like Bryant, was one of the first to see this wild and lonely continent as a theme for art."

A brilliant small oil on panel by William Merritt Chase (1849–1916), undated, bears the title *The Lone Fisherman*,[10] but it conveys no such awesome solitude or hermetic darkness as marks Doughty's image of perhaps seventy-five years earlier. A stout seawall backed by piled-up rocks leads us violently on a diagonal—perhaps suggested by compositions of Degas—to the fisherman, who seems much more actively engaged than Doughty's prisoner of nature primeval. The sea is a dazzling blue. Such intensity is unusual in Chase's work; and his landscapes are generally much more placid. If you will turn the illustration upside down, you will discover how powerful is the play of diagonals in this picture. Technically, Chase was a virtuoso who managed in his later years to combine the high-intensity palette of the French Impressionists with the spirited brushwork of John Singer Sargent. He spent five years in study abroad, including nine months in Venice with the American Frank Duveneck. Returning in 1878, as E. P. Richardson says, "with a halo of European success," he opened a studio on West Tenth Street in

10

New York and also taught at the newly organized Art Students League. As a teacher, he was enormously influential. When John W. Twachtman died in 1902, Chase took his place in a group of New York and Boston painters who first exhibited in 1898 in New York under the name of Ten American Painters. Including such masters as Frank W. Benson (see MA 168) and Childe Hassam (see MA 182), they formed, in Richardson's words, "a kind of academy of American Impressionism."

It is no great leap in time, but light-years in the development of modern art, to turn from Chase to *Guitar on a Table*[11] by Pablo Picasso (1881–1973). An oil 2 feet high painted in 1912/13, it is some five years later than Boston's *Standing Figure* (MA 87) and about six years before *La Table*, owned by Smith College (MA 185). Between 1908 and 1920, in close association with Georges Braque, Picasso developed Cubism to its nearly monochromatic gray-and-tan stage and then gradually reintroduced color into the century's most important visual invention. The Dartmouth picture, once owned by Gertrude Stein and later by Nelson A. Rockefeller (a Dartmouth graduate), is a superb example of the early return of color to Cubist painting. It is not strictly an "oil" because Picasso first drew the major lines in charcoal and introduced sand into the oil medium for textural effect. As of 1911 he began to work in collage (pasted papers), partly for their texture and chiefly as a means of achieving a playful dichotomy between reality and illusion. The papers, usually printed newspapers, patterned oilcloth, or simulated wood grain, are "real" but their reality is clearly at best only incidental to the picture's content; it is therefore illusory. What is real is the illusion of objects disassembled and reconstructed according to the painter's imagination. Quickly following on the first collages, the idea came to Picasso to paint illusions of them, to achieve, as it were, his own complete reality. Paintings of this period are much flatter than those of tan-and-gray Cubism of 1910/11, and they look like assemblages of papers laid onto the picture surface. The Dartmouth example is finely composed with its activity revolving around its black center. Pale ochers, greens, and blues gently enliven the varied near-whites. The guitar has been taken apart and its basic shapes rearranged to form the design. For a true collage of the same period, but still lingering in Picasso's gray-and-tan tonal limits, see *Glasses and Newspaper* by his younger compatriot and protégé, Juan Gris (MA 184).

From the series of frescoes by José Clemente Orozco (1883–1949) in the Baker Library, one called *The Departure of Quetzalcoatl* is illustrated here.[12] Orozco spent two rather frenetic years (1932–34) on this

11

12

important commission: such tension is hardly surprising when a highly temperamental artist is set in a traditional center of learning. Although the murals are certainly not conducive to the sense of restfulness and quiet essential to a study area, the visitor should know that Orozco did not select the location for his frescoes and was by no means happy about it. Nevertheless, the series as a whole ranks among the best works of Mexico's most gifted painter. As such, it contributes significantly to the cultural life of the college. Moreover, one should not forget, any more than medieval monks did in their time, the importance of owning an object of pilgrimage. Dartmouth is increasingly discovering its debt to those intrepid souls who brought Orozco to Hanover. The frescoes seem to some extent the victim of their own propaganda, but they serve as a reminder of cultures other than our own; and since they commemorate the overthrow of oppression in Mexico we may be reminded, however obliquely, of our own Revolution. Measuring 10 by 17 feet, *The Departure of Quetzalcoatl* is one of the largest of the frescoes. As legendary god and Toltec ruler, Quetzalcoatl stands for the forces of light and goodness in their combat with darkness and evil. To him is ascribed the discovery of maize, the arts, science, and the calendar.

In approaching the art of Jean Dubuffet (born 1901) we should clarify the meaning of *l'art brut*, with which he is closely associated. Such art is indeed brutal at times, but the word means rough or unrefined, as in rough-cut diamond or *champagne brut*. In an important exhibition held in 1961 at the Museum of Modern Art, "The Art of Assemblage," the title came from a word championed by Dubuffet himself. He felt that *collage* should be reserved for "collages made in the period 1910–1920 by the Dadaists, Picasso and Braque, etc." For some years Dubuffet had extended the original idea of collage to all manner of unexpected materials and into three dimensions as well. "I have always loved—it is a sort of vice—to employ only the most common materials in my work, those that one does not dream of at first because they are too crude and close at hand and seem unsuitable for anything whatsoever. I like to proclaim that my art is an enterprise to rehabilitate discredited values."

In an age without heroes such an artistic program is surely relevant. Well trained in the academies of Paris, Dubuffet quickly challenged their axioms and assumptions, collected and exhibited the art of the insane, explored graffiti scratched on urban walls, promulgated the art of children, loaded his canvases with soot, debris, and cut-up scraps— and in general exploited his belief that art should be "stripped of all the tinsel, laurels and buskins in which it has been decked, and be seen naked with all the creases of its belly."

Dartmouth's *Topographie au Nid de Pierres*,[13] an assemblage of 1958 on a canvas measuring 3 by 5 feet, belongs to a series made from various paintings of basic elements composing the earth's surface; these were then cut up and the pieces newly juxtaposed. His project was "the execution of a cycle of large paintings celebrating the ground." The title of the Dartmouth picture is essentially untranslatable, but we may venture a paraphrase to the effect that this is an impression (but in no sense a description) of bare rocky ground seen from above. In his comment on these paintings in the catalogue of the Museum of Modern Art's Dubuffet retrospective of 1962, the artist wrote of being captivated by the "opportunity afforded of composing paintings by the simple method of juxtaposing textures on which there were no objects with clearly defined contours."

Our last selection, a construction of iron, steel, and wood measuring 11 by 18 by 10 feet and entitled *X-Delta*,[14] was acquired in 1976 and erected on the lawn of the Baker Library. A brief look at our first selection, the ancient Roman marble relief, will indicate dramatically the long road that sculpture has traveled; it will also help explain why not all the citizenry of Hanover approve of this enormous interloper. The history of the Orozco frescoes, however, suggests that time will heal all wounds. The artist of this piece is Mark di Suvero, born 1933 and in New York circles considered the leading monumental sculptor of his generation. *X-Delta* was the sensation of the Whitney Museum's Annual in 1970, the year of its execution. In the tradition of David Smith (see MA 88), but much closer to modern skyscraper and bridge construction, and in some ways suggestive of the paintings of Franz Kline (see MA 279), it stretches its powerful diagonals, while a free-swinging metal platform introduces actual movement whenever it is pushed.

Our survey of Dartmouth's important collection has had to omit many fine works. Artists we should have liked to discuss include Alma-Tadema (see MA 258), Thomas Eakins (MA 17), John Sloan (ME 17), Fernand Léger (CT 84), Fritz Glarner, and especially Mark Rothko. Dartmouth's Rothko, an oil of 1953 nearly 10 feet high, is accurately described by its title, *Orange and Lilac over Ivory*. The values are so close, however, that a photograph would show only meaningless grays. It is one of the very fine works of the artist (1903–70), whose influence has been as profound as the magic of his veils of color.

The collection of modern art at Dartmouth, with generous representation in all media, and extending from Cubism to the present, makes it one of New England's five or six leading centers in this field.

13

14

The Currier Gallery of Art

Location: 192 Orange Street
Hours: Tues.-Sat. 10-4, Sun. 2-5; closed national holidays
Admission: Free. Ⓗ

This fine museum opened to the public in 1929. It was built in memory of Moody Currier, a governor of the state of New Hampshire, on the site of the Currier mansion in pleasantly landscaped grounds. Under a series of discriminating directors and wise trustees, it has become one of the leading small museums of New England. The most important acquisitions are published in a bulletin, and a well-illustrated handbook (including some thirty excellent color plates, but with no descriptive text) was published in 1979.

Also celebrating its fiftieth anniversary, the gallery inaugurated a building campaign that will provide balancing wings at the rear of the original structure. This welcome addition of space for exhibitions and services should be completed about the time of the appearance of the present book.

Apart from its paintings and sculptures, the gallery offers fine displays of decorative arts, principally American, with emphasis on furniture of New Hampshire origin. Some of New England's leading silversmiths are also represented, notably John Coney (1652–1722) of Boston, in one of his best designs, a sugar box of the 1690s.

Two items of particular local interest are *Amoskeag Canal*,[15] painted in Manchester in 1948 by Charles Sheeler (1883–1965) on commission from the gallery, and the *Merino Ram Weather Vane* of c. 1855, possibly made in the metalwork shops of the Amoskeag Manufacturing Company. While Sheeler's image of Manchester's factories, celebrated for their architectural purity, is not quite so "immaculate" as his *Upper Deck*, discussed at the Fogg Art Museum (MA 132), there is a kind of

15

16

Roger Sherman Spartanism (CT 75) about this industrial scene. Yet it is more complex than it at first appears. The varieties of red and pink are subtle, as are the variations on that endlessly repeated shape, the rectangle. The most important of these, the rise in window height at the left, occurs in the building itself, but we can easily imagine that Sheeler would have invented it if it had not existed.

The *Ram Weather Vane*, with its lightning rod, is one of the largest of its kind (73 inches wide and 11 inches across the body), and one of the finest in design. According to tradition it came from a mid-nineteenth century woolen mill, and it is worth noting that the Merino strain of sheep was early introduced into America to improve the quality of the wool. The ram is made of two layers of welded sheet copper, and there are traces of the gold leaf that once covered it. In profile, note how the curve of the horns finds echoing ripples and droops along the underside. Not to be missed, however, is the broad-beamed frontal view, with its impression of great strength. Like so many of the Early American limners, designers of weather vanes remain anonymous.

From a pair of superb portraits, subjects unknown, by William Jennys (active 1795–1805), we have selected the *Portrait of a Woman* for illustration. Comparison with the *Reuben Hatch* at New London (CT 87), signed and dated 1802, will quickly indicate that the unsigned Manchester portraits are by the same hand. They can be safely dated in approximately the same year. Fetchingly ugly in her pink dress, with face tones of pink and much gray, this woman has the harsh but native dignity seen in Walker Evans's photographs of the Depression years. Her husband, likewise popping into view in his oval inner frame, is perhaps more conventionally portrayed, but his stringy hair is yet another instance of the uncompromising honesty of this gifted American painter.

As impressive as it is rare outside Italian museums and churches is an anonymous Tuscan painting of the *Madonna and Child*,[18] in tempera on

18

17

panel measuring 37 by 20 inches. Its date, c. 1275, places it near the time of the birth of Giotto (see MA 33) and some fifty years before Simone Martini's altarpiece at the Gardner Museum in Boston (MA 34). Its formula is wholly Byzantine, but a Florentine inflection already appears in the squatter proportions and in the relative emphasis on physical bulk. The scarlet mantle projects brilliantly from the surrounding greenish gray of the robe and coif. Originally the curtain behind the throne was dark green, while the upper background and the frame were coated with silver foil. The frame was rectangular, not semicircular as now: an original section remains above the Virgins's head. This image may be called half icon, half relief sculpture in its total effect. Already Tuscan art is moving in the direction of Giotto. On the basis of its style, the picture has been attributed to the Florentine master Meliore, or to his circle.

At the head of the main staircase hangs a magnificent *Gothic tapestry*[19] woven at Tournai about 1490. This is a well-known example, often illustrated in books on tapestry making. As was usually the case, it formed part of a series for the decoration of a large hall. Others in the series have been preserved, two of them in the Corcoran Gallery, Washington, D.C. The scene is generally identified as *The Visit of the Gypsies*. Arriving at the left, they are met by the lord and lady of the castle, but it is not at all certain that they will be admitted. A hunt is in progress high up in the background. The escutcheon at the top was added about 1600 by a new owner. The Gothic tapestry makers characteristically limited themselves to about thirty different wools, with the result that the colors, in which reds and blues predominate, stand out well at a distance. Similar results were obtained in medieval stained glass. Because the designers had no thought of natural illusion, they were free to make the decoration of a wall an occasion for creating an enchanted world. Sacheverell Sitwell chose this tapestry as his point of departure in writing "The Gothick North."

To what extent the North felt the influence of the Italian Renaissance may be seen in a comparison of Manchester's *Self-Portrait*[20] by Jan Gossaert, called Mabuse (c. 1478–1532), with the *Portrait of a Lady*[21]

19

20

by Lorenzo Costa of Ferrara (1460–1535). Both are about 18 inches high, and both were painted in oil on panel, although the Costa has been transferred to canvas (a difficult operation necessitated by warping and cracking of the original panel). The more squarish shape of the Italian picture (18 by 14 inches as against 17 by 12 for the Gossaert) corresponds to Italian-classical traditions as against Gothic verticality, as also seen in the architecture of the two regions.

Gossaert, whom we shall see again at Providence in an ambitious drawing of *Adam and Eve* (RI 10), started his career at Antwerp, but a trip to Italy about 1508 turned him from inherited Flemish forms toward uniting them with Italian ones. Identified as a self-portrait by two authorities independently, it can be dated around 1518–20. The eyes look as if into a mirror, while the right hand (assuming this is a mirror image) is hidden to disguise the fact that it is engaged with the pencil or brush. We can admire the skill of Gossaert's mannered Italianate nudes (RI 10), but only in his portraits do we sense that he was free from a desire to show off. Face and hand are equally expressive, and the several blacks contrast superbly with the red hat and the bright green ground.

Lorenzo Costa, after painting in Ferrara and Bologna, had the good fortune to be called to Mantua in 1506 by that great patroness of the arts, Duchess Isabella d'Este. He remained there until his death in 1535. The Currier's portrait was formerly thought to represent Eleonora Gonzaga, of the ruling family at Mantua, but in 1978 the gallery's *Bulletin* published a long study by John E. Schloder that demonstrated the error of such an identification, and through an elaborate study of Costa's known work set the date of the picture back from c. 1506, as previously believed, to c. 1497. Whoever the lady may be, she is shown against a black ground in a green dress with a red bodice and sleeves of brownish-red and yellow. Against this mass of hard color her delicate skin contrasts with stylish pallor. To keep it so, the artist has held the shadows to a minimum; he has achieved the desired sculptural effect through a web of thin lines (bodice, necklaces, headdress, wisps of

21

hair). It is worth looking closely to see how Costa has made them push inward and outward to model the form.

Compared with the Gossaert portrait, this Renaissance image is characteristically big in scale, solidly planted on its invisible base, aggressively modeled, and serenely confident, whereas Gossaert seems to look at himself through the eyes of one of Jan van Eyck's pious donors.

The *Madonna and Child* by Pietro Perugino (1445–1523) can match neither the expressiveness nor the strength of modeling of the *Sepulcrum Christi*, discussed at the Clark Art Institute (MA 250); but its authentication as a work of the master by a long list of experts would be difficult to refute. That it was long ago proclaimed to be the work of Raphael, however, may be taken to demonstrate the advance of modern connoisseurship. The picture has a distinguished provenance, almost back to the time of its execution, around 1500, and to the famed collection of Agostino Chigi for his Villa Farnesina in Rome. Truth to say, it is fully characteristic of Perugino's flaccid art; and thus it offers yet another reason to wonder how Perugino could have been totally responsible for the marvelous picture in Williamstown.

The *Holy Family*[22] by Joos van Cleve (1485–1540), born in the lower Rhenish town of his name but, like his contemporary Jan Gossaert, active in Antwerp, illustrates once again a Northerner's attempt to graft Italian humanism onto inherited traditions. Renaissance effects are found in the soft flesh modeling and in the Italianate column. Flemish elements remain in the precise detail, in Joseph's wooden pose (and his straw hat), in the foreground still life and the landscape background, in the Gothic hand of Joseph's scroll, and in the carved Gothic paneling below it. A similar composition is owned by the Metropolitan Museum of Art, New York. The suggested date of c. 1520–25 places the Currier's picture as almost exactly contemporary with Jan Gossaert's *Self-Portrait*.

By the seventeenth century, Italian painting was in full Baroque sway. In the *Martyrdom of St. Bartholomew*[23] by Mattia Preti (1613–69) the Currier Gallery has a potent example. A canvas over 6 feet square, it

22

23

dates from c. 1655–60. The head of the bearded old Saint has much in common with Bernini's clay head of *St. Jerome* at the Fogg Art Museum (MA 121), of approximately the same period. Born in Calabria, Preti studied in Rome under the strong influence of the followers of Caravaggio (see CT 12), and worked primarily in Naples. The Manchester painting was part of a triptych—probably the central element—which also represented the martyrdoms of Saints Peter and Paul. The massive figure of Bartholomew, his eyes turned to heaven, is dramatically spotlighted while his torturers go about their terrible work in half darkness. The Saint's right arm has already been flayed. As we have suggested in other instances, the power of the design—its clashing diagonals and its tight clusters of figures at the extremities—will come through with great force if the illustration is turned upside down. (It does so right side up, but you can easily overlook it as you explore the formidable interest of the details.) In the proper position note the power of the three heads at the lower right, one jutting forward, one erect, the third turned away. Of such "push-and-pull" combinations—to borrow a phrase from the modern abstractionist Hans Hofmann—Baroque art produces its explosive energy. It also exploits textural contrasts, as here in the opaque highlights as against the thinly applied darks that allow the grain of the canvas to show through. Seen against a cold greenish-blue sky of low intensity, the Baroque drama reaches a pitch seldom matched in seventeenth-century paintings in American museums.

That the spirit of the Baroque was not limited to martyrdoms, or to Italy, will quickly be discovered in a superb Dutch landscape, *View of Egmond-on-the-Sea*,[24] signed and dated 1648 by Jacob van Ruisdael (1628/9–82). A smallish (26 by 20 inches) oil on panel painted when the artist was only twenty years old, it prefigures his masterly marine at Boston (MA 74) by two decades. It is so highly regarded that in 1954 the Metropolitan Museum of Art included it in a memorable exhibition of "Dutch Painting in the Golden Age," the greater part of which was lent from major European collections. Among painters prior to Ruisdael, landscape was almost always conceived as the background to something else; in the century after him it fought a losing battle against the con-

24

ventions of the Rococo park, the classical ruin, or the storm-racked coast. *View of Egmond* is landscape as pure as those of Constable and Monet in the nineteenth century. Yet it is still touched by the medieval sense of wonder, in the artificially darkened foreground with its strange formations and shadowy figures—and the unforgettable tree. How it swirls around its axis, propelling us along the picture's serpentine course deep into the distance! Baroque? Indeed it is; in the disguise of nature this wildly contorted trunk is nothing less than a twisted column from Bernini's bronze *baldacchino* under the dome of St. Peter's.

Much of this spirit lingers in *The Storm*,[25] painted in 1759 by Claude-Joseph Vernet (1714–89). For all its headlong rush, however, the action seems more restricted to the surface than Ruisdael's movement of powerful masses into space. An early exponent of what was to become nineteenth-century Romanticism, Vernet was inspired more by the *idea* of nature untamed than by creative imagination. The canvas is choked with awe-provoking clichés of disaster: ships leaning at dangerous angles, a blasted tree (à la Salvator Rosa), a grim castle surmounting a lonely rock, lashing waves, gesticulating people, an expiring victim. A single hole of blue pokes through the leaden skies. What is lacking here is the *painter's* equivalent of James Thomson's apostrophe to Winter in his poem of 1726 ("Cogenial horrors, hail!"), or of the storm in the third movement of Beethoven's Sixth Symphony. Discussing a very different work by Vernet in the Louvre (*The Ponte Rotto, Rome*)—one that magically links Claude Lorrain with Camille Corot—Paul Jamot wrote that it shows "what he was capable of, had he been able to resist the dictates of fashion" (*La Peinture en France*; Paris: Plon, 1934).

As for Corot himself (1796–1875), the Currier owns a small masterpiece, *Grez-sur-Loing: Bridge and Church*[26] of the 1850s, slightly later than Yale's limpid *La Rochelle* (CT 78) and a quarter-century after Smith College's crystalline *Jumièges* (MA 177). Situated just south of

25

26

the forest of Fontainebleau, Grez attracted many painters of the Barbizon
School. Since Corot was one of the primary sources for the art of Claude
Monet (1840–1926) and the Currier also owns a major early work by
this leading Impressionist, *The Seine at Bougival*,[27] a comparison is appropriate. Despite the long interval between the births of the two artists,
the pictures are not far removed in time: the Corot is fairly late and the
Monet was probably painted in 1869 in the outlying Parisian village
frequented that year and later by Renoir (see MA 83). In both paintings
the space is fenced off by a series of small elements parallel to the picture surface. Monet works in a deeper space, but Corot is at pains to
emphasize the bridge and the church. Monet is dazzled by his new discovery of light and fresh color, to which the oil and watercolor sketches
of Constable may have contributed. The apple greens, rust reds, oranges,
and pale blues shine out from this world of slate and buff; and Monet
is on the verge of moving into the full Impressionism of the "rainbow
palette." It is possible to admire this stage of his art more than the later
realization; the point is mentioned because Monet's early work is too
easily passed off as a step toward something else. If he had died in 1870,
he would still rank as a master of consequence.

Corot worked at a lower emotional pitch, and his color intensities are
appropriately muted. Through his subtle "feathery" screen we are led
to his well-modeled architectural masses. The strongest light establishes
the not-quite-exact center of his composition. How dull a series of arches
parading left to right might have been! But Corot makes each one different, profits by the break left of center, and like the Little Dutch
masters he so admired discovers all manner of detail to enliven this long
link between the two extremes of his picture.

Before we move into the twentieth century, a listing of paintings
omitted with regret, and only because of restrictions of space, is inserted
here. For the seventeenth century, the large *Banquet of Anthony and
Cleopatra* by Jan de Bray of Haarlem, possibly alluding to the artist's
own marriage in the year he painted this picture; and a superb *Still Life*
of c. 1650 by an unknown Spanish artist more delicate and precise than
his formidable predecessor, van der Hamen y León (see MA 274). For

27

the eighteenth century, *The First Lessons in Love* by Jean-Baptiste Greuze, in which a miracle of painting overcomes the pettiness of its theme. For the early nineteenth century, the *Portrait of a Musician* by Pauline Auzou (1809), almost comparable to the work of Jacques Louis David (see MA 125), whose strong influence she felt; and John Constable's *Dedham Mill* (c. 1820), a bit smoother than usual, but already rich in the greens that helped liberate French landscape painting from the domination of Old Master browns. For American nineteenth-century landscape, excellent examples by Bierstadt, Birch, Cropsey, and a Heade (*Marshfield Meadows*) that rivals the one discussed at Bowdoin College (ME 14).

There are several fine American paintings from the first quarter of the twentieth century. Leading the list is a late portrait by Thomas Eakins, *Miss Florence Einstein* (1905, one year after Smith College's *Mrs. Edith Mahon*, MA 176). Robert Henri's *Girl*, c. 1910, is even more characteristic than Mount Holyoke's example (MA 207); Charles Demuth's watercolor of rooftops close to Williams's *Trees and Barns* of 1917 (MA 276); and Edward Hopper's *Bootleggers* of 1924 not yet in the full stride of Andover's *Manhattan Bridge Loop* (MA 20).

One would not ordinarily think of Walt Kuhn (see ME 42) and Georges Rouault together, but they were both born in the 1870s and the Currier's fine examples date from 1939 and represent circus people. *Lancer*, a healthy American girl, rather like a drum majorette dressed in red, white, and blue, contrasts strikingly with Rouault's *Wounded Clown*,[28] an unusually large oil-on-paper-on-Masonite measuring 6 by 4 feet. As so often happens in such comparisons, we see a brash new world juxtaposed with an introverted, complex old one. Both painters load the brush heavily, but it is Rouault who lingers over his strokes, introducing subtle variations within a color area, and so manipulating the textures as to provide a wonderful sense of light shining through from behind. Kuhn portrays his subject objectively, as he saw her; Rouault's three figures are somehow symbolic of the human condition. The ambiguity of his title is appropriate. Which clown is wounded? The old one, seated at the left as if exhausted? The young clown and/or

28

his companion, sadly preoccupied with the book they hold? We do not require an answer. Blacks play a major role among the dominant reds and blues of this picture. Heavily outlining the rich color areas, they help create the illusion that we are looking at a Gothic stained-glass window. They also model volumes: stomachs, knees, thighs. Behind the head of the old clown they hollow out an ominous cave.

Twenty years ago, to come upon Picasso's *Woman Seated in a Chair*,[29] a 51-by-38-inch composition of 1941, was an astonishing experience in the generally conservative atmosphere of this museum. Much has happened since to give it company, but still its *modernity* is here unsurpassed. We should perhaps point out that it was not a purchase but a gift in 1951, and an anonymous one. If the community has not wholly taken the lady to its heart, she at least serves as a reminder that time marches on. Picasso's precarious vertical constructions and the importance of the dagger shapes in his disquieting art for a disquieting era have been pointed out (see MA 185). Here the full range of color that we might find in the Alhambra is called into play, together with its superposition of patterns. The composition was influenced by Matisse in the big curves of the chair, binding together all these stacked angles. We hesitate to call this chair a Windsor, and we should never call this personage a Woman. The painting is an object in its own right, flat yet spacious, abstract yet sinister, gaudy yet harmonious; an optical jam session if you will, but featuring a star performer.

Another *Seated Woman*,[30] this time nude and with arms clasped behind her head, brings us to sculpture and to Picasso's chief rival in modernity, Henri Matisse (1869–1954). For evidence of modernity, contrast this bronze with Augustus Saint-Gaudens's lovely *Diana* of 1893 (NH 3), of which the Currier owns a small bronze replica. Purchased in 1964, the Matisse figure was completed in 1925 and cast in an edition of ten. In profile it exists in an imaginary square some 32 inches on a side; but it should be seen from many angles, for it is over a foot broad and the transitions as you walk around it are subtle indeed. Its vitality is extraordinary, emerging in part from the risky balance of the pose, in part from the powerful jut of the elbows and the raised

29

30

left knee, and perhaps most of all from the harsh shift of planes in the modeling itself. Such modeling relates directly to Matisse's painting, especially in the mid-1920s following a relaxed period of soft, rather indolent odalisques. It marked a return to his normally vigorous style, influenced from the start by the painting of Paul Cézanne.

In his ambitious monumental creations the modernism of Sir Jacob Epstein (1880–1959), New York–born but working in England from the age of twenty-five, is gross and now sadly dated. But as a portraitist Epstein was one of the leading figures of his generation. He intensified the realism of Rodin (see MA 308), giving it an almost Etruscan effect of actuality. *Portrait of Kitty*,[31] the third version of a likeness of his daughter, was modeled in 1957. Its green patina is especially effective in catching the light on its churned surfaces. The deeply hollowed pupils give strong focus to the gaze, as does the tousled bobbed hair. We are made very conscious that this head was conceived and executed in clay; and the superb casting does not betray that origin. As such, the precariousness of the head's support on a very thin neck and very narrow shoulders is all the more remarkable and expressive. Through kinetic means a feeling of empathy is somehow enlisted.

The American sculptor Dimitri Hadzi, born in New York in 1921, gained international acceptance during the 1960s. *Floating Helmets*, a major bronze of 1965, has a prominent position in the sculpture garden of the Yale University Art Gallery (a smaller study for it is owned by Mount Holyoke College). In 1978 the Currier purchased *Hephaestus III*,[32] a bronze of 1971/2, 6 feet tall, the second cast of an edition of seven. Unlike Epstein's *Kitty III*, this piece was designed for its ultimate realization in metal—and very heavy metal indeed. The great double-ax shapes, though irregular, evoke memories of ancient Crete. If Hephaestus (the Roman Vulcan) frequented Mt. Olympus rather than Mt. Ida, and the volcanic islands of the Aegean Sea and Sicily rather than Crete itself, we shall not quarrel, for the forms are most appropriate to the god of fire and metalwork. Their power is portentous; such images can suggest

31

32

destruction. Too many people, hurrying into Avery Fisher Hall at Lincoln Center to hear the New York Philharmonic, have not noticed in the lobby Hadzi's *K. 458 The Hunt,* inspired by a Mozart quartet.

In our survey of paintings in the Currier Gallery we ended on the theme of modernity with Picasso's *Woman Seated in a Chair.* But that work dates from 1941; in the interim modernity has spawned new forms in painting as in sculpture. In the past few years, the gallery has been active in filling in the gap with admirable purchases of paintings by such artists as Olitzki, Anuszkiewicz, Albers, and Gottlieb. Adolf Gottlieb (1903–73) was a leading member of the so-called New York Abstract Expressionists. His 6-by-8-foot canvas, painted in 1956, bears the title *From Midnight to Dawn.*[33] As always in such art, we should resist the temptation to "read" the painting from associations suggested by its title —which was almost certainly an afterthought. (The alternative would have been *Number X, 1956,* but Gottlieb preferred more specific iden- tifications.) His canvas is a huge, dark blue field, varied in texture like a Mark Rothko, with light seeming to shine through from behind, and boldly marked with strokes of deep black. Activity sputters across the top—in a frieze suspended over the void.

33

Vermont

Vermont

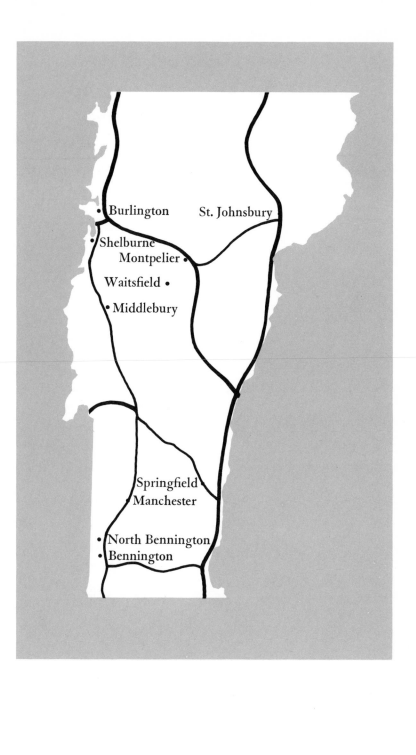

Bennington Museum

Location: West Main St. (Vermont Route 9), 1 mile west of Route 9 inter-
section with U.S. 7
Telephone: (802) 442-2180
Hours: 9-5 daily, including Sun. and holidays; but closed December, January,
and February, and on Thanksgiving Day
Admission: Charged. Ⓗ but phone ahead

Primarily a museum of southwestern Vermont history, with a supporting
research library, this well-appointed building also serves as an art
museum. It contains mementos of the Battle of Bennington (1777),
an array of U.S. flags (including the oldest one in existence, now so
faded as paradoxically to resemble a modern Jasper Johns version in
gray oils), military collections, costumes, the largest collection anywhere
of ceramics made in Bennington, a superbly shown and very extensive
display of American glass, fine furniture, household items, and dolls
and toys.

Early American paintings include Ralph Earl's *Portrait of Captain
Elijah Dewey*, commander of the Bennington militia at the Battle of
Bennington (his house, now the nearby Walloomsac Inn, appears in the
distance); William Jenny's *Portraits of Governor Paul Brigham and
His Wife* (comparable in quality to CT 87 and NH 17); and several
oils by William Morris Hunt (unfortunately skied and in need of
cleaning).

An especially good weather vane featuring horse and driver came
from the Putnam barn in the vicinity. Outstanding among the sculptures,
however, are two animal groups by Antoine Louis Barye (1796–1875)
and a small bronze by Auguste Rodin (1840–1917). *Leopard with
Prey*,[1] about 3 feet long and the larger of the Barye bronzes, was
modeled in 1850. This version was exhibited at the Paris World's Fair
in 1889. While many New England museums represent this major
sculptor in small bronzes, few can show him at a scale that does full
justice to his power. It is a commonplace to call him the alter ego in
sculpture of Eugène Delacroix (1798–1863); but it would be equally
appropriate to reverse the two names. Comparison with MA 120 will

1

indicate the connection. Exact contemporaries and lifelong friends, they studied wild animals together in the Paris zoo (better known as the Jardin des Plantes). The strength of the leopard in this superb design finds expression in Baroque forms whose source leads back to Bernini and the seventeenth century. Traces of gilding persist in this piece, but its true "color" comes from its carefully marked surfaces, modeled as only a sculptor knows how to model them, and then drawn upon.

The little Rodin bronze, only a foot high, is a greenish patinated cast of a plaster in the Musée Rodin in Paris, there listed as *Petite Ombre, Numéro 1* and dated 1888. A second "Small Shade," strained and emaciated like the first, likewise found its place in the sculptor's vast project for the *Gates of Hell*, inspired by Dante's *Inferno*. (For another work connected with this project, see MA 308, a head that, reworked, became a portrait of Eleanora Duse but is known as *Sorrow*. That title, while also appropriate for the Bennington figure, has the disadvantage of causing confusion.) Bennington's *Petite Ombre* is deeply expressive from all points of view, and like the *Leopard* bronze of Barye, by whom Rodin was profoundly influenced, it should be exhibited free-standing in order to allow such inspection. As for this particular bronze cast, which bears the stamp of the great Rudier foundry, it is difficult to tell when it was made. Casts of Rodin's plasters were produced in his lifetime and frequently after his death; the posthumous ones did not always record the ultimate subtleties of the original.

Sculpture of a very different kind appears in a 10-foot *Monumental Piece* created by Christopher Fenton's U.S. Pottery Company of Bennington for the 1853 Crystal Palace Exposition in New York. It incorporates most of the known processes for which Bennington ceramics became celebrated. The Madonna at the summit and the bust of Fenton are of unglazed white Parian ware; pedestals and pillars are of multicolored glazed flint enamel; the molded columns lower down are in the mottled brown glaze properly called Rockingham rather than Bennington; and the bottom section is of scrodded ware worked to resemble veined marble. Aesthetically this creation leaves something to be desired, but it is perhaps captious to say so.

A carved and gilded wooden *Eagle* of 1795, nobly impressive, will not be overlooked by the visitor; but a painted *British Drum* of 1757 could well escape the attention. This object was captured at the Battle of Bennington; its figured circumference is not uninteresting.

An extra attraction here is the gallery of paintings by "Grandma Moses" (Anna Mary Robertson, 1860–1961), who took up painting in the early 1900s, but did not make a career of it until 1938, at the age of seventy-eight. In her remaining twenty-three years she produced some fifteen hundred pictures. In 1972 the old schoolhouse that she had attended more than a century before was moved from nearby Eagle Bridge, N.Y., to form a separate extension of the Bennington Museum. It had been fitted out as the Grandma Moses Schoolhouse Museum by the artist's son, Forrest Moses, and his wife. The memorabilia include the stained-glass window of the W. D. Thomas pharmacy in Hoosick Falls, N.Y., where she sold her first paintings (at three dollars and five dollars, depending on the size). Since she lived in Bennington for eight years, from 1927 to 1935, it is fitting that her memorial should be here. She died nationally honored, and particularly acclaimed by another amateur artist, Dwight D. Eisenhower.

Visitors to the museum should not fail to visit the nearby First Congregational Church, a gem of the Federal Style built in 1806 by Lavius Fillmore, and its graveyard with excellent examples of the stonecutter's craft.

In the fall of 1981, announcement was made of the acquisition of Ralph Earl's important, large, and very fine *Landscape of Bennington*, painted in 1798. The gambrel-roofed house of Capt. Elijah Dewey, whose portrait is mentioned above, appears again in the landscape view of the original town. Earl's portrait of Mrs. Elijah Dewey will also be added to the collection.

Bennington College

Location: From Route 7 north of Bennington, exit west on Route 67A and follow to the entrance to the campus, on the right
Hours: Daily except from mid-December to mid-March, when the college is not in session
Admission: Free

An important center for the study and practice of contemporary modern art, Bennington College has resisted a policy of forming a permanent collection. Through the years it has attracted leading figures as instructors, and its alumnae (and now alumni)—including Helen Frankenthaler (see MA 222)—have made their mark. The Usdan Gallery, located off the entrance to the college's vast Visual and Performing Arts Center, offers frequently changing exhibitions, primarily of the work of artists in New York City. Scattered about the grounds and in various college buildings, however, the visitor may come upon work by such sculptors as David Smith, Anthony Caro, and Isaac Witkin, and paintings by Helen Frankenthaler, Pat Adams, Paul Feeley, Kenneth Noland, and Jules Olitski.

The college owns a bronze *Portrait Bust of John Dewey* by Sir Jacob Epstein (see NH 31), one of two such casts of a clay original of 1927. The other was purchased by Dewey's students at Columbia University and presented to Teachers College. As the guiding spirit of progressive education, Dewey became a kind of father figure for Bennington College at the time of its opening in 1932. Of his bust, Epstein has written, "Dewey's son-in-law said . . . that I had made him look like a 'Vermont horse dealer.' This was not a bad characterization, as Professor Dewey came from Vermont; and he pleased me with his Yankee drawl and seeming casualness. He was a man absolutely straightforward, simple, and lovable in character. Professor Dewey said of his bust that it pleased him and he 'hoped he looked like it' " (*Let There Be Sculpture*; New York: Putnam, 1940).

The Park-McCullough House

Location: Park St., near the center of town; from Route 7 north of Bennington exit west on Route 67A

Hours: May 1-October 31, Mon.-Fri. 10-4, Sun. 12-4

Admission: Charged. Ⓗ projected

For a description of this great house, built in 1865 of white clapboards over brick and containing thirty-two rooms in its high-ceilinged three stories, see the companion volume in this series, *A Guide to Historic Houses of New England*, by Margaret Supplee Smith. On the lawn, do not miss the dollhouse replica of the cupola atop this imposing pile.

A hundred years after its construction, the house was opened as a museum and has developed into an active cultural center in the community. The elaborate furnishings are notable, and they include paintings by Kensett and Bierstadt of the Hudson River School.

Robert Hull Fleming Museum, University of Vermont

Location: Colchester Ave. Take exit 14W off I-89; from Williston Rd. turn left onto East Ave., go to the end and turn left onto Colchester Ave. The museum is about 200 yards farther
Hours: Mon.-Fri. 9-5, Sat., Sun. 1-5; closed on national holidays
Admission: Free. Ⓗ in progress

The present Neo-Classical building, dedicated in 1931 as a memorial to Robert Hull Fleming, an alumnus of the university, contains collections of art and archaeology, geology, paleontology, and natural history. It provides eight galleries on two floors adjoining a marble entrance court. The art collections have developed from an original "cabinet of curiosities" of 1826. While the Shelburne Museum surpasses them in the quality of its paintings and in American folk art, the Fleming Museum still ranks as the largest in Vermont and the one with the greatest coverage of world art. It is especially rich in the art of primitive cultures, and no other museum in the state regularly open to the public offers so rich a sampling of modern art.

Near the entrance the visitor will find a superb example of ancient Assyrian relief sculpture, a life-size image of a winged human deity from the Palace of Ashurnazirpal (883–859 B.C.). It is similar to reliefs from the same site owned by Amherst, Bowdoin, Dartmouth, Middlebury, and Williams colleges. The group as a whole is discussed in the section on Amherst College (MA 1).

A Gandharan *Head of the Buddha*, in black schist some 11 inches high, rivals in quality the full figure discussed at Yale University (CT 64).

The collection of so-called primitive art includes a wide range of examples from North, Central, and South America, Africa, the Asian mainland, the Philippines, and the South Pacific. Many were given by the painter Henry Schnakenberg, several of whose works are owned by the museum.

The masterpiece of this distinguished assemblage is a brass *Head of a Princess*[2] from Benin (Nigeria), of the sixteenth or seventeenth century.

2

The very broad collar extending to the mouth abruptly defines the cylindrical shape, while the conical hairdo, curving forward, echoes the prominent bulge of the forehead and the sharp projection of the nose. The features, simply delineated, are kept subordinate to the shape of the head as a whole. Most African sculpture is carved from wood, but the Benin kingdom, presumably under European influence, developed metal casting by the lost-wax process to a very high degree of craftsmanship. The classic description of the process itself is contained in the *Autobiography of Benvenuto Cellini* (Book II, chapters 75–78). The event —the casting of the *Perseus and Medusa*—occurred in 1550, but the manuscript was not published until 1728, well after the execution of the Benin sculptures. For Cellini, see MA 42; and for further discussion of the art of the Benin kingdom, see the section on the Peabody Museum of Harvard University.

The conical top of the Burlington head appears only on princesses (or queens). The head thus reaches a height of 15 inches, as against the 10½-inch height of an equally superb male example at the Peabody Museum. Both the neck and the Princess's high coiffure are bound in strands of coral; rosettes are set at her temples. As is customary in such heads, there is an opening at the top for the insertion of an elephant's tusk. During 1980 an exhibition, "Treasures of Ancient Nigeria: Legacy of 2,000 Years," selected by the Nigerian Federal Department of Antiquities, was shown in Detroit, San Francisco, and New York. It included heads of this kind, plaques like our MA 143, and work in terra-cotta, ivory, and stone. While Benin metal sculptures are generally referred to as bronzes, brass is a more accurate term.

Archaeological interests at the University of Vermont have not slighted local finds. The *Colchester Jar*,[3] discovered in 1825, came from a site less than ten miles north of Burlington. It was apparently left behind by New York Iroquois on a hunting trip to Vermont. In a letter of June 12, 1827, Luther Loomis described how it was found by Captain John Johnson "of whom I bought it yesterday. . . . If you think it worthy a place in the College of Nat. Hist. you will please accept it from your Humbl. Servt."

Such Indian pottery was made by the women, who used a paste of clay and powdered feldspar, mica, quartz, and other materials. When the basic shape of the jar was built up, it was finished with a finer clay

3

surface. After several days of drying, the design was scratched in, then fired.

The museum's extensive collection of paintings and drawings is strongest in the American field, but it includes two oils by Corot, a drawing of horses by Delacroix (and small bronzes by his colleague Barye—see VT 1), and English portraits by Michael Wright (seventeenth century), Kneller, Romney, Joseph Wright of Derby, and Lawrence, in addition to the Thomas Hudson *Portrait of Miss Ann Isted*,[4] which we now consider.

One of England's most influential painters, Hudson (1701–79) trained or indirectly affected the work of such varied talents as Sir Joshua Reynolds, Joseph Wright of Derby (see MA 152), and Joseph Blackburn (see ME 11), making his influence felt on both sides of the Atlantic. Yet his importance as a creative artist need not be exaggerated. To speak truthfully, his work is more competent than inspired. Hudson's rather tame variation on the prevalent Rococo style is nonetheless interesting because it demonstrates that the sources of High Georgian art were relatively plain and modest, as was likewise the case with painting in the American colony. Miss Isted's silver-gray dress with its blue ribbons contrasts well with the red chair and curtain, but without the intensity of John Singleton Copley (1738–1815). Copley's early career in Boston (see Deerfield, page 216) was developing at just the same time that Hudson painted Miss Isted (1756).

A portrait of about 1758 by John Wollaston well represents American Colonial painting, as do miniatures by James Peale and Edward G. Malbone in the Federal period. The mid-nineteenth-century Vermont portraitist Horace Bundy is seen in a characteristically sober pair. American landscape is here in some quantity, with good examples by Bierstadt, Blakelock, Cole, Sanford Gifford, Hinkley, and Wyant.

The Scratching Tree,[5] painted in 1848 by Thomas H. Hinkley (1813–1896), is composed like the idyllic pastoral scenes of the Hudson

4

5

River School, but its minuteness of detail and disarming insistence on what the bull is doing echo the work of such seventeenth-century Dutch painters as Paulus Potter, whose celebrated *Young Bull* (The Hague) has been aptly described as being as effective as it is prosaic. That Hinkley was subject to well-established formulae is shown by similarities between the Burlington landscape and one owned by Colby College, Waterville, Maine, painted in the following year.

As for the German-born American still-life painter Severin Roesen (active 1848–71), we have an embarrassment of riches as between the university's large *Fruit on Table*[6] and an equally fine version at the nearby Shelburne Museum. Little is known about Roesen's early training in his homeland, but his endless patience with detail seems a natural inheritance. Totally at variance with still lifes of such classic restraint as those of Chardin (see MA 216), and of such unobtrusiveness as those of Thomas Badger (see ME 36), Roesen gives us a galaxy that could be called Baroque were it not for the brittle edges and wiry precision of all these forms. Color runs to high intensities and rhythm to rapid movement. The wonder is that, turned upside down, the illustration shows that this profusion is visually coherent—that is, more than the sum of its parts.

From the American twentieth century you will find here drawings by Peggy Bacon and Isabel Bishop, a watercolor of 1915 by Charles Demuth (see MA 276), a pastel by Preston Dickinson, a wash drawing by William Kienbusch, several watercolors and drawings by Reginald Marsh (see VT 8) and by the Vermont painter-composer Carl Ruggles, and—from the very modern end of the spectrum—an oil by Ilya Bolotowsky (born 1907). *White Abstraction,*[7] 37 by 19 inches, painted in 1934/5, is published in Barbara Rose, *American Art Since 1900* (New York: Praeger, 1967, page 146). In the 1930s painters like Fritz Glarner and Josef Albers were also working in a vein distantly inspired by Piet Mondrian (see CT 85) and also related to compositions of the late 1920s by Pablo Picasso, such as *The Studio,* in the Museum of Modern Art. By the 1950s Bolotowsky moved closer to Glarner's so-called relational paintings (e.g., Glarner's enormous mural in the lobby of the Time-Life Building, New York City) and to their primal source, Piet Mondrian. Mondrian had led the way toward their own goal, an art totally divorced from the illusionistic representation of nature.

6

7

Southern Vermont Art Center

Location: Off West Road
Hours: July 4 to mid-October, Tues.-Sat. 10-5, Sun. 12-5; open Mon. if a holiday
Admission: Charged

The beautiful Manchester-Dorset region has long attracted artists of high competence and generally conservative stripe. A group of them incorporated in 1933 and inaugurated summer exhibitions that have become a major attraction of the area. In 1950 Southern Vermont Artists purchased their present attractive quarters, consisting of a large house and 375 acres with an imposing view eastward to the Green Mountains. Eleven of the original twenty-eight rooms were converted into galleries, and the studio-barn was refitted for classes in art instruction. In 1956 the Louise Ryals Arkell Pavilion opened for its annual series of musical concerts and film showings.

Through the years a permanent collection has been developed, with emphasis on the work of Vermont-associated painters, sculptors, print-makers, and photographers. Apart from Reginald Marsh, whom we shall discuss, the more established painters seen here are Carl Ruggles, Eugene Speicher, Peter Hurd, John Steuart Curry, Herbert Meyer, Dong Kingman, and Ogden Pleissner, whose large watercolor *Normandy Farm* is especially noteworthy. Sculptors include Simon Moselsio and Ossip Zadkine.

On the Bowery,[8] a 1946 watercolor and gouache measuring 27 by 40 inches, is a characteristically powerful work by Reginald Marsh (1898–1954) in a style developed in the Depression years that effectively expressed the prevailing spirit of the times. The New York Bowery became a favorite subject, and he never lost interest in it. Crowds of bathers at Coney Island also took on artistic significance under the magic of Marsh's brush. Unlikely as it may seem, both themes assumed a kind of grandeur under the inspiration of Michelangelo—not so much the Michelangelo of the Sistine Ceiling as the later and wilder Michelangelo of the *Last Judgment*. An ashen hue streaked with dissonant color, strong rhythmic connections between figures, and vigorous brushwork are major elements in Marsh's art.

8

The Johnson Gallery, Middlebury College

Location: At junction of Routes 7 and 30; turn west on Route 125 to bottom of hill below marble Catholic church, turn right, then second left up the hill to student parking lot B

Hours: Mon.-Fri., Sun. 12-5; Sat. 9-12, 1-5; closed during college vacations

Admission: Free. Ⓗ

Although Middlebury is one of New England's older colleges (opened 1800), its art museum is one of the youngest (opened 1968). An acquisition of the 1850s, an Assyrian relief from the Palace of Ashurnazirpal (see MA 1) is still shown in Munroe Hall rather than in the new gallery, where much of the available space is normally occupied by temporary exhibitions.

Near the museum entrance is a stainless-steel sculpture, 12 feet high, by George Rickey (see MA 163), *Two Open Rectangles/Excentric, Variation VI*, of 1976. Within, the permanent collection is strongest in small sculptures, of which we shall consider four examples. There are also landscapes by Kensett and Théodore Rousseau (Barbizon School, 1812–67); a landscape drawing by Fragonard; an extensive collection of Old Master and modern prints; African sculptures; and Far Eastern paintings, sculptures, and porcelains. A large sixteenth-century painting, *Judith with the Head of Holofernes*, is an interesting "problem piece": probably but not necessarily Italian, not authentic Bronzino or Parmigianino, yet impressive in design, drawing, and color. Like Pirandello's Six Characters, it is in search of an author.

In addition to our four sculpture selections, the following are noteworthy: the George Rickey already mentioned; a Calder mobile (*Black, Two Discs in Air*, c. 1960); a small South German wood *Madonna* of the first half of the eighteenth century; *Jaguar Devouring a Hare*, a bronze by Antoine Louis Barye (see VT 1); and a bronze cast of Falguière's *Diana*, of which we discuss the marble version at Wellesley College (MA 238).

In including the marble *Bust of the Greek Slave*,[9] by Hiram Powers

9

(born at Woodstock, Vt., 1805, died in Florence 1873), we make a flagrant exception to our policy to discuss only unique works of art. But the *Greek Slave* (marble of 1846 in the Corcoran Gallery, Washington; one of 1851 at Yale University; four others known, including the "original" of 1843 in an English private collection) was so popular that Powers and his many assistants were kept busy meeting the demand. The situation resembles that of Gilbert Stuart's "Athenaeum" Portraits of George Washington—the more so when we consider that the *Greek Slave* generated three additioral marble replicas at two-thirds size (all posthumous, but carved by Powers's assistants), and the list of marble replicas of the bust reaches a total of no less than eighty in Donald M. Reynolds's doctoral thesis (Columbia University, 1975). At a height of 24 inches, these are at two-thirds the size of that portion of the original figure. Replicas identical to the Middlebury bust will be found at the Berkshire Museum, Pittsfield; the Addison Gallery of American Art, Andover; and a smaller one at the St. Johnsbury (Vt.) Athenaeum—to mention only New England collections open to the public.

However that may be, Hiram Powers is without much doubt Vermont's most distinguished sculptor, the *Greek Slave* is his most celebrated work, and he lived at a time when both sculptors and painters were delighted to keep abreast of the demand for replicas by employing specially trained assistants, usually adding final touches themselves to the approved product. Why, then, eliminate the *Greek Slave*?

We should note that Powers, like many ambitious Americans, established his studio abroad, and that from 1837 to his death he worked in Florence. If his glistening white nude females are safely within the Neoclassical formulae set by Antonio Canova and other sculptors well before 1800, they have an American air of bland moral purity, as if created by an artist determined not to be seduced like the mythical Pygmalion. To return to the question of mass production: Powers's signature, under the back, means only that the work came from his studio.

Head of a Gaul,[10] a fierce-looking bronze 14 inches high (including the base), is signed by the great progenitor of French Romantic sculpture, François Rude (1784–1855). His place in the history of sculpture is roughly equivalent to that of Théodore Géricault (1791–1824) in painting, except that Géricault's life was cut short much earlier. Comparison with the latter's *Madman-Kidnaper* (1822/3) at Springfield

10

(MA 218) or his wash drawing of a *Negro Soldier* at the Fogg Art Museum (MA 127) will illuminate the connection.

The plaster for the Middlebury head is in the Musée de Dijon, and illustrated in the handbook by P. Gasq and F. Marion (Paris: Henri Laurens, 1934, page 47). Dijon, where Rude was born, has in recent years remodeled a former Baroque church as a special and additional Rude Museum, and here can be seen full-scale plaster casts of his work, including one of his vast stone relief for the Arc de Triomphe in Paris, representing the *Departure of the Volunteers in 1792*. The Gaul in question is the main figure beneath the allegorical flying image of War. The great arch was originally commissioned by Napoleon in 1806, but not completed until 1836. Rude received the order for all four sculptures on the main facades, but through political intrigue three of them went to inferior competitors. Nevertheless, "La Marseillaise" commands the view as you approach up the Champs-Elysées, on the right side of the arch. Over 40 feet high, it was completed between 1833 and 1836. Whether Middlebury's obviously much smaller bronze of the Gaul's head was made from the original plaster model in Rude's lifetime, or later in the nineteenth century, is a specialist's problem that awaits solution. The demand for such small replicas was not of the immensity of that for the *Greek Slave*. If we break our general rule once again, by including this replica, our reason for doing so is partly that Rude's work is rarely seen in the United States, partly that the Arc de Triomphe relief is his masterpiece, partly that the Gaul's head dominates its exact center, and partly that the quality of this particular bronze is high. As in the case of Hiram Powers's *Bust of the Greek Slave*, the artist's signature is no guarantee that it was made in his lifetime.

With the *Head of Pierre de Wiessant*[11] by Auguste Rodin (1840–1917) we have no such problems. A cast in plaster and plasteline, it was given by Rodin himself to a friend, the engraver Jean Paricot. Numerous versions of this head exist in various sizes and media as studies for one of the six figures in Rodin's celebrated *Burghers of Calais*, a commission on which he worked from 1884 to 1887. The story of his trials and frustrations with the authorities of Calais, who desired a monument to

11

the city's heroic struggle against the English in the Hundred Years War, is recounted in detail by Albert Elsen in his *Rodin* (Museum of Modern Art, 1963). The installation, which did not take place until 1895, was doubly ironic. By an act of local pique, the group was not placed, as originally intended, in front of Calais's medieval town hall, but in a public garden; and elevated on a high pedestal, not on the tradition-breaking low base that Rodin rightly felt would emphasize the immediacy of his image. The six burghers who offered themselves as hostages to save their city were not allegorical abstractions, but local citizens. Not until 1926 was the monument placed where Rodin desired and on the low base he designed for it. A knoll in front of the town hall provides all the elevation it needs.

I have omitted so far any indication of the size of the Middlebury head. As I write these words, I am looking at an 8-by-10-inch photograph, and its impact is nothing less than majestic. The same is true of the work itself, although it measures less than 4 inches in height. From the 85-inch height of the final monument, I estimate the head of Pierre de Wiessant at about 12 inches. Except for its size, it resembles Middlebury's little masterpiece with minor differences. A date of close to 1884 seems appropriate for the latter. On page 75 of his *Rodin*, Elsen illustrates a bronze version of the head at heroic size, owned by the Cleveland Museum of Art, which he dates as "by 1889." In other words, this particular head is probably an "afterthought"—of the same character as various heads by Picasso that followed his mural painting of 1937, *Guernica*, and not to be confused with the many studies that preceded that great composition. The Cleveland head carries the expression of inner torment still further than the Middlebury head or the figure in the completed monument. The sequence here is paralleled in Rodin's *Walking Man* (M A 190), developed from an earlier figure, as we have seen in the section on the Smith College Museum of Art. At three greatly differing sizes—under 4 inches (Middlebury), about 12 inches (completed monument), and 32 inches (Cleveland)—the head of Pierre de Wiessant remains faithful to Rodin's early conception of it and yet becomes more deeply expressive. At whatever size he worked, however, Rodin's imagination operated on a plane of grandeur.

Bimbo Malato (Sick Child),[12] a wax over plaster bust of 1893 by Medardo Rosso, completes our survey of Middlebury's small but dis-

12

tinguished group of sculptures. Born in Turin in 1858 and working in Paris in the 1880s and 1890s, Rosso had a relationship with Rodin, his senior by eighteen years, that has puzzled and intrigued scholars for a long time. We know that he arrived in Paris in 1884, became an assistant to Dalou (see MA 239), and met Rodin; that he soon returned to Milan (where he had grown up and received early training) but exhibited at the annual Paris Salons; that by 1889 he was back in Paris; that in 1894 Rodin wrote him an enthusiastic letter after visiting his studio; and that from 1890 to 1910 Rosso enjoyed an international reputation second only to Rodin's. When Rodin exhibited his plaster of the final (clothed) version of the *Balzac*, Rosso became convinced that Rodin "had taken a great deal" from him. This charge, otherwise unspecified, did not improve the relationship; but it is possible that it contained a general truth. A look through Margaret Scolari Barr's book on Rosso (Museum of Modern Art, 1963) will demonstrate similarities in the Impressionistic surfaces and the shadowy-garbed figures of the period 1893 to 1895. On the other hand, Rosso's debt to Rodin from the very outset of his career is obvious. What seems to have happened is that a normal relationship between two highly gifted artists was spoiled by lack of generosity on the part of an older titan and by hypersensitivity on the part of the younger man.

However that may be, Middlebury has been fortunate in acquiring Rosso's haunting image of a sick child, one that would make an interesting comparison with Edvard Munch's various representations in oil and lithography of his invalid sister—beginning as early as 1885. Rosso's special technique of modeling the top surfaces in wax over a plaster base is wonderfully appropriate for expressing impermanence and flux; but the moment in time that he caught was not joyous, as in the paintings of the Impressionists, but one of tormented uncertainty and disintegration—an Impressionist technique, but used for Expressionist ends. It does not seem irrelevant to add that Middlebury's bust was once owned by the philosopher Ludwig Josef Johann Wittgenstein.

Sheldon Museum

Location: Park Street
Hours: June to the end of September, Mon.-Sat. 10-5; October to the end of May, Tues. and Thurs. 1-5; closed Sundays
Admission: Charged

The museum was founded by Henry Sheldon in 1881 in an early nine-teenth-century brick house, to exhibit Vermont life at various times in its history. A modern rearrangement includes paintings and furnishings from about 1780 to about 1890. There is an emphasis on folkways, on the tools people have used, the clothes they wore, their books, games, medicines; on the essentials and the trivia of human existence.

From the point of view of the present book, the most interesting items are two portraits by William Jennys, who flourished in the Connecticut River Valley in the 1790s and early 1800s, of the wife and the daughter of Gamaliel Painter, a founder of Middlebury College. There is also a modern copy of Jennys's portrait of Painter himself, of which the original hangs in the office of the president of the college. We have discussed this expressive portraitist in examples at New London (CT 87) and Manchester (NH 17), and outlined his connection with Richard Jennys, who was either his father or older brother, in the section on the Connecticut Historical Society. It is interesting to find him working as far north as central Vermont.

Behind the museum a well-appointed research library serves students and scholars.

Thomas Waterman Wood Art Gallery

Location: Kellogg-Hubbard Library, 135 Main Street
Hours: Tues.-Sat. 12-4; in summer, Tues.-Fri. 12-4, Sat. 9-1
Admission: Free

More than a hundred paintings by the Montpelier painter Thomas Waterman Wood (1823–1903) are preserved here. After training under Chester Harding and study in Paris, Wood practiced in New York and as far afield as Kentucky before returning to Montpelier, where he opened a gallery to exhibit his own work and that of some of his contemporaries. The collection was moved from Wood's old house to the second floor of the Kellogg-Hubbard Library. In addition to works by nineteenth-century painters like Asher Durand and Alexander Wyant, the collection now includes paintings by such twentieth-century artists as Joseph Stella and Reginald Marsh (see VT 8).

Wood specialized in portraiture and genre scenes. His hard style of painting and his observant eye were well suited to his descriptive intention.

The Vermont Museum

Location: 109 State Street (near the state capitol)
Hours: Mon.-Fri. 8-4:30, except legal holidays; during July, August, and foliage season also open Sat., Sun. 10-5
Admission: Free ("small donation appreciated"). Ⓗ by Taylor St. entrance

Described as "a history museum dedicated to telling the Vermont story," The Vermont Museum succeeds admirably in fulfilling that task. It is housed on the first floor of the New Pavilion, built soon after the razing of the old, mansard-roofed Pavilion Hotel, of 1870 vintage, and designed to resemble it. The Vermont Historical Society moved its headquarters here in 1971, and for the first time in its 138 years of existence had a museum properly equipped to display its wide-ranging collections. These include some good portraits from the first half of the nineteenth century, country furniture, textiles, glass, pottery, and metalware.

The rear of the exhibition area opens onto the foyer of a modern office building, and here—as well as in the nearby state-capitol complex —you will find modern paintings and sculptures acquired by the Vermont Council on the Arts. A large landscape, *Champlain Valley* (1976/7, 33 by 84 inches) by Thelma Appel, who worked in the Bennington area for some years before moving to New York City, achieves the difficult combination of surface interest through linear brush strokes and an impression of deep space without resort to perspective or a horizon line. The range of color is exhilarating, as fresh as a Schubert song.

Elsewhere in the complex is a big stainless-steel sculpture[13] by Isaac Witkin (born 1936), formerly a member of the art faculty of Bennington College, but now centered in New York. *Spill XII*, measuring

13

76 by 116 inches in height and width, dates from 1976. Designed like rings of fire receding in depth, it is one of a series utilizing spills collected from a steel factory and assembled according to the dictates of the artist's imagination. The elements are patinated with varying acid combinations to produce colors and textures that have the appearance of being brushed as in a painting. Witkin has exhibited widely and enjoys an international reputation. Other examples of his work are at the Massachusetts Institute of Technology, the Hirshhorn Museum in Washington, and the Tate Gallery in London.

Locations of works acquired by the Vermont Council on the Arts are subject to change, and inquiry at its offices at 136 State Street (not far from The Vermont Museum) is advisable.

The St. Johnsbury Athenaeum and Art Gallery

Location: 30 Main Street at Eastern Avenue, junction of U.S. 2 and U.S. 5
Hours: Mon. and Fri. 10-8, Tues.-Thurs. 10-5, Sat. 10-2
Admission: Free

The handsome library building, completed in 1871 from designs by John Davis Hatch of New York, and its gallery wing, completed two years later, were the gift of Governor Horace Fairbanks, whose fortune derived from the invention of the platform scale by Thaddeus Fairbanks of St. Johnsbury. While the Art Gallery is not the oldest in the United States—the gallery of the Wadsworth Atheneum in Hartford, for example, dates from 1842—it may well be the oldest still in its original form.

An attractive illustrated catalogue of the collection lists some ninety paintings and nine marbles. With paintings superimposed two and three deep and some displayed on easels, and with mauve-textured walls broken by dark green pilasters ornamented in gold with classical motifs, the ensemble sets a tone that has strong nostalgic appeal in an age accustomed to antiseptic white backgrounds and dramatic isolation of individual works. The small white marbles provide sparkling accents in the generally dark scheme.

The entire end wall is occupied by a major work of Albert Bierstadt (1830–1902), whom we have seen in early pastorals at Framingham (MA 154) and the Fruitlands Museum at Harvard (MA 158), and in the operatic *Seal Rock*, of 1872, at New Britain (CT 44). *Domes of the Yosemite*,[14] nearly 10 feet high and 15 feet long (without frame), was painted in 1867. Governor Fairbanks acquired it from a New York collector, and it has dominated the gallery ever since. Bierstadt traveled to the Far West in 1863 with Fitz Hugh Ludlow, and Ludlow described their adventures in the *Atlantic Monthly* for June of the following year. His response to the Yosemite was cleary shared by Bierstadt: "I never could call a Yosemite crag inorganic, as I used to speak of everything not strictly animal or vegetable. In the presence of the Great South Dome that utterance became blasphemous." From his many oil studies made on the spot, Bierstadt developed a long series of Yosemite can-

14

vases; it is estimated that over a quarter of his finished paintings were devoted to that subject. An earlier view, more peaceful and taken at a greater distance from the crags (1866), is owned by the Wadsworth Atheneum, Hartford. In the summer of 1873 Bierstadt, with his wife and a few friends, spent several weeks camping in and around Hetch-Hetchy Valley, some fifty miles north of the Yosemite. Of the many paintings resulting from that trip, examples can be seen at Hartford and at the Mount Holyoke College Art Museum (see page 280).

It must be acknowledged that Bierstadt depended heavily on the impressiveness of his subjects, and that his paintings seldom reached the poetic intensity of Frederic Church's, as seen at the Berkshire Museum, Pittsfield, MA 195. One of the few disappointments in St. Johnsbury's fine collection of painters associated with the Hudson River School is the absence of a work by this master.

Jasper Cropsey (1823–1900), born on Staten Island, N.Y., took two long European trips for study in Italy and England before settling at Hastings-on-Hudson. Besides painting on the Hudson and the Susquehanna and in the Catskills and the White Mountains, he frequented Lake Greenwood and the Ramapo Valley on the New Jersey–New York border. *Autumn on the Ramapo River*,[15] 37 by 64 inches and painted in 1876, is a lovely idyll of the season he liked best, when the fall foliage gave him an opportunity to indulge his passion for rich reds, dappled on in quick small strokes. (At Hartford, however, there is a *Winter Scene* painted in the Ramapo area.) Comparison with Corot's *Grez-sur-Loing: Bridge and Church*, at the Currier Gallery, Manchester (NH 26), will show the great difference between American interest in poetic light and Romantic love of nature, and French concern with compositional structure. Corot's bridge is a rhythm of strong shapes and a connector between the two sides of his painting; Cropsey's, a flimsy support for a diminutive couple engaged, no doubt, in amorous dialogue. The Currier Gallery owns another fine Cropsey, but of nearly twenty years earlier, *Indian Summer Morning in the White Mountains.*

Cropsey's contemporary Sanford R. Gifford (1823–80) grew up in Hudson, N.Y., just across the river from Catskill, where Thomas Cole (1801–48) maintained a studio. *South Mountain, Catskills*,[16] 23 by 40 inches, was painted in 1873. The horizontal format is typical of the work of Gifford, who preferred wide panoramas to towering masses. His extraordinary sensitiveness to effects of light has been mentioned in connection with examples at New Bedford and in the George Walter Vincent Smith Museum at Springfield, Mass. Like Martin Heade and

15

Fitz Hugh Lane, he was one of our visual poets. Gifford's early work shows the influence of Cole, but gradually his forms became dissolved in a new radiance. Like Bierstadt, with whom he traveled in Europe in the 1850s, and like Church, he sought out exotic scenery, venturing as far afield as Turkey and Syria, the Rockies, and Alaska. But Gifford's was a calm spirit, to whom aqueous mirages and luminous skies spoke more directly than scenic wonders.

A historical curiosity here is a dozen or more nineteenth-century copies made in the European galleries of works by Andrea del Sarto, Raphael, Paolo Veronese, Guido Reni, Carlo Dolci, Fra Angelico, Van Dyck, Murillo, and—surprisingly—Rosa Bonheur. Such copies, often well painted, were regular fixtures in museums of the time, but they are rarely seen today.

As for the St. Johnsbury marbles, most are anonymous but have the appeal of subjects like Psyche, Hermes, Venus, Diana, and Julius Caesar. But the prominent Neoclassicist Antonio Canova (1757–1822) is represented by a *Dancing Girl* (height about 20 inches), and Vermont's own Hiram Powers by yet another bust of the *Greek Slave* (this example only 13½ inches high), discussed at Middlebury College (VT 9). Another good American sculptor, John Quincy Adams Ward (1830–1910), is represented by a portrait of special local interest: Governor Horace Fairbanks himself.

16

Shelburne Museum

Location: On U.S. Route 7, about 7 miles south of the center of Burlington. Parking available

Hours: 9-5 daily from mid-May to mid-October

Admission: Charged (two-day tickets can be purchased). Ⓗ

A full day, or two days, for an unhurried visit to this superb enterprise will be well repaid in interest, aesthetic delight, and educational value. There are thirty-five buildings to inspect, most of them full of art or artifacts, on forty-five acres of parklike setting of fruit trees, formal gardens, and well-tended lawns. At the Toll Booth and Information Center a useful map is provided.

The Shelburne Museum was founded in 1947 by Mr. and Mrs. J. Watson Webb to preserve Vermont's traditions of building and craftsmanship. Like the marine museum at Mystic, Conn., it is not a static display, nor is it a reconstruction of a vanished town in the manner of Colonial Williamsburg. Described as a "collection of collections," it is enlivened by things to do as well as to see, and by skilled guides and craftsmen from whom one may learn much. Installations combine the highest order of historical accuracy and good taste. The care for detail is extraordinary, and it extends to the hundreds of explanatory labels. Indeed, many an established museum of fine arts could profit from a study of methods used here to develop effective public education.

First of all, the museum is a collection of buildings of the eighteenth and nineteenth centuries: houses, barns, an inn, a meetinghouse, a school, a lighthouse, a jail, a blacksmith shop, a general store, a railroad station, a Shaker shed, and a covered bridge. Almost all of these came from Vermont sites—some ten from Shelburne itself or nearby Charlotte, and frequently saved thereby from imminent destruction. Endleaf pictorial maps in the superbly illustrated book *A Pictorial History of the Shelburne Museum* (Shelburne, Vermont: Shelburne Museum, 1972), show the original locations.

Second, the museum is a collection of American crafts exhibited in appropriate architectural settings: interior decoration and furnishings, household utensils, rugs, quilts, pewter, glass, and ceramics. Third, it contains what is probably the finest collection of native American sculpture in existence. Fourth, it is a museum of transportation, with an outstanding collection of luxury carriages, coaches, wagons, sleighs, and of horse-drawn fire equipment; and of ship models, ship paintings, and marine prints. Poised at the Shelburne Depot is an engine and the private car "Grand Isle," built about 1890 by the Wagner Palace Car Company and presented by its president, Dr. W. Seward Webb (the father of J. Watson Webb), to the governor of Vermont, Edward C. Smith. It contains an observation room, two staterooms, a parlor, a secretary's stateroom, a porter's room, and a kitchen. Mahogany paneling and furnishings are in the best style of the period. Not far away is the

892-ton side-wheeler *Ticonderoga*,[17] hauled two miles overland to its present resting place and imaginatively tilted to give you the feeling, on board, that you are under way. *Ticonderoga*'s engine was built at Hoboken, N.J., by Andrew Fletcher and Sons; her hull, by T. S. Marvel on the Hudson River and shipped to Lake Champlain by the Champlain Canal; and her joiner work was completed in 1905 at the Shelburne Harbor Shipyard of the Champlain Transportation Company. She plied the lake from 1906 to 1953.

Metal weather vanes, wood figures for commercial enterprises, and ship's figureheads rival those discussed elsewhere in this book. While sculpture was the slowest of the visual arts to develop in the American colonies and the early Republic—no doubt because of its relative infrequency in English art and because of the Puritans' fear of idolatry—it would be easy to exaggerate its rarity. We must keep in mind, however, that until about 1850 it was almost entirely utilitarian.

The Stagecoach Inn houses a varied supply of weather vanes, cigarstore figures, trade signs, circus figures, symbolic eagles, and ship's figureheads. Most of the weather vanes take the form of an animal: a horse, ram, boar, cow, fish, butterfly, peacock. Occasionally the human figure appears: an Indian archer, a classical centaur, a mermaid. The railroad engine was also a popular theme; a sheet-zinc example here includes a brass and iron lightning-rod attachment above the smokestack. Found in Rhode Island, it is thought to have been used on a railroad station. Whether this object was cut flat from sheet metal or hammered into half-round relief, its silhouette against the sky was its chief visual element. The artisan simplified his forms with an unerring eye for clarity and expressiveness.

The making of bird decoys gave the carver further opportunities to set down characteristic positions of head and body. A collection of over a thousand of these decoys is shown in Dorset House, near the covered bridge. Of special delight for circus lovers is the Circus Parade, stretching more than five hundred feet around the interior of a horseshoe-shaped building near the Shelburne Depot. Carved and painted by Roy Arnold and four other craftsmen over a period of many years were sixty Lilliputian bandwagons, cage wagons, and other spectaculars, some 450 horses (no two alike), animals, riders, clowns, and musicians. On the walls is a running display of posters that cover the history of the American circus.

The exterior of public buildings gave the carver his most challenging opportunity. The great wooden eagles were, so to speak, decoys raised

17

to the level of fine art. One of them with a wingspread of sixteen feet (shown in the Stagecoach Inn) came from the Marine Base at Portsmouth, N.H. More rarely the human figure was employed. The personification of Justice,[18] 10 feet high, that greets you in the entrance hall of the Webb Gallery once adorned the top of the courthouse at Barnstable, Mass. Carved from pine, the blindfolded figure holds a metal scale and a sword. Its rough planes give it unusual vigor; and both the subject and the date of c. 1800 make it extremely rare. In 1958 *Justice* was exhibited at the Brussels Universal and International Exposition in the section on American art.

In the entry for Old Deerfield we have discussed rather briefly the emergence of quilting as an American art form (see MA 149). Throughout the Shelburne Museum one becomes increasingly aware of the American artist's sensibility to shape and color, but especially in rug design and in the elaborate productions of the quilting bee. The textile display in the Hat and Fragrance Unit (beyond the Stagecoach Inn at the northern end of the museum) is very large, and the quilts and coverlets are as magnificent in design as they are spectacular in workmanship. Perhaps the most extraordinary of the quilts is the *Star of Bethlehem*,[19] almost 9 feet square (partly turned under at the bottom of our illustration). Its date is thought to be early nineteenth century. The appliqué design is made of a patchwork of chintzes and English calicos in a symmetrical pattern. Diamond-shaped pieces in the border are made of the same materials. The corner squares are fashioned of cutout chintz on a white background. Three bands of yellow and red material worked with a design of interlaced circles form the wide border, together with the diamond-shaped pieces already mentioned. As would be expected in such a virtuoso performance, the quilting of the background is superbly managed.

Earlier in this account of the museum, we listed four types of collections. We turn now to two others, which from the point of view of this book are the most important of all. In 1960 the Webb Gallery opened as a showcase for the collection of American paintings that Mrs.

18

19

Webb assembled while amassing the many thousands of pieces of Americana that fill the various buildings here. In the same year, 1960, Mr. and Mrs. Webb died. She had inherited from her parents, Henry O. and Louisine Havemeyer, an important share of their magnificent collection of European art, the bulk of which went to the Metropolitan Museum of Art in New York—one of the greatest acquisitions in its history. Mrs. Webb had long planned to bring to Shelburne what remained of this inheritance after further gifts by the Havemeyers' children to expand the great bequest to the Metropolitan. Her own children decided instead to create a memorial to their mother by installing the present collection exactly as it appeared in the Webbs' Park Avenue apartment. Six rooms were reconstructed in a fine new building of Greek Revival style overlooking the southern end of the museum complex, not far from the Webb Gallery. The Electra Havemeyer Webb Memorial opened in 1967.

As a result of these two additions, Shelburne became the leading art museum of the state of Vermont—though its range is much more limited than the collections of the nearby University of Vermont—and indeed one of the finest in New England outside the great cities. From these riches we have selected four masterpieces of French nineteenth-century art (works by Corot, Courbet, Manet, and Degas) and two American paintings of high quality (by Peto and Wyeth). As always in our survey of a collection of great importance, limitations of space have proved constricting and our selections have had to fit into an overall plan to present a well-rounded picture of the history of art.

Two Rembrandt portraits in the living room of the apartment, dating from 1632 and 1643, make a good appearance but cannot match the examples discussed at the Gardner Museum (MA 48) and the Fogg Art Museum (MA 124). A *Portrait of the Princess de la Paz*, in one of the bedrooms, is close to Goya, but because of a certain flatness and lack of spirit it is merely attributed to him. Mary Cassatt's pastel *Portrait of Mrs. Henry O. Havemeyer* (1899), hanging nearby, has greater energy. Artist and subject were close friends, and it was Cassatt (see CT 98) who advised the Havemeyers in their collecting activities in Paris, especially in the field of nineteenth-century French art.

Greek Girl: Mademoiselle Dobigny,[20] by Jean Baptiste Camille Corot (1796–1875), about 33 inches high, is probably unsurpassed among

20

the many late figure paintings of this artist. The date is c. 1868–70. It has been widely exhibited: at Chicago, the New York World's Fair (1940), Philadelphia, the Louvre, and the Metropolitan Museum of Art, among other places. Emma Dobigny, one of Corot's favorite models, posed for it. Fugitive colors animate a predominantly grayish picture, and fugitive also is the girl's facial expression. The forms are softly rounded, yet structurally firm. In this Vermeer-like world of silence, it is hard to believe that the artist was an almost exact contemporary of Delacroix (see MA 120) and an exact one of the sculptor Barye (see VT 1).

Our next two selections, *Still Life with Fruit*[21] by Gustave Courbet (1819–77) and *Blue Venice*[22] by Edouard Manet, both about 22 by 28 inches, are paired on a landing of the memorial's beautiful staircase. For his alleged activities in the destruction of the Vendôme Column in Paris during the Commune uprising, Courbet was sentenced to six months in the Ste.-Pélagie prison. He was confined there from September to December 1871, but because of illness he was allowed to serve the remainder of his term at a Neuilly clinic. Although the Shelburne picture is signed and inscribed "71 Ste. Pélagie," it is possible that it was painted at Neuilly and so inscribed to advertise what Courbet considered a gross miscarriage of justice. One such still life, so inscribed, was scornfully rejected at the Salon of 1872. During his confinement Courbet could paint only fruit or flowers (although there is a self-portrait from this time), because he was one of those rare artists of genius who are helpless unless the motif, or its elements, is literally in front of their eyes. Some of the Ste.-Pélagie or Neuilly still lifes, stark and devoid of accessories, rival the solemnity and geometrical purity of Chardin and Cézanne. Others, like the Shelburne picture, are given landscape backgrounds and otherwise encumbered. The weakest part of

21

22

this picture is the landscape, precisely because Courbet had to imagine it. In his violent espousal of the doctrine of Realism each tangible object reinforced his stand; as a result, there is often a plethora of forms. The basket here is indeed heavily laden. Color is much stronger than in the Smith College picture of almost twenty years earlier (MA 178). By 1871/2 the much younger Impressionists were emerging; while they were greatly influenced by Courbet's themes and by his application of heavy masses of the oil medium, it is very doubtful that their color had much interest for him. As for Courbet's later years, he spent the last five of them in exile in Switzerland, out of touch with what was happening in Paris.

What was happening in Paris was the First and Second Impressionist exhibitions (1874 and 1876), Renoir's *Moulin de la Galette* (Louvre), and boating pictures painted at Argenteuil by Renoir, Monet (RI 16), and Manet, whose *Boating at Argenteuil*, exhibited at the 1874 official Salon, was eventually bequeathed to the Metropolitan Museum of Art by the Havemeyers. In the early fall of 1875, Edouard Manet (1832–83) visited Venice in the company of James Tissot (see RI 19) and brought back two magnificent scenes of the Grand Canal. A vertical canvas, 23 by 19 inches, is in San Francisco; Mrs. Webb's *Blue Venice*, of similar height but 28½ inches wide, is more daring in its elimination of the conventional sky and in its concentration on water reflections, the blue-striped mooring poles, and a shining black gondola placed at the very center. This picture was once owned by Tissot and it has been exhibited many times—in Paris, New York, and especially at the major Manet retrospective of 1966/7 at Philadelphia and Chicago. Black contrasted with prismatic colors: that is Manet's forte—black inherited from Courbet but more directly inspired by Velázquez, black continued from Manet's own pictures of the 1860s (CT 2). In the distance, not the expected hues of Renoir and Monet, but earth-browns and whites. In his turn to Impressionism he remained faithful to the work of those earlier years, but what a dazzling maze of brush strokes in the new Impressionist technique!

Edgar Degas (1834–1917), a great favorite of the Havemeyers, is seen here in four superb pictures, especially the whitish vision of *Two Ballet Girls* in the living room, and in a bronze cast of *The Little Dancer, Age Fourteen*,[23] about 38 inches high. A similar cast is in the

23

Clark Art Institute, Williamstown, and others are in major museums in the United States. The original wax version dates from 1880; the Shelburne bronze, purchased by Mrs. Webb, is the tenth of an edition of twenty-two cast by the Paris foundry of Hébrard in 1922. We should not forget that, as in the case of sculpture by Honoré Daumier, all Degas bronzes are posthumous.

The original wax figure, now in the collection of Mr. and Mrs. Paul Mellon, Upperville, Va., was listed for inclusion in the Impressionist exhibition of 1880, but as it was not completed in time, Degas exhibited it the following year. The ballerina was dressed in a real bodice, a white muslin tutu, a wig (probably of horsehair), a blue satin ribbon tied around her pigtail, and satin slippers. All these additions except the tutu and the slippers were coated with wax to make their texture agree with the rest of the figure, and this also facilitated the later casting. On the advice of Mary Cassatt, the Havemeyers sought to purchase it, but negotiations with Degas broke down; in due course they acquired the first bronze cast in the Hébrard edition of twenty-two. That cast was given to the Metropolitan Museum of Art.

No less than seventy-two wax figures by Degas were cast at the Hébrard foundry between 1919 and 1922. Except for *The Little Dancer* and a nude study for it of the same size (a cast of the nude version is in the Albright-Knox Gallery, Buffalo), these were figurines that Degas used as models for paintings of ballet subjects and racing pictures. According to the contract between Degas's heirs and the Hébrards, the wax originals became the property of the foundry. Until the 1950s it was thought that they were lost, but discovery that they had survived the German occupation of Paris in the Second World War in the basement of the Hébrard house led to their exhibition, for the first time ever, in 1955 at the Knoedler Galleries in New York. While their dull finish could not match the glint of light that animates the bronzes, the extreme subtlety of their surfaces was a revelation, surpassing even the expertly cast replicas.

In the bronze versions, the tutu (again a real one) has turned a dirty greenish gray, and the real hair ribbon was sometimes omitted, or subsequently lost. Chemical patination successfully reproduced the already oxidized tones of the original wax, especially in the bodice area. A fine account of *The Little Dancer* is in John Rewald, *Degas: Sculpture* (London: Thames & Hudson, 1957), which contains six superb plates of the dressed figure and two of the nude version. Rewald points out that the developments of Degas and Renoir were diametrically opposed —Renoir moving away from Impressionism toward firmer line, Degas toward increasingly pictorial effects. He quotes a penetrating statement about the *Dressed Dancer* by Sacha Guitry: ". . . a kind of hallucinating mummy . . . You would have to go a long way, a very long way, right to Egypt and into its ancient past to discover a work of art to equal her."

A large still life in the Webb Gallery, 56 by 33 inches and signed "John F. Peto/ 1887," bears the title *Ordinary Objects in the Artist's Creative Mind*.[24] The title is an accurate statement of the credo of John Frederick Peto (1854–1907): homely objects elevated to the plane of art. A green door with rusty locks and hinges serves as background for

a blue-covered book, a photograph of a woman, a wood engraving of a
boy and girl on a beach (by Winslow Homer, appearing years before
in *Harper's* magazine), a canvas still life of Peto's with edges curled
out, a music book with a torn reddish cover, a trumpet (on which Peto
played expertly), and a sign AT DINNER hanging from a nail. This
modest assemblage agrees entirely with the character of Peto's *Discarded
Treasures* at Smith College (MA 187), returned, as we have indicated, to
Peto's oeuvre despite its Harnett signature. It contrasts strikingly with
the luxurious array of objects in Harnett's *Emblems of Peace* at Springfield (MA 220). Both these Philadelphians were masters at fooling the
eye, but Harnett's choice of objects aimed at attracting affluent patrons
and as a result he had a much greater success. He often influenced Peto,
six years his junior, nowhere more so than in the Shelburne picture,
which may be called a poor man's version of Harnett's relatively elegant
After the Hunt (1885, at the California Palace of the Legion of Honor,
San Francisco). While it is clear that Harnett was the more expert
composer, in the tattered array that Peto has given us, a new note of
pessimism prevails. This has been remarked upon by Gerdts and Burke
in *American Still Life Painting* (New York: Praeger, 1971), and by
Alfred Frankenstein in *After the Hunt* (Berkeley: University of California Press, 1953) with his apt phrase, "the pathos of the discarded."

At the Payson Gallery in Portland, we shall encounter Andrew Wyeth
(born 1917) in an early tempera landscape of 1940 (ME 20).
Shelburne owns one of his most impressive works, painted ten years
later. *Soaring*,[25] tempera on Masonite, is 4 feet high and more than 7
feet wide. A huge brown-black turkey vulture—one soon discovers two

24

25

others far below—straddles most of the picture surface, wings outstretched on a dramatic diagonal. A diminutive house and shed inform
us of the vulture's great altitude, but without distracting from the force
of Wyeth's flat design. Spears of deep brown woodland project into the
bare gray-greenish-ochered fields and unobtrusively echo the vulture's
shape—all this beneath a narrow ice-pale sky. Gone are the rich
Burgundy reds of 1940 and even the forlorn pink of the dress in
Christina's World, 1948 (Museum of Modern Art)—still, in the
opinion of many, Wyeth's finest work. Since 1950, Wyeth has continued in the dour vein and tonality of *Soaring*, at times repetitiously—
as appears when a great number of his pictures are shown together—
but often striking deep emotional chords. As for *Soaring*, it deserves
comparison with the great gilded eagle in the Stagecoach Inn, carved by
an anonymous craftsman perhaps a century ago. Power triumphant
there (and then); in Wyeth, power turned gloomy and ominous.

Springfield Art and Historical Society

Location: 9 Elm Hill. From I-91 take exit 11 or 12 onto Route 11 into Springfield. Beyond the center of town look for a right turn up a steep hill onto Elm St., and then take the *first* right turn onto Elm Hill and destination. Follow these directions with care! Parking available

Hours: Mon.-Fri. 12-4:30, weekends by appointment

Admission: Free

As I near the end of this book, it is a pleasure to make an appeal to the public-spirited reader to support a deserving institution. Springfield is not a large town, and the existence of the Art and Historical Society does it credit. Nevertheless, the handsome building of the 1860s, given in 1956 by Mr. and Mrs. Edward W. Miller, needs considerable repair, and a number of the good pictures it contains are in dire need of a conservator's tender, loving, and expensive care.

Other than the paintings and objects of primarily historical interest, the collections include Bennington pottery, pewter by Richard Lee, dolls, toys, quilts, and costumes. Of special local interest, but now gaining increasing attention, are four portraits of the Chase family by Asahel Lynde Powers (1800–81), a native of Springfield who also painted in New York State and in Ohio. Powers was brought from obscurity by the American specialist Jean Lipman, in an article in *Antiques* for June 1959, and in her subsequent books on American painting. The New York Historical Association at Cooperstown (more often visited than Springfield) has Powers's *Portrait of Charles Mortimer French as a Child*, painted in 1839, some seven years after the Chase portraits, but folk-art enthusiasts should see the examples in Springfield itself to gain a more extended impression of this artist's uncouth, but strangely provocative, forms. His combination of different perspectives has an unexpectedly modern air; and if his deeply lined facial features make every person, regardless of age, seem venerable, Asahel Powers was by no means unique in this respect.

Another Vermont artist, better known than Asahel Powers, is Horace Bundy (1814–83), who came from Hardwick. A portrait and sometime landscape painter in Vermont and New Hampshire, he was in Jamaica shortly before his death, on commission by an English planter. There he also made sketches of tropical scenery. A portrait of 1841, *A Vermont Lawyer*, in the Garbisch collection at the National Gallery of Art in Washington, which is among his best works, is generally comparable to one of 1845 at Springfield. Bundy has received much attention from scholars and collectors in the American field, and his career is now well established. Springfield owns seven of his portraits and a landscape.

Bundy Art Gallery

Location: On Route 100 about 4 miles south of the village. From I-93 turn south on Route 100 at Waterbury. Parking available
Hours: Open July and August, Mon., Wed.-Sat. 10-5, Sun. 1-5
Admission: Free

Described as a country museum dedicated to contemporary art, European as well as American, the gallery was founded and designed by Harlow Carpenter and named in memory of his mother, Helen Bundy Carpenter. It opened in 1962.

Modern sculptures, many of them placed on the grounds and along paths and in clearings of the beautiful woodland property, include works by Dino Basaldella, Roger Bolomey, Luciano Minguzzi, Louise Nevelson (see MA 147), and Sahl Swarz. Among well-known modern painters represented here by major works are Afro (Basaldella), Karel Appel, John Grillo, Ivor Hitchens, Conrad Marca-Relli, Pierre Soulages, Janis Spyropoulos, Antoni Tapiès, and Esteban Vicente.

Changing exhibitions feature selections from the large permanent collection and work by avant-garde Vermont artists. Free concerts are also a part of the gallery's program.

Maine

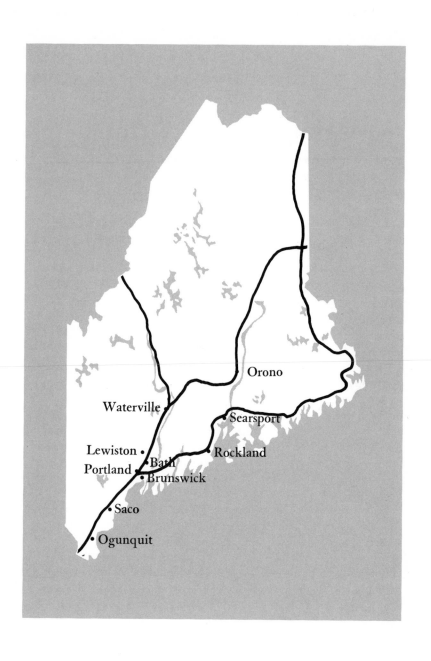

Waterville

Orono

Searsport

Lewiston
Bath
Portland
Brunswick

Rockland

Saco

Ogunquit

Maine Maritime Museum

Location: 963 Washington St. Take Maine Tpke. exit 9 for coastal Route 1 through Brunswick to Bath; take exit 209 from Route 1 onto High St., which parallels Washington St.; turn left (north) on Washington St. Sewall House is at the near right corner of North St.

Hours: Daily 10-5 from mid-May to late October; after that on Sun. 10-5

Admission: Charged

The museum occupies Sewall House, a superb mansion of 1844, and, with additions, provides 5,600 square feet of space for exhibition of the maritime collections. Ship models are here, 200 of them, from early sailing craft to J. P. Morgan's *Corsair* (3,100 tons)—built at the Bath Iron Works—to ships built for the U.S. Navy. Bath is the oldest still active shipbuilding city in the United States. The basement of Sewall House has been admirably fitted out for exhibition of these modern activities.

There are a few carved ships' figureheads, but not of the magnitude of those at Mystic Seaport. The many maritime paintings are of high quality. One of the most interesting represents the U.S. ship *Samaritan* in three views: approaching, broadside, and departing. The painting is attributed to a British artist, R. B. Spencer, but the ship itself was the last one built by the Bath firm of Clark & Sewall, which closed in 1855. A scene of great violence is projected by a hinter-glass painting of *The Brig Caledonia in a Storm* (built 1828), by the Antwerp artist Petrus Weyts.

A "please touch" room, with ship's wheel and bell, is popular with children.

According to the *New York Marine Journal* (1891), "A Bath man can no more help building ships than he can help breathing; and a Bath man when he isn't building ships, sails them." By 1900 Bath had produced half of the large wooden vessels sailing under the American flag. During the Second World War the Bath Iron Works built more destroyers than the entire Japanese navy.

The Maritime Museum administers three additional sites. The Winter Street Center, at 880 Washington Street, a former church, is used as a working center for the museum's staff and for changing exhibitions of seafaring life. The riverside Apprenticeshop, at 375 Front Street, offers an eighteen-month training program in constructing models, boat building, and seamanship. The Percy and Small Shipyard, well down the Kennebec River at 263 Washington Street, is the only surviving shipyard in America of those that built large wooden sailing vessels.

An additional attraction is the unique steam tug *Seguin*, the oldest U.S.-registered wooden steam vessel. Her restoration and new ship-house are open for public inspection.

Bowdoin College Museum of Art

Location: Walker Art Building
Hours: September-June: Tues.-Fri. 10-4, Sat. 10-5; July and
August: Tues.-Sat. 10-5, Sun. 2-5; closed Mon. and holidays
Admission: Free. Ⓗ

An art collection has existed at Bowdoin almost since the inception of
the college itself. The earliest acquisition of major importance was a
group of 142 Old Master drawings bequeathed in 1811 by the Honorable James Bowdoin III, son of a governor of Massachusetts, and
himself a U.S. minister to France and Spain. Among many treasures—
appraised at the time for $7.50 the lot—this bequest contains a superb
pen-and-ink landscape by Pieter Brueghel the Elder. The collection
was the first of its kind in America. James Bowdoin III's Old Master
paintings came to the college two years later, in 1813.

Although various portions of the college's art collection were on
view during the first half of the nineteenth century, it was not until 1855
that a special gallery devoted to them came into being in the college
chapel. This was made possible by a gift from Theophilus Wheeler
Walker, a cousin of Bowdoin President Leonard Woods. As a memorial
to Walker his two nieces, Harriet Sarah and Mary Sophia Walker,
donated funds in 1891 for the erection of the present museum building,
designed by Charles Follen McKim of McKim, Mead & White. Four
tympana murals of *Athens, Rome, Florence,* and *Venice* by John
La Farge, Elihu Vedder, Abbott Thayer, and Kenyon Cox, respectively,
decorate the museum's Sculpture Hall.

The museum contains one of the most important collections extant
of American Colonial and Federal portraits, including works by Smibert,
Feke, Blackburn, Copley, Stuart, Trumbull, and Sully. Among the five
examples of Robert Feke's work is the full-length likeness of *General
Samuel Waldo,* generally regarded as among the finest American
portraits of the first half of the eighteenth century. Nine works by
Gilbert Stuart include the so-called official portrait of *Thomas Jefferson,*
as well as its pendant, *James Madison.* A complete catalogue of this
collection, *Colonial and Federal Portraits at Bowdoin College,* by
Marvin S. Sadek, was published in 1966.

The holdings in Ancient art include sculpture, pottery, bronzes, gems,
coins, and glass of all phases of the Ancient world. The most notable
benefactor in this area was Edward Perry Warren, the leading collector
of classical antiquities of the first quarter of the twentieth century. Five
magnificent ninth-century B.C. Assyrian reliefs from the Palace of
Ashurnazirpal II, the gift to the college of Henri Byron Haskell,
Medical 1855, are installed in the museum's Sculpture Hall. *Ancient
Art in Bowdoin College,* by Kevin Herbert, a descriptive catalogue, was
published in 1964 by the Harvard University Press.

In recent years, the college has been the recipient of a Samuel H. Kress Study Collection of twelve Renaissance paintings; a large collection of medals and plaquettes presented by Amanda, Marquesa Molinari; a fine group of European and American pictures given by Mr. and Mrs. John H. Halford; a collection of Chinese and Korean ceramics given by Governor and Mrs. William Tudor Gardiner; and 19 paintings and 168 prints by John Sloan bequeathed by George Otis Hamlin.

In the fall of 1964, the college was the recipient of the major portion of a collection of Winslow Homer memorabilia, which until that time had been in the artist's studio at Prout's Neck. This material, the gift of the Homer family, and now known as the Homer Collection of the Bowdoin College Museum of Art, includes the artist's first watercolor, a significant group of letters he wrote over a period of many years to various members of his family, and a considerable number of photographs of Homer, his family, and of Prout's Neck. More recently, a large group of woodblock reproductions of Homer's drawings that appeared in *Harper's* magazine was purchased to augment these holdings and create a major center for the scholarly study of Homer's life and work. The museum already owned a significant number of Homer's oils, watercolors, and drawings.

Other nineteenth-century American painters well represented here are Eastman Johnson, Thomas Eakins, George Inness, and Martin J. Heade; while for the twentieth century—in addition to the large collection of the work of John Sloan—William Glackens, Marsden Hartley, Andrew Wyeth, and Leonard Baskin are shown to advantage.

The museum is active in well-displayed temporary exhibitions, accompanied by scholarly catalogues meticulously designed. The Bowdoin College Traveling Print Collection is made available gratis to educational institutions in Maine. The museum also sponsors symposia and special lectures. Since 1973, symposia on American furniture, nineteenth-century decorative arts, American Indian art, nineteenth-century American architects, and conservation have been held.

Exhibition space in the Walker Art Building was more than doubled following an extensive renovation made possible by gifts to the 175th Anniversary Campaign Program and completed in 1976. Three galleries for exhibiting the museum's permanent collections and a temporary-exhibition gallery were added on the lower levels, and the previously existing galleries on the ground level were redecorated.

A handbook of the collections nears completion as of this writing.

McKim's masterly building (a Palladian adaptation of Brunelleschi's Pazzi Chapel in Florence), the impressive and wide-ranging holdings that we have outlined, and the sensitive taste of a series of directors have combined to make this the leading art museum in the state of Maine. Ambitious plans for the Portland Museum of Art may eventually make this statement obsolete, but certainly not in any near future. There is no visible abundance of James Bowdoin IIIs or of Edward Perry Warrens.

The five Assyrian reliefs, one of the larger groups received in the 1850s by New England colleges, primarily from missionary alumni serving at Mosul on the Tigris, are similar to those at Dartmouth,

Harvard, Middlebury, the University of Vermont, Williams, and Yale. We discuss them in the entry on Amherst College (MA I)—because of its alphabetical priority and because it owns six.

Mr. Warren, the distinguished connoisseur who was Bowdoin's great benefactor in the field of Greek and Roman art, also contributed to the early development of the classical departments of the Boston Museum of Fine Arts and the Metropolitan Museum of Art in New York. From Bowdoin's Warren collection of Greek vases we have selected three Attic examples of quality to illustrate three methods of applying decoration to the clay surface, and to give some idea of stylistic range from the beginning of the fifth century B.C. to a high point of achievement at the middle of the century. (In architecture and architectural sculpture the same span would take us from the late Archaic temple at Aegina to the Temple of Zeus at Olympia.)

In the small *Black-figure Lekythos*,[1] an oil jar about 8 inches high dating from c. 490, the two foot soldiers were painted directly on the red clay in black silhouette, but their internal contour lines had to be laboriously scratched through the film of paint to reveal the red under-surface. This method had dominated most vase painting during the sixth century; but about 525 B.C. a much less confining process began to gain acceptance. It is seen in the *Red-figure Hydria*,[2] a three-handled water jar twice the height of the *lekythos* and dating from c. 460–450. Here the figures were drawn, both in outlines and in interior contour lines, and the background was then filled in with flat black paint. (A comparable reversal of an earlier process to gain greater freedom can be seen in the development of medieval enamels from Byzantine cloisonné to French champlevé as practiced during the thirteenth century at Limoges.) A third method, which brought vase painting still closer to what we think of as normal painting procedure, is seen in the *White-ground Lekythos*,[3] about 10 inches high and dating from c. 450. Here the entire vase was given a white slip, and then the artist drew and painted—as on a gesso panel or a canvas sized white—as he pleased. The second of the three methods eliminated the necessity of scratching lines through previously applied paint; the third avoided the difficulty of making the black background end exactly at the edges of the figures.

2

I

3

In its figure style, the *Black-figure Lekythos* recalls late sixth-century Archaic sculpture somewhat more than it does the relatively advanced sculpture of its own time, c. 490. Some Greek vase painters kept pace with sculptors in this voyage of anatomical discovery; others settled for accepted convention. An enormous advance in this direction is seen in the *Red-figure Hydria* of 460–450—but not without loss of ornamental appeal, for now something approaching an *independent picture* is wrapped around the vase. It is assigned to the Niobid Painter, one of the most skilled of his generation. Often such artists signed their names, but this one remains anonymous. In the case of the Niobid Painter, named after the subject of one of his major works in the Louvre, scholars have developed an impressive oeuvre. Here the subject is the rape of Oreithyia by Boreas as Athena watches and other figures flee from the scene. Greek painting was, of course, not limited to the ornamentation of vases, and leading fifth-century artists like Polygnotus are known to have made great wall paintings. It is very difficult to assign with any certainty connections between such masters and their modest counterparts who decorated vases, but scholars have succeeded in demonstrating that the Niobid Painter was indeed influenced by the art of Polygnotus himself. The *White-ground Lekythos* is assigned to the School of the Achilles Painter, one of the greatest figures of mid-fifth-century vase painting. But its quality by no means matches that of the master's works, for all its haunting charm. Such vessels, used frequently in burials, as frequently portray mourning persons like this man in a dull red himation before a stele and the woman on the reverse, offering red sashes.

In our concern with decoration we must not forget the vases themselves. Utilitarian objects, more often than not mass-produced (two hundred like our first illustration have been assigned to the same workshop), they attain great elegance even in their shape. Attempts have been made to discover complex mathematical formulae controlling their subtle outlines; but, as Rhys Carpenter has pointed out, the simplistic diagrams used in the demonstration are misleading. We do not *see* vases this way. However that may be, shapes of vases developed in ways similar to the evolution of Greek architecture and figured sculpture and painting. The two *lekythoi*, several decades apart, offer an example. The earlier one is relatively wide; the later, suavely elongated. Even the two lips are strikingly different. In the same order we note a change from a shape very much like the bearing portion (*echinus*, or cushion) of an Archaic Doric capital to a shape so narrow and vertical that it is clearly liberated from dependence on any such architectural model. The lovely Greek *kylix* (drinking cup) seen in MA 169 also seems related to the Doric *echinus*, and its evolution closely follows the development from Archaic Doric temples to the Parthenon.

Among the sculptures in the Warren collection is a superb marble *Statuette of a Nude Youth*,[4] dating from the Hellenistic era. Only the torso remains, its front somewhat marred by erosion and chipping. The position of three fingers on the left hip indicates that the left arm was held akimbo. With the entire weight held on the right leg, the figure takes a pronounced S-curve, first seen in the fourth-century sculptures of Praxiteles and Lysippos. The refinement of the carving precludes any possibility that this is a Roman copy of Greek work. The Swedish sculptor Carl Milles once told me that he collected Greek marbles because of the magnificence of their backs. The visitor is advised to observe this example accordingly. The figure may have represented a satyr, Hermes, or Narcissus.

The marble *Portrait Head of the Emperor Antoninus Pius*[5] (A.D. 138–161) is widely regarded as perhaps the finest Roman portrait in America. The flesh has a fine sheen, contrasting well with the rough hair passages. The eyes, with iris and pupil incised, bring the marble to life, and about the mouth there is a highly individualized suggestion of hesitancy.

All of this makes a fascinating contrast with a thirteenth-century French Gothic limestone *Head of a King*[6] from no less a source than Chartres Cathedral. At 6½ inches in height, it is about half the size of the Roman example. This crowned head is no royal portrait, but a biblical personage. The abstracted eyes and generalized mouth reveal no inner personality. The features remain close to the surface, without the projections and shadows of the Roman portrait. The fine rhythms of the flowing hair and short beard are an exercise in abstract design. They frame a three-dimensional shape that could be described in simple geometric terms. The unknown artist's intention was clearly to make

4

5

6

this head relate directly to architecture built of the same limestone; and we may assume that the body reflected similar architectural restrictions.

The identification of this head with Chartres Cathedral was made by Brooks Stoddard, at the time a teacher of art history at the college who specialized in medieval art. Knowing the Bowdoin head well, and remembering that Chartres had been suggested as its possible origin, he explored the crypt of the cathedral, where there are many fragments, especially of the screen (*jubé*) that once separated the choir from the nave. A headless draped figure seemed to have the same break as the Bowdoin head. Stoddard then had a cast made at Harvard of the Bowdoin head, took the cast to Chartres, and placed it on the headless figure. The fit was perfect.

Included in the gift of the Samuel H. Kress Study Collection is a small oil on canvas representing *Apollo and Daphne*.[7] Its companion, *Cupid and Apollo Disputing the Power of Their Arrows*, went to Bucknell College (Lewisburg, Penn.). Formerly attributed to Andrea del Sarto, they are now generally agreed to have been the work of his important pupil Jacopo Pontormo (1494–1557) at the time of his apprenticeship. In 1512 the Medici were reinstated in Florence, and the youthful Lorenzo and Giuliano—more famous for their tombs by Michelangelo than for the wisdom of their tenure—decided to dazzle the public with elaborate festivals including floats. Andrea del Sarto was a chief designer of them, and the ornamentation went in for readily intelligible symbolism. Both Medici organized companies of retainers; Giuliano's honored Lorenzo the Magnificent with one of three floats symbolizing the Ages of Man. This float, *The Triumph of Summer*, used the Apollo and Daphne myth to refer to the great Lorenzo, who had adopted the laurel as his own device. Daphne, it will be remembered, escaped the ardent Apollo by being transformed into a laurel tree. The unusually reduced color, black and white only—almost like a chiaroscuro drawing—was presumably dictated by the design of the float itself.

It was mentioned earlier that James Bowdoin's gift of drawings, so poorly thought of by the appraiser, contained a pen-and-ink sketch by

7

Pieter Brueghel the Elder (c. 1525–69). This *View of Waltersburg*,[8] a town at the headwaters of the Rhine, is inscribed "Waltersspurg," in the old spelling. Brueghel went to Italy in 1551, and this drawing presumably dates from that time, because Waltersburg is on the old route between Flanders and Italy. While Brueghel's paintings show the result of his study of Renaissance anatomy and perspective, it is clear that what most impressed him on his trip was the rugged Alpine scenery. There are many Brueghel drawings of this sort in European collections today. He used them for the landscape backgrounds in some of his most famous pictures. Why it so closely resembles Chinese landscape art is hard to explain, but Benjamin Rowland, Jr., spotted such a similarity long ago. In *Art in East and West* (Harvard University Press, 1934), he pointed out that, like the Chinese, Brueghel drew from memory—I interject that though the Bowdoin drawing represents Waltersburg it can almost be exchanged with his other Alpine views. He developed a vocabulary of shorthand strokes to suggest the structure of rocks and trees, as the Chinese did. Rowland's comparison, illustrated by his plates 33 and 34, is based on the Brueghel *Alpine Landscape* in the Fogg Art Museum at Harvard.

After Brueghel, the next great leap in Flemish painting was taken by Peter Paul Rubens (1577–1640). We have discussed Rubens in full Baroque magnificence in an oil panel for the Whitehall Palace ceiling (CT 52), and we shall meet him several times again; but at Bowdoin there is a surprising little gem of a pen drawing of about 1602–05, *Thisbe Committing Suicide*.[9] Less than 4 inches high, it belongs with five other studies for this figure on a sheet in the Louvre (illustrated by Julius S. Held, *Rubens: Selected Drawings*, London: Phaidon Publishers, 1959, vol. II, pl. 9). These rapid little preliminary sketches, probably executed during his early sojourn at the court of the Gonzaga at Mantua, show Rubens already well launched toward his virtual invention of Baroque form, whereas his paintings of the same period are cramped and stiffened.

Little is known about Robert Feke (1707–52) before 1741, when he painted the *Family of Isaac Royall* in Boston (owned by Harvard Law School), and even less is known about him after 1750. It is apparent,

8

9

however, that he was influenced by Smibert's stiffened variation on the English Baroque of Kneller. (Compare CT 74 at Yale.) Smibert's Baroque interests are represented at Bowdoin by his copies, made in Italy, of Tintoretto, Poussin, and Van Dyck, and by his *Portrait of the Reverend James McSparran* (1735). But Feke refined Smibert's meaty grossness in favor of polished surfaces, clean lines, and decorative beauty. Thus he became the true precursor of Copley.

The *Portrait of James Bowdoin II*,[10] painted in 1748, is one of five Feke portraits at Bowdoin, all of that year. If the full-length *Brigadier General Samuel Waldo* (8 feet high) outstrips the others (all 50 by 40 inches) in size, the *James Bowdoin II* equals it in quality, and may even surpass it. In color, James's rich brown coat is set against cold blues and blue greens, his yellow-trimmed glistening white silk vest guiding our eyes swiftly up to his face. In the companion portrait of his wife the brown and blue sequence is reversed, but the whites serve a similar directional purpose. An ardent patriot and near the end of his life a governor of Massachusetts, he was twenty-two when the portrait was painted, and his wife of that year was seventeen.

To the Americanized Baroque of Smibert and Feke we may contrast the Anglo-American Rococo of Joseph Blackburn, painter of the primly elegant double portrait of *Elizabeth Bowdoin Temple and James Bowdoin III as Children*.[11] In his early training in England, Blackburn seems to have been influenced chiefly by Thomas Hudson, the master of Sir Joshua Reynolds. (A work by Hudson at the University of Vermont is discussed, VT 4.) Blackburn arrived from Bermuda in 1754 and painted in Boston, Salem, Portsmouth, and Newport until he returned to England in 1763. To judge from the age of James Bowdoin III (born 1752), this picture dates from well into Blackburn's American period. We need only remind ourselves of exactly contemporary portraiture at the court of Louis XV by Boucher and Nattier, or of Gainsborough's early work (see CT 54) to judge how far Blackburn was removed from the fashionable Rococo trends. Still, it would be hard to deny that in the Bowdoin children he painted a portrayal as delicious as it is improbable.

There is no evidence for the suggestion that Blackburn returned to England because John Singleton Copley (1738–1815) gave him too

10

11

much competition. But that Copley continued the purer American vein of Feke can easily be seen in his superb *Portrait of Thomas Flucker*,[12] painted c. 1770. A rabid Tory, Flucker was the last Royal Secretary of the Province of Massachusetts. By his first marriage he was the brother-in-law of Governor James Bowdoin II; by his second, the son-in-law of General Waldo. He wears a gray coat with gold buttons. The head is modeled with great force, and the expression is remarkably penetrating, even by Copley's high standards. Copley's American period ended in 1774, when he went to England, never to return. Occasionally he rose to his earlier heights (the *Mrs. Seymour Fort* at the Wadsworth Atheneum, CT 25, is an English work), but on the whole he became just another rather good English painter.

Gilbert Stuart (1755–1828) studied in Edinburgh when he was seventeen and went to London when he was twenty. He worked there from 1775 to 1787, when debts drove him to Ireland, where he remained until 1792. Except for a brief period in his teens at Newport (where his Copley-inspired *Portrait of Benjamin Waterhouse* is; see RI 1), Stuart was obviously a product of European training. He returned to America in 1793. His mature style was an important factor in what is sometimes called the release of American painting from its provincialism. I reserve the right to believe that the price of this artistic ransom was rather steep. I think that American portraiture suffered a confusing European-inspired deviation about 1800, and was only brought back on the track by the George Caleb Binghams, the Winslow Homers, and the Thomas Eakinses of later generations.

Be that as it may, Stuart's *Seated Portrait of Thomas Jefferson*,[13] commissioned by James Bowdoin III in 1805, is one of those significant points of contact that link a great personage with a leading artist of his own day. When we realize that Jacques Louis David began to paint the *Coronation of Napoleon* in Paris in the same year, it becomes clear that Stuart clung to the tradition of Sir Joshua Reynolds and resisted the swing to Neoclassicism that dominated most painting and sculpture at the turn of the century. Stuart's is without question the "classic"

12

13

portrait of the great President. Nevertheless, his image is at variance with Jefferson's well-known classical tastes, and with his equally strong French leanings. It is a Georgian image, though Jefferson himself deplored Georgian architecture and its decoration. If we therefore find this famous picture rather un-American, despite the understandable patriotic sentiment that has become attached to it, we certainly do not minimize its quality as a portrait and as a work of art.

For James Bowdoin III, Stuart also painted (again in 1805 and in 48-by-40-inch size) a *Seated Portrait of James Madison.* Here the status symbols such as the column are less emphatic, the pose more informal, and the characterization more intense. In their brilliant displays of scarlet drapery, chairs, and tablecloths the two presidential images make a sumptuous pair.

Martin J. Heade (1819–1904), discussed in the entry on the Benton Museum at Storrs, Conn. (CT 100), is represented at Bowdoin by a less ominous and more typical example, *Newburyport Marshes: Passing Storm*[14] (c. 1865–70 and 15 inches high). A serpentine stream leads us in and there is the expected little fringe of trees at the distant horizon. But here, long before Claude Monet appropriated them as a major theme, are two haystacks, one in shadow, the other catching the light from its left. A serene gentleness pervades the scene, which may have been painted from sketches made on Plum Island, off Newburyport. Unlike Monet, however, Heade did not work on his canvases out of doors, nor did he fragment his haystacks with light. He painted tender idylls, not symphonic color poems.

It is appropriate that Bowdoin and Colby, as colleges in the state of Maine, should own fine works by Winslow Homer (1836–1910), for his later career developed there. From the Bowdoin collection let us look at a very unusual example. It is not the best from a critical point of view (I should nominate a late watercolor, *End of the Hunt,* for this distinction), but it is in some ways the most interesting. The *Fountains at Night*[15] was painted in 1893 after Homer visited the World's

14

15

Columbian Exposition in Chicago. That makes its subject exceptional enough. Equally remarkable, however, is the fact that Homer painted it in oils using gray tones only. There exist many other monochrome studies by Homer, but usually in gouache. Bowdoin has one (*Wolf's Cove*, Quebec, 1895) and the Farnsworth Museum at Rockland has another. Homer's oil shows Frederick MacMonnies's fountain by electrical illumination and the Venetian gondolas that plied the lagoons of the "White City." Such a work helps us to understand how important Homer felt the neutral tones were when he painted a watercolor like *End of the Hunt*.

Of the four lunettes in the elegant entrance rotunda, *Athens*,[16] painted in 1898 by John La Farge (1835–1910), is richest in color. The blues run deep; a dozen years earlier La Farge had preceded Gauguin in imbibing the colors of the South Seas. He had always admired the great Venetians. A statuesque calm, befitting the occasion, prevails. The figures are almost sufficiently generalized to avoid the disturbing thought that Victorians are posing in make-believe Greek costume. La Farge was intimately associated with architects: McKim, of course, and also H. H. Richardson, who chose him to decorate the interior of Trinity Church, Boston, with murals and designs for stained glass. It was the monumental sculptor Augustus Saint-Gaudens who recommended him to McKim for the Bowdoin commission. Of La Farge his ardent admirer Henry Adams wrote that he "owned a mind complex enough to contrast against the commonplaces of American uniformity, and in the process had vastly perplexed most Americans who came in contact with it."

Soon after the turn of the century, painting in America reacted strongly against the high idealism of artists like La Farge and the high-society images of John Singer Sargent. The revolt was led by Robert Henri and included seven others: Glackens, Luks, Shinn, Davies, Prendergast, Lawson, and John Sloan (1871–1951). From Bowdoin's

16

important representation of Sloan's work we have selected *Sunday Afternoon in Union Square*,[17] painted in 1912—a year before the opening of the riotous Armory Show in New York. Another 1912 picture by Sloan, *Sunday: Women Drying Their Hair* (Addison Gallery of American Art, Andover) was exhibited there, uncomfortably jostled by works of the European avant-garde. Sloan learned much from the competition, and applied it in his later painting. But in 1912 he was very much the Impressionist, sunlighting his bright colors and spicing his everyday images with an American's sharp observation of detail.

A branch of the Bowdoin Museum commemorates two famous Arctic explorers (and Bowdoin alumni), Admirals Robert E. Peary and Donald B. MacMillan. The display is located on the first floor of Hubbard Hall, for many years the college library.

17

Treat Gallery, Bates College

Location: From the Maine Tpke., take exit 13, drive northwesterly through the town to the college campus. The gallery is on the ground floor of Pettigrew Hall
Hours: Mon.-Fri. 1-4:30 and 7-8, Sun. 2-5; summer hours Tues.-Sat. 1-4
Admission: Free. Ⓗ

The gallery has an active schedule of temporary exhibitions. Until present hopes for expanded quarters materialize, the permanent collection is only sporadically on display. It contains a small number of good paintings, including portraits by Gainsborough and Beechey, and a composition of Roman ruins by Panini (or a follower); nineteen prints by Mary Cassatt; and gouaches and crayons by Carl Sprinchorn (1887–1971). There are many nineteenth- and twentieth-century prints and photographs.

The chief attraction, however, is a collection of ninety-nine drawings and two small early oils by Marsden Hartley (1877–1943) given in 1951 by the artist's heirs. A catalogue of the drawings, prepared by William J. Mitchell, was published by the college in 1970. The gift was made in accordance with Hartley's wish. He was born in Lewiston and spent the first fifteen years of his life there. After study and work in Europe, especially Berlin (see CT 30), and intermittent travel elsewhere, he repeatedly returned to his native state, and in his final decade divided his time between Maine and New York City. For a very fine late oil, see MA 21.

Pallid Spring,[18] signed and dated 1909 and dedicated to the artist's sister, precedes his pioneering modernism. A poetic little Impressionist landscape, vigorously brushed with small strokes of thick paint, it has something of the patterned surface effect of Maurice Prendergast's oils of the same year (see CT 99). The glories of Hartley's color in later years are already in evidence here.

18

The drawings range from delicate pencil sketches of landscape to aggressive work in pen and litho crayon, and from c. 1913 (Berlin) to Hartley's death. *Seated Man with Wide Collar*,[19] in litho crayon c. 1938/9, is typical of his latest phase. The bequest also includes many photographs of Hartley and his friends.

19

Museum of Art of Ogunquit

Location: Approach Ogunquit by Route 1; the museum is 1.4 miles south of
Ogunquit Square on Shore Rd. Parking available
Hours: July through Labor Day, Mon.-Sat. 10:30-5, Sun. 1:30-5
Admission: Free

The museum, built in memory of Charles Godfrey Strater and Adeline
Helme Strater, was completed in 1953. Constructed of cinder blocks
and granite on three levels sloping down to the sea, it serves as a cultural
center for the area. The collection is restricted to American art, with
emphasis on recent painting, sculpture, graphic arts, and ceramics. Each
summer there is a major temporary exhibition, usually based on the
permanent holdings but supplemented by loans from elsewhere. These
include broad surveys and one-artist shows. The museum owns fine
examples of such painters as Bacon, Brook, Burchfield, Demuth, Hartley,
Homer, Karfiol, Kuhn, Kuniyoshi, Luks, Marin, Marsh, Wyeth, and
the founder, Henry Strater; and sculptures by Greenbaum, Lachaise,
Zorach, and the ceramist Carl Walters.

One of the phenomena of modern art has been the decline of importance of the human figure as a subject. Abstract form is not, however,
the only artistic alternative in a world beset by superhuman forces. A
number of recent artists have found symbolic images in the animal and
the bird kingdoms. The Ogunquit Museum allows us to compare two
very different uses of the bird image. The sculptor John Flannagan
(1895–1942) has expressed in *Pelican*[20] (1931) a timeless essence
much in the character of ancient Egyptian art. Morris Graves (born
1910) has brushed *Bird with Spirit Mask*[21] (1953) with the magic of
the Sung painters of ancient China. Both are modern in their emphasis
on the fragment: Flannagan's bird is deliberately broken, while Graves's,
its identity masked, is but an evocation. Flannagan found certainty in
the durability of sandstone; Graves, in a world of spirit beyond the
world of appearance. It is worth knowing that Flannagan carved *Pelican*
during a year's stay in Ireland, where the rugged forms of the great

21

20

stone crosses made a lasting impression on him, and that Graves comes from the Pacific Northwest, whose museums are rich in Far Eastern art. Graves went to Ireland, too, in 1955/6, but the Ireland that interested him was another Ireland, one of mist-laden landscape.

Our final selection is by Mark Tobey (1890–1976). Though he came from Wisconsin and trained in Chicago, Tobey had, like Graves, a long association with the Pacific Northwest. After 1922 he lived in Seattle, but traveled to France, England, and the Far East, where he studied calligraphy and Zen. He eagerly absorbed Chinese and Persian philosophies stressing the unity of man and nature. *Meditative Series, Number 7*,[22] painted in tempera in 1954, may seem a meaningless labyrinth. It is indeed one, but so are the heavens on a moonless night. "Among and floating free above matted grasses, delicate threadlike structures rise and float . . . wind blown as the summer passes." This is a characteristic statement by Tobey; it may provide some bearings for his voyages into the infinite—all, in our example, at a size of only 18 by 12 inches.

In 1958 Tobey became the first American artist since Whistler (in 1895) to win first prize at the Venice Biennale. Three years later his European reputation was such that the Musée des Arts Decoratifs (in the Louvre) gave him a one-man exhibition of 286 works. Paris had given Whistler such a retrospective, at the Ecole des Beaux-Arts in 1905—two years after his death. Since that time no other American artist had been so honored—and Tobey still had fifteen years left him. In 1962 the Museum of Modern Art in New York energized lagging American acclaim with a retrospective of 135 works. It was also shown in Cleveland and Chicago.

22

The University of Maine Art Collection

Location: On the Penobscot River, about 15 miles north of Bangor
Hours: Open daily (but see below)
Admission: Free. Ⓗ

Since the university's large collection is placed in various public areas around the campus, the visitor should inquire at the curator's office in Carnegie Hall about the specific location of items. An illustrated catalogue is available there, without charge. Those concerned about security are reassured that proper vigilance is enforced.

The collection is primarily devoted to American art but it includes examples from abroad to assist in the teaching program. The print collection is extensive in the modern American field; it is supplemented by representative works by European masters from Dürer to Picasso. There are paintings of the Barbizon School here (Daubigny, Diaz) and one by Bouguereau (see MA 257). Among the Americans, Marsden Hartley, Childe Hassam, George Inness, William Kienbusch, John Marin, Waldo Pierce, Carl Sprinchorn, Abbot Thayer, and Andrew Wyeth are represented by oils, watercolors, or drawings. The most impressive sculpture is a bronze relief, *Awakening*, by the New York artist William Zorach, who spent much time working in Maine.

The Elm,[23] an oil by George Inness (1825–94), signed and dated 1864 and 3 feet high, is a serene and accomplished example of his early phase, in the vein of the Hudson River painters. We discuss Inness's further development in the 1870s as seen in works at Andover (MA 16) and Mount Holyoke College (MA 206).

23

A Bit of Cape Split,[24] signed and dated 1940, is one of two water-colors by John Marin (1870–1953) owned by the university. Marin's earlier career is discussed in examples at Waterville, Maine, and Rockland, Maine, and at Williamstown, Mass. (MA 275); the Orono selection carries his shorthand vocabulary almost to the point of Chinese calligraphy. As for color, only black and greenish grays are allowed to compete with the azures of Maine waters. Cape Split, the easternmost point in the United States, was "nearer his heart than any place in the world," according to Mackinley Helm, Marin's biographer. Like Winslow Homer before him, Marin found an escape on the lonely Maine coast—at Cape Split, Pleasant Bay, Schoodic Point, and Deer Isle. To find one in an earlier day, Homer had to venture only as far as Prout's Neck, below Portland.

24

Portland Museum of Art

Location: 111 High St. (corner of Spring St.); from Route 295 turn right on Forest Ave.; follow it to Congress St. (dead end), left to Oak St., then right on Spring St.

Hours: Tues.-Sat. 10-5, Sun. 2-5; closed Mon. and holidays

Admission: Free. Ⓗ projected

The museum was founded in 1882 as part of the Portland Society of Art, which also governs the Portland School of Art, founded in 1911. Its first permanent home came in 1908 through the bequest of Mrs. Lorenzo di Medici Sweat in memory of her husband, citizen of Portland and member of Congress. She left her home, erected in 1800 and now a Registered National Landmark, and funds for the construction of a gallery wing, opened in 1911.

The house itself is an exceptionally beautiful example of the Federal style. It was built by John Kimball, a local housewright, for Major and Mrs. Hugh McLellan. Its neighbor on Spring Street, the Charles Quincy Clapp House, built in 1832, and the McLellan-Sweat House itself form a distinguished island of historic New England architecture in a modern commercial city.

As of this writing, the museum is planning an ambitious expansion into a fifty-four-thousand-square-foot addition beyond the gallery wing and fronting on Congress Square. Designed by I. M. Pei & Partners, the architects of the already celebrated East Wing of the National Gallery of Art in Washington, it will bring the museum complex very much up to date. As always happens in such bold architectural ventures, there are shouts of joy and cries of protest; but if the Washington case is any parallel this will eventually settle down to a condition of municipal pride. The new building itself should stimulate future growth toward realization of the museum's goal of becoming Maine's chief cultural resource.

The museum displays works by Winslow Homer, the state of Maine collection, decorative arts, and temporary exhibitions; and it offers a full range of educational programs. The permanent holdings focus on the works of artists with Maine associations. Recently announced is a gift from Mr. Charles Shipman Payson of seventeen paintings by Winslow Homer ranging from 1868 to 1897. The Hamilton Easter Field collection, the gift of the Barn Gallery Associates in Ogunquit, includes among fifty-three works paintings by Bacon, Bouché, Davis, Field, Hartley, Karfiol, Kuhn, Kuniyoshi, Pascin, Spencer, Sterne, and von Schlegell; and sculptures by Gross and Laurent.

Other artists represented in the permanent collection include Arp, Badger, Brewster, A. B. Davies, Harding, Henri, Lachaise, Marsh, Motherwell, Nevelson, Prior, Renoir, Rivers, Steinberg, Frank Stella, Stuart, Whistler, Wyeth, and Zorach.

New York–Paris Number 2,[25] an oil 30 by 40 inches, was painted
by Stuart Davis (1894–1964) in 1931. His early training under Robert
Henri (see MA 207) directed him toward the social-realist themes of
the so-called Ashcan School. Soon he turned toward modern abstraction
but not until three or four years had elapsed since the Armory Show
of 1913. By the time of Davis's year-and-a-half stay in Paris, in 1928/9,
his work was already well advanced in the new direction, but the Paris
experience gave him further confidence. The Portland example, painted
eighteen months after his return to New York, shows how important
it was to him. During the Depression years, Davis painted many murals
under subsidy by the federal government. Other commissions included
a mural for the men's lounge of Radio City Music Hall (1932), appropriately titled *Men without Women*; recently cleaned, it is still *in
situ*. In 1978 the Brooklyn Museum organized a major retrospective of
his work; the catalogue, by John R. Lane, is the most important study
of many devoted to this important American artist.

25

The Joan Whitney Payson Gallery of Art, Westbrook College

Location: Take exit 8 from I-95 onto Route 25; go east about 1½ miles to Stephens Ave., turn left and follow to the college. Free parking

Hours: Tues.-Sat. 10-4, Sun. 2-5

Admission: Free

The collection of twenty-eight paintings and drawings formed by Mrs. Payson came to Westbrook College as the gift, in her memory, of her son John and his wife Nancy, an alumna and trustee of the college. They also gave the fine little cubic building, designed by The Architects Collaborative of Cambridge, in which it is so tastefully housed. The gallery opened to the public in 1977. Thus art in Portland is, so to speak, bounded by Payson donations—Mrs. Payson's collection at its west end and the massive contributions of her husband, Charles Shipman Payson, to the Museum of Art in the old city to the east.

The pictures are displayed on the ground floor and around a little balcony overlooking it. In the basement there is space for small temporary exhibitions. Most of the works are of good to very fine quality, and one masterpiece, Vincent van Gogh's *Iris*, is unforgettable. Even a list of the artists represented should whet the appetite: Chagall, Courbet, Daumier, Degas, Gauguin, Glackens, Homer, Ingres, Marquet, Monet, Picasso, Prendergast, Renoir, Reynolds, Rousseau-le-douanier, Sargent, Sisley, Soutine, van Gogh, Whistler, and Wyeth. We illustrate and discuss four of them and regret that space precludes the inclusion of more. Unfortunately, too, the great Courbet, *Stormy Weather at Etretat*, does not photograph well in black and white. I should like to have compared it with Homer's imposing but less potent marine, *The Backrush* (close by), painted at Prout's Neck at least twenty years later, in order to commit a pun for which I hope I shall be forgiven: that Courbet's vision was the more Homeric.

In *A Painter*,[26] a drawing in crayon, pen, and wash, Honoré Daumier (1808–79) is seen in his late, free phase. For contrast, see the early lithograph of 1834, CT 41. Highly sculptural contour lines now re-

26

place the former laborious modeling in light and shade, and subtle washes of shadow reinforce them. Darker washes plunge the image into a Rembrandtesque gloom. In his oils, few of which date from before 1850, Daumier adopted a technique much like this.

Little need be said about Vincent van Gogh's *Iris*[27] except that it was painted in the spring of 1889 at Saint-Remy in Provence, a full year later than his pen-and-ink *View of Arles*, now in Providence (RI 20). Masterpieces have a way of being self-explanatory. You will not overlook the spiked rhythms of the green leaves, repeated or introduced in the orange-red foreground, or the variant greens at the top of the canvas, or the shrill contrast between blue and orange blossoms, or the single white blossom at the left—somehow suggesting a woman's bonnet. Is this really a flower piece, or is it an allegory of the human condition?

Jungle with Monkeys,[28] by Henri Rousseau (1844–1910), painted in 1909, has the scary big scale, although it is only 2 feet high, and the harsh color contrast of his latest work, as well as the power of his very large pictures. New England has few examples by this mysterious, mostly self-taught artist. It is surprising to realize that he was a contemporary of the Impressionists, from whom he differed so markedly. (Compare the oranges with Renoir's onions, for example, in the Clark Institute's picture, MA 256.) A modest customs agent (*douanier*), Rousseau painted at off hours and then indulged in it full time; but he attracted little notice until the avant-garde discovered him. A big jungle painting of Rousseau's hung in the main gallery of the anti-Salon (of the Independents) in 1905 along with works by the Fauves. In 1908 he was the guest of honor at a strenuous banquet staged by Picasso and attended by Apollinaire, Georges Braque, Gertrude and Leo Stein, Alice Toklas, Marie Laurencin, Maurice Vlaminck, and many others. For further details, see Roger Shattuck's fascinating volume, *The Banquet Years* (Garden City, N.Y.: Anchor Books, 1961).

If you can manage to attend a concert without knowing what the program will be, you are sure to listen with the greatest concentration and learn much from the experience. (Is this really by Mozart, or is it

27

28

Haydn, or a minor contemporary?) In the same way, I suggest you look at *Road Cut*[29]—whether in the original or in our illustration—before reading further. If you are actually visiting the Payson Gallery don't look at the illustration, because it is the color of this picture that gives it much of its powerful expression. Go to the original! Even though the painter is well known to you, you may be in for a surprise, as I was. The brittle tempera medium, the harsh wiry lines, the bare tree, the stark loneliness—these ring bells in the memory. But these deep russets, close to the color of red wine? If you are on the right track, you expect only sepia browns, blacks and grays, pale acid greens and sooted bleached yellows. The following information may or may not help: the picture was painted in 1940 when the artist was only twenty-three. Nearby is another of his works, *The Chair*, a dry-brush painting on paper, a minor but fully typical example of his developed style. Now I suspect you know who he is. But if so, a question remains. Did he develop significantly from his marvelous beginnings? An answer to this question is suggested in our discussion of a major work of the artist's later years, at the Shelburne museum (VT 25).

29

William A. Farnsworth Library and Art Museum

Location: On Route 1 (Main St.), turn west on Museum St. There is a parking lot at the Union St. end of the block
Hours: June 1-September 30: Mon.-Sat. 10-5, Sun. 1-5; October 1-May 31: Tues.-Sat. 10-5, Sun. 1-5. Closed legal holidays. The homestead is open only June 1 to mid-September, at the same hours as the library and museum
Admission: Free

In accordance with the will of Lucy C. Farnsworth, of Rockland, the museum, completed in 1948 as a memorial to her father, has become a cultural and educational center for the Penobscot area. The nationally registered Farnsworth Homestead, built in the Greek Revival style of the first half of the nineteenth century, stands on the adjacent property. The house, with its interior furnished in the Victorian style, is maintained exactly as when the Farnsworths occupied it.

The Farnsworth Library, handsomely appointed, is a rich source for the study of Maine history, maritime life, and art history. The permanent collection of the museum specializes in American paintings, drawings, and prints of the eighteenth century to the present. A complete catalogue of them was published in 1975. European and Oriental art are also represented.

In the summer season the museum often stages a major exhibition of the work of an artist with Maine associations. Two of the most memorable were devoted to Fitz Hugh Lane (see MA 155), who often painted scenes of Rockland harbor, and Louise Nevelson (see MA 147), whose early years were spent in Rockland. Since these exhibitions sometimes occupy most of the available gallery space, visitors who wish to see the permanent collection should take that into consideration.

In addition to the four painters discussed below, other prominent Americans represented here include Washington Allston, Thomas Eakins (small oil studies for *William Rush Carving the Nymph of the Schuylkill* and *The Thinker*), William Harnett (a large still life of quality comparable to the example we discuss at Springfield, Mass.), Edward Hopper, William Jennys, Eastman Johnson, John F. Kensett, Fitz Hugh Lane (three oils and a drawing; see our discussion of his work at Gloucester Mass.), Maurice Prendergast, Gilbert Stuart, Thomas Sully, and the Wyeths—N.C., Andrew, and James—permanently displayed in an upstairs gallery.

Storm Clouds on the Coast,[30] an oil of 1859 by Martin J. Heade (1819–1904), is very different in mood from the summer idyll we have studied at Bowdoin College (ME 14); but it shares much in ominous immensity with the smaller *Rye Beach, New Hampshire* at the University of Connecticut (CT 100). Here the generous size (20 by 32 inches) gave Heade a more extended range. A rocky island and a sailboat, diminutive but crisply silhouetted, mark its outer limit. The approaching wave is no monster, yet its fringe has great energy.

A calm sea sets the mood for *A Girl in a Punt*,[31] a small gem of a watercolor by Winslow Homer (1836–1910). The freely brushed strokes, very liquid and transparent, accentuate a restful horizontality. The punt does not disturb it, nor does the sailboat, not far away. A foreground rock points toward the girl, but her oar blocks further passage off to the left. She is the darkest and the largest element in the picture, and inevitably she leans across the direction defined by the rock. Homer signed the picture but did not date it. A second watercolor, *Sailing Ships in Harbor*, in opaque white gouache on brown paper, is signed and dated 1880. Comparison with a large number of watercolors and gouaches painted that summer at Gloucester, Mass., suggests that *Girl in a Punt* also dates from that year. Compared with Homer's earliest watercolors of the mid-1870s, there is now a larger scale, a more liquid wash, greater freedom in the use of the medium, and a darkening color and atmosphere. There are only two oils of 1880 (one a beach scene in the Springfield Museum), and they too are sunless and serious. All of this, we should not forget, was produced before Homer went to England in 1881 and changed his basic theme into one of the struggle of man against the sea.

The schooner in our next picture is in dangerous waters. The scene is off the great cliffs of Monhegan Island, the date is September 1913, and the artist is George Bellows (1882–1925). *Boating out to Sea*[32] is one of three of his oils owned by the Farnsworth Museum. *Autumn—Camden*, twice as large, is more typical, but it lacks the concentrated power of our selection. Lowering color and vigorous brushwork underlie the ominous impact.

30

31

32

Marine Landscape,[33] a watercolor by John Marin (1870–1953), is an offbeat masterpiece. The tenderly applied washes recall Marin's work of around 1910–13 (see ME 38); there is virtually no evidence of the harsh, jagged strokes that mark his watercolors of around 1920. This example was painted in 1919, as the abbreviated signature makes clear. The colors are gentle too, and that is most exceptional. They are like a Whistlerian symphony in pale pastels. Yet behind this delicate surface lies a firm, rectangular structure, not found in the early watercolors; and the scale has Marin's mature boldness. What one normally expects from him can be seen in the smashing example at Williams College (MA 275).

In addition to the artists listed or discussed above, the Farnsworth Museum offers an opportunity to study the work of lesser but talented masters. Three ship painters deserve close attention: James Baldridge, Robert Salmon (five oils here, from 1822 to 1832), and William Stubbs. Do not miss the examples by Frank Benson (see MA 168), Alfred Bricher (see MA 161), Charles Codman, Alvan and Jonathan Fisher, Waldo Pierce, and Paul Sample.

33

Dyer-York Library and Museum

Location: Main St. (Route 1) at intersection of North St.; from Maine Tpke. take exit 5
Hours: In summer, Tues.-Sat 1-4; in winter, Tues. and Thurs. 10-4, Sat. 1-4
Admission: Free

The York Institute Museum was incorporated in 1867; its present home was erected in 1926 and a gallery wing was added in 1968. The neighboring Dyer Library, including a well-equipped research center, occupies the remodeled former home of the Deering family.

The front portion of the museum contains a Colonial kitchen, Empire and eighteenth-century bedrooms, and furnishings and artifacts from the family of Colonel Thomas Cutts, Saco's great landowner and shipbuilder of the Revolutionary period. Those interested in the genre plaster groups of John Rogers, mid-nineteenth century, will find some twenty examples. Of special local interest is a small oil painting of an Anti-Slavery meeting at the old Gibbs Hotel by Charles H. Granger, a Saco artist.

In connection with Smibert's full-length *Portrait of Sir William Pepperrell* at Salem (MA 196), it is interesting to find, at Saco, silver presented to him by Commodore Peter Warren, whose British squadron assisted Pepperrell's force of 4,240 New England farmers and tradesmen in taking the French fortress of Louisburg. That was in 1745, and all these fine pieces bear hallmarks for the same date. Such was the hurry on Warren's part to make this presentation in the year of the victory that each piece was made by a different craftsman, and the pineapples in the Pepperrell shield were inadvertently reversed. The two large double-handled and covered cups are particularly magnificent.

From the point of view of the scope of this book, however, the greatest treasure here is a group of thirteen portraits by John Brewster, Jr. (1766–1854), a deaf-mute itinerant painter born in Connecticut. We have discussed a portrait of his at the Connecticut Historical Society (CT 7), and now refer the reader to articles on Brewster in that society's *Bulletin* for October 1960, and in *Antiques* for November of that year. The York Institute has published a small brochure on the artist's remarkable career. Apparently he spent several months about 1800 at the Cutts mansion in Saco and painted the whole family. Not surprisingly, the largest pictures are the full-length ones of Colonel Cutts himself and of his wife Elizabeth. The *Portrait of Colonel Cutts*[34] (1736–1821), aged about sixty-five, may be described as a stiffened American Holbein. Black and white dominate this stark icon. Everything is rigidly vertical except the colonel's fingers, crossing exactly at right angles the black-and-white diagonal of his cane. How the cane stays put is not revealed, but where in painting is there a diagonal more incontrovertible?

In 1980 the portraits of Colonel and Mrs. Cutts traveled to a major exhibition of American folk painting at the Whitney Museum of American Art, New York.

34

Penobscot Marine Museum

Location: Church St., just off Route 1
Hours: Open Memorial Day weekend through October 15, Mon.-Sat. 9:30-5, Sun. 1-4
Admission: Charged

Marine museums are fascinating places and art is no stranger to them. To our entries on those at Bath and, in other states, Mystic, New Bedford, and Salem, we are happy to add this account of six neighboring houses in a charming village at the head of Penobscot Bay.

The museum was incorporated in 1936, when Searsport presented to the trustees its original Town Hall, built in 1845 from funds given by David Sears of Boston, the town's eponym. Purchase and restoration of "the Captain's House," the former home of Captain Jeremiah Merithew (c. 1816), facilitated the exhibition of a rapidly growing collection relating to Maine shipping and coastal life. Four other buildings provide quarters for special exhibitions, a small craft exhibit, workshops, and an intimate presentation of life at Searsport in times long gone. The main displays, in the Old Town Hall and the Captain's House, show the same taste and expertise that mark the Maine Maritime Museum at Bath. A research library is one of the features of the Captain's House, along with displays of furniture, glass, ship models (including the *Charles W. Morgan*, the original of which can be visited at Mystic Seaport), memorabilia of the China Trade, and large eighteenth-century panels depicting various phases of whaling. The Old Town Hall features half-size models of Maine-built ships and ship portraits. The collection of marine paintings, shown throughout the complex, is regarded as one of the finest in the state.

Gerald Brace, my favorite writer on Maine, sums it all up toward the end of *Between Wind and Water* (Norton, 1966): "The people on the old coast of Maine were not romantic philosophers or poets—they were not at all bookish or self-conscious—but they did seem to provide the evidence on which philosophy could build. They illustrated what could be done when the right people and the right place and climate and conditions all collaborated in a harmonious and at best beautiful way of life." On page 67 you can find out why "nor'west" and "sou'west" are correct, and why "nor'east" and "sou'east" will instantly betray you as an ignoramus.

Colby College Art Museum

Location: From I-95 take the Waterville exit; the college is located on a hill to the west of the city

Hours: Mon.-Sat. 10-12, 1-4:30; Sun. 2-4:30; closed holidays

Admission: Free

With the opening in 1959 of the Bixler Art and Music Center, Colby's already important art collection was at long last appropriately housed. The new building immediately stimulated enthusiastic support from the Friends of Art at Colby and impressive donations. Like all college museums, Colby's is indispensable for the teaching of art history and studio courses. As of this writing, Colby College is the leading center for the study of advanced modern art in the conservative state of Maine. While the Ogunquit Museum shares that distinction, it is open only in the summer months.

The Colby collection, however, is by no means limited to the modern field. Its range extends from a large and fine group of Colonial and Federal portraits and nineteenth-century American folk art through major masters of the nineteenth century. While the emphasis here is on American art, Europeans from the Dutch seventeenth century, British portraits, and moderns like Utrillo, Kirchner, Klee, and Philip Guston are represented. Decorative arts are well represented too, notably by the Bernat collection of three hundred examples of Oriental ceramics. There are many fine drawings and prints.

As the only noncoastal art museum of significance in Maine, Colby's has attracted the interest of residents and artists with Waterville connections. (The important art school at Skowhegan is only twenty miles to the north.) The two most extensive of the earlier donations were the Helen Warren and Willard Howe Cummings collection of American paintings and folk art, and the American Heritage collection of American primitive paintings and drawings, the gift of Mr. and Mrs. Ellerton Jetté. Since 1949 a precious selection of the work of Winslow Homer has been on extended loan from Mrs. Harold T. Pulsifer. Mr. and Mrs. John Marin, Jr., have given twenty-five works by Mr. Marin's father, ranging from an 1888 watercolor to a 1952 oil. Two distinguished sculptors contributed: William Zorach gave a bronze of his well-known *Mother and Child*, and Louise Nevelson (see MA 147), twenty of her drawings, twelve small sculptures, and four paintings.

If our selections skip over the Early American portraits, that is because they are in such quantity in New England and we wish to emphasize more recent art here, for reasons given above. The collection has good examples of Smibert, Wollaston, Joseph Badger, McIlworth (see MA 174), Earl, Copley, Charles Willson Peale, and Gilbert Stuart; and among the anonymous portraits one of *The Reverend Silas Ilsley*, c. 1840, is outstanding.

We begin our survey with *Landscape with River and Temple*,[35] signed and dated 1773 by Richard Wilson (1714–82). A master rarely seen in New England museums, he was the virtual founder of British landscape painting. Until he was thirty-five he painted portraits; then he set out for Italy. There he remained about five years and mastered the landscape art of Claude Lorrain and Gaspard Poussin, with their dark foreground *coulisses* starting the viewer on a journey back into a distant light. On his return Wilson seems to have studied the Dutch landscape painters. In this late example we find an eighteenth-century flattening of the extreme spaciousness of his seventeenth-century models, and some lessening of their solidity. Irregularities like the scarred bark of the tree at the left and the picturesque cliff beyond it unsettle Claude's soft calm. While the scene is probably imaginary, it could pass as the depiction of a real place. Color and brushwork, held in restraint, await the Constables and Turners yet to come. As is well known, there was little demand for such pictures in Wilson's lifetime; recognition for his brave departure did not come until well after his death. At the end, he retired to his native Wales, a broken man.

Still-life painting had an enormous vogue in nineteenth-century America. Of many examples at Colby, *Still Life with Oranges*, by William J. McClosky, is memorable, but perhaps surpassed by *Still Life with Melons and Fruit*,[36] by Thomas Badger (1792–1868). The latter, no doubt influenced by similar assemblages by Raphaelle Peale, has produced a sumptuous dining-room ornament, given it a substantial pyramidal structure, and displayed a virtuoso's technique. Little details

35

36

like the spilled seeds from the watermelon did not escape his notice. For a later and still more elaborate production, compare the work of Severin Roesen (VT 6).

We have discussed an early oil by Winslow Homer (1836–1910) at Yale (CT 80) and a watercolor of 1880 at Rockland (ME 31), but at Colby we can study to advantage Homer's earliest ventures into the difficult watercolor medium. *The Berry Pickers*,[37] signed and dated July 1873, comes from the very first year he worked in watercolor. Though he was later to carry it to unheard-of marvels—such as *Three Men in a Boat*, 1890, also at Colby—this example, once seen, has a way of returning to the memory as one of his masterpieces. This despite a certain tightness and dependence on preliminary drawing, and on opaque white wash (gouache) to increase the solidities. Perhaps that very hesitancy contributes to the image's tender and nostalgic appeal. Henry James's reaction to such innocents has already been quoted; in the presence of *The Berry Pickers* it seems incomprehensible. But then, James recommended Algiers and Capri as proper subjects for painting.

Brooklyn Bridge,[38] a watercolor of 1912 by John Marin (1870–1953), is as loose and liquid as *The Berry Pickers* is taut and brittle. Curiously, Marin progressed in the opposite direction from that of Homer, as may be quickly seen here in a comparison with *Stonington*, a watercolor of 1925, or with the 1940 example discussed at Orono (ME 24). Painted a year before the Armory Show, *Brooklyn Bridge* precedes Marin's gradual absorption of European Cubism, with its interpenetrating planes, and Italian Futurism, with its angular collisions of industrial and urban forms. We marvel at how these little puddles

37

38

of color manage to shape a whole vista of Manhattan seen from the Brooklyn waterfront.

We continue with two landscapes, both street scenes and both painted between 1910 and 1916. Here the similarity ends, for the Childe Hassam (1859–1939) *View of Broadway: Newburgh, N.Y.*[39] has an American freshness and charm, while the Maurice Utrillo (1883–1955) *Street in Le Vésinet*[40] is weighted down with Old World cares in its leaden gray loneliness. In its company the Hassam, a watercolor, sparkles with optimism. The blue air and waters of the Hudson carry through the holiday mood set by the flags. Hassam often made hackneyed variations on the work of the French Impressionists. Here he stands on his own.

The Utrillo is an early oil from his best period (c. 1910). The design is tautly laced by the sharply receding planes. No breeze, no people animate this suburb. Eventually, Utrillo drank himself to death, and unlike two colleagues in alcoholism, Toulouse-Lautrec and Modigliani, he injured his artistic powers in the process. Toward the end, he tossed up repetitious confections based on tourist postcards. Utrillo's streets always lead in the same direction, and eventually they led him to a vacuum.

With *Agricultural Experimental Plan for Late Fall*,[41] a fantasy in watercolor and ink by Paul Klee (1879–1940), we truly enter the realm of modern art, despite its long-ago date in the 1920s. The title, inscribed in Klee's spidery hand, is his own; and it is our guarantee that this image is no pure abstraction. A master of line, shape, color, and space, Klee exploited the medium of painting at its purest to express profound ideas about life and death. This example is about life, and how to generate it; after the mid-1930s, when the Nazis came to power, he was concerned with death. Swiss-born, he worked primarily in Germany, and after 1920 at the celebrated Bauhaus until the Nazis dissolved it

39

41

40

in 1933. Ultimately he returned to his native Bern, to end his days there in deepest pessimism. But in the 1920s he was much affected by the architectural discipline of the Bauhaus exerted by its founder, the architect Walter Gropius, as was his Russian-born colleague Kandinsky (see CT 83). It is too easy to compare Klee's works of this period with intricate Swiss toys; but they do invoke a world of magic as if seen under a magnifying glass. Klee's paintings—all unrepetitive nine thousand of them—are little poems to personal privacy and to the freedom of the artist's imagination. That is why the Nazis declared his art "degenerate."

By Klee's standards, our next two American oils are obviously conservative, even though they date from the next decade, or later. It is surprising to discover that Walt Kuhn (1877–1949) was a near contemporary of Klee's; but the American concern with describing an image in readily understandable terms was not yet prepared to yield to European countertraditions. Thus for Kuhn the clown *Mario*[42] was the portrait of a man, and not, as for Rouault (see NH 28), a symbol of fragile existence on the edge of life. For all that, it is solidly painted, strongly designed, and expressively characterized. The date is 1938.

Shell and Feather,[43] by Georgia O'Keeffe (born 1887), might seem without its color a superb photograph of two objects sensitively selected and as sensitively arranged. But the aesthetic appeal of these whites and near whites and shell pinks is considerable, as is the controlled smooth brushwork. Set in a nowhere space, the objects tell us much about shapes we have seen but not really observed.

Colby's sculpture collection is small. The best examples are American primitive or modern. We conclude with two examples of the latter. Set

42

43

out of doors, *Stranger III*,[44] a bronze nearly 8 feet high, is a fine example of the work of the English artist Lynn Chadwick (born 1914). It is the gift of Jere Abbot, a former director of the Smith College Museum of Art celebrated for his eye for quality in modern art. Dating from 1957–59, this disquieting three-legged personage spreads its ominous wings under the flattened square of an inhuman head. In his brief monograph on the artist (Universe Books, 1961), the critic J. P. Hodin describes another piece in the *Stranger* series: "The animal form suggests the human, a metamorphosis which by way of a shock gives the beholder a sensation of the unprecedented. The transitoriness of all living substance, be it man, animal or plant, is suggested as well . . . although there is no primary intention to produce a series, a formal problem can show itself so interesting that it demands further investigation or formal exploitation until the fascination ebbs away."

Torso,[45] a ceramic sculpture 20 inches high, is the work of the Japanese-American Isamu Noguchi (born 1904). After responding to its powerful simplification and its formidable stance, you will not be surprised that Noguchi studied with Brancusi (see CT 68) in Paris, and became his assistant. That was in his youth, in 1927/8. This piece comes from thirty years later, when he had succeeded in fusing his Japanese heritage with the sculptural inventions of modern Western art. Note the importance of the straps that bind the hips, the subtly flattened rib cage and its transition to the abdomen—the very antithesis of explosive Baroque, and of Rodin. One nipple is simply a hole, informing you that the piece is only a shallow shell; but a hole is the opposite of a bulge, as Henry Moore has often pointed out, and hollows formed in rocks by the action of water are a potent form of sculpture in nature. Therefore, a hole is simply a bulge seen inside out.

44

45

Index

Numbers refer to pages, not illustrations. In longer entries only the first page is indicated.

NOTES

NOTES

NOTES

NOTES

NOTES

The Art Museums of New England

was designed by Jean LeGwin and set in linotype Garamond, a face designed by Claude Garamond, who died in 1561. Garamond lived and worked at a time when black-letter fonts were in course of being superseded in France by types based on the Renaissance hands we now call roman and italic. He derived his inspiration from the Aldine old face, and the influence of his work dominated European typefounding for the succeeding two centuries. Many punches cut by other hands were subsequently ascribed to him, including the historical prototypes of many of the revivals bearing his name at the present time. The roman is based on fonts recorded as Garamond's work in specimens issued in Germany between 1592 and 1702, and its italics derives from originals ascribed to Robert Granjon of Lyons in the same specimens. Both series were the work of R. Hunter Middleton, and were issued in 1930.

THE ART MUSEUMS OF NEW ENGLAND was composed by Lamb's Printing Company, Clinton, Massachusetts and printed on Monadnock's Greenfield Opaque. Halliday Lithograph, West Hanover, Massachusetts was the printer and binder.